From 1982 to 1985 the Sudan was devastated by drought—a natural disaster that became horribly familiar to Westerners through news coverage of the famine it created. In A DESERT DIES, Michael Asher provides a first-hand report of the drought, in what is not only a remarkable work of front-lines journalism, but also a memorable personal story of friendship and courage.

Asher lived with the Kababish, a nomadic tribe of the Sahara desert, during these years of drought. In an area racked with hunger and torn by civil war, he learned the ancient customs of the desert Arabs, their language, their traditions, and their skills—an unchanged way of life that had endured for centuries in one of the world's least hospitable environments.

A DESERT DIES shows the pride and strength of the Saharan nomads who have, over the centuries, learned to live with the implacable natural forces that surround them. As he roamed the Sahara with the Kababish, Michael Asher witnessed, and came to share, their loyalty, hospitality, and generosity—and above all, their passionate love for the desert. It was the desert that had molded the nomads, given them their identity and the merciless codes by which they lived and died. For the Kababish, the town was crowded, dirty, and confining. The desert was freedom. But when the drought struck, the land that the nomads loved turned against them. And what began for Michael Asher as a piece of travel writing ended as a quest for survival.

With A DESERT DIES, Michael Asher joins a distinguished line of writer-adventurers ranging from T. E. Lawrence and Wilfred Thesiger to Peter Matthiessen. He has given us a dramatic account of existence on the margin of life and death, and a celebration of the values of a vanishing culture.

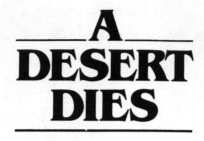

A
DESERT
DIES

By the same author

In Search of the Forty Days Road

MICHAEL ASHER

A DESERT DIES

The parched eviscerate soil,
Gapes at the vanity of toil,
Laughs without mirth,
This is the death of earth.
T. S. Eliot, 'Little Gidding', Four Quartets

St. Martin's Press
New York

Library of Congress Cataloging-in-Publication Data

Asher, Michael, 1953–
   A desert dies.

    1. Kababish.   2. Sudan—Social life and customs.
3. Droughts—Sudan. I. Title.
DT155.2.K32A84 1987   962.4   87-4459
ISBN 0-312-00720-5

First published in Great Britain by Viking Penguin Books Ltd.

First U.S. Edition

10 9 8 7 6 5 4 3 2 1

To my mother and my father

Contents

List of Plates

List of Maps

Acknowledgements

I could not have written this book without the help of many friends amongst the ruling house of the Kababish. I should like to thank the late nazir, Hassan Wad at Tom, whose tolerance and understanding enabled me to gain my first foothold amongst his people. I am also indebted to the present nazir, At Tom Wad Hassan, and to his brothers Salim, Mohammid, Ali and Fadlallah. I owe a special thanks to my friends Salim Wad Musa and Ibrahim Wad Hassan Wad Khalifa. These two will always remain for me the epitome of the noble Arab.

I should like to thank the following members of the nazir's people for their hospitality and generosity: Sheikh Musa Wad Ali, Sheikh Ali Wad Salim, Sheikh Jami' Wad Ali, Mohammid Reyd Wad Fadlallah, Ali Shiekh Wad Mohammid, At Tom Wad Mohammid, Mohammid at Tom Wad Mohammid, Mohammid Dudayn, Ibrahim Wad Hassan Wad al Faki, Ali at Tom Wad Mohammid, Salim Wad Ali, Marghani 'Al Faki', Hamid Wad Digerr, Abdallah Abu Kajarna.

I could not have made initial contact with the Nas Wad Haydar without the help of Mansour Abu Safita and Mohyal Din Abu Safita in El Fasher. I am deeply grateful for the trouble they took on my behalf.

I should also like to express my gratitude to those British teachers who gave me hospitality during my years in the Sudan, especially Indra Roy, Rob Hydon, Peter Midgeley, Jane Ellis, Joanna Christina, Mike Farrell, Julian Mountfield and Charles Mitchell.

I am grateful to Indra Roy and Eric Lawrie for warm friendship and valued counsel, and to John Garvey, who was always willing to provide me with a base in London when I was in transit.

I cannot repay my debt to my parents, who dealt so patiently with my correspondence while I was writing this book in the Sudan. Neither can I fully express appreciation for the patience and understanding of Maria Antonietta Peru, who besides drawing the maps with meticulous attention, has been my sole critic and untiring advisor.

Finally, I have listed my travelling companions separately. I shall never forget the million acts of friendship, great and small, which they performed. We were men from different worlds, yet there is a bond between us that time cannot erase.

My Companions

The Migrations in South Darfur 1982

Mohammid Wad Dayfallah ('Dagalol')	Nas Wad Haydar
Hassan Wad Dayfallah	"
Musa Wad Dayfallah	"
Abboud Wad Mohammid	"
Hassan Wad Mohammid	"
Ahmad Wad Ballal	'Atawiyya
Mohammid Wad Habjur	Nas Wad Haydar
Habjur Wad Kurkur	"
Ali Wad Hassan	"
Sayf ad Din	Mima
Hamdan	"

The Journey in the Bahr 1982

Sheikh Hassan Wad at Tom	Nurab
Mohammid Wad Hassan	"
Mohammid Dudayn Wad Hassan	"
Ibrahim Wad Hassan Wad al Faki	"
Sharif Mohammid	"
Khamis Wad Bambidu	"
Sa'ad Wad Siniin	"

The Journey in Dar Kababish and the Jizzu 1982

At Tom Wad Hassan	Nurab
Salim Wad Hassan	"
Juma' Wad Siniin	"
Adam Wad ash Shaham	"

Abdallah Wad az Zayadi	Nurab
Mahmoud Wad Affandi	"
Abdallah Wad Fadul	"
Ja'adallah Wad Hussayn ('Mura'fib')	"
Ibrahim Wad Mohammid	"
Hamid Wad Markaz	"
Juma' Wad Tarabish	"

The Journey to El 'Atrun 1982

Fadlal Mula Wad Arba'ini	Sarajab
Mohammid Wad Fadlal Mula	"
Balla Wad Ahmad	Hamdab
Ballal	Ruwahla
Ali	"
Sulayman	Sarajab

The Journey to Egypt 1983

Bakheit	Duwayih
Sannat	'Awajda
Musa	Meidob
Mohammid	Bani Jarrar
Musa Adam	Awlad Rashid
Bakkour	"

The Journey to Nukheila 1984

Juma' Wad Siniin	Nurab

The Journey to Ed Debba 1984

Rabi'	Kawahla
Musa	"
Ahmad	Awlad Rashid
Mohammid	

The Journey to Abu Tabara and Selima 1985

Jibrin Wad Ali	Awlad Huwal

A desert is not uninhabitable
through lack of wells, but through
lack of grazing, which in
turn depends on the sterility of the
ground as well as upon rainfall.
Ralph Bagnold, Libyan Sands, *1935*

The Kababish
Family Tree of the
Ruling House

Nazirs of the confederation shown in capitals

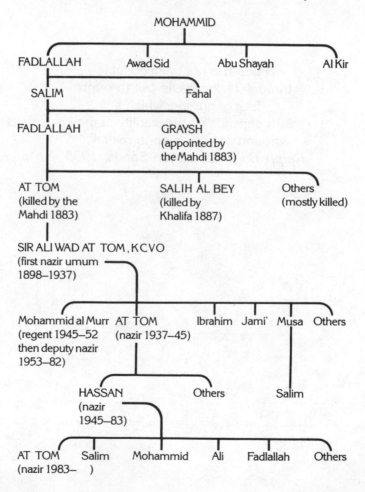

MOHAMMID

FADLALLAH   Awad Sid   Abu Shayah   Al Kir

SALIM   Fahal

FADLALLAH   GRAYSH
(appointed by
the Mahdi 1883)

AT TOM   SALIH AL BEY   Others
(killed by the   (killed by   (mostly killed)
Mahdi 1883)   Khalifa 1887)

SIR ALI WAD AT TOM, KCVO
(first nazir umum
1898–1937)

Mohammid al Murr   AT TOM   Ibrahim   Jami'   Musa   Others
(regent 1945–52   (nazir 1937–45)
then deputy nazir
1953–82)

HASSAN   Others   Salim
(nazir
1945–83)

AT TOM   Salim   Mohammid   Ali   Fadlallah   Others
(nazir 1983–   )

Part 1
The Kababish

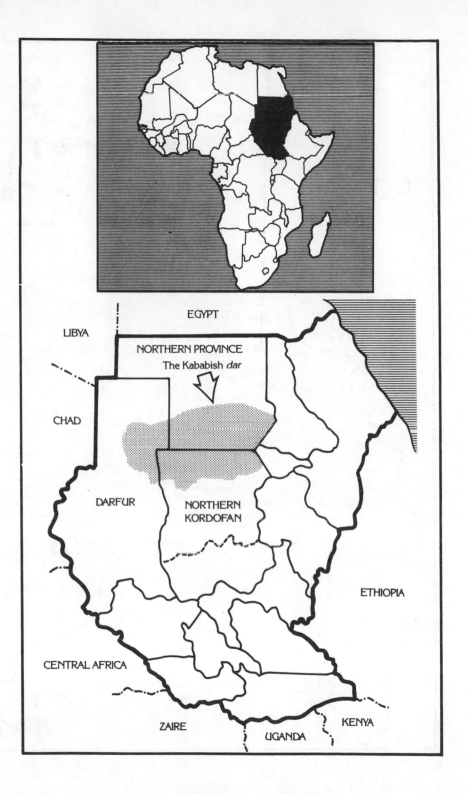

EGYPT

LIBYA

NORTHERN PROVINCE

The Kababish *dar*

CHAD

DARFUR

NORTHERN
KORDOFAN

ETHIOPIA

CENTRAL AFRICA

ZAIRE

UGANDA

KENYA

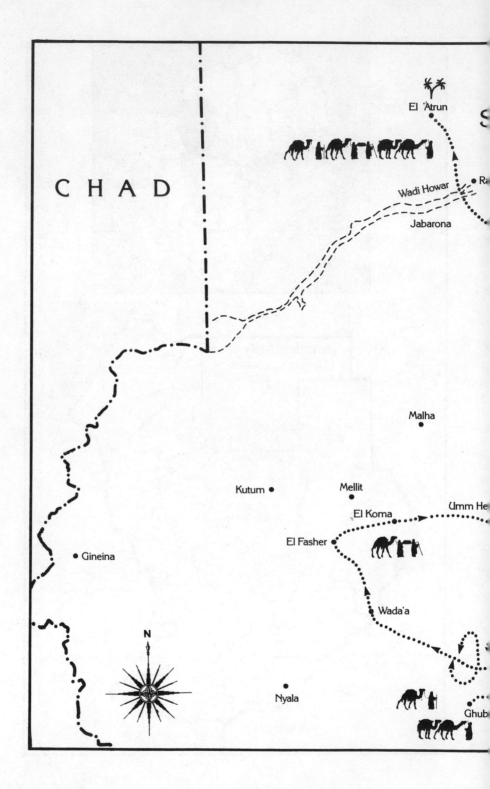

CHAD

El 'Atrun

Wadi Howar

Jabarona

Ra

S

Malha

Kutum

Mellit

El Koma

Umm He

El Fasher

Gineina

Wada'a

N

Nyala

Ghub

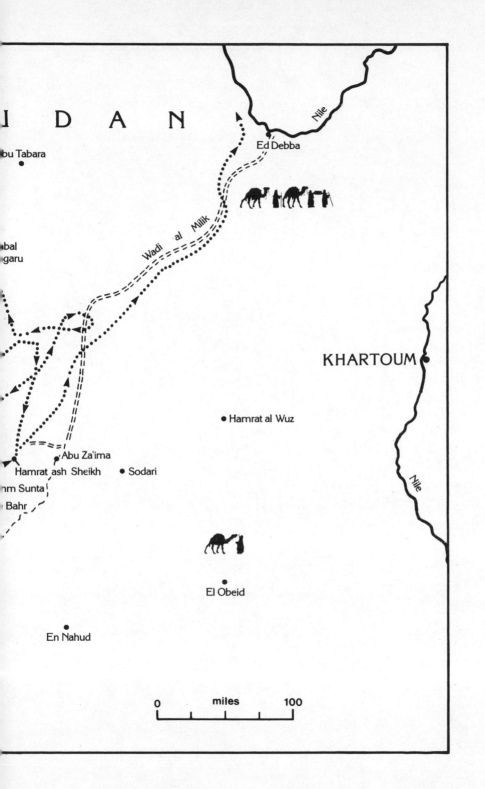

IDAN

bu Tabara

Nile

Ed Debba

Wadi al Milik

bal
garu

KHARTOUM

Hamrat al Wuz

Abu Za'ima

Hamrat ash Sheikh   Sodari

nm Sunta

Bahr

Nile

El Obeid

En Nahud

0   miles   100

1
Heart of
the Herdsman

Strong is the Sheikh of the Arab
in the season of the rains.
Arab saying

Five minutes after my plane touched down at El Fasher airport, I
knew that something was wrong.

The rains had been due weeks ago, but the air outside the plane
was dusty and dry, and the trees that stood on the edge of the runway
were as stark as scarecrows. There was no water in the wadi that
plunged down to the camel market, and the thorn bush that lined it
was brittle and dead.

The feeling of desolation increased as I looked out of the Toyota
truck that took me into the town. Nowhere was there a fleck of green
grass or a tree in leaf. As we pulled into the road that led to the
market, I noticed with surprise that the rainwater *fula* was empty. It
was normally brimming at this time of year, the great *siyaal* trees
around it pulsing with the cries of ten thousand water birds. Now its
bed was a carapace of cracked earth on which some men were
making bricks. The trees around were empty.

I turned to the driver and asked 'What happened to the water?'

'The rains did not come. They are later than ever.'

'I have never seen the *fula* empty at this season.'

'Neither have I,' he told me, 'and I was born here!'

I was to remember that scene many times over the next three
years. It reminded me that from the moment I had arrived in the west
of the Sudan to fulfil my ambition of living amongst the Kababish
nomads, there had been signs of the powerful changes that were
already in motion.

El Fasher was already a place of many associations for me. It
was from there in 19°0 that I had set out with a guide called Abu
Sara and six other nomads on a five-hundred-mile camel trek to

7

Dongola in the Northern Province. That experience had been my first taste of life in the desert. At the end of it, exhausted and a stone lighter, I had realized that here was the environment that offered the challenges I craved. Amongst these nomadic herdsmen I had discovered comradeship that could overcome even the deeply rooted barriers of culture and race.

While working as a teacher in the Sudan for three years I had spent almost all my spare time travelling and living in the harsh world of the nomads. I had ridden across the rolling savannah of Central Kordofan and explored the then little-known country along the Chad border. I had journeyed with tribesmen of the Zaghawa and the notorious Bedayatt. I had suffered many setbacks: once my camel had been taken, and on another occasion I had been arrested by the police under suspicion of being a Cuban mercenary. Undeterred I had set out again across the country of the Bani Hussayn between Gineina and Kutum, and from there had ridden through the Tegabo hills and penetrated into the narrow chasms of Jabal Meidob. I had travelled with nomads of the Mahamid as they drove their camel herds on their annual migrations through the acacia forests and across the plains of West Darfur, and visited families of the Baggara, the cattle-Arabs, who planted their winter crops on the hills outside Gineina. I had stayed with nomads of the Awlad Zayid and Awlad Janub as they wintered with their herds in Wadi Habila, and crossed the Fur country of Jabal Kawra where I had watched half-naked Fur women hunting porcupines in the thickets. I had been into the desert and felt its vastness. I had seen the great ergs spreading out before me to every horizon, day after day, without a blade of grass or a tree, seeing no one but my companions, until it seemed that there was nothing in the world but this huge emptiness and this handful of men who were with me.

These brief tastes of life in the vast ranges only served to whet my appetite. My time was always limited. I always had to return to my classroom, where I felt suffocated and inactive. This was not the fault of my students: they were gracious, affectionate and on the whole eager to learn. But all my life I had felt the need for a challenge that would tax both my mind and body to extremity. Some men had found the answer to that challenge in the high mountains and the seas, others in the jungles, the uncharted rivers and the poles. I found it in the desert.

This time I had come to El Fasher to resign my job as a teacher, and to take on the challenge that life amongst the nomads offered me. I had decided to live and travel amongst the nomadic Kababish.

The Kababish were the nomads who inhabited the deserts and desert steppes in the northern third of the Sudan, west of the Nile. They called themselves Arabs, and spoke Arabic, yet their origins were many and varied, and almost certainly included non-Arabic elements. I chose them because they were the heirs of the thousands of generations of nomads, African and Arab, who had occupied this most arid of regions.

The tribes I had travelled with previously were peoples of the Sahel and the desert fringes. They ventured into the desert wastes as outsiders, and were never totally at ease in a hostile world. Nothing could change the affection I felt for those like Abu Sara, for the men who had been early companions. But to live with the Kababish represented an even more exacting test. I went amongst them to live the life of the desert and to understand the demands made by one of the most desolate places on earth.

The day after my arrival in El Fasher I handed in my letter of resignation to the Province Education Office. The same evening I visited my friend Mohyal Din Abu Safita, in the Brinjiyya district of the town.

I had met Mohyal Din the previous year. He was a camel merchant. His family, the Abu Safitas, were people of Libyan and Mauritanian extraction, with the blood of half the races of the Sahara in their veins. They were the richest merchants in Darfur, but their wealth was founded on the camel trade. They had contacts amongst all the camel-rearing tribes of the west, and I hoped that Mohyal Din would be able to give me a letter of introduction to the nazir of Kababish, Hassan Wad at Tom.

Mohyal Din was a well-built, imposing figure, with an uncompromising manner and a face that was grained with the toughness that comes of countless transactions. Although a prosperous merchant, he was no stranger to the desert. His ancestors had come to the Sudan by camel and he maintained the tradition, travelling with the herds and riding and hunting like a nomad. There was little he did not know about camels and the tribes that bred them, and he and his brothers owned some of the finest racing dromedaries in Darfur.

As I sat in the courtyard of his house on that day, he mulled over my project with a thoughtful face. 'I can easily give you a letter to Hassan Wad at Tom,' he told me. 'He is my friend. I have entertained

9

him here at my house. But if you visit him now, you will not find any camels. All of his camel herds are moving to South Darfur because the rains have not fallen in their own lands.'

He explained that some rain had fallen on the pastures around the city of Nyala, and that the nomads of many tribes had been gathering there for some weeks. He thought a little more, then he said, 'I am going to visit my herd in a few days. It is being grazed near Ghubaysh in the region of Nyala. You can bring your luggage and ride in my truck, then I can introduce you to any Kababish that we find in the area. You can buy a camel and travel with them until they move back north. That way you can learn their customs before you go into the desert.'

I knew that South Darfur was Sahel savannah, and hardly the environment I had envisaged for my first meeting with the nomads of the desert. Nevertheless, it would be greatly to my advantage to have Mohyal Din introduce me to these Arabs, and to spend time learning about their ways before moving into the harsher world of the north.

'Are you sure they will accept me?' I asked.

'Of course they will accept you,' he replied. 'They are Arabs. Arabs never turn away a guest!'

As I left the house that night, I was electric with anticipation. I wondered with excitement what awaited me amongst the Kababish, and what I should discover over the next years of my life. In the soft moonlight the *fula* gaped, dark and empty.

When we arrived in South Darfur several days later, the grass was thick and tall, and the thorn trees were burgeoning with green leaf. There were seams of grey cloud across the azure sky, and the air was cool and full of moisture.

We arrived at the village of Ghubaysh in the afternoon. Mohyal Din had already sent word to some Kababish of the Nas Wad Haydar tribe to meet us there, and their two camels were couched outside one of the compounds of broken cane that made up the village. Otherwise the village was deserted. There were a few grass huts on the verge of collapse, their thatched walls and roofs eaten by creepers that had burst into purple flower.

Mohyal Din hooted violently, and almost at once two men came out of the compound. One was a striking if unhandsome figure. He was short and stout, with a bulging black face and a protuberant belly: it was this, I learned later, that had earned him the nickname

'Dagalol', which meant 'little pot'. He stopped and waited for us to get out of the truck, his feet planted firmly apart. A Kalashnikov rifle was slung from his shoulder and a bandolier of bullets sagged across his stomach. His woollen cap was tilted over one thick eyebrow.

Dagalol's companion, Mohammid Wad Habjur, was taller and slimmer, with a square, solemn face marked with small-pox scars. Like Dagalol he wore a cotton shirt yellow with age, with the addition of a dirty rag of cloth twisted across his forehead like a bandage. He carried a heavy Belgian rifle cradled against his elbow.

The Arabs greeted us warmly, clasping our hands and releasing them again and again, and repeating, 'God's blessing on you! God give you peace! Welcome in peace!' At first they met my gaze with averted eyes, which was the custom amongst nomads, but after a while I noticed Dagalol peering at me appraisingly through the greetings; his small, intense eyes held me for an instant in their powerful glare. When the greetings finally fizzled out, Dagalol invited us to sit in the shade of the compound wall. I squatted down, and Mohyal Din sat with the Arabs a few yards away. The servants who had been riding on the back of the truck jumped down and leaned against the wheels, smoking cigarettes.

The Arabs spoke with Mohyal Din in low voices and in an unfamiliar dialect of which I could pick up only odd words. Occasionally one of them shot me a questioning glance. I had no doubt they were discussing my future, and I felt awkward and conspicuous in the new white *jibba*, cotton *sirwal* and headcloth that I had put on for the occasion.

It seemed a long time before Mohyal Din called me over and said, 'It is all arranged. You can travel with these men until they move north. They are Kababish of the Nas Wad Haydar, and their camp in Kordofan is near the camp of Hassan Wad at Tom.' Then he turned to the Arabs and told them, 'His name is Omar. He can speak Arabic and he knows how to ride a camel. You can sell him one – a good one, not a camel of fools.'

'Very well,' Dagalol said, speaking in a slurred, harsh accent. 'But does he know that the life of the Arabs is very hard? There are no beds to sleep on, no bread and no vegetables. We move every day and we wait for no one.'

'He will survive,' Mohyal Din answered, shrugging. 'God is generous.' Then he took a clip of ten Kalashnikov rounds from his

11

pocket and gave it to Dagalol. The Arab did not smile or thank him, but I could see from the way he quickly put the gift away in the folds of his shirt that it was much appreciated. 'He could not be in better hands than ours,' he said.

'That is good,' Mohyal Din commented, 'for I shall be listening for news of him.'

Then he wished me good luck and told me, 'Come and see me in El Fasher when you return.' I agreed to do this, and thanked him. We shook hands and he told the servants to dump my equipment in the grass.

In a few moments the truck stuttered into life and was off, cruising into the bush. I watched it until the landscape swallowed it up, and only the angry buzz of its engine remained. Then that too disappeared and there was silence. The men standing a few feet away seemed to belong to an alien world. For a split second loneliness engulfed me. The landscape seemed to come alive with a sudden shock of sensation. I saw the sunlight glittering on the sea of grasses and smelt the peppery scent of the acacias in bloom. There was a whiff of petrol lingering in the air from the truck, and from somewhere else came the richer fumes of woodsmoke. I saw my equipment in the grass around me as if under a microscope: the saddle and the leather saddle-bags, the new waterskins smelling of tar, the canvas, blankets and sheepskin. I felt the taut restriction of the money-belt under my *jibba*, which contained 1,000 Sudanese pounds.

Then Dagalol held up a bowl of water and said, 'Come and drink. There is no fresh water on the ranges.' I took the bowl and hunkered down to drink. As I passed it back, he said, 'I do not know why you have come here, Omar, but this land is a hard land, a dangerous land. There are men here who would kill you for nothing. Keep your wits about you always. You understand?'

'I understand.'

'God is generous.'

It was a short ride from the village to Dagalol's camp, but for me the journey represented far more than the distance covered. Once again I was crossing the divide between the world of the town, where the international culture of motor-vehicles and mass communications reigned, and the timeless dimension of the nomad.

I rode Dagalol's camel, while the Arabs shared the other. The camels were both magnificent animals, moving gracefully through the bush, flowing with that suppressed power that had become familiar to me on my many journeys. We rode across a carpet of tribulus decorated by millions of yellow flowers. Here and there were patches of sand bright orange in colour; there were seams of taller grasses, some with ripe ears white and bobbing, and others with waxy, bulbous leaves and purplish flowers. Everywhere the thorn trees wore a mantle of rich green, and occasionally we saw vast grey baobabs rising like monuments above the lesser shrubs. We saw no other men. Once or twice Dagalol pointed out the movements of camels, no more than furry white blots on the rolling plain.

It was almost sunset when we came to a grove of acacias, where a man and a boy sat twisting ropes out of bark. They stood up as we approached shouting, 'Welcome! Welcome in peace!' and 'Your return is blessed!' We made our camels kneel by them, and they shook hands with me. The man had a pleasant face, nut-brown and oval as an egg, and hair shaved down to the skull. The boy was about twelve years old, and much darker; his face was lopsided, with an ungainly and irrepressible grin. Both were dressed in the same mould-yellow shirts rent with tatters that had been stitched and restitched. The brown-faced man was called Ahmad Wad Ballal, and the boy was Dagalol's younger son, Hassan. They took our camels and led them over to a place where saddles and gear had been piled into neat little pyramids. In the midst of it stood a V-shaped support of wood, from which were draped five or six bulging goatskins of various sizes. Wad Ballal and Hassan untied my equipment and helped me to arrange it in a place that Dagalol chose with great deliberation. Then Mohammid Wad Habjur mounted his camel, saying that he was going to his father's camp, and rode away.

I sat down awkwardly near my belongings, not quite knowing what to do next. 'Give Omar some milk, boy!' Dagalol told his son. I watched as Hassan drew a bowl of murky liquid from one of the skins. When he handed it to me I saw that it was unlike any milk I had ever drunk. Its surface was a coagulated mass of greyish lumps with a fine smattering of dust. I drank some. It was unexpectedly sour and I winced involuntarily. Dagalol chuckled. 'This is what the Arabs call *gaaris*,' he said. 'Do not drink too much or you will be running to the wadi!' Hassan giggled, and Wad Ballal smiled. 'This is all we have on the migrations,' Dagalol explained. 'Milk, and what we can hunt. There is no bread for us here, that is for women. But the Arabs want for nothing when they have milk!'

13

I will never forget the sunset on that first day amongst the Kabab-ish. The last shards of sunlight lay red and gold across the western skyline, hung like streamers on the grey outlines of the thorn trees. The whole of the great plain was washed with a sheen of soft gold that lent it an insubstantial, dreamlike quality. As the sun set, two great herds of camels came drifting out of the bush, one after the other. The animals moved in tight groups, shoulder to shoulder, so that the herds seemed to glide silently in a corporate mass. They were being driven by three dark figures, two small boys who swung knotty sticks and an older youth with a camel-whip. The coaxing, clicking sounds they made came clearly across the range.

Men had been driving their camels into the safety of their camps at sunset for generations. Before the camel had come to Africa, for thousands of years when all the Sahara was as rich and verdant as this savannah, men not unlike these had brought their cattle home at the end of the day. Since those days most of that vast landscape of three million square miles had been reduced to wasteland by unstoppable environmental changes and the overabundance of the stock itself. Only these Sahelian grasslands were left as a reminder.

Hassan began to kindle a fire between three stones, blowing into the embers with long whooshing breaths. Wad Ballal and Dagalol took their whips and went out to meet the herds. Soon the camping-place was besieged by camels that loomed over my head like giant reptiles. They stamped and snarled, heaved and squeezed, and the Arabs pressed them back, shouting, 'Deh! Deh! Deh!' which was the signal to halt. 'Come here, Omar!' Dagalol called, and as I approached he said, 'Stand here and keep them together while the boys hobble them.'

I took my whip and stood on guard at the back of the herd. They were unruly animals, heavy with fat, squabbling and snapping at each other in the half-light. Several times a beast would shuffle backwards towards me, forcing me to leap out of the way to prevent myself being trampled. Dagalol saw me, and scoffed, 'Don't be afraid. Use your whip, by God!' Meanwhile the Arabs moved amongst them carrying masses of hobbling-loops that clinked as they worked. The loops, known as 'uqals, were about a foot long and attached to a wooden peg. To hobble a standing camel the herds-man would seize one of its front legs by the hock, bending it upwards until it was parallel with the thigh, before fixing the loop around both parts of the leg and securing it with the peg on the outside. This gave the animal only three free legs, and it would soon get tired and settle down comfortably in the grass. Sometimes the camels resisted, letting out a blood-curdling roar and edging away from the herdsman, who would grab the animal by the shoulder and slap it hard, crying, 'Khyaa! Khyaaa!' until it sat down. Then he would scrape out a little tunnel under the heavy foreleg and fasten the 'uqal around it from beneath.

By the time darkness was thick around us, all the camels had been hobbled and the Arabs sat down amongst their equipment. Dagalol introduced me to his elder son Abboud, a tall, slender Arab, not long past manhood. The two other boys were aged about ten or eleven, and were as alike as two peas. They were called Sayf ad Din and Hamdan. As they greeted me shyly, Dagalol explained in a gruff and mocking tone that they were his 'little chickens' from the Mima tribe. In fact, they were hired boys who worked as herdsmen, though 'chicken' was a euphemism for 'slave'.

It was tranquil in the evening, sitting by the fire watching the yellow flames knitting a complex pattern around the dry wood. Across the dark plain many fires blinked and trembled, but their number was insignificant beside the galaxy of stars that stretched to eternity across the sky above.

That night the nomads questioned me about my tribe and my land. Dagalol wanted to know if my *Ingleez* were the same as those who had once ruled the Sudan. 'Where did they go?' he asked me. 'Why did they leave the Sudan?' I told him that my people had returned to our own country.

'Where is that?' he inquired.

'It is to the north-west, beyond Libya.'

'Beyond Libya, by God! Then it is surely a long way. How many days by camel?'

'The camel would not arrive there. My country is surrounded by water. Only a boat or an aeroplane can enter it.'

'Do you have camels there?' Wad Ballal asked.

'No, we have only cattle and sheep and some horses.'

'Are the cattle and sheep as fat as those of the Kababish, or are they of the poor kind?'

Here I thought I had some aces up my sleeve. I had brought with me photographs of prize Suffolk rams and champion steers from the Royal Show. I presented the cards triumphantly in the light of my torch. But my triumph faded when I noticed the Arabs puzzling over the pictures, turning them over and holding them upside down. I realized with surprise that these men had no concept of pictures and could not make out the shape of an animal in two dimensions. It had never occurred to me that this was a learned concept. There had been superb rock paintings and carvings in the Sahara for millennia, and the men who made them were certainly nomads. But these nomads had lost the art of drawing. Their only artifacts were things that were essential to them on their wanderings, and their arts were poetry, storytelling and song, which could be transported anywhere.

Later, when I traced the outlines of the animals with my finger, they soon recognized them, declaring, 'No God but God, see how fat they are!' Wad Ballal asked me if we lived on their milk. I explained that we drank a great deal of cow's milk. Then, just to be devilish, I added, 'We milk the cows twice a day with a machine that sucks the milk out of their udders and pours it into a bucket!'

They looked at me in obvious disbelief. 'How can that be?' Dagalol said. 'Surely it is easier to milk them by hand. That is something that any child can do!'

'Not in my country,' I told him. 'Some of my people have never seen a cow. They buy milk in bottles and don't even know where it comes from!'

The Arabs were eager to know about women and marriage. I was always a little ashamed to admit to nomads that I was unmarried, for I knew that for them celibacy was ridiculous. It was the aim of every nomad to marry as soon as possible and become a master of a household. Old men who had not married were figures of fun.

'Do your people marry, or do they just take a woman?' Wad Ballal asked.

I told him that we had both systems.

'But if you just take a woman, what happens to the children?'

'There may be no children. We have medicine to get rid of them.'

'God protect us from the devil!'

Dagalol explained that a man must have children, especially sons, to look after his livestock. 'You should have at least three,' he declared. 'One for the goats, one for the sheep and one for the camels.'

'What about daughters?'

'They are just incidental.'

I asked why there were no women here. 'This is the *shogara*,'

16

Dagalol told me, 'the southern migration. Only the men go on the *shoqara*. The women stay in the north in the *damar* camps. They look after the goats until the rains come, then they move. That is why we have no tents here. The tents are for women.'

The fire had burned down to a pool of glowing ashes. The camels were drowsy and had stopped chewing the regurgitated forage of the day. One by one the Arabs got up from the fire and unfolded the sheepskins and canvas sheets they slept on. Before he retired, Dagalol told me, 'There are plenty of robbers in these ranges. The thieving is worse than it has been for years. Now you can hardly rest a single night for fear of bandits, by God! Do you have a weapon?' I told him that I had a ·22 revolver. 'Hah, that is no use,' he said. 'Tomorrow I shall give you a shotgun. It is necessary in this land. And do not sleep too soundly. We call that the sleep of the donkey. The man who sleeps like a donkey may never wake!' And with these words of encouragement, the Arab stalked off to bed.

I lay down on my sheepskin, my head awash with thoughts and ideas. For a long time I stayed awake staring at the stars and sensing the wall of camels around me, smelling their smell and hearing the occasional sighs and scuffles from their midst.

I knew little about the Kababish except that they were a confederation of about nineteen tribes and some smaller subsections who shared a common culture and a common nazir, or paramount chief. They were of different origins. Most of their ancestors, however, came originally from Arabia. In 1048 the Fatimid Caliph Mustansir allowed his vizier to unleash the bedouin of the Bani Hillal, the Bani Sulaym and kindred tribes against the people of North Africa. Each Arab was given a piece of gold and a camel on the understanding that he would settle in the conquered territory.

The tribes ravaged and pillaged the new lands, settling along the Libyan and Tunisian coast. Some of them pressed west as far as the Maghreb and south into the Sahara, where they eventually mixed with tribes of Berber origin. Others began to trickle into the deserts west of the Nile.

In the Nile valley itself the Christian kingdoms of Nubia had long resisted the Arab threat. Eventually though, cut off from their spiritual heartland by the Muslim domination of Egypt, the kingdoms grew weak and succumbed to the invaders. The first Muslim ruled in Dongola in 1315. The Arabs obtained control of Nubia by marriage, as it was the custom in Nubia that inheritance was passed through

17

the female line. By giving the Arabs their daughters as wives, the Nubians acceded control to the Arabs while ensuring that the character of their land remained essentially Nubian, as it still does today.

But in the deserts west of the river, the ancestors of the Kababish roamed as they had always done. The fourteenth-century Arab historian Ibn Khaldun commented, 'There is no vestige of authority in the land, but they remain nomads, following the rainfall like the Arab of Arabia.'

In 1982 little had happened to change that pattern. The Kababish remained nomads like their fathers and grandfathers, herding camels, goats, sheep and a few cattle throughout the deserts and desert steppes of the western Sudan.

In Arabia the bedouin were camel breeders; the sheep-breeding tribes remained separate. While the Kababish saw themselves as camel-men, they managed to rear all types of livestock. This was possible because of the complex system of migrations they had developed, in which different parts of the family moved to different places at certain times of the year. Those who herded the camels could live adequately on milk, but the Arabs who kept goats and sheep required grain to sustain them while the camels were away. The Kababish traded their animals in local markets and as far afield as Egypt in return for grain and the essentials that they could not produce themselves, such as salt, tea, sugar, cloth, dates, seasoning and metal goods.

The camel was the most important of their animals. It provided milk and occasional meat; its hair was the main component of Kababish tents. The camel gave them the mobility they needed to traverse the vast distances they covered each year. It carried the Arab scouts on their search for grazing. It carried a man's belongings, his tent and his wives, his children and his supplies, ferrying his small, portable world across the wilderness. Without the camel, life in these desiccated latitudes would not have been possible.

I spent a restless night. The camels around me shifted continually, lurching up suddenly on their three legs and hopping about with ponderous, pounding steps within a few feet of my head. Dagalol was up constantly, cursing at the camels and swearing at the herdsboys, 'Down you son of the uncircumcised! May the Zaghawa take you! Where is that slave! Hamdan! Get up, you lazy black!'

The morning was full of the acrid smell of camel, and the animals

18

seemed to be everywhere, thick around the hearth and hugging the bases of the thorn trees. They were all shapes and sizes, from enormous stud-bulls to fluffy calves a few weeks old. Many of them were she-camels, gigantically pregnant or carrying bulging udders that cried out for milking.

The Arabs were already gathering around the fire, on which a pan of camel's milk bubbled. No one seemed to speak much at that hour of the day. Even the camels seemed unwilling to move from the cosy configurations in which they had arranged themselves. There was a pristine stillness that seemed to hold everything in its power. The Arabs, wrapped in their ragged woollen *tobes*, possessed a strange dignity as they rested silently by the hearth as if in meditation on the approaching day. Only the Mima boys moved carrying heavy bowls of milk fresh from the udder and filling up the goatskins that hung from the central pole. I watched one of them, Sayf ad Din, as he went through the ritual of milking. He chose a big she-camel and released her from the hobble so that she stood up, lazily shaking herself until her fat hump wobbled. Then the boy spoke to her softly, massaging her udder. His fingers worked lightly on the teats while he held the bowl in his left hand, balancing on one leg as the milk splashed into the vessel. The fresh milk was covered in froth and slightly salty. The Arabs called it *halib*. It was stored in long goatskins that hung vertically by the upper end. The larger skins, made of either goat or sheep hide, were used for carrying water.

We drank tea mixed with milk for breakfast. The mixture was bitter, for the Kababish thought it a waste to use milk and sugar together. They drank out of miniature enamel mugs, which they laid in the sand before the pourer after they finished each one. They drank five or six cups of this tea every morning, for there was no shortage of milk.

After we had tea, I went with Dagalol to visit the camp of Mohammid Wad Habjur, which was pitched about a hundred metres away, across a carpet of *diffir* grass. We were welcomed by Mohammid and his father, a stumpy man with a wedge-shaped face and a head of grey hair. 'Welcome!' said the old man, Habjur. 'You are the *Ingleezi* who wants to travel with the Kababish? Don't you know that the life of the Arabs is difficult? The people of the town cannot stand it! The Arabs carry hunger and thirst. Their way is the way of men, by God! There is no comfort here!' He said this in a chaffing, jocular tone, but I realized that underneath it lay the traditional

19

distrust that the nomads felt towards townsmen like myself. They regarded themselves as superior to all settled people, white or black. Anyone who was not a European or a free Arab was referred to as being one of the *'Awwala* – the slaves. The Kababish called themselves *Al 'Arab* and would scarcely concede that there were any Arabs more noble than themselves.

The lives of these men were austere simply because they were nomads, and because they could not afford to own goods other than those they could carry. It was this very austerity, however, that gave them their sense of aloofness. From the beginning I was regarded as inferior, partly because I was a townsman and partly because I simply could not do what they could. I had not come amongst these Arabs to be an observer. I wanted no less than to become one of them. I knew that it was an almost impossible task, yet I was rigidly determined to follow their customs and faith and to do as they did, no matter how hard it proved. Only in this way could I show myself to be worthy of them, and open up the way for acceptance.

After we left Habjur's camp, Dagalol took me on a tour of his camel herd in order to find one that would suit me. He owned more than two hundred animals. Only a small number of them were trained riding camels. These were all males, and could be distinguished from the others by their low humps and the patchwork marks on their backs where a saddle had rubbed against their hide. Riding and baggage camels were known as *jumaal* to differentiate them from the herd camels, or *ilbil*.

The Kababish had three types of camel: the *ashab*, the *'anafi* and the *'arabi*. The *ashab* was a racing dromedary, imported from the Beja tribes in the east of the Sudan. It was distinguished by its off-white colour, small head and curved neck. It was lightly built, full-muscled and extremely fast and smooth, much prized as a riding animal for raiding and hunting. The *'arabi* was a massive beast, ponderous and powerful. This was the animal that carried the Arabs' belongings and the colourful litters in which their women rode. It was generally beige, red, white or light-brown in colour, and could be recognized by its large forefeet. The *'arabi* was the breed developed by the Kababish themselves and was well adapted to the desert. It was enduring and patient and often used as a riding camel for long-distance treks such as those to Egypt. The *'anafi* was a hybrid, produced by the interbreeding of the other two types, com-

20

bining the characteristics of both. Some of the fastest and most enduring camels the Kababish owned were of the *'anafi* type.

It was an *'arabi* that I selected from the camels Dagalol offered me, since I knew that over the next months I might be covering a great distance. The animal was a huge fawn-coloured male and Dagalol told me that his name was Wad al 'Atiga. 'A good choice, by God!' he commented. 'This camel will take you anywhere. But he will cost you a great deal.'

I asked how much, and he told me, '1,000 pounds!'

I gulped. This was all the money I had in the world. I offered him 400. The Arab shook his head, pityingly. 'You know I would not sell him except for your sake, and because of Abu Safita. He is an excellent animal. I have reared him from a calf. His mother was sick with the mange and recovered. That is why I called him Wad al 'Atiga – it means "The Son of the One that was Sick and Recovered".' I knew that the Arabs hated to sell their camels, but that they were also masters at sales talk. We were opponents, and I was obliged to strike the best bargain I could. I offered 450. 'May God open!' he said in the traditional way. We argued for about half an hour. At the end of that time I had managed to bring the price down to 600. I suspected that Dagalol would not shift any lower, so I said, 'Very well, 600.'

'It is a very good bargain for you,' he told me, clasping my hand, 'Wad al 'Atiga will bring you luck.'

'Do all your camels have names?' I inquired.

'Of course. How else would we know them?' he replied.

By the time we returned to Dagalol's camp, the sun had risen and clean golden light was flooding across the ranges. The boys had released most of the herd from their hobbles and already the camels had spread out into the wedges of thorn bush, browsing amongst the prickly leaves or tearing up the thick grasses. Far across the plain I could see the sunlight reflected on the massed bodies of other herds, tiny islands in the immense ocean of grass.

Now the meditative mood of the early morning was gone and the camp was in uproar. Half a dozen camels were being loaded and the boys were running about with saddle-bags and goatskins, shouting and swearing. I saw Abboud and Hassan stop to wrestle over the headrope of a camel that seemed too young for riding. 'He is mine!' Hassan wailed, 'I am training him!'

'You!' Abboud snorted. 'How can you train him? You are not trained yourself yet!'

They pushed and pulled at each other in a miniature tug of war until the little animal, roaring and trying to back away, gurgled up a mess of green vomit. Most of it fell on Hassan. I could smell the nauseating stench from where I stood. The boy let go of the rope at once and shivered in disgust. Dagalol rumbled with laughter. 'That camel knows what is best for him,' he chuckled. 'You will never be a man while you give up so easily!'

As the loading continued, Dagalol called me over to him. He opened a long, narrow, tightly clasped saddle-bag and took out the pieces of an old shotgun, which he assembled. It was an unusual but handsome-looking weapon, made by the travelling gunsmiths of the Zaghawa tribe. 'Here,' he said, 'this is what you need. It will not be much use at long-range, but if anyone tries to steal your camel in the night, you can blast him, by God! He will not escape!'

'Is it really necessary?'

'I told you that the land is full of bandits. The tribes have gone mad. Only a few weeks ago we had seven camels stolen. This is not a place for games. What will you do if someone steals your camel in the desert? You may as well ask God to save you, for there will be no other chance. Take the gun and do as I say. This place is a land of men and not for the shade dwellers. This gun is old, but it is better than nothing!'

I realized that I was up against sales talk again. But I knew from my previous travels that there was much in what he said. The desert and the Sahel were more disturbed than they had been for decades. The tribes were at each other's throats in a way unheard of since before colonial times. The British had succeeded in keeping tribal competition to a minimum by the Native Administration Ordinance, which had concentrated power into the hands of nazirs and omdas. The system had worked well, but the present government had removed it, placing power in the persons of local officials who often knew little of the tribes and cared even less. Old rivalries, still smouldering during colonial times, had erupted into flames once more. The violence grew worse.

I parted with another sixty pounds for the gun, then went quickly about preparing Wad al 'Atiga for riding. I was anxious to demonstrate to these nomads that I was well versed in the ways of camels.

I adjusted the girth of my saddle to fit him. As I began to saddle, Dagalol shouted, 'Hey! That is not the way to do it!'

I protested that I had been riding camels for several years, and certainly knew how to saddle, but he brushed my objections aside, saying, 'You hang the waterskins on first, one each side for balance.' He generously allowed me to take two of the fullest skins, which we loaded together. They did not hang properly, so we lengthened the loops with hobbling-ropes. Then he told me to fit my two saddle-bags, one over each skin. 'Now fold up your canvas carefully and lay it over the saddle,' he said. 'Yes, that is the way. Now your sheep-skin, with the head pointing towards you as you mount. Now the blankets, you fold them and lay them over the sheepskin. Then the saddle-cushion. Good. Your water-bottle comes next. Hang it over the saddle-horn, then hang your shotgun on the right side so that you can grab it if there is trouble. You understand? If you fit the camel like that always, there will be no problems.' All this luggage made the saddle very high, and hard to mount. It was necessary to step on the camel's withers, with the right hand gripping the rear saddle-horn. As soon as the beast began to stand up, the rider would hook his knee around the front horn and swing into the saddle as the camel reached full height. Trained camels tended to rise as soon as they felt the rider rest the slightest weight on them, and I had once seen an inexperienced rider break his arm when the camel rose suddenly in this way. The trick was to leap quickly and without hesita-tion, at the same time holding the headrope taut in the left hand so that the animal could not rise more than a few inches prematurely. It was a simple matter of timing.

The Kababish used the double-horned riding saddle that orig-inated in North Arabia. It had probably come to the Sudan with their Bani Hillal ancestors. The main problem of camel saddle design was to find a way of accommodating the rider on the beast's back in spite of the protruding hump. In South Arabia they had solved the problem by seating the rider behind the hump, whereas the Tuareg had saddles that placed the riders on the withers in front of it. The Somalis, who had probably been the first to bring camels to Africa, had never solved the problem, and their crossed slats of wood only served for carrying baggage. For this reason they never rode their camels.

The North Arabian saddle design placed the rider above the hump. Its four 'feet' rested on pads of leather filled with goat-hair, which protected the animal's back, and the two wings of the seat were separated by a gap that allowed the top of the hump to press through. A good saddle had its wings inclined in such a way that the rider was never in contact with the hump. The Kababish also had a pack saddle, the *hawiyya*, which was much cruder, but of the same basic design. It was supported by pads of sacking or straw, though the Kababish of the north used palm fibre. The riding saddles were made by the Kababish men, and were often ornate.

It took no more than half an hour to load everything and clear the camp. As I watched the Arabs strapping on saddle-bags, fitting their pack saddles and lapping them around with rope, folding blankets and canvas sheets and draping on waterskins, I marvelled how everything they had fitted life on the move. There was no dross, and almost everything was adaptable. The canvas sheet was a relatively new item, imported from Libya or Egypt, yet it was one of the most useful. It was a groundsheet and a tent; it could be used as a trough for watering animals, or as a sling for carrying heavy items or loads of hay. The Kababish had little use for rugs in these latitudes, since they could be eaten by termites. Before the arrival of canvas sheets they had used thick sheets of cowskin. The leather saddle-cushions, oblong and about two feet long, were used as seats and pillows, and the sheepskin served as a mattress or an extra blanket in extreme cold.

Almost all Kababish men carried rifles or shotguns. These weapons were symbols of their freedom in their vast, wild land, where a man's security depended on himself. Many Arabs, like Dagalol, carried modern weapons: Kalashnikovs, FNs, and Heckler-Kochs. However, the bolt-action Lee-Enfield ·303, known as Umm 'Ashara ('Mother of Ten Shots') was still a favoured rifle. I saw many Kababish with Martini-Henri breech-loaders, some stamped 'Sudan Government 1899' yet still in perfect condition. Rifles and shotguns like the one I had bought were made by travelling gunsmiths of the Zaghawa tribe, who carried their workshops by camel and followed the nomads from camp to camp.

A Kabbashi was not dressed without his dagger, which was never worn in the belt but always on the left arm. It was a straight-bladed, double-edged weapon carried in a leather sheath, usually decorated with geometric patterns and coloured patches. In the same sheath the Arab would carry a pair of tweezers for removing thorns, and a curved packing needle, always useful for mending equipment. Many

Kababish carried swords, most of them long-bladed weapons imported from the east. All these steel weapons were made for the Arabs by settled blacksmiths, for the Kababish considered the practice of metalworking a disgrace; I only ever heard of one Kababish family who had taken up the trade.

When everything was lashed on the baggage camels and the riding animals were saddled, Dagalol fetched his own *ashab* and mounted. A few hundred metres to the east old Habjur, his son and herdsmen were already in the saddle, pushing their herd out in long columns. Beyond them were two or three herds belonging to other members of the clan, trickling slowly towards the northern horizon. One by one the Arabs who were with me mounted, flicking their camels with sticks and whips. I picked up my own whip and climbed aboard Wad al 'Atiga. Within moments we were half a kilometre from the camp that had been home for a night, the place where my life with the Kababish had started.

As I rode, all the familiar feelings came back to me in the slow, lumbering gait of the herd and the sharp cries of the herdsmen. We moved very slowly, so that the camels could graze as they went, in and out of the thorn thickets and along the sandy banks, bursting with grasses. It was deliciously peaceful in the cool of the morning, moving gradually north across the vast panorama of Darfur. The savannah undulated gently, a soft sheen of lush grass scattered with beds of flowers where insects hovered in sparkling colours. There were acacias of many shapes, with trunks bulbous and delicate, silver-grey, lime-green and red. There were trees with nests of orange berries, and waxy-leafed *mukhayyit* with ivory fruit, like bunches of pearls. The sky was full of birds. Hornbills ducked and pitched on their uncertain trajectory between the trees, and I saw the deep blue of Abyssinian Rollers in the bushes. There were kites and lanner falcons circling high above us. The red sand between the patches of grass was littered with the tracks of ground-squirrels and gerbils, and there were many craterlike pustules of ants' nests. Amongst the thorn brake rose the amber sculptures of great termitaries.

Four thousand years ago, a man might have ridden north from this place for more than a thousand miles, as far as the coast of the Mediterranean, and found the land everywhere as rich as this. He might have seen herds of elephants in the middle of what is today the Sahara, and found tribes of nomads herding the ancestors of

25

today's cattle. He might have skirted lakes that brimmed with fish, and wandered over mountainsides covered in cedar trees. Now, no more than thirty kilometres north of these savannahs, the vegetation began to dwindle and the rich carpet of grasses gave way to parched earth.

All morning the herds seemed to drift on at their own volition, scattering into loose formation on the richer pastures and drawing up tight again where the grazing was sparse. There was no sense of hurry. All the world moved at the measured pace of the camel, minute after minute, hour after hour, as the sun changed shape from a bloated globe of orange to a tight yellow fireball. It was a pleasure to meander along, taking in the details of the landscape, the richness of the trees and herbs, the tell-tale signs of previous migrations. In one place there were piles of black droppings that indicated an overnight camp, and pieces of blackened wood beside the white bones of a bustard picked clean by the ants. In another there were a few fragments of bark where a man had twisted a rope, and five neat hollows in the earth where a camel had been couched.

By midday we had come to a concave bowl where the *siyaal* trees grew thick and low, and where silver boulders peeked out of the covering of grass. Dagalol told me to couch Wad al 'Atiga, and all around me the others began to make their animals kneel. 'This will be our *taya*,' Dagalol declared. 'This is where we stay the night.' We untied our saddles and laid our equipment in the grass, and Dagalol told me to hobble my camel with the foreleg-hobble, or *gayd*. This was a thick rope of cowskin with a knot at one end. It was looped around the camel's hocks and fastened so that he could shuffle about grazing, but could not walk normally. Only the riding animals were hobbled in this way, so that they were able to graze, yet would be easy to find if needed quickly. Putting on the *gayd* was a dangerous operation. The rider held the headrope in his teeth in case the animal tried to bolt, and then bent down near the camel's forelegs. Camels were often bothered by flies under their chests, and would raise their legs and stamp down hard to disperse them just as the rider was about to fix the hobble. The beast's legs were as powerful as pistons and could easily crush a man's arm. I soon learned that the job should be done at arm's length, and as quickly as possible.

After hobbling, the boys went off to watch the herd and I joined Wad Ballal, clearing the ground of deadwood and droppings and laying out saddles and bedding in a neat line. The wooden support, which had been cut from an *inderab* tree, was firmly planted in a hole and we slung the heavy skins from it before covering them with canvas against the heat. They could not be left on the ground, for the liquid would seep out or they might be ruined by termites.

It was already very hot. Beyond the forest of acacias that stretched for miles north and south, I could make out the flat, red ledge of a mountain wall. Not far away to the east were knots of gargantuan baobab trees, their trunks stripped and raw. The Arabs used their supple bark for rope-making. The tribulus beneath my feet was full of silver centipedes about six inches long, whose segmented bodies reflected the light brilliantly. There was plenty of shade around us, and I wondered why Dagalol had chosen to make camp in the open. 'This is uncertain country,' he told me. 'It is better to stay away from trees so that bandits cannot use them for cover after dark.'

A few minutes later Wad Ballal drew a massive bowl of sour milk from one of the skins. The cheesy-tasting liquid was cool and very refreshing, and I began to understand why the Arabs cherished it. There were several points of etiquette to remember when drinking milk. Like water it was supposed to be drunk squatting down, not standing. It was very impolite to allow the nose to dip into it, and the generous proportions of mine gave me a disadvantage in this. It happened several times that I withdrew it with milk dripping from the end, and received withering glances from the Arabs.

After the milk had been drunk, we moved away from the *taya* and into the shade of the nearby trees. In Kababish country the Arabs would have no qualms about leaving their *taya* all day and even overnight. The *taya* was almost like a sacred sanctuary, and to steal from one was an utter disgrace. If travellers discovered a *taya* unattended, though, it was quite acceptable for them to help themselves to the milk, for they were considered the guests of whoever owned it. But in this savannah country there were many tribes who had no respect for Arab customs and who could not be trusted.

Wad Ballal took out some long strands of bark that he had stripped that morning from a baobab tree and placed them in a bowl of water to soak. Later I watched him as he anchored several of them amongst his toes and began plaiting them together with a twisting motion of the palms. 'In our country we make ropes out of wool,' he told me, 'because there are no baobabs in the desert, but here we

27

use bark while we can get it.' It took about twenty minutes to make an *'uqal*. When it was finished, the loop was fixed around a peg of wood that the Arab cut from a bush nearby.

In mid-afternoon five camel riders appeared suddenly out of the brush and couched their mounts near our camp. They were all muscular, heavy-set men with broad black faces and tufts of spiral hair, bearing a family resemblance, like a stamp. Few of the Nas Wad Haydar looked like Arabs; their features reminded me more of the Beja tribesmen from the east of the Sudan, whom I had seen in Omdurman. Their clothes were filthy and in tatters, yet their riding saddles were immaculate, carefully greased and polished. Most of them carried automatic rifles that they braced on tripods of wood when they sat down.

As they approached the camp, Dagalol called out, 'Welcome! Welcome in peace!' and we lined up to greet them. The greeting consisted of the repeated hand-shaking and releasing, and the reciting of the rhythmic formulas over and over again. These formulas were meant to be question and response – 'I hope you are well?' and 'Thanks be to God, I am well!' – but in practice the Arabs just rattled them off without particular order and without waiting for a reply. Some of them jerked out the phrases at the speed of a machine-gun with hardly a pause for breath. Often the exchanges struck me as unbelievably comical, a contest to see who could rattle loudest and longest; I once timed a series of greetings between two Kababish at fifteen minutes. Eventually, though, the custom grew on me, and I began to view the brief greetings of townsmen as brusque and rude.

Our guests sat down in the shade with great dignity, each one laying his rifle on its tripod before him. One of them was a tall man with a distinguished bearing whom I discovered was Dagalol's elder brother, Haj Hassan. Another was a curious, gnomelike little man with a frail body and an overlarge head covered with a quiff of hair. His appearance was so childlike that I was surprised to learn that he was Ali Wad Hassan, the chief scout of Nas Wad Haydar. The Arabs began to ask Dagalol about me: where was I from? What tribe did I belong to? My host began to recite my story, repeating things I had told him the previous night, and embroidering here and there to give the tale extra weight. In his mouth it sounded like an epic, and I realized that it was an expression of the Kababish love of storytelling for its own sake.

As we talked, Wad Ballal made a fire between three stones and set on it a blackened kettle. Abboud brought the guests dates and a bowl of sour milk. The tea was black, and stiff with sugar; the Arabs drank it with loud, appreciative sips. The kettle went back on the fire time and again in the course of the afternoon.

Dagalol asked, 'What of the grazing? What kinds of grass have you seen?' One by one the men gave accounts of the grasses and trees they had seen that morning. They had an encyclopedic knowledge of the plants and animals in their environment, and excellent memories for locations. They had sharpened the art of description into an exact science, and had a large vocabulary of words with fine gradations of meaning for geographical features. When the talk of grazing faded, Ali Wad Hassan said, 'I saw a *gom* of Zaghawa riding north-west this morning. There were twelve of them on fast camels. They were all carrying rifles. Their camels had the brand of the Artaj, and one of the men was Awdi Mohammid who took three camels from the 'Awajda last year. They might have been going to the market, but you do not need rifles in the market.'

'They were bandits and no doubt!' Haj Hassan commented.

'Curse their fathers!' Dagalol declared. 'They are a pestilence since they came south!'

The Zaghawa were one of the semi-nomadic tribes speaking a central-Saharan language who inhabited the semi-deserts of North Darfur. They had been the rivals of the Kababish for generations. Since the late 1970s, however, their lands had been severely affected by drought and desertification. Many had abandoned their villages and fled to the cities. Others had moved south with the remnants of their herds, where they had come into conflict with other tribes intent on using the southern grasslands.

The next day we moved off soon after sunrise, coursing through the forests of acacia and moving steadily north towards the granite ridge I had seen on the previous day. The camels strode on, lowering their cranelike necks as they went, and consuming the luscious herbage by the ton. The grasses became sparser as we moved north, and Dagalol sent Abboud off on his fast little camel to find the best pasture. Throughout the morning we twisted north-west and north-east, turning and circling in search of better grazing. At noon we made camp on a plain of tribulus beneath a shining wall of grey rock, which was the edge of a range of hills to the west. Nearby we

29

saw the conical roofs of a village called Ereja, inhabited by cultivators of the Berti tribe.

After we had made the *taya* I rode off with Dagalol and Mohammid Wad Habjur in search of a she-camel that had been lost during the morning. We found her several kilometres away, lying near a *siyaal* tree. She was still alive, but when the Arabs examined her they found that one of her rear legs was broken. Mohammid said that she had probably been kicked by a bull-camel trying to mate with her. 'We shall have to slaughter her,' Dagalol said, 'and we can sell some of the meat to the Berti.'

Leaving the animal, we mounted up and rode to the nearby village. It was similar in appearance to Ghubaysh, but slightly larger, with the usual beehive huts and tottering compounds of cane. We couched our camels outside one of the houses and were greeted by a tribesman of the Berti, a thin little black man wearing a cotton singlet and a skull-cap. As they dismounted, slinging their rifles across their shoulders, I noticed an almost imperceptible change come over the Arabs. Suddenly their manner was reserved and distant, as if they were in the presence of an inferior; as they walked into the compound they seemed to summon a condescending dignity that was not far short of swagger.

We sat inside one of the grass huts, and a woman brought us a bowl of hot polenta. It was greenish-grey in colour with the consistency of dumplings, and was covered in a gravy made of onions, dried tomatoes and okra. The hut contained little except two rope-beds and some tin boxes piled against the wall. As we ate, Dagalol explained that he had some meat to sell. The Bertawi nodded, and said that he would fetch all the men of the village who would ride out and butcher the animal. After he had gone his wife came to collect the empty bowl. She was a small woman with a very dark complexion and short, spiral hair. She was probably not long out of her twenties, though she looked worn and thin from childbirth and hard work. To my amazement Dagalol called the woman over and said, 'Your people are coming with us to slaughter a she-camel. While they are out of the village I will come back to see you. You understand?' At first I thought I must have misheard, but the woman nodded, her face expressionless, and said, 'Very well.'

My thoughts were interrupted by shouts of 'Peace be upon you, people of the house!' We stood up to greet two nomads of the Zayadiyya tribe, both carrying rifles, who sat down with us in the hut.

The men were very excited and told us that they had just returned from chasing some Zaghawa who had stolen six of their camels in the night. 'The slaves made camp in a wadi not far from here,' one of the men told us. 'So we dismounted and made a circle round them. Then we opened fire. I shot one of them dead and my brothers shot two more. The rest of them ran away, leaving the dead ones. We let them go, and just collected our camels. They will not come looking for our stock again. No, they will not forget that lesson, by God!'

'What was their tribe?' Dagalol asked.

'They had the brand of the Artaj.'

'Were there twelve of them?'

'Yes, but there are only nine now.'

'We spotted them moving north-west yesterday. May the curse be upon them, the sons of dogs!'

As Dagalol talked to the Zayadiyya, some of the arrogance dropped from his manner and he assumed a cordiality that seemed exaggerated after his distant manner with the Berti. I had heard in El Fasher that there had been clashes between the Kababish and the Zayadiyya recently, and I expected my host to treat these men more as enemies than friends.

Not long afterwards the Berti assembled with their camels and donkeys, and we rode out to butcher the she-camel. She was still lying where we had left her, and at once Mohammid Wad Habjur slaughtered her, stabbing her in the neck with his dagger, then slitting her throat. Before the Berti set to work to cut up the meat, Dagalol agreed on a price with them for the carcass. Then he told them that he would ride back to his herd, and rejoin them before the work was finished. No one paid him much attention as he mounted his fine camel and slipped off across the ranges. I sat with Mohammid and watched the men carving red slivers of meat and hanging them on the thorn trees. One man severed the head with an axe. The camel still looked very peaceful, lying coiled in the sand. It seemed an ignominious end for such a noble beast, yet I realized that this was the law of the nomads. Those which could not keep up with the herd had to die.

Dagalol returned as the men were dividing the meat and stowing it in leather bags. His face wore an inscrutable expression as he dismounted and watched the final stage of the work.

Later, as the three of us rode back to camp, he bragged, 'I made

31

sixty pounds for the camel and only paid two for the woman! These Berti women never refuse, by God!'

'What would have happened if they had caught you?' I asked him.

'Death!' he smirked, though he did not make clear whose death it would have been.

For a week we moved north-west, circling around the hills of Karkur and Bat-Ha, searching for rich pasture. The days faded into one another, indistinguishable except for small events. As my body became accustomed to the new pattern of life, this unchanging rhythm became a soothing heartbeat, which at times brought me a deep sense of peace and tranquility.

The mornings were grey and heavy, the sky overcast with billows of cloud, grey and Prussian blue. Occasionally the air was moistened with a scatter of raindrops, but there was no cloudburst of the kind the Arabs hoped for. The plains were crowded with nomads. There were tribesmen from other sections of the Kababish: the Nurab, the Haworab and the Barara, as well as unrelated tribes such as the Zayadiyya, the Zaghawa and the Meidob. Mostly, however, these nomads moved with their camels and fat-tailed sheep like unseen clippers below the horizon. It was only at night, when scores of campfires twinkled out of the darkness, that the scale of the great migrations made itself felt.

In the evening, after the meeting with the Zayadiyya, Dagalol became even more circumspect. He would post one of the Mima boys as a sentry and expect him to stay awake all night. In the morning there would often be acrimonious arguments about one of them having fallen asleep. My sympathy was with the boys, for I noticed that they always got the lion's share of the work and I did not blame them for being exhausted at night. They were little more than children, yet they did the work of adults. They seemed perfectly at ease amongst the camels and I often watched them riding, some-times bareback, perched like crows on the rumps of huge bulls, handling them with the confidence of masters. Though the Mima were villagers like the Berti and owned few camels of their own, many of them were apprenticed to Kababish herd owners from a very early age. They were paid in livestock, and each boy received a young camel at the end of a year. Sayf ad Din and Hamdan had been working for Dagalol for almost two years. I once asked Sayf ad Din what he would do when he had finished working here. 'I will have a herd of my own,' he told me, 'and I will grow millet and sorghum and ride a white donkey. I will be a rich man like Dagalol!'

Indeed, Dagalol was rich by Arab standards. Apart from his large camel herd, he owned goats, sheep and cattle that were still in Kordofan. Like most Kababish, he did not display his wealth in his manner of living. He ate the same meagre food, wore the same tattered clothes and lived the same hard life as his fellow-men. Amongst the nomads a man's position in society depended not only on the number of livestock he owned, but also on his generosity. The Kababish disliked selling their animals and always maintained herds and flocks that were as large as possible. They never culled the weak animals to improve the strain. I once asked Wad Ballal if this maintenance of large herds was purely to improve a man's position. 'It is good to have many animals,' he told me, 'but that is not the only reason the Kababish have large herds. In times of hardship, when the rains do not come, the weak animals will die anyway. The man with a hundred camels may be left with twenty, but the man with twenty will be left with nothing. But no matter how many animals a man has, if he is not open-handed he is nothing. The man who does not slaughter animals for his guests is not a man. It is better to have a few camels and be renowned for generosity than to have many and be known as a miser.'

'And which is Dagalol?'

'He is mean, by God! I would not work for such a mean one if I had the choice. I am a freeman from the 'Atawiyya, the Arabs of the desert. My family lost their herds years ago and I have to work as a herdsman. I get paid one adult camel every year, and usually I have to sell it. Still, God is generous. There are many who have less than me.'

I learned much from such conversations, and it soon became clear that the Kababish was by no means a society of equals. The bedouin tribes of Arabia were groups of independent freemen in which the sheikh held power by consent of the others. Amongst the Kababish, though, there were at least five distinct levels in the hierarchy. First, there were the livestock owners, like Dagalol and old Habjur, who formed a kind of upper crust. These were the Arabs who had the leisure to visit each other in the afternoons: the warrior class who carried automatic weapons and rode on *ashab* camels. After them came the herdsmen, who were divided into Arab freemen like Wad Ballal, and *'Awwala* herders like the Mima boys. They were

33

paid for their work, though the next level, the slaves, were not. They were bound to their masters by a reciprocal arrangement in which the freeman was obliged to feed and clothe them. Legally, of course, slavery did not exist in the Sudan, for it had been outlawed by the British in 1924. Kababish slaves could not be prevented from leaving their former masters, and many of them had done so. Others, however, had opted to remain in their position, valuing the sense of security that they were not assured of finding in the town or the city. Another class consisted of 'clients'. These were freemen who belonged to another tribe or family, and who might attach themselves to a powerful individual. There were no clients amongst the Nas Wad Haydar, though I met several later during my stay with the nazir.

Despite the sense of tranquility that engulfed me, there were inevitable times when the strangeness of the new culture weighed down on me like a heavy load. In the mornings I hardly noticed the time passing, but the afternoons were vacant spaces in which the day stretched out like a desert to the far-off horizon of the night. I was not accustomed to idleness, and my body was still geared to the constant stimulus of the town. I found that I had to make an effort to slow my body down to the ticking-over rate of the Arabs. They were never bored, and the words 'interesting' and 'boring' had no place in their vocabulary. If there was nothing to do, they merely retired into themselves, preserving their valuable energy for the next burst of activity. I had not yet learned to do this, and for a long time it remained my most difficult problem.

Language posed another problem. I spoke Arabic more or less fluently, but the Kababish spoke a dialect that I found difficult to understand. Not only was their pronunciation different, but they also used many words that were specific to their way of life and that only a nomad would have known. I set about learning as many of these words as I could, noting them down in my pocket-book in phonetic script, but the task was an unending one and the dialect seemed to get more difficult as I tried to pin it down.

In the afternoons the talk was always about raids and bandits. Old Habjur was the most aggressive and outspoken of the family. 'I have been through good times and bad,' he would say, 'and I am not going to let these slaves eat my livestock now! You see this rifle? It is an excellent weapon. It cost me the price of a camel, by God! I may have grey hair, but I still know how to shoot!'

Once he told me, 'I do not like this country. These slaves stop us watering our herds. They hold us back at the watering-place and say, "The wells are dry!" or they tell us, "Pay us money and we will let you water!" Curse their fathers! In the old days the Kababish would not come near this land of blacks! The grazing was good in the north then. You could stay in the desert and find everything you needed. If you wanted meat there were oryx and ostrich to hunt. Where are they now? I have not seen an ostrich in two years, by God! The best ranges have gone and we come further south every year.'

It was true that the settled tribes that controlled the bore-wells in the south resented the nomads' increasing activity in their land, and charged them high prices for water and sometimes even for grazing. If a camel strayed into cultivated land, the farmers would seize it and refuse to return it until the Arab paid a hefty fine. Often the owner had little cash and might have to sell the animal in order to pay.

Each day we seemed to pass deeper into the timeless zone of the ranges. We rode through prairies where the sand was obscured by the valuable *baghayl* grass with its tiny wheatlike ears and stalks of spun gold. We drove the massed herds under the sweeping back-drop of the Darfur mountains on the edge of the Marra range, through bristling acacia woods and out into the flat lagoons between volcanic atolls that rose from the valley floor like broken teeth. At other times there were few features by which to measure distance and time, and often little relief for the eye from the ocean of green stretching to every skyline. Sometimes I would forget where I had come from and where I was going. My life became free of past or future, just an ever-present now focused here in the tranquil, changeless undulation of the great herds across the land.

Often in the mornings the boys would sing. In clear voices they sang the four-line rhyming verse that the Kababish called *dobbayt*. The songs spoke of tall grasses and rich hunting, of races to the watering-place, of men who had fallen in camel raids, and of maid-ens with eyes like gazelles'. They sang of the things that lay close to the heart of their culture, and always the theme returned to the rain and the camel, the camel and the rain, over and over the melody repeated itself and the song went on and on as the camels paced and grazed. The song, the singer and the animals seemed to merge into a single euphonic harmony, regulated only by the slowly chang-ing intensity of the sun's heat.

Occasionally we moved so slowly that Wad Ballal and I would

dismount and let our camels graze with the herd. We would wander along behind them, stripping bark from a baobab tree or watching for game. There were some bustards here; once Dagalol brought one down with his Kalashnikov, and we ate meat. Another time he shot a massive shoebill, but after he had turned the great carcass over with his foot he said, 'Its meat is no good,' and he left it lying there for the ants and vultures. Once Wad Ballal bagged a wildcat by simply hurling his axe at it as it popped out of its hole at sunset. Its meat was tough but not unlike rabbit.

The days passed, and the nomads made no attempt to move further north. The rains had not yet fallen in Kordofan except in scattered places, and the Kababish were reluctant to drive the herds back without more encouraging news. I was still thinking about the desert and my meeting with Hassan Wad at Tom, and was afraid of being stuck in Darfur all winter. I told Dagalol about this and he said, 'Wait a few days, then we shall decide whether to go or stay. There will be a meeting if no news comes in a few days.' I agreed, and it was during those few days that the most memorable incident of my stay occurred.

We were camping on a gently rising bank covered with tribulus. About a hundred metres away to the west lay a wadi, veiled with acacia trees. It was late and the boys were already curled up on their sheepskins. I lay in my space nearby, writing up my journal in the light of my torch. I could see the dark figures of Dagalol and Wad Ballal hunched up near the remains of the fire, a pool of faintly glowing embers. There was a gentle murmur of talk from the Arabs. Beyond them were the shadowy outlines of the camels. The night was full of the sound of their chewing and the sweet–savoury smell of their bodies.

Suddenly I saw Dagalol stiffen. 'There are men in the wadi!' he hissed in a half-whisper. Both men turned their ears to the west and listened intently. 'Yes, by God!' Wad Ballal said. 'There are men with camels!' The Arabs were up in an instant and there was a metallic click as Dagalol cocked his rifle. Wad Ballal grabbed his torch and club. 'Abboud! Watch the camels!' Dagalol shouted. 'Omar! Get your gun!' I was already fumbling with my sandals. The boys threw back their covers and ran towards the herd. I snatched my shotgun and some cartridges, but already the two men had plunged into the darkness. I hovered on the perimeter of the camp for a moment, not knowing what Dagalol had intended, crashing a cartridge into the breech of my weapon and snapping it shut. Just then a camel roared somewhere to the west and suddenly three sharp reports cracked out of the darkness. My heart burst into activity and I ran towards the wadi with my shotgun held ready. I hoped to God that if I had to use the weapon it would not explode in my face as these home-made guns had been known to do.

There were no more shots; everything seemed quiet. I called out Dagalol's name and at once saw the flash of a torch from the trees. 'Omar!' someone called. 'Over here!'

I ran towards the light of the torch and found the two Arabs standing in the bed of sand beyond the trees. They were examining the ground, and in the torchlight I saw that it had been churned up by the feet and bodies of three or four camels. It was littered with fresh droppings and there were dark patches where the animals had staled. 'They must have heard me cock the gun,' Dagalol declared. 'A moment earlier and I should have got them!'

'They were bandits and no doubt,' Wad Ballal said.

Wad Ballal began to follow the tracks leading out of the wadi to the west. For a few moments he was screened from my sight by the trees and I could follow only the dim circle of the torchlight. Then he came shuffling out of the shadows and held up something. It was a hobbling-loop made of twisted cowhide. 'It was certainly someone from Darfur,' Wad Ballal said. 'The Kordofan tribes do not use this type of 'uqal.'

'Zaghawa!' Dagalol declared. 'Without doubt!'

Abboud appeared, and the four of us walked back to the camp together. 'The thieves got nothing this time,' Dagalol said, 'but they will be back!' Then he commented, 'I thought you were never coming, Omar! What happened to you? You must change those foreign sandals for some Arab shoes if you do not want to be caught out here!'

The next day some Nurab came into our camp at midday. They were quite different in appearance from the Nas Wad Haydar. There were two of them, both carrying old shotguns. One was a tall old man, whippet-slim and naked except for a pair of *sirwal* and a length of cloth that crossed his torso and fell down his back like a cloak. The other was a tremendously strong-looking Arab with an old *jibba* whose sleeves had been cut away to make room for his enormous biceps. Both men were lighter in colour than Dagalol's family and

37

were much more Arab in appearance, with straggling beards and grey-blue eyes.

After they had drunk tea, the strong-looking man took me aside, some distance from the camp, and asked for a cartridge for his shotgun. I gave him one, hiding my reluctance, and he put it away in his pocket.

'I have some advice for you,' he said. 'Do not stay with Dagalol any longer. He is a bad one. Remember one thing in this country. Never trust a fat Arab!' And before I could reply, he made off back to the camp, and was soon on his way with his companion.

That evening came the long-expected meeting. It was held after sunset, when the camels had been brought into a tight circle around our camp. A desultory fire trembled in the hearth and its poor light reflected on the shirts of the guests who came out of the darkness one by one. They shook hands and sat down with their rifles in front of them. Soon there were more than twenty Arabs sitting shoulder to shoulder. I recognized the faces of Habjur and his son amongst them, and the tall figure of Haj Hassan with a younger brother called Musa. The last to arrive was the diminutive Ali Wad Hassan. They looked as wild and primitive as savages sitting there in the firelight, but there was nothing primitive about their culture; it was a sophisticated and efficient adaptation to the demands of their environment.

It was Dagalol who spoke first. He described what had happened the previous night, and went on to say that it was time they moved north. 'Every day we remain here, we run the risk of losing stock,' he said. 'Those Zaghawa have no honour and they do not fear God. They will be back! Meanwhile we must pay much money for water, and half the time the herds go thirsty.'

'I am not with you!' Haj Hassan cut in. 'There is plenty of trouble in Kordofan and Darfur with the Zayadiyya. They are worse than the Zaghawa . . .'

'Do not bother about the Zayadiyya, brother,' Dagalol said. 'They are our friends.'

'They may be your friends,' the other said, with heavy and sarcastic emphasis, 'but they are not mine. I have no love for the Zayadiyya.'

I sensed under these words a deep resentment that referred to something I did not know about. I thought about the words of the Nurabi earlier that day, and wondered if there were a connection.

'We must be patient,' Haj Hassan continued. 'You have no patience, brother. It is better to stay here where there is grazing than to go back to nothing, just because we want cow's milk and porridge!'

Dagalol snapped back angrily, 'You are the one for the cows, not I!'

Suddenly the booming voice of Habjur chimed in, 'God knows I hate this land of blacks! But I am not going to see my camels grow thin because of a few slaves of the Zaghawa. No, by God! I am going to stay here and fight them. I may be old, but I can still shoot, by the life of the Prophet!'

Before he had finished, the piping voice of Ali Wad Hassan interrupted him, saying that if they did not move now, then there would be no grazing left on the way to Kordofan. Someone else said that many of the other Kababish tribes were already moving back. Another Arab with an uncut, frizzy mop of hair declared that he supported the Haj. Everyone seemed to talk at once, and the discussion continued for what seemed like hours, shuttling back and forth between the two opinions.

In the end it was the rhetoric of Haj Hassan and the power of old Habjur that carried the day. Dagalol agreed sulkily to wait until there was more definite news from the north. 'But there will be trouble, I tell you, brothers!' was his last word. In the event he was proved right.

I knew that this decision meant that I should have to travel north alone. I decided to set off the following day. That night I told Dagalol I was leaving, and thanked him for his hospitality. Whatever his shortcomings, and whatever the mystery surrounding him, he had not fallen short in his duties as my host. It was under his instruction that I had learned my first lessons about the Kababish. He told me that I was welcome to visit him in his *damar* at Umm Qozayn, and wished me good luck. 'But take care in the north,' he said. 'Do not sleep alone on the road. Always sleep with people. There are many bandits there, by God!'

I was up at first light the next day and saddling Wad al 'Atiga. Dagalol presented me with a skin of sour milk that he tied on the rear horn of my saddle. Then he shook hands and said, 'Go in the safe-keeping of God.'

I trotted my camel through the brakes of acacia and climbed a high ridge from which I could see the hills around the village of Wada'a, which lay across my path. Far away to the south I made out the herds of Nas Wad Haydar already moving out of their overnight camps. I had been with them only a matter of weeks, yet it seemed like a lifetime. For a few moments I watched them, tiny white dots on the vast landscape, moving in perfect harmony with the days and the seasons.

Then I flicked the rump of my camel and rode down towards the green fields of Wada'a.

2
Good Things in Humble Guises

The jerboa, or desert-rat, is one of the
most successful desert-dwellers. It can
live its life without ever drinking, breaking
down the dry plant material which it
eats to manufacture its own water.
*Henri Lhote, 'When the Sahara was
Green', The World's Lost Mysteries,
1976*

North of Wada'a the landscape changed with dramatic suddenness. Here the surface was a sheet of bone-dry clay, cracked and lifeless, through which the stalks of the acacias groped like petrified claws. The land was desolate. Gone were the mat of tribulus and the baobab trees. The edge of moisture in the air was replaced by wafts of choking dust, and the heat, reflected from the bare soil, was scorching. The familiar birds were no longer to be seen in the desiccated branches, and beneath their split and twisted roots lay the skeletons of dead cattle and donkeys.

I rode Wad al 'Atiga at a trot. Continually he turned his head left and right, searching for a mouthful of succulent grass in the arid landscape. Nowhere did there seem to be a rash of grass or a single tree in leaf. There were patterns in the earth where men had planted crops, but the sorghum and millet had not germinated. Many of the villages I passed looked broken and deserted. The straw huts were derelict, bleached grey by the sun and toppled over by the wind. The places had the look of ghost towns, stranded on the hard shoulder of the earth where cultivation would sustain them no longer.

No rain had fallen here for months. The farmers of the Berti and Mima tribes had abandoned their villages and moved south into the skirts of Jabal Marra. I wondered how those who remained managed to survive in this waterless land.

As soon as night came I made camp amongst the acacias. After

41

I unloaded, I hobbled my camel with the *gayd*, hoping that he might find a few withered leaves to appease his hunger. I set about making a small fire to brew some tea in the way I had learned from the Arabs. I collected three stones and laid them in a triangular pattern, then searched for a handful of dry straw to kindle the fire. It was difficult to find: only the brittle and less woody straw burned fiercely enough to ignite the wood. There was none underfoot and I eventually took some from an old bird's nest in a tree, as I had seen the Arabs do. I picked up a few tiny pieces of bone-dry wood and laid them on the straw in between the stones of my hearth. Then I set a match to the kindling, lighting the straw from beneath and lifting it so that the draught would spread the flame. When the tiny pieces of timber caught fire, I slowly added larger and larger pieces until the flames were hot enough to burn the two or three branches I had collected. Each stage of the process had to be carried out with a ritualistic attention to detail, for if the kindling was rushed the fire would be smothered, which was extremely irritating after a hard day in the saddle.

I made tea and drank three cups, then began to look around for Wad al 'Atiga. He was nowhere to be seen. Thinking that I should soon spot him, I skirted around the bushes on the perimeter of the camp. Nowhere could I make out the camel's dark shape, nor could I hear his chomping. I picked up my shotgun and made a wide circle around the camp. The moon was out, casting an eerie silver light over the silent landscape. The dead acacias stretched for miles, and in the moonlight there was nothing to distinguish one from another. Within a few metres I was totally disorientated and had to search for my footmarks in the grey dust in order to retrace my steps.

I stared into the night and listened carefully. No sound reached my ears. I skirted around once more, and found the track of what I thought was a hobbled camel. I began to follow it. The track wound in and out of the trees, half circling around, then twisting east and west. I followed it for about ten minutes until it performed a double-helix around a *tundub* tree and turned back in the direction from which I had come. My heart sinking, I hurried back towards my camp, realizing that I had been following the wrong track. Again I could not locate the camp. The colourless night disguised any feature that would allow me to navigate. Painstakingly I found my own tracks once more, and followed them to where my saddle and equipment lay, next to the burned-out fire.

I knew that my only chance lay in finding the camel's tracks, otherwise I would search the whole night and find nothing. But I now saw that there were scores of camel tracks around me. An Arab guide would have been able to spot Wad al 'Atiga's hoofmarks at once, and indeed would have scoffed at me as a fool for not knowing the distinct prints of my own camel. I still lacked this skill, and could barely tell the difference between the marks of a hobbled camel and a loose one. I selected a particularly visible track, which seemed fresh, and began to follow it south, armed with my torch and my shotgun.

I was so intent on the trail that I did not see the huts of the Mima village until I was almost on them. Suddenly a dog barked and I looked up to see a nest of six or seven grass buildings in the darkness. There were people here. I caught the scent of woodsmoke and glimpsed the flickering light of a fire inside one of the stockades. A few steps further on and I noticed the figures of two young women, clearly silhouetted in the moonlight. I hurried towards them, hoping desperately that they had seen my camel. I had scarcely opened my mouth to ask, when one of them let out a piercing scream, and shouted, 'The devil! The devil!' The other girl screamed too, and both took to their heels and charged off towards the nearest compound at a sprint, still yelling, 'The devil!' and ignoring my protests.

This reaction was a little disconcerting, and I stood still for a few minutes, wondering what to do. I had no wish to frighten these people further, especially as fear could be very dangerous, yet I was desperate for their help. I decided to approach the compound and behave as humbly as possible.

I knocked at the closed gate and shouted, 'Peace be on you, people of the house!' At first there was no sound, but after a few minutes a bent and bearded old man shuffled towards the gate, carrying a woodcutter's axe over his shoulder. He shook hands with me gingerly and eyed my shotgun. I explained as well as I could that I had lost my camel. After a moment the old man said, 'He has not come this way. That track you followed must be an old one.' Then with no further hesitation he asked me where my camp was, and declared, 'The camel will be found. Come, let us go!'

Moments later we were tracing my steps back towards my small *taya*. I felt much more confident now this man was with me. I knew that he was a villager, yet he seemed quite sure that he could find the animal. 'I am from the Mima,' he told me, 'but I was brought up as a herdsman for the Kababish. I know the tracks of camels very well, better than some of the nomads. Tonight we are blessed because the moon is out. If there were no moon, it would be difficult. With the moonlight – if God wills – we shall have no trouble.'

He told me that his name was Hamud.

When we reached my camp, Hamud examined the place where I had couched Wad al 'Atiga, then began walking in a series of tight circles around the camp, his path slowly widening, his eyes always riveted to the ground.

'Here!' he said suddenly. 'This is it!' I looked down with him, but I could make out no more than the faintest broken crust of sand. I wondered how he could possibly be sure. He darted off towards the bushes and I followed closely. Fifty metres away he began circling an acacia tree that bore a few wrinkled leaves, again widening the circle as he walked. Then he darted off again at a different angle to another tree, a few yards away, where he employed the same circling technique. 'A camel wanders from tree to tree when he is hungry,' Hamud told me. 'He will never go in a straight line.'

Many minutes went by as the little man, bending over the ground like a tracker-dog, shuffled quickly from tree to tree. Several times he lost the trail and had to return to the previous tree and begin circling again. I tried vainly to follow the tracks as he did, but the surface was hard and I could rarely make out more than the vague outline of a padmark. 'You see,' he commented, 'the trees are bare. Your camel is hungry, that is all. He is searching for food.' I was weary after my long ride, and my brain was unreceptive and unable to take in all the small lessons I might have learned. At times I began to doubt if we should ever find the camel.

After what seemed like hours Hamud said, 'Hah! There he is! Thank God that we caught him. He has broken the hobble!' The camel was browsing calmly in a thorn tree not more than ten metres from where we stood, yet I had not spotted him. The hobbling-rope hung loosely from one of his legs. The old man walked carefully up to him, and refastened the *gayd*. The camel did not stop eating. 'See, you did not tie it properly,' the man said. 'It had only come undone! You will lose him again if you do not tie it properly!' I felt embarrassed, but tremendously relieved. 'It will take a long time to get him back to the camp,' I said.

'We will not take him hobbled,' Hamud replied. 'We will lead him.'

'But I did not bring the headrope.'

'No matter,' the Mimawi said, staring around him. He selected a tree, then began digging in the soil beneath it with his axe. He uncovered a long, ropelike coil of root and stripped it out of the earth, severing it with the axe. It was about seven feet long. He fashioned it into a rough bridle and fitted it over the head of the camel. 'That will make it easier for us,' he said. 'You can find almost everything in the bush if you look for it!'

I should never have been able to find my camp alone. The thorn trees were a maze without exit or entrance. But Hamud led the camel back with unerring certainty and without even glancing at the tracks he had followed.

Back in the camp I rekindled the fire and made more tea. The old man sat on my sheepskin and stared into the flames. His face was black and as wrinkled as an old waterskin, yet his eyes shone with life. 'Are all the Mima skilled as trackers?' I asked him. 'Not all,' he said. 'But those who have worked for the Kababish know everything about the tracks and the hunt.' He explained how the track of a laden camel differed from that of an unladen one by the depth of the prints. 'The prints you followed to my village were those of a heavily laden camel,' he chuckled. 'They could not possibly have belonged to your animal.' Then he told me how the veins and wrinkles that could be seen on a day-old track faded quickly, becoming more obscure every day until only the vague outline was left. 'Much depends on the weather conditions, the wind and the rain,' he said. 'You must be careful to remember the changes in the weather when you read a track.'

He told me that many of the Mima were excellent hunters and knew the whereabouts of the gazelles, the hares and the wildcats. 'But the game has gone since my father's time,' he told me. 'Now even the crops will not grow.' I asked how it was possible for his people to survive in this drought. In answer he pointed out some tiny marks at intervals around the base of a bush. 'See, the mouse of the desert!' he said. 'He lives, even though there is no water on the land. He eats the little plants that grow in the wadis, that you hardly notice! My people are like the jerboa. As long as there is some moisture, they can survive.' He told me how the women would gather the wild grasses like *gau* and *haskanit* and grind them into flour on their stone hand-mills, and how the flour could be made into a polenta that was almost as good as that made from sorghum or millet.

These were not new skills. Rather, they were a survival of an ancient knowledge that had been handed down since the Stone Age. The desert was littered with grinding and milling stones that had been used for grinding wild grasses by the neolithic people of northern Africa before agriculture was invented.

There were other wild fruits that men could eat, the Mimawi explained. The nuts of the *mukhayyit* tree could be ground up and made into porridge, though they had to be prepared in a certain way to rid them of their poison. Many trees, like the *tundub*, carried edible berries; the green nuts of the *nabak* tree provided sustenance. There were small melons called *handal* that could be used to feed donkeys, and another species of dwarf melon that humans could eat. The green herb from the *harjal* bush was a substitute for tea, and the grass called *jibayn* was used for making cheese. Wild okra was a valuable herb, and men could eat the gum of the *siyaal* and the *samuk*, or gum arabic tree. Locusts were a delicacy, and there were many kinds of grubs and caterpillars that were edible. Hungry men could even eat lizards and snakes, or the hardy desert-rat itself.

It was a fascinating lesson for me, and at the end of it I was much impressed by what I had learned of the Mima. They were one of the strange tribes from the west of the Sudan who seemed to combine the traditions of the Arabs and the Africans equally. The nomads treated these men as inferiors, but I saw that like the desert-rat, they hid a strong and resilient spirit under a humble exterior.

Before he left me, Hamud said, 'Do not linger on the road to El Fasher. There are bandits from the Bedayatt who have come from Chad. Only a few weeks ago they attacked a market near Kobka-biyya. They stole tea and sugar and a large amount of money. Two men ran for help and the bandits shot them. Then they rode back to Chad on their camels. Those men have no mercy, and certainly will not spare a white man on a camel. Go in the safe-keeping of God.'

I left at dawn the next day and moved north-west across the unrelenting wasteland south of El Fasher. I could see all day the faint shadow of Jabal Sarjayn, the double-peaked outcrop that stood on the plain near the city. Everywhere I was reminded of the drought and desertification that was devastating the land.

It was popular to blame the nomads for this destruction of veg-etation and even for the diminishing rainfall. Certainly over-grazing

46

by camels and sheep had played its part in reducing plant cover, just as the practice of cutting trees for fuel had encouraged the blight of deforestation in the ranges. But no one had yet proved a connection between over-grazing and deficient rainfall that was powerful enough to have created this drought. Drought was endemic in the Sahara and the Sahel, and had occurred at intervals for millennia.

The fertile area that became the Sahara, the world's largest desert, died because of a decrease in the monsoon rains that fed it before about 2000 BC. No one knows why these rains began to diminish, though it is known that at some stage an imbalance occurred between rainfall and evaporation. A change in only one degree in rainfall distribution could bring drought to thousands of square miles of land. Before 10,000 BC the Sahara was desert as it is today, and even after the monsoons were supposed to have ceased there were wet periods, one of which ended as recently as AD 500. Though nomads may have affected changes at local level, I believe that the drought that reached its nadir in 1984 was far too vast to have been brought about by a few tribes and their animals. Those who blamed the nomads were reluctant to admit that they were unable to explain the colossal natural fluctuations of which this drought was but a minor part.

I arrived in El Fasher two days later. No rain had fallen since I had been away and the Wadi Halluf, which fed the lake in the centre of the town, was still bone-dry. Many Zaghawa, who had fled from their villages in the north, poured into the area, setting up shanty towns around the cattle market or moving in with families already established there.

I was anxious to press on as soon as possible. My route lay north-east, through Zayadiyya country, to the tiny village of Umm Sunta on the Kordofan border, where the nazir of the Kababish, Hassan Wad at Tom, had pitched his camp, or *dikka*. Many Arabs I spoke to in El Fasher market told me, 'The Zayadiyya and the Kababish are killing each other. There are many bandits on the road. If you keep your eyes open you will be all right.' It sounded as if the Kordofan–Darfur borders were more disturbed than ever. When I last rode across this land in 1980, there had been a truce between the Kababish and the Zayadiyya. I wondered what had happened to aggravate their peaceful relations.

I left El Fasher in mid-afternoon, riding across the cultivated plain of green, orange and buff. Some farmers were planting millet in the sandhills, still hoping for rain. Soon the town fell behind me and I was in a great grey desert with the Wima hills towering amongst the bluish mist on the skyline. I rode past outcrops of black rock and across orange sand dunes, climbing up into the saddle of the hills as night fell and making camp in a dry-wash under the rock wall. As I made camp, I saw the flash of a torch in the hills. It was impossible to say how far off it was. After all the tales I had heard of bandits, it disturbed me to know that there were others moving about in this lonely place after dark. I loaded my shotgun, and kept it close to me as I slept.

The next morning I moved into the belly of the hills. For the first hour I skirted through the wadis on the lower slopes, seeing the solid grey wall looming up before me. I knew that there must be a way through it. As the land began to slope steeply upwards, I dismounted and led the camel by hand. Soon I saw a cleft in the rock face, through which a water-course meandered, lined with trees. I began to head-haul the animal up the ravine. In one place our way led over smooth granite boulders and the camel suddenly refused to move. He dug his feet into the soft sand, and though I tugged and strained on the headrope I could not budge him. I cursed at him loudly in English and Arabic, as a hot sweat broke out across my forehead. Still the animal would not move. I realized that my only choice was to go back. Edging my way behind the animal, I pulled gently on the headrope. Wad al 'Atiga dug in his feet even more firmly. He was not going up, but neither was he going down. I yanked the rope more determinedly. Equally resolute, he spread his legs out and braced himself backwards, ducking his neck to relieve the strain on his head. I managed to master my anger, and tried speaking to him gently, coaxing him sideways. Along the side of the wadi was a narrow strip of firm ground, which led upwards past the obstacle of the rocks. There was a scattering of goats' droppings on the path. Slowly I nursed him towards it, talking soothingly. At last his resolution wavered. He took a tentative step forward, trembled a little, then took another. Then he was standing on the ledge, with myself in front of him. Step by step I manhandled him past the rocks, and after about ten minutes we came to a place where the path was wider and less steep. I heaved a sigh of relief. Soon, though, the path disappeared and we were on a steep scree of stones that led up to the summit of the hill. Again the camel refused to go on. Exasperated anew, I gripped the headrope over my shoulder in a mad effort to drag him up. Amazingly it succeeded, and inch by agonizing inch I drew the animal to the top of the scree.

Below me was a vast plain stretching as far as the horizon, a patchwork of brown and beige reflected vividly in the growing sunlight. I descended through a thicket of tangled bush and came out into a sheltered bay where about twenty camels were drinking from a pool between the rocks. I noticed that the camels bore the distinctive lightning-flash and star brands of the Bedayatt. I became wary, for I knew it was unusual for these nomads to graze so far east. I wondered if the torchlight I had seen the previous night might have belonged to them. I saw no herdsmen. It gave me an eerie and vulnerable feeling to know that they might even now be watching me. Involuntarily I scanned the rock walls around me. At the same time Wad al 'Atiga began to pull towards the camel herd. I pulled him back, staying clear of the Bedayatt animals and striding firmly towards the plain, feeling, even as I did so, unseen eyes boring through my shirt.

There had been a gun battle in these hills only a few weeks previously, when an Arab of the Zayadiyya, Abdal Rahman Umm Badda, the court bailiff of the Zayadiyya chief, caught up with some bandits whom he had been tracking. The bandits, from the Bedayatt, had hidden themselves in the hills and opened fire on the Zayadi as he approached, leading his camel. Luckily no one had been shot, but the Bedayatt had escaped by leaping on to their fast mounts. I did not hear this story until I reached El Koma, which was still in front of me, but had I done so, I should certainly have thought twice about wandering alone through the Wima hills.

When we reached the valley floor, I swung into the saddle and rode across the semi-desert plain. In the centre stood a few villages of grass huts and beyond them the black canines of mountains along the skyline. The plain was deserted. A forest of broken trees lay in ruins in the sand and the grass had been burned crisp by the long and rainless summer. Everywhere there seemed to be the bones of dead beasts, bleach-white and wrapped in shrouds of rock-hard leather.

Without its tree covering this area might soon be desert, like so many parts of the western Sudan. Here the rains had always been uncertain and the needs of the vegetation were precariously balanced. Nomads and farmers together had tipped the scales in the direction of disaster by chopping down the acacia trees, which they needed for fuel. The process was unstoppable because the people of this region had no alternative source of fuel. The villagers used charcoal, which was more economical than firewood, but which also depleted the forested land. Charcoal was impracticable for the nomads, who had to carry all their supplies by camel.

The areas most seriously affected by desertification were those around towns and villages, where the livestock of the settled people grazed. Although their herds and flocks were far smaller than those of the nomads, the destruction they caused was much greater; the nomads had the range to make use of even the most remote pastures, whereas the animals of the settled people were concentrated in one place for most of the year. The animals destroyed the young shoots so that plants could not reproduce. Without the plants to hold the topsoil, the wind and rain leached it away, leaving only the sterile skin of the desert beneath. Year by year the volume of grazing around the villages diminished. In some areas the problem was made worse by the shifting sands of the desert, which were capable of burying acres of arable land and of drowning entire villages within a few years.

I spent the night near the volcanic cone of Jabal Tantara and the next morning arrived at El Koma. I sought out an old acquaintance of mine, Ibrahim Munzal, who was an *umbasha* of police in the village. Ibrahim invited me to his house at once. It was built of cane, like those of the Berti and Mima, and yet was far larger, with more interlocking courtyards and huts. The Zayadiyya, to whom Ibrahim belonged, were nomads and semi-nomads, though they lived in straw houses and had no tents as the Kababish had. Of mixed African and Arab origin, they were an offshoot of the much larger Dar Hamid tribe of Kordofan, though they had lived in Darfur for generations. El Koma was a watering centre for the Zayadiyya, and the village was centred on two bore-wells, run by diesel engines. To the north-west lay the wells of Abu Ku', from where I had set off to Mellit in 1980 with two Zayadiyya nomads, Tahir and Ahmad.

As I sat in the shade of Ibrahim's grass compound, we were joined by a hoary, grizzled-looking man who carried a long-barrelled Martini rifle. This was Abdal Rahman Umm Badda, whom I knew by reputation. He was the *ghaffir*, or bailiff of the court of Mohammid Jizzu, sheikh of the Zayadiyya. His job was to bring to the court those who had been convicted. In this wild land only someone who had a detailed knowledge of people and places would have been capable of doing this job. Rolling a cigarette from the local chewing-tobacco, he told me that he had been involved in several gun battles over the past few months, including the one in the Wima hills.

When I told him that I was on my way to meet the Kababish nazir, he grimaced and said, 'This is a bad time to cross into Kababish country. There has been fighting all year. Seven of the Zayadiyya have been killed by Kababish in the last few months. The Kababish dare not come near El Koma now.' I asked him if he knew Dagalol, and he grinned nastily. 'Yes, I know him well,' he said. 'He is the only friend I have amongst the Kababish.' Just then Ibrahim cut in and said, 'Do you remember Tahir, the man you travelled with to Mellit, two years ago?' I told him that I remembered him well. 'He was one of the Zayadiyya killed by the Kababish. He was with three companions, and they were attacked by twelve Kababish one morning as they left camp. They had no chance. Two of them escaped, but Tahir and another were killed.'

I was shocked by the news, and I asked why it had happened.

'Tahir was a bandit.' He shrugged. 'The Kababish knew him and the Zayadiyya knew him. But whether he had stolen camels that day only God knows!'

I wondered again what lay at the heart of the problem. Umm Badda told me, 'Zayadiyya land is rich and the Kababish have always wanted it. This grazing is ours. If they graze their camels on our land there will be trouble. The Kababish are many, but we are ready to fight them, by God! Not a month ago I met one of the Kababish sheikhs, Ibrahim Wad Ali. He said to me, "If there is any more trouble we will bring twenty truckloads of weapons, then we will finish the Zayadiyya. And we will finish you!" I just got up and left. No one dared to stop me.'

It sounded as if the tribes were on the verge of a major conflict. As always the ultimate trouble was over grazing land. The diminishing rain, coupled with the rise in population of men and animals in recent years, fanned ancient feuds that had lain dormant for decades.

I left El Koma two days later, climbing up to a high tor of purple rock. I looked down over a carpet of grey and amber, hemmed in by an archipelago of dunes and decorated by thorn trees.

Before me lay a journey of more than two hundred and fifty kilometres, in country where the tribes faced each other with daggers

51

drawn. I decided to stay away from the tracks as everyone had advised me and to travel on a compass-bearing. For two days I rode through dead thorn scrub, seeing no one and nothing. Wad al 'Atiga kept up a steady, rhythmic trot, and I rode for eight hours a day, covering more than forty kilometres between sunrise and sunset.

Just before sunset on the second day, I came to the bore-well at Umm Hejlij. There was a spray of fine dust over the water-yard and the last gold beams of the sun illuminated its particles, drawing a gilded veil over the huts and thorn trees. Zayadiyya men and women were driving away herds of cattle and knots of camels and goats through the sand.

I led my camel into the well-compound, hoping to water him and fill my waterskin. As I stood there, the watchman told me, 'There is no water. The engine is going off.' I protested, saying that I had ridden from El Fasher, but the man hardly listened to me and seemed intent on my camel and riding gear. 'It is too late,' he argued. 'I am going to the sunset prayers and the engine is going off.' I had never experienced such a lack of hospitality before; it was very unusual for a well-keeper to turn away a lone traveller. I knew that it was the custom for local people to invite strangers to stay with them at sunset, and though I never relied on hospitality, I was surprised that no such offer came. The man told me sourly, 'Your people are camping out there.' He pointed to the desert. 'There are some Kababish with goats. You can camp with them and come back in the morning.' With that he ushered me out of the compound and snapped the gate firmly shut.

It was dark by the time I led Wad al 'Atiga to the nearest grove of thorn trees. I had a little water left in my canteen, but I knew that it would not be enough and that I should go thirsty that night. I was irritated by the lack of hospitality. In a land where there were no inns, it was the custom for travellers to rest with local villagers. Not only was this an Islamic rule, it made good sense. The nomads said that anyone who camped alone must have something to hide. It was only after I had made camp that it struck me that the watchman might have taken me for a Kabbashi. I remembered how he had examined the brand on my camel's leg very carefully. It had been almost dark when I met him, and my head had been cowled in a headcloth and shawl. Many Kababish were light-skinned and their accent was very different from that of the Zayadiyya; perhaps he had taken my foreign pronunciation for that of the Kababish. If this were true, then it showed how deep ran the feelings between the tribes.

The man's hostility had made me uneasy and I loaded my shotgun again before retiring, placing it next to me broken, with a cartridge in the breech.

Just after settling down on my sheepskin, I heard the sound of hoofbeats in the darkness. From somewhere a man was approaching me on a donkey. I sensed that he was coming directly towards me, and in a moment I glimpsed a shadowy figure moving through the trees. Instinctively I seized my shotgun and snapped the breech shut. There was a resounding metallic clang and almost simultaneously the rider broke through the cover. 'Who is it?' he shouted, wheeling the large white donkey round in a half-circle and sliding off the saddle.

'Peace be on you!' I said, holding the gun before me.

'What are you doing here?' the man said, ignoring the greeting. I saw that he was thin, with a fringe of beard. He seemed nervous.

'No one invited me to stay in the village,' I told him.

'There are plenty of Kababish with goats. Why do you not stay with them?'

'I am comfortable here,' I answered, 'as long as I am left alone.'

The man grunted and leapt on his donkey again. Soon the footfalls faded away into the distance.

I was both hungry and thirsty when I set off the next morning. It was hot, but I rode on at a trot for five hours through the thorn bush, hoping that I should find someone from whom I could beg water. At noon I stopped to rest under a *kitir* tree. I tried to eat some dates, but my mouth was too dry. As I sat there, a shadow fell across me and I looked up to see an Arab couching his camel. He had approached so silently that I had not heard him. He was fair-skinned, with the swarthy, dark hair of a gypsy, and wore a shirt that was covered in patches. I noticed that a ·303 rifle was slung from his saddle. I stood up to greet him, and invited him to sit in the shade and eat some dates. After a few minutes he asked me, 'What is your tribe?'

'*Ingleez*,' I told him.

The man grinned. 'You are the *Ingleezi* who was with Dagalol, aren't you? Your name is Omar.'

'Yes. How did you know?'

'I am Salim Wad Ahmad from the Haworab. My brothers were

travelling on the *shogara*, near Dagalol. The news gets passed along.'

I smiled in surprise, and explained that I was travelling to Umm Sunta to meet the nazir.

'You will not find him in Umm Sunta,' Salim told me. 'He is here in the Bahr, with his cattle. I saw his people yesterday. You will find his camp tomorrow. For tonight you can stay with us.'

The Haworab had made camp in some trees about two kilometres away. With them was a herd of about thirty camels scattered across the plain, grazing on green grass. After I unsaddled, I greeted the three other Arabs who were there, Salim's father and two brothers. They brought me a bowl of fresh milk and made tea, into which they poured unmilled millet. Afterwards one of them asked me, 'Are you not afraid to sleep alone in the bush?'

'No, why should I be?'

The man clicked almost pityingly and then said, 'The English captured this land once. Perhaps they want to do so again. Perhaps you are their spy!'

'If the English wanted to spy on this land, they would not send a man on a camel!' I told him, but I could see that he was unimpressed.

After sunset the wind roared through the trees, but no rain fell from the darkling sky. The Haworab lit a blazing fire and brought their camels into the *taya*. The deadwood crackled in the hearth and the camels chewed rhythmically. I asked the Arabs if the rains had been good in this area.

'There has been some rain,' Salim said, 'but only in a few places, like this area – the Bahr. We call it by that name because the water collects here in many pools, like a river. But there is not enough grazing for all the Arabs.'

We were interrupted by two Arabs who couched their camels hastily beside our *taya*. They belonged to the 'Awajda, slim men with flattened headcloths and well-used rifles. One of them had prominent teeth and wore a silver earring in his right upper-ear. 'Brothers,' he said, 'we have just seen a *gom* of twelve men from the Zayadiyya. They are coming back from Umm Qozayn with some stolen camels. The camels belong to the Meidob, and there was a battle yesterday. Someone was killed. I advise you to stay alert tonight. Those men mean trouble. They will be passing here very soon.'

At once the Haworab doused the fire, and ran around the herd, making sure that all the camels were collected. I brought Wad al 'Atiga close to my sleeping-place. Salim and his brothers cocked their weapons, and two of them moved into the bush several hundred metres away. The 'Awajda stayed with us, sitting together in the midst of the herd. No one spoke and the minutes passed with no sound but the slow mastication of the beasts around us.

About an hour later Salim and his brother came walking back from their position, saying, 'They passed by, going towards Umm Hejlij. There were twelve of them with five loose camels.'

'Why didn't you stop them?' I asked.

'They were Meidob camels, and no concern of ours. Besides, there were too many of them.'

The 'Awajda bid us goodnight and rode away. After they had gone, I lay down and thought about the next day. I hoped that it would bring the meeting I had looked forward to many times over the past months. I should meet Hassan Wad at Tom, the Sheikh of Sheikhs, whose family had ruled the most renowned nomads of the Sudan for generations.

3
Lord
of the Drums

In 1898 a young man called Ali Wad at Tom was living in a village west of Omdurman. A British intelligence report described him as 'a man of modest wealth'. The Kababish legend, however, has it that Ali Wad at Tom was born with no more than two little she-camels to his name, yet he died the richest nazir in the Sudan.

Ali was a man of uncommon charisma and powers of concentration. He was handsome, charming and intelligent, with the mind of a strategist. His photograph, taken in middle age, reveals features that are dark, brooding and aristocratic. His father, At Tom, the hereditary chief of the Kababish, had been put to death for his refusal to join the Mahdi's revolution. Many more of his family had died in battle against the Mahdi's forces, and others had been captured and executed in Omdurman. The Mahdi had appointed his uncle, Graysh, as nazir of the tribe, and Ali grew up in Graysh's household, dreaming of revenge against the Mahdi, and his successor, the Khalifa Abdallahi.

In that same year the necessity for revenge was removed when 12,000 of the Khalifa's followers, the Ansar, were killed on the field of Kerreri near Omdurman; they had recklessly charged a British position defended by Maxim machine-guns and Lee-Metford rifles. With the British once more in control of the Sudan, Graysh was summarily dismissed, and young Ali Wad at Tom appointed in his stead. It was an excellent choice, both for the British and for the Kababish. Ali remained firmly loyal to the *Ingleez* throughout his

56

life, but also took the pathetic remnants of a tribe decimated by persecution, drought, famine and disease, and within forty years re-established them as the most powerful nomadic people in the Sudan.

Under Ali's leadership the Kababish pushed west year by year. They crossed the Wadi al Milik, which was then the border of the independent Sultanate of Darfur, and clashed constantly with Darfur tribes, such as the Zayadiyya, the Zaghawa and the Bedayatt. They attacked the oasis of El 'Atrun and skirmished in the remote pastures of Chad with warriors of the Gur'an. The Darfur tribes retaliated, raiding Kababish territory, and these raids were immediately reported to the British as evidence of the Darfur sultan's readiness to attack British land. This reinforced Ali's position, in British eyes, as the guardian of the Sudan's western marches.

When the sultan, Ali Dinar, joined forces with the revolutionary Senussi brotherhood of Libya, he wrote to Ali, inciting him to join the 'holy war' against the unbelievers. The nazir refused and referred the matter to the government, which responded by supplying him with shipments of rifles. In 1916, when Darfur was invaded by British forces, Kababish irregulars were part of the occupation group.

Evidently profits for the nazir were great. Within sixteen years his two little she-camels had become a herd of 3,000 head. 'And that,' as British Inspector Reginald Davies commented drily, 'had not accrued by the slow process of nature.'

Ali spent the latter part of his life moulding what had been a scattered grouping of tribes into a unified confederation. He worked to reduce the power of tribal sheikhs and to concentrate authority into his own hands. He was much assisted by the British, who found it more convenient to deal with a single powerful family than a score of smaller chiefs. When he died in 1937, he was Sir Ali Wad at Tom, KCVO, one of only three Sudanese ever to receive the peerage. It was Sir Ali's grandson, Hassan, who had become nazir in 1945, whom I met in the Bahr in the summer of 1982.

Not long after dawn I rode with Salim across the *goz* to Sheikh Hassan's camp. The Bahr was a land of gently rolling downs, covered with yellow grasses, still green at the roots, and clothed in thorn bush, *kitir*, *la'ot* and *siyaal* like twisted, delicate carvings. Spits of earth, ochre and carmine lay between the wedges of grass, and the downs were slashed by shallow washes that grew wider as they fed into the broad depression where muddy pools of rain-water had collected.

We rode out of the scrubland and into the sea of wind-riffled herbage. My companion pointed out to me a group of figures under a single *kitir* tree. Near them was a *zariba* of thorn branches and a place where the grass had been cropped short by cattle. Far beyond the camp I could see the blue outline of the Qoz al 'Ajura, with its spine of broken granite stretching away north and towering over the acacia scrub.

'That is Sheikh Hassan,' Salim told me. 'The dark man sitting in the shade. The other men with him are his scribe, his holy man and his servants.' The Arab wished me the safe-keeping of God, and rode back in the direction of his herd. I approached the camp slowly, couched my camel nearby, then walked over and greeted the company.

Sheikh Hassan received me with gracious dignity, and showed no surprise when he saw that I was a European. He was a thick-set man with dark skin and the same heavy, rather brooding features I had seen in a photograph of his grandfather. He was dressed very simply, in a shirt of white cotton and *sirwal* like any ordinary tribesman. A Martini carbine lay propped against the rope-bed on which he sat, and scattered around him was a clutter of chipped saddles and saddle-bags worn shiny by use. A brace of waterskins hung in a nearby bush.

I had been looking forward eagerly to my meeting with Hassan since I first decided to live amongst the Kababish. He was paramount chief of the entire confederation of tribes, and his authority extended not only to the borders of the Kababish *dar*, or homeland, but far beyond into the open reaches of the desert itself. It was a vast area. The *dar* alone was 48,000 square miles, and the desert was perhaps four times that size. The nazir's power was acknowledged as far as the oases of El 'Atrun and Nukheila, near the Libyan border, and even along the palm groves of the Nile as far as Dongola.

When I met Sheikh Hassan, the power of the nazirate was already on the decline. Only a month before I arrived in the *dar*, Hassan's uncle, Mohammid al Murr, had died. Al Murr was the eldest son of Sir Ali, though due to his mother's status he never inherited the title of nazir. Nevertheless, he had been the real power amongst the Kababish for decades and when he died something of the old spirit of Sir Ali Wad at Tom died with him. I greatly regretted not meeting this famous Arab.

Sheikh Hassan introduced me to his clerk, Mohammid Dudayn. He was an olive-skinned Arab, dressed in a spotless *jallabiyya* like a townsman. I later came to admire Dudayn: he was the son of a holy man, the Faki Hassan, who had been a client of the nazir's and had originally come from the Jawa'ama tribe. Dudayn was one of the most perceptive and intelligent men I met amongst the Kababish. The other man was the Sharif Mohammid, a lean and austere figure with close-cropped hair. He was an Arab of the Kunta tribe from Mali and had practised as a holy man amongst the Kababish for many years.

The nazir called for a negro servant to unsaddle my camel and set it out to graze. Another servant brought a canvas sheet for me to sit on, and a little later gave me tea and a handful of dates. As I ate and drank, Sheikh Hassan asked me questions about my journey. He was interested in everything: the state of Dagalol's camels, the grazing in the south, the latest stories of camel raids and the condition of the country between there and El Fasher. He was particularly interested in news about the Zayadiyya, and seemed very impressed that I had ridden from El Fasher alone. 'You were lucky to get through alive!' he exclaimed.

Later, when I tried to explain why I had come to live with the Kababish, he waived my explanations aside as if he already knew them. He told me that two outsiders had lived with his family before. One was the anthropologist Talal Asad, and the other a German traveller called Farid. 'You are welcome here,' he told me. 'You are British, and the British have always been friends of my family. This land is your land.'

It was not until much later that I realized how much I owed this reception to my colonial predecessors, men like Reginald Davies, Harold MacMichael, Douglas Newbold, Bill Henderson, Guy Moore and many others. They were remembered with affection, and their age was thought of as a golden one. They had been admired for their toughness, honour and sense of justice; they were men who had devoted their lives to this country and knew its language and customs well. The Kababish were a hard, wild people much in sympathy with the uncompromising yet incorruptible attitude of the colonial administrators. The scores of outsiders – teachers, medics, nutritionists and aid-workers – who poured into the Sudan after the drought never replaced the colonialists in the affections of the Kababish, despite their liberal pretensions, which were as alien to the nomads as if they had been written on the moon. 'The British were honest and just, and their word was one word,' the nazir told me later. 'They ran this district with one inspector, two clerks and five police troopers. Now there are two hundred doing the same job and doing it less efficiently!'

Later that morning Sheikh Hassan's son Mohammid arrived with two more negro servants and a squad of five white donkeys that he had watered nearby. He was a tall, quiet lad, with a tangled mass of long hair: this, I learned, was a sign of mourning for the death of Sheikh Mohammid al Murr. We were joined by a slim, pleasant-faced Arab of about twenty who carried a ·22 rifle. He was Dudayn's younger brother, Ibrahim, who was chief herdsman of the nazir's cattle, which were grazing out beyond the skyline. At mid-morning one of the servants brought us a dish of polenta. It was a hemi-spherical cake of millet, known as *kisri*, over which cow's milk had been poured. We ate in the shade of the *kitir* tree, crouching around the bowl and eating with our right hands.

I stayed in the Bahr with Sheikh Hassan for ten days.

Each morning I would awake as the first red streak of dawn fired in the sky and the dark shapes of the cattle and baggage camels around me came into silhouette. The cattle herd would be massed in a semicircular laager, rank upon rank of humped bodies with passive, peacefully chewing heads. A score of calves would be low-ing a few yards away in the *zariba*, where they had been enclosed for the night. Cattle could not be hobbled as the camels were, but by enclosing their offspring the Arabs ensured that the cows would not wander off in the darkness, and also that the calves would not drink their mothers' milk.

The Arabs would get up one by one from their rope-beds, upon which all but the servants slept. They were light structures known as *'angarebs*, sprung with ropes of palm fibre, which were easily car-ried by camel. As they arose, the servants would bring round jugs of water with narrow spouts for the ritual ablution. Each man would retire some distance and wash his private parts, then return and complete the ritual. He would wash his hands, mouth and face each three times, splashing the water over the forearms up to the elbows, dragging wet palms through the hair and forcing wet fingers into the ears. Finally he would pour water over his feet, washing them as high as the ankles. This sequence was performed only when water was plentiful. In the desert those who prayed used a shorter form of ritual in which sand was substituted for water.

Each man prayed in his own space, facing Mecca. He would compose himself, whispering the call to prayers, then raise his hands with a final: 'God is great!' He would clasp both hands before him, staring at the ground and repeating the first verse of the Qur'an, 'Al Fatih'. This would be followed by another prayer, brief or long according to his choosing. Then the Arab would make his prostration, first bowing, then kneeling and crouching so that his forehead and the bridge of his nose touched the ground before him. For the morning prayer only two sets of prostrations were required. The Arabs also prayed at midday, afternoon, sunset and evening. For each of these prayers four sets of prostrations were performed, except for the sunset prayer, which required three.

Generally the Kababish were not religious, and knew little about Islam. Some families, like Nas Wad Haydar, never bothered to pray; others prayed when they felt like it. The nomads were not fanatic Muslims; though they had some superstitions they were not fanatically superstitious, for they were essentially a pragmatic people.

After the prayer the Arabs sat in private meditation until the servants brought tea and fresh milk. In the nazir's camp everyone was served tea individually, with his own teapot. This, and the presence of rope-beds, distinguished Sheikh Hassan's camp from any other encampment.

The servants were mostly negroes from the nazir's household slaves. They were referred to as the 'Ol. Almost all of them were second or third generation descendants of men and women who had been captured during raids in the time of Sir Ali Wad at Tom. One of the servants with us was Sa'ad Wad Siniin, whose father had been part of the spoils of Sir Ali's raid into the country of the Gur'an. He was a huge, powerful man with enormous hands and feet, and an unkempt mop of spiky hair. Another was a thin, wiry fellow called Khamis; his father was a famous Dinka slave known as Bambidu, who had taken part in many raids against the Kawahla tribe.

After tea Ibrahim and the herdsmen would release the calves from the *zariba* and drive the cattle out into the pastures. The Kababish were famous as camel-herders, and I wondered why the nazir was travelling with his cattle. Sheikh Hassan told me, 'The Kababish are camel-men, but we have all types of animals. It was my grandfather, Sir Ali, who first introduced cattle to our family. One day he asked his people, "Which is the richest tribe of the Kababish?" They thought for a bit, then said, "It is the 'Awajda, for they have many camels." He said, "It is not the 'Awajda." They thought a little more and said, "Then it is us, the Nurab. We are the richest." "It is not the Nurab," he told them, "it is the Shilaywab." "But the Shilaywab have far fewer camels than us," they said. "Yes, but the Shilaywab have all kinds of animals, not only camels. That is why they are richest. We should be like them." So from that time we started getting cattle.'

Sheikh Hassan explained that cows were an important source of milk for the families that could not travel with the camel herds on the distant migrations. The cattle had to be kept near the nomads' semi-permanent camps, as they needed water every two days.

The nazir's emphasis on cattle meant that his family were already in transition from the free life of the desert to that of semi-settlement. The descendants of Sir Ali Wad at Tom had become the ruling élite of the Kababish, and all the magistrates and government representatives were taken from this family. Distracted from their livestock by their other duties, these men could no longer spare the time for long-range camel migrations, and though they still owned thousands of camels, these were in the hands of slaves and hired men. Denied the benefit of camel's milk, they had turned instead to cows. But cattle were not resilient enough to resist even mild drought: by 1985 the nazir's magnificent herd of over a hundred cows had been reduced to only fourteen head.

When the cattle had moved out, Sheikh Hassan and Dudayn would prepare for the work of the day. A canopy of canvas would be slung up in the thorns of the tree and the beds moved into the oblong of shade beneath it. The nazir received visitors constantly. They were mostly Kababish tribesmen with weathered bedouin faces, belonging to any of the nineteen tribes that composed the confederation. They wore *jibbas* of soiled cotton, and patched *sirwal* with yellowish strips of headcloth and cowskin sandals. The majority were small men with stringy beards and brown eyes. They wore wooden rosary beads around their necks, and carried rifles and daggers. They would couch their camels in small nests about twenty metres from the camp and stack their weapons at a respectful distance before approaching the nazir, stepping gracefully out of their sandals and squatting down in the dust before his couch.

Many of these Arabs came with complaints about livestock thefts. One old man told the nazir, 'The Zayadiyya took twelve of my camels last night, by God! I knew nothing until I awoke this morning. They are sons of dogs, curse their fathers!' Another Arab of the Nurab came to report that two of his she-camels had been driven off from the watering-place by Zayadiyya, in broad daylight. 'I shall take the first two Zayadiyya camels I find, by God!' he declared. Always the nazir listened carefully to the complaints and Dudayn recorded the details in a thick ledger. Within a few days the list of such incidents had become considerable, and always the Zayadiyya were blamed. 'The Zayadiyya will soon have a proper war on their hands,' Dudayn commented. 'Once they were nothing, but now they have grown rich in herds and weapons. When the Kababish first came to the area of Umm Qozayn, there were few Zayadiyya here. Now they claim it is their territory, and that the grazing belongs to them. They have no official *dar* as we do, and they cannot stop us grazing in their territory.' Both Dudayn and Sheikh Hassan were delighted when I produced my map of the region. It was a copy of the 1940 survey made by the British, though it showed clearly the border between Kordofan and Darfur. 'See,' said Dudayn, pointing to the map, 'Kordofan is marked as Kababish country, but the Zayadiyya are not marked at all!'

The grazing land in the west of the Sudan was owned communally, and officially no tribes could prevent others from grazing their animals on any part of it. However, the Kababish had so-called '*dar* rights' in their own homeland, which meant that they could forbid strangers from making permanent camps or buildings or from sinking wells there. I asked Dudayn how the troubles had started. He told me that they had begun when a Zayadi called Karusha had come into the Kababish *dar* in the previous year, with a Kalashnikov rifle for sale. 'He disappeared,' the Arab said, 'and only God knows what happened to him. Then the Zayadiyya sent a *gom* of sixty men into our *dar* to search for him. They found nothing, but soon after that many camels were stolen from our land. It was the Zayadiyya, and no doubt. One day a raiding party of four Zayadiyya were surprised by a group of twelve Kababish. Two of them were shot dead, and the others escaped.' This was the story I had heard in El Koma, of the incident in which Tahir had died.

I could imagine how it had happened – the four tribesmen waking at dawn with their stolen camels, hidden amongst the thorn bush, thinking they were safe. A spiral of smoke from their fire rising slowly above the trees as they hastily made tea and saddled their camels for leaving. The sudden shuffle of camels' feet on the sand. The realization that they had been caught. The hard bronze faces of the Arabs coming out of the acacia brakes – then the last desperate effort to mount their camels before the volley of shots came spitting towards them. The two bodies jumping as if they had been stung, the shrieks of the camels and the streaks of blood on the earth. The frantic gallop of the two survivors as they whipped their mounts out through the thorn trees and back towards Darfur. The flies settling on the silent bodies as they lay dead in the sand. Tahir's body was found to contain twenty bullets.

'The police arrested twelve men of the Kababish for that incident,' Dudayn continued. 'But no one knows how they got their names. Someone must have told the Zayadiyya. I do not know who it was, but I have a very good idea.'

He told me how the Zayadiyya had taken their revenge. In February 1982 a Kababish youth named Hassan Wad Esa was herding his camels near Umm Qozayn. It was a warm moonlit night, and Hassan and the three little boys with him were about to lie down on their sheepskins, when there was a commotion amongst the camels. Hassan seized his rifle and ran to the edge of the herd. Not ten metres away he saw three dark figures driving off one of his camels. He called out a terse warning and was answered by a salvo of shots that cracked out of the shadows, spinning off the rocks around him and hitting several of the camels. The animals screamed in agony, and the boy dodged between them, throwing himself into the shelter of a boulder. More bullets whizzed above his head. The stricken camels wailed pitifully and the other camels reared up and stampeded, bounding madly away and breaking their hobbles. The bandits pumped bullets into five or six more for good measure, shouting, 'We are Tahir's people!'

Hassan shouted back, 'Then take me for Tahir!' and was again answered by a blaze of bullets. While he lay in the cover of the rock, the Zayadiyya quickly collected the scattered animals and mounted their own camels, driving the stolen herd before them and disappearing into the night.

Fourteen of Hassan's camels had been shot. Some were dead and others lay moaning in bloody pools about the camp. 'Stay here,' he told two of his young cousins. 'We will follow the bandits and get those camels back.' He took the other lad with him and together they began to track the Zayadiyya in the moonlight. It was hard going, for the thieves were mounted and Hassan and his companion were on foot. After four hours he sent the little boy off to find a riding camel and some water. By Kababish law a tribesman pursuing raiders could requisition a camel from any camp and was not liable should that animal be injured in the pursuit.

The boy went, and Hassan continued on the trail until dawn came like a blessing. He knew that the bandits would stop to make tea and was certain that he would catch them. Sure enough, he came upon them in a shallow depression amongst some rocks. Stealthily he took up a firing position, and moments later shot one of them dead with a single bullet. The other bandits dropped into the dust and fired back before picking up their dead companion and jumping on to their camels, leaving the stolen herd. When some Kababish came on the scene later that day, they found Hassan's body still propped up in a firing position. He had been shot four times, and was stone dead.

I realized then how sacred was the quality of courage amongst these men. A herdsman was expected to guard the tribe's animals with his life. Hassan had been little more than a boy, but his pursuit of the Zayadiyya had been in keeping with all the epic traditions of the Arabs, unchanged since pre-Islamic times.

Amongst the Kababish and neighbouring tribes livestock raids were small, impulsive affairs, usually carried out at night and rarely well organized. If a man's camels were stolen, he could apply to the sheikh of the bandit's tribe for return or redress. By the Arab law of 'urf it was the sheikh's responsibility to provide either camels or compensation. If neither was forthcoming, then the Arab was legally justified in taking the same number of camels from any member of the bandit's tribe. In this way raids and counter-raids multiplied, soon becoming complicated by blood feuds between the tribes.

If a tribesman was killed in a raid, his family's first reaction would be to demand a life from the enemy tribe. When they had cooled off a little, however, they might be persuaded to accept a payment of blood money, or *dia*, instead. The settlement of *dia* was the responsibility of the sheikh. The usual course of events amongst the Kababish was for a series of killings and revenge killings to take place before all parties agreed to make a settlement; then the losses on both sides would be calculated and payments made accordingly.

65

No matter which tribe of the Kababish was involved in the matter, the entire confederation shared in the payment of *dia*, provided the case concerned an enemy tribe outside the confederation.

Often during my stay we would change camp in order to find new grazing for the cattle. The camp clutter would be packed up in the early morning, with the nazir bellowing orders at anyone within range, including myself. When everything was packed the Arabs would mount their donkeys as the great procession moved out into the scrub. Sheikh Hassan rode on a large white donkey, a resplendent figure with his carbine slung over the back of his saddle. Then came Dudayn, also riding a white donkey, and the Sharif, mounted on a smaller, mottled beast. Then came the cattle, a mass of tawny backs and sleek, shining hide, plodding on after the herd leader, a gigantic roan bull. Behind them came the camel riders like myself, and the slaves carrying all the encumbrances of the camp. We would ride on sometimes for nine or ten hours through the acacia scrub. The downs were full of Kababish camels returning from the south, as numerous as locusts on the pastures. In the afternoon the nazir would select a tree from the millions around us and say, 'This is our *taya*.' Before anyone dismounted, Sheikh Hassan would send forward the Sharif on his donkey. The thin old man would chant out the call to prayers in a loud, stentorian voice to rid the place of any jinn that might be lurking there.

The Sharif was one of many Arabs of Moorish origin who lived amongst the Kababish. They formed an entire subsection of the Nurab tribe known as the Shanagit, after the famous oasis of Chinguetti in Mauritania. Many of them lived in the camp of Umm Ejayja north of the nazir's *dikka*. They had come across the desert in small groups, on foot or by camel and donkey. Many of them had been intent on making the Haj, the holy pilgrimage to Mecca and Medina. The tradition of Islamic learning had always been strong in the western Sahara, and many of the religious men, or marabouts, had memorized the entire Qur'an. However, their most valuable function amongst the Kababish was the writing of charms, which the Arabs wore in leather pouches on their arms. They believed that these charms, usually consisting of a verse from the Qur'an, were proof against gunshot wounds and knives. The belief was very strong throughout Africa, although it had no real foundation in Islam.

Very few of the Kababish were able to read or write, and, like many illiterate peoples, they considered the written word a source of magical power rather than a means of communication. Often while I was with them, they would peer at me intently as I wrote up my journal, as if I had been engaged in some fascinating magical rite. Often I was asked, 'Why don't you become a faki – a holy man? Then your writing would have some use!' In reply I would relate an amusing story that had occurred while I was a teacher in Darfur.

A merchant friend of mine, Mohammid Zakariyya, had been approached by a faki, who said that he had a very special charm for sale. It was effective against guns and knives, and the price he asked was 100 pounds. '100 pounds!' Mohammid told him. 'If it is as good as you say, I shall give you 200!' Then he instructed the holy man to bring the charm to his garden the next Friday. On the appointed day the faki had turned up with his charm and Mohammid had turned up with a fat sheep and his shotgun. 'Tie the charm round the neck of the sheep,' Mohammid told the man. After he had done so, Mohammid said, 'We shall see if this charm is effective against guns!' And so saying, he shot the sheep at point-blank range. The animal dropped dead instantly. 'Well?' Mohammid asked. 'I must have made a mistake in the writing!' the faki commented sadly. The reaction of the Kababish to this tale varied. Some laughed uproariously, while others sniffed and muttered, 'Even fakis can make mistakes.'

The charms made by fakis were sold to tribesmen for cash or livestock, and some of them had grown rich on this trade. The belief was not as innocent as it seemed. The Simba wars in the Congo had been based on the fanatic conviction that the Simba warriors, protected with their charms, were invulnerable against the bullets of their foes.

At night we slept on our rope-beds with our rifles near at hand. The Bahr belonged to the disputed interface between Kababish and Zayadiyya country and it was not impossible that Zayadiyya bandits would attack such a promising herd, even though it belonged to the Kababish nazir. As the days passed the reports of thefts and bloodshed continued. One night, just before sunset, we were visited by four tribesmen of the Meidob. They were tall, black-featured men, led by a negro who wore the saffron-coloured headcloth of a court bailiff. They couched their camels nearby, but carried their rifles with them as they sat down before the nazir: they were armed with ·303s, and they carried heavy bandoliers of cartridges across their stomachs. The negro told Sheikh Hassan that they had been tracking some Zayadiyya who had stolen five camels from their kinsmen in the region of Umm Qozayn a few days before; the bandits had come in daylight and the Meidob had opened fire on them. The Zayadiyya had shot back and one of the Meidob had been killed. The four men had been sent by one of the sheikhs of the Meidob to track down the murderer. I realized that the bandits who had passed by while I had been with the Haworab were the ones, and I told the four men all I knew. Fortunately they did not ask why the Haworab had not stopped them; it was well known that the Meidob and the Kababish were bitter enemies and had been so for generations.

On the fifth day after my arrival, we watered the cattle in the muddy shallows of a rainwater-pool where the liquid lay like a green mould over the mud-flats, full of algae. There were many white cattle-egrets perched at the water's edge, waiting to hop on the shoulder of a cow. These birds fed on the ticks that were found on the skin of cattle and camels. We saw one or two wild duck, which took flight before anyone could shoot them. There were some Arabs of the Hamdab at the pool, watering about twenty camels. They were dapper little men with oval faces of walnut-brown, who carried old service rifles. Two of them stood calf-deep in the gelatinous mud, keeping their camels together as our flying picket of cattle came tromping down to the water, wreathed in a veil of dust, and charged into the mud-slick beyond the water's rim. We dismounted from our riding animals and greeted the Arabs. They referred to the nazir as 'Sheikh Hassan', but otherwise showed no sign of self-effacement. The nazir told me, 'These men are Arabs of the desert. You will not find Hamdab in these parts very often.'

I had met men of the Hamdab on a previous journey and knew that they were one of the Kababish tribes scattered around the wells at the northern edge of the *dar*, where the Wadi al Milik turned towards the Nile. In summer their camel-hair tents were to be found amongst the thick *'ushur* and *markh* bushes in the wadi-bed, while in winter they herded their camels and goats out north and west into the desert pastures. They rarely ventured this far south. Once the Hamdab had grazed their animals beyond Jabal al 'Ain and Jabal Abyad, deep into the Libyan desert. Those grazing lands had disappeared for ever, and now the Arabs were forced to move farther and farther south each year.

The Hamdab were only one of the Kababish tribes who had adapted themselves to life in the inner desert. The other desert dwellers were the 'Atawiyya, the Awlad Huwal, the Awlad Sulayman and some sections of the Sarajab. Each of these tribes was of different descent. The 'Atawiyya were the Bani 'Atiyya, a branch of the Bani Hillal whose relations had settled in Constantine. The Awlad Huwal were a smaller offshoot of the Hillal, while the Awlad Sulayman were a bedouin tribe who had settled in the Fezzan in Libya, where they had been decimated in a war with the Berber Tuareg. In 1850 they moved into central Chad, where many still remained. The Sarajab were a branch of the noble Kinana tribe that had been left behind when the rest of the tribe moved south to settle in the central region of the Sudan.

The Nurab, to which the ruling house of the Kababish belonged, were one of the largest sections of the tribe. They were Arabs of the Sahel who rarely ventured far into the desert wastes. They lived side by side with the Barara, another large tribe thought to be descendants of the Juhayna Arabs, because unlike the other Kababish they branded their camels on the left side. Another tribe whose homeland lay to the north-west of the Nurab was the 'Awajda, one of the richest of the Kababish groups. The tribes who were to become the Kababish had moved south over centuries, until they found the rich pastures of North Kordofan, which they claimed as their own. Their possession of these pastures was disputed by tribes such as the Zaghawa of Kajmar, the Bani Jarrar and the Dar Hamid. The Kababish eventually pushed these three tribes southwards and established their *dar*. Though a loose confederation the Kababish invented the mythical ancestor 'Kabsh' to explain their relationship: *kabsh* was the Arabic word for 'ram'.

Each of the nineteen tribes that now constituted the Kababish had its own Sheikh of Sheikhs, depending on its size. These sheikhs were responsible for collecting the annual *tulba*, or herd tax, of which they were allowed to retain 10 per cent. The tax was passed on to the nazir, who did not retain a percentage, but whose family was exempt from the tax. The royal family also had the right to requisition livestock from any other tribe in the confederation in the form of tribute; this was often exercised if animals were required for a feast or an expedition.

The title of nazir, or paramount chief, had existed for generations amongst the Kababish, but originally belonged to the Awlad 'Ugba, who were the direct descendants of the Bani Hillal. The 'Ugba were now humble sheep breeders living in the eastern part of the *dar*.

69

The story went that a man called Kirban purchased the nazirate from the 'Ugba, who had grown weak. The price he paid was twenty pure-white she-camels, each with its calf, twenty roan cows, twenty pure-white sheep and a grey stallion with its handler. Kirban was the founder of the Nurab, and the remote ancestor of Sheikh Hassan. Ironically, the Nurab were probably the least pure of all the Kababish Arabs; they were first heard of in the Dongola region, and were almost certainly a mixture of Arab and Beja blood. There still remained a Beja tribe in the Nubian desert called the Nurab.

All the Kababish tribes acknowledged the leadership of the nazir, and the symbol of his authority was the *nahas*, a set of copper kettle drums that were sounded in time of war or on auspicious occasions. The Nurab possessed a *nuggara*, a wooden drum that was sounded for setting up and striking camp during the migrations. Only the royal house was entitled to a *nahas*, which was the standard of the tribe, though other sections might possess a *nuggara*. The only other section of the Kababish owning a *nuggara*, however, was the Barara.

At the end of August we left the cattle herd and rode back to the nazir's *dikka* at Umm Sunta. It was a large camp of camel-hair tents with walls of white cotton, set under thick groves of *siyaal* trees near the wadi of Umm Sunta. There were fifty or sixty tents of various sizes, arranged in widely spaced groups. The nazir's tent was noticeably larger than the others. On one side it consisted of the usual roof of thick camel-hair, while on the other it had been extended by timber and straw into a spacious reception area draped luxuriously with carpets and cloth hangings and containing the sheikh's divan of palm ribs. Decorated saddle-bags of many shapes and sizes hung on the walls and a number of rifles and shotguns were propped up by the door-gap. A pack of ferocious-looking guard-dogs bounded up to greet us when we arrived.

As we dismounted, the nazir's two eldest sons came out to welcome us. The eldest was At Tom, a man of about my own age with a broad, serious face and a mop of jet-black hair. His brother, Salim, was a handsome, tough-looking lad with a quick and humorous expression. At Tom spoke in a well-modulated voice that contained strength and charm. Salim's manner was abrasive and mercurial; he displayed a wit that had little patience with the dull. Both brothers were dressed alike in shirts and *sirwal* of brilliant white, embroidered with silk braid of red and blue. They were the future leaders of the

70

Kababish. Both had been educated at the High Secondary School in El Obeid, but while At Tom had been carefully instructed in the ways of tribal diplomacy, Salim was a herdsman *par excellence* who had spent every vacation hardening himself in the ranges and mountain plateaux, scouting, hunting and tracking raiders.

The servants dumped my luggage and saddlery in a small guest's retreat, about thirty metres from the main tent. They then turned Wad al 'Atiga out to graze with the household camels.

During the day many Arabs came to greet me, curious to see the new foreigner in their midst. One of them was the nazir's cousin, Salim Wad Musa. He was quite different in appearance from the rest of the family, slim, small, graceful, a shade lighter of skin. He was the son of one of Ali Wad at Tom's younger offspring, and had been trained as a teacher. He knew some English and was far more aware of the outside world than most of the Arabs, yet retained a deep commitment to his people and his culture. Salim became my closest friend in the royal family, and always remained for me the embodiment of all that was noble, courageous, generous and enduring amongst the Kababish.

I stayed in the *dikka* for more than a month, sleeping in the guest tent, either alone or with visitors who happened to arrive. These were often tribesmen who had come to petition the nazir or had been summoned to appear in his court, and I learned much from conversations with these men. My strangest companion was a travelling dervish of the Awlad Rashid. He stayed with me for two nights, and in that time hardly spoke at all. He owned nothing but a water-bottle, a staff, a rosary and a prayer mat; he spent much of the night repeating prayers and making prostrations. When I finally asked him why he had come here, he merely answered that he was travelling 'in the path of God'.

Every morning, after we had tea with goat's milk, one of the servants would call the visitors over to the nazir's tent. I would usually accompany them, and we would find Sheikh Hassan in the shade outside with two or three of his guards and several of his sons. Often he was called upon in his capacity as judge to deliberate in some dispute.

In one typical case a tribesman complained that a neighbour had slaughtered one of his cows. The neighbour was brought, and told Sheikh Hassan, 'The animal was dying. It had got stuck in a bog and there was no chance for it. I passed it by once and the next

71

morning it was still alive. I slaughtered it so as not to waste the meat.'
Several of the onlookers applauded his action. There was no attempt
to keep them quiet, and it seemed that anyone could express an
opinion, even the servants who had sat down to listen. Finally, however, the nazir said, 'The case is clear. By the law of *'urf* no man is
entitled to slaughter an animal belonging to his neighbour, no matter
what its condition.' He nodded to the defendant. 'The mistake is
yours. You must repay your neighbour the cow you took from him.'

The nazir's authority as judge was maintained by a corps of
court bailiffs, or *ghaffirs*, who drew a small salary and were officially
entitled to carry arms. There were twelve or fifteen of them, mostly
belonging to the Nurab. The majority were of the slave caste. A few
were 'clients' of the royal family who had originally come from other
tribes and settled with the Nurab, such as Adam Wad ash Shaham
and Mahmoud Wad Affandi, who had originally belonged to the
desert Awlad Huwal. Adam was an old man, unusually tall for an
Arab, with a muscular frame and a cavernous face, scarred by years
in the sun on the trail of bandits and lost camels. His relative, Mahmoud, was a small man who always looked as if he were about to
burst out laughing. He had been badly kicked by a camel in the
previous year, and walked with a limp.

Many of Sheikh Hassan's guards were renowned for their toughness and tenacity. Some, like the notorious Abdallah Wad Fadul,
had been desperate bandits in their younger days, lifting scores of
camels from the tribes. Wad Fadul was a man of about fifty with a
crop of silver stubble, a wide moustache and foxy eyes. He was as
neat as a professional soldier and always kept his equipment in
immaculate condition. He had once lived in Darfur, where he had
become involved in so many blood feuds with the Zayadiyya that he
had fled back to Umm Sunta, where Sheikh Hassan had made him
a *ghaffir* in recognition of his great potential.

Umm Sunta was the summer quarters or 'dammering' centre
of the nazir's family, and the *dikka* was pitched near to the well-
fields in the wadi so that the herds could be watered frequently there.
Some of the wells were hand-dug pits; others were permanent deep-
wells called *sawani*. There was a bore-well several kilometres from
the camp run by a powerful engine, though the scarcity of fuel meant
that it was often idle.

In the first days of my stay I rode to the market near the bore-
well with At Tom Wad Hassan. It was a bleak day and the settlement

looked incredibly desolate. The wind blew silver lashes across the square, beating at the frail doors of the shops. There were a few Arab women about, dressed in wrap-around loincloths or flowery dresses, wearing nose-rings of gold or thick chunks of amber around their necks. Most of the six or seven stores were built of timber and straw, though a few were of mud-brick; they were owned by merchants of the Jallaba tribes from the Nile valley, who had lived with the Kababish for years and were under their protection. They sold tea, sugar, salt, cloth, grain and perfume and were paid either in cash or in livestock, which they sent to Omdurman. The other inhabitants of the village were retired slaves who cultivated tiny plots in the wadi, kept a few goats and chickens, or worked as labourers for the merchants. I asked At Tom why none of the Kababish lived in the village. 'That would mean settlement,' he told me, 'and for the Arabs settlement is like death.'

I soon got tired of living in the guest tent and told the nazir that I should like to build a tent of my own. He frowned and was reluctant to agree. Later I went with At Tom on a tour of his family's tents. They were all of the same basic design, with the tilted roof of thick, woven wool stretched over a central frame of two uprights and a cross-piece. There were two poles, one at each end, which supported the corners of the tent. The roof was held in place by tightly bound guy ropes, and its edge stood about two metres from the ground.

The tents of the nazir's family were far more lavish than those of the other Kababish tribes. They had been extended with local materials such as cane, grass and wood. The extension was often draped in white cotton or in matting of black goat-hair, which the Arabs called *khesh*. Outside the tent stood a wooden cabin, made by piling up lengths of deadwood. This was known as a *tukul*, and was used as a kitchen. The *tukul* was abandoned when the nomads moved camp, but often stood for years as a forlorn monument to a past campsite.

The roofs were made of four pieces of woven wool that were stitched together. The strips were grey, off-white, cream and brown in colour and were made of camel-hair with some goat-hair mixed in. The camels were shorn at the end of winter, when their long coats had grown. The Kababish made a great festival of the event, inviting their neighbours and slaughtering sheep or goats for a feast. When the wool had been sheared, it was carded and spun into thread. The lengths of tent material, known as *shuggas*, were woven on a hand-loom with a frame about five metres long. It was identical to the loom used by the Arabian bedouin, though it was curious that the bedouin used goat-hair instead of camel-hair. One Kababish woman told me, 'Camel-hair keeps out the heat in summer and the rain in the rainy season. Goat-hair keeps out neither, that is why we only use it for walls and not for roofs.'

Many of the tents were beautifully decorated inside with ornaments of leather and wool. The basic item of furniture was a double bed made of palm ribs bound with strips of leather. The bed rested on pegs about a foot from the ground, though it could easily be rolled up and carried by camel. Along the sides of the bed, forming a small antechamber around it, were two sheets of plaited gazelle hide decorated with cowrie shells. These were works of great skill and subtlety in which the leather was woven like thread. They were practical as well as ornate, and when folded could be used as voluminous shelves. Behind the bed were usually two enormous wedge-shaped saddle-bags made of cowskin. They were often decorated with elaborate patterns, and were used for carrying grain during the migrations. Most of the ornaments of the tent had a practical value as well as a decorative one.

Though the nazir finally agreed to allow me to have my own tent, it was with some reluctance, and I wondered why this should be. One night Salim Wad Musa took me aside and told me, 'Omar, you cannot really have your own tent. Tents are for married men and you are not married. The tent is the property of the women. If you have a tent, it means that you must receive guests and to receive guests you must have a woman to cook. To fail in hospitality would be a disgrace.' At once I saw my error, and thanked him for his frankness. 'Of course,' he added, 'if you want a woman a wife can always be found. You should marry at your age. Why not marry an Arab?' I told him that I should consider it, and went back to the guest tent a wiser man.

It was the first week in September, and still no rain had fallen in the *dikka*. The rains were two months late in this area and the summer was turning into a test of patience for the nomads. The days in the camel-hair tents were unendurably hot; at night the lightning danced temptingly in the sky, but no rain fell. There was a palpable sense of frustration amongst the Arabs that darkened into depression as the dry days passed. The afternoons were seething hot. The sky sparkled like polished marble and the thorn trees bristled in the sun. The white cotton walls of the nazir's tent shimmered brilliantly under the trees, and hour after hour the heat spilled down like molten brass. There was not a leaf of green here to ease the harsh colours, the stark ochre and glaring pink of the earth. The tents were the only hiding place from the strafing sun. Often hot winds would rake over the camps, tearing at the cotton walls and dragging a fine mist of dust over the woollen roofs.

Everything was difficult here. The wells were far away, and water had to be brought from them by donkey; often there was none for washing or even drinking. The water was always stored in the nazir's tent; to get a drink one either had to call a servant or brave a pack of viciously snarling dogs. In the deep-wells the water-table had sunk progressively lower; now camels had to be used to draw up heavy buckets. Water was never available to wash clothes, and I was reluctant to ask the servants to work for me, since I had no money to give them. It was difficult for me to visit the wells or the market, for my camel was far away, grazing with the other camels in the wadi, and these places were too far to reach easily on foot. The Arabs had donkeys that they used for local transport while their camels were grazing, and though the nazir always assured me that I could help myself to any of the donkeys, there never seemed to be one available when I needed it. I once spent ninety minutes walking to the market and a further ninety minutes walking back, only to be called into the presence of Sheikh Hassan who told me, 'Do not walk to the market. Do not go there without transport, for the Arabs will say that I am a bad host, and that will be a disgrace for me.' I appreciated his point, but at times the *dikka* seemed like an island in space, cut off from everywhere without the magic carpet of camels to provide connection. I often wondered why on earth the nazir had chosen this benighted, desolate place for his headquarters. The answer always came back: 'For the animals!' To the nomads livestock was everything, and a campsite was always chosen for the availability of food for the animals, no matter how inconvenient for the men. The *siyaal* trees in which the camp was pitched were almost the only source of food for the goats, which were the animals kept in the *dikka* during the summer months.

There was no news from the nazir's camel herds, the so-called *nuggara*-herds that were still in the south. The Arabs could do no more than watch and wait. I realized then how hard the lives of these men were. It was not the thirst, or the heat, or the lack of food, or the desolation of the desert that crippled one, but this constant inactivity of the summer months. It seemed an existence of mono-chrome dreariness that dragged on and on without respite. I had expected hardship and challenge here, but this soul-destroying idle-ness was something I had not bargained for.

The gloom was deepened by the sense of mourning in the camp after the death of Sheikh al Murr. The period of mourning was set at an entire year, and this meant that for that time there could be no weddings, no singing, no dancing and no celebrations of any kind. The men of the family allowed their hair to grow long and unkempt until the mourning period was over; they also reversed the sheep-skins on their saddles so that the side without fur was uppermost. Female relatives wore simple dresses of white cotton instead of colourful robes for the whole period.

When Sir Ali Wad at Tom died in 1937, Al Murr had been passed over for the nazirate in favour of his younger brother At Tom, Sheikh Hassan's father. The new nazir had depended much on his elder brother's advice. When he in turn died in 1945, Hassan was a lad of only seventeen years. Al Murr had been regent of the tribe until 1952, and thereafter had been deputy nazir. Al Murr was much feared for his merciless attitude to enemies, though I learned that he had been charming to those he liked. The power of his personality had undoubtedly shaped the Kababish in the years since Sir Ali's death, and his death in 1982 was in many ways a symbol of the end of the old Kababish and a portent of the years of disaster that were to follow.

During September the nazir fell ill and was confined to his tent. I learned that he was suffering from diabetes and from a mysterious allergy. Occasionally I would sit with him as he lay outside in the shade. He related how he had been to Britain as a young man and had visited Buckingham Palace, where he had met the Queen and the 'Dook', as the Sheikh called him. He described with amusement how the sun had once come out from behind a cloud during his stay, and how he had been amazed when everyone had begun to remove their clothing. He commented that Britain was 'a place with-out sun nor empty talk!' I asked the nazir whether Kababish migrations had changed in recent times. 'There were certain set routes once,' he told me. 'Everyone went on the same day. We would sound the *nuggara* as a signal to start. Each family moved parallel

76

so as not to use up the other's grazing. The Nurab took precedence over the other tribes, but there was plenty of grazing and no one worried. Now there is just not enough grazing for our animals. We can dig new wells, but they will not bring more grass. It gets worse every year. Now everyone goes his own way and looks after himself.'

The tedious days were only lightened by the visits of other outsiders. Three tribesmen of the Berti from Darfur shared my tent for almost a week. They were simple, good natured men with round, black faces, who spoke Arabic with a strange accent, reversing masculine and feminine cases. They had come to claim compensation from the nazir for some camels that had been stolen from them by the 'Atawiyya. I asked one of them what had happened. He told me, 'One of my brothers was herding his camels with his son, when four 'Atawiyya came into his camp. They ate and drank with him, then left. Then they came on him at night and beat him with their rifles until he was senseless. The boy ran off, even though they shot at him, and fetched help. The Arabs went off with thirty camels.' He related how the Berti had shot one of them dead. Two of the 'Atawiyya had run away and the other had been captured. 'But they killed seven of the camels on the way, that is why we are claiming compensation,' he added.

When I later asked the nazir about the case, he told me, 'Those 'Atawiyya were pursuing Berti raiders at the time, and they were entitled to take camels from them by the law of 'urf.' The Berti did not get their compensation, and at the end of the week I watched them riding back towards Darfur.

Some days were so hot I could neither think nor sleep. I lay in the tent watching flocks of goats pawing the dusty ground outside, tended by a negro slave-girl of about fourteen. She had closely cropped hair and a smooth black face that I thought incredibly beautiful. She had a well-developed figure and very large brown eyes. She noticed me watching her and a few moments later her cheeky face appeared at the gap in my tent. 'Would you like to come for a walk with me?' she said.

Totally aghast, I replied, 'What?'

She repeated the offer, and by this time I had gathered my wits enough to say, 'Yes, come back at sunset.' Much to my disappointment, she did not return. Later I asked Salim tentatively about her. 'She is just one of the *'Ol,*' he said. 'Her mother is a slave and she has no father. There are many like that in the camp. Has she asked you to go for a walk with her yet?'

In the heat of an afternoon I watched a knot of camel riders coming through the haze towards the tent of the nazir. As the men dismounted, I recognized the familiar figure of Dagalol, and the squat outline of old Habjur with some other Arabs of Nas Wad Haydar. They had come to perform the ritual of 'Al Fatih' for the nazir, as a way of expressing condolences for the death of Al Murr. This ritual was practised whenever a tribesman or woman died. Instead of having to compose a speech of condolence, the Arab would seek out the deceased person's nearest relative, and before greeting him present his hands in supplication while reciting the first verse of the Qur'an. After that nothing further was needed to be said. It was a system that removed any awkwardness and required no special imagination.

After the ritual I talked with Dagalol. He seemed nervous and ill at ease, refusing to join me in the guest tent. I asked him how it had been in the south, and he told me bitterly that six more of his camels had been stolen after I left. Remembering the argument with Haj Hassan, I could hardly suppress a grin. I found his shifty behaviour surprising, and wondered why he was so anxious to get away.

Some days later I met Mohammid Dudayn, and Dagalol came up in the conversation. I told Dudayn how strangely he had behaved.

'I can explain it,' the Arab said. 'It was guilt, by God!' Then he told me that he had always suspected Dagalol of informing on the Kababish, of telling the Zayadiyya who had shot Tahir. 'He is the only Kabbashi who has Zayadiyya friends!' he said.

'Why should he inform them?'

'Because he is afraid. He is a rich man, and his *damar* is near Zayadiyya country. He is afraid that they will rob him as they do others. He is not a man, neither is he a Kabbashi. If we had proof of his treachery, we should put an end to him!'

Later I went to visit Sheikh Hassan and asked if he were feeling better. He told me, 'I shall be better when I hear that the rains have come and the herds have returned. This has been the longest summer I remember. When I was a boy there was nothing like this! My father's *dikka* was in Hamrat ash Sheikh, and we had grass right up to the door-gap every year! Now the rain comes in patches, but does not satisfy the tribe. There are a few good places, like the Bahr, but the rest is drying up. Soon there will be nothing. If next year's rains are not better, then the Kababish are finished!'

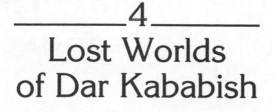

4
Lost Worlds
of Dar Kababish

He has safely weathered one more dread
summer, the life-giving rains are
coming, and with them abundance
once again.
H. R. P. Dickson, The Arab of the Desert,
1949

One morning the nazir's young son Fadlallah came rushing into my tent shouting, 'Omar! The camels have come back from the south! They are grazing a few days away and they will water at Umm Sunta next week!'

That day the camp was full of excitement. There was also news of some rain in the north where the depressions scattered across the desert steppes had filled up with water. This was the signal for all those of the tribe who were able to begin the great move north, out of the sweltering camps of the hot season. The women would pack up their tents and roll up their palm beds. Their baggage camels would be draped with all manner of saddle-bags and fitted with the light-framed litters in which the young women rode with their small children. A Kababish family on the move was a fine sight. There might be twenty or thirty camels carrying the black-swathed litters, which rocked gracefully back and forth to the rhythm of the camels' step, followed by the baggage animals that bore the rolled-up beds, containers of leather and basketwork, folded *shuggas*, tent-poles and ropes, the great waterskins of cowhide, carved platters of black wood, pots of liquid butter and sacks of grain.

The families would pitch their rainy-season camps by the water-filled depressions in the north, choosing the pools where the grazing was most abundant. Large groups of Kababish from various tribes — Nurab, 'Awajda, Haworab, Barar, Awlad Tarayf and Ribaygat — would congregate at the depressions until the rains were truly over and the

79

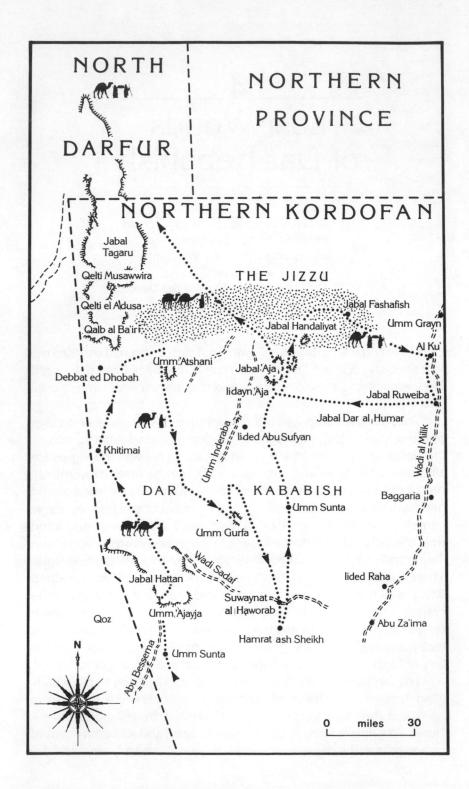

NORTH

NORTHERN

PROVINCE

DARFUR

NORTHERN KORDOFAN

Jabal
Tagaru

Qelti Musawwira

THE JIZZU

Qelti el Aldusa

Jabal Fashafish

Qalb al Ba'ir

Jabal Handaliyat

Umm Grayn

Al Ku'

Umm 'Atshani

Jabal 'Aja

Debbat ed Dhobah

Iidayn 'Aja

Jabal Ruweiba

Jabal Dar al Humar

Iided Abu Sufyan

Khitimai

DAR

KABABISH

Baggaria

Umm Sunta

Umm Gurfa

Iided Raha

Jabal Hattan

Wadi Sadaf

Suwaynat
al Haworab

Umm 'Ajayja

Abu Za'ima

Qoz

Hamrat ash Sheikh

Umm Sunta

N

0   miles   30

water dried up. Then some would drive their animals north into the almost legendary desert pastures called the *jizzu*, which in good years might extend as far as Chad or the borders of Libya.

Many of the young men of the nazir's family began to clean their equipment and prepare their rifles. Their best *ashab* riding camels would be brought in from the wadi of Umm Sunta, and they would get ready to join the herds on the way north. This was the time the Arabs looked forward to all year. The milk yields were usually high and the women travelling with the *ilbil* made clarified butter. Each morning they would draw off the fresh milk and pour it into a small skin slung from a tripod outside their tent. After half an hour of shaking, the butter would be poured off and the buttermilk residue would be used as seasoning for the *kisri*. The nazir's herds were tended by slaves and herdsmen, but at this season anyone who could spare the time took his rifle and his saddle-bag, and rode out to spend three tranquil months in the ranges of *dar* Kababish.

A few days after the news reached us, Sheikh Hassan sent for me. True to his word, he seemed much better, and I found him sitting up in his tent with his sons At Tom and Salim and three of his guards. I recognized one of them as Ja'adallah Wad Hussayn, a bald negro with bulging muscles and a vicious grin, which had earned him the nickname Mura'fib — the local name for a hyena. The others were a tall, spidery man with a dignified beaming Abdallah Wad az Zayadi, and the foxy-faced Abdallah Wad Fadul. As I sat down, the nazir told me that in the next few days At Tom would be leading an expedition into the remote reaches of the *dar*. The object of the journey was to collect camels from each tribe in the confederation. 'We need a hundred camels,' the nazir explained, 'and it will not be easy to get them. There will be eight or nine of my *ghaffirs* with At Tom, and Salim will go as well. They will have to visit every tribe of the Kababish. The camels are for the government, in return for the hospital they built in Hamrat ash Sheikh. It is the first hospital in the region, and it needs money to keep it going. Our taxes do not cover the cost, so I decided that the Kababish should give a hundred camels instead of cash. Each section of the Kababish will be required to give a camel or several camels depending on its size. There will be some problems because the Kababish hate to give up their camels.'

Sheikh Hassan said that he thought the expedition would be a good opportunity for me to meet all the sections of the Kababish.

81

'No other outsider has had this chance!' he said. I could hardly believe my luck. Now all the days of waiting seemed worthwhile: at last I had found the action I craved. I knew that once in the north I would be closer to a chance to visit the salt-oasis of El 'Atrun, which had been my ambition for years.

I asked At Tom about the journey. 'This is the third time we have collected camels for the government,' he told me. 'That is why we are calling this the "Third Requisition". We will use the list that we have for assessing the animal tax. It lists all the families of the tribe and tells us how many camels they own. Of course it does not contain the real number – no Arab will ever tell you how many animals he owns – but it gives us a rough idea. We will take the camels from the rich families who have many camels, as long as they have not given camels before. The brothers and cousins will have to pay the owner of the camel their share. In the end they will only pay a few pounds each.' I asked the nazir's son if I might have an opportunity to visit El 'Atrun. 'We shall not go that far,' he said, 'because there are not enough families in that part of the desert to make it worthwhile. But at this time there are always salt caravans going there. If we meet one then I will see that they take you with them.'

The following day some of the *ghaffirs* arrived in the camp with eight riding camels that were to be used for the expedition. Close behind them came three Arabs of the 'Atawiyya who couched their mounts by the nazir's tent and hustled in to see him. I walked over to the tent to hear what was going on. As I entered, one of the 'Atawiyya was saying 'Sheikh! Your men have taken eight of our camels. We need them for our families, for we are poor men!'

'You have plenty of camels,' the nazir answered calmly. 'We are borrowing these eight for the "Third Requisition". You are lucky, by God! Other families will have to give us the camels – you will get yours back after the expedition.'

'But Sheikh, you have plenty of camels yourself!' another of the men protested. 'Why can you not use them?'

'If I used my own camels for every official journey, I should soon have none left!' Sheikh Hassan replied.

In the guest tent that night I asked the 'Atawiyya if they thought the hospital a worthwhile project. 'Hospital!' one of them answered. 'What use is a hospital to us? We live in the desert. We have no need for hospitals!'

The next morning Wad al 'Atiga was brought in from the wadi with two *ashabs* belonging to the nazir's sons. He looked well fed and rested, though coarse and bulky beside the two trim dromedaries. We left the *dikka* at noon, riding the dry-wash outside the camp with two of the *ghaffirs*, Mura'fib and a silent Arab called Ibrahim Wad Mohammid. We found the rest of our party in the wadi where they had made camp under some *siyaal* trees. As we made our camels kneel, I spotted Mahmoud Wad Affandi and the tall, full frame of old Adam Wad ash Shaham. Abdallah Wad Fadul was there, sitting on a saddle-cushion, next to a small man with a grizzled face as black as mahogany. He was Juma' Wad Siniin, the half-brother of big-boned Sa'ad who had been with us in the Bahr. He was an experienced tracker and guide and was to become one of my most valued companions amongst the Nurab. He was brewing tea on a fireplace of three stones and at once made us laugh by declaring, 'Anyone who has no cup will have to drink with his arse!'

The men were cheerful and full of jokes, chaffing each other unmercifully, making startling declarations followed by the phrase, 'I will divorce my wife!' if the others doubted them. If they lied they really were supposed to divorce their wives, though if this had happened in practice the entire tribe would have been composed of divorcees.

As they talked, the lanky Wad az Zayadi appeared with a lad called Hamid Wad Markaz. The two Arabs were leading a baggage camel that carried most of the supplies for the expedition. As the men unloaded it, I saw that the luggage contained flour, oil, seasoning and a biscuitlike substance in broken pieces. There was also an enormous cowskin of water and a metal camp-bed for At Tom. After this party came the three 'Atawiyya I had seen in the nazir's tent, who were to ride with us as far as the bore-well at Khitimai.

Soon the camping-place was piled with equipment, and many camels were feeding in the trees around us. The raised voices of the Arabs filled the air. I watched them with fascination. They looked different from the Arabs I had been with previously. They had the well-oiled confidence of fighting men and looked equally capable of raiding camels or arresting bandits. Many of them wore bits of old uniforms: a cap, a shirt or a pair of boots; all of them carried rifles, shotguns or even submachine-guns. The impression was more of some ragtail guerilla army than of a group of nomads.

I noticed that the three 'Atawiyya sat apart and did not join in

83

the general conversation. They were reserved and self-conscious in front of so many strangers, and their appearance was startlingly different from that of the *ghaffirs*. They were very Semitic looking, with narrow, aquiline faces and lean bodies. They were nomads accustomed to lives of solitude in the remote reaches of the desert, and beside them the nazir's men seemed almost brash and worldly-wise.

We left the wadi under the cover of darkness, surging in a caval-cade into the eye of a fresh wind from the north. A current of excite-ment ran through the company as everyone sensed that the long summer was now over and at least they were heading north. The camels paced out, anxious to get back to their homelands. The moon had not yet risen, but the starlight gleamed upon their bodies, giving them the streamlined look of racing camels as they lurched forward into the night.

We rode for three hours and spent the night with some Nurab under the granite scar of Jabal Azraq. The next morning we left at daybreak, climbing over the smooth stone of the hill from where we could see the vast clay plains beneath, clothed in their dress of low scrub. To the west the trees were thicker along the curving wadi of Abu Bassama, where I could make out the rigid arms of several baobabs thrusting out of the thorn scrub. Far in the distance was the grey line of Jabal Hattan, the great plateau that formed the northern boundary of the valley. In these steppes there was hardly a sign of life. Some of the acacias in the wadi were in bloom, but apart from them the acres of bush were as stark as a graveyard.

As we swept through the plain, our camels formed and broke in endless patterns, sometimes trotting, sometimes walking. Every-where we came across abandoned camps, the square frame of a tent or a *tukul* left behind when the nomads had moved north. Around these, the skeletons of the nomads' summer-places, were scattered useless waterskins hardened by the sun, bits of broken pottery, old tins or torn hobbling-ropes. As we rode, the camels kicked up the powdery dust so that it layered the air above us, and their hoofs sank into the scarlet sand beneath, making gashes like open wounds along its surface. We followed the line of the wadi, seeing no one, though everywhere there were reminders of how recently this area had been populated. We crossed the massed hoof-prints of many goats, sheep and camels; many of the trees displayed raw, yellow scars where the nomads had cut them with axes. In the

84

wadi the baobabs were lifeless. I saw one that had crashed amongst the thorn scrub, its enormous roots hanging in the air like the limbs of a dead dinosaur.

Juma' Wad Siniin rode beside me for a while, pointing out places that were familiar to him. 'This place is not as it was,' he told me. 'By God, it was a rich place when I was a boy! The old nazir, Sheikh Hassan's father – may God have mercy on him – used to pitch the *dikka* at the watering-place here in winter. There was grass everywhere then, and it grew tall and green. There was game of all sorts. By God, you could find oryx even in the wadi in those days! There were no bore-wells then; no one had even heard of them. The Arabs watered from the hand-wells in summer and the rainwater pools in winter. The rain was more plentiful in those times. Even if the rains failed, as they did some years, there was enough grazing left from the previous years for the animals to eat.'

Undoubtedly the increase in the numbers of livestock owned by the Kababish had played its part in reducing the abundance of grazing in these ranges. Before the 1960s the numbers had been restricted by the availability of water, but this situation had been changed by the new bore-holes drilled by the government around that time. The livestock had boomed and the pressure on the grazing land had increased to a point where the land could no longer sustain all the herds. There was no evidence, however, that the herds had destroyed the pastureland irreversibly, for the seeds of these grasses were very enduring and might remain in the sand for decades, needing only a cloudburst to bloom again. Satellite pictures had shown that there had been no major change in the plant cover around the edges of the Sahara for years. It was the diminishing rainfall that had destroyed these pastures, not the herds of nomads like the Kababish.

We watered the camels in the wadi of Abu Bassama, near the place where the old nazir had once pitched his winter-camp. There was nothing left of the old watering-place now but a sheen of liquid an inch deep on the grey mud. The camels floundered and slithered as they lowered their great heads to suck it up. The sunlight fell over the water in a network pattern, beaming through the tangled branches of acacia and *inderab* trees that were desecrated by axe cuts and the browsing of goats.

In the afternoon we rode towards the tortoiseshell of Jabal Hattan, which had already come into focus on the horizon. Wad Fadul was our guide for this stretch. He rode his own red camel, which bore the crocodile brand of the Gur'an tribe from Chad. He carried a shotgun on one side of his saddle and a Sterling submachine-gun on the other, and was dressed immaculately in a white cotton shirt and an old police cap with a brass badge that I often saw him polishing. I was curious to know what the badge was, and he told me, 'It is an official badge to show I am a *ghaffir* of Sheikh Hassan.' Later I found a chance to examine it properly. It was a brass fleur-de-lis, with the words 'Boy Scouts' etched beneath in English.

All day we moved slowly, letting the camels go at their own pace and allowing them to browse wherever there was a little grass or a few trees in leaf. We passed through miles of waist-high *la'ot* trees, their reddish branches spreading out from ground level, and groves of *gafal* whose thick and tuberous limbs curled around the central trunk in a clawlike cage. There were few Arabs about. One night we halted by the campfire of some Nurab and called out a greeting. At once the answer came back, 'Welcome! Come and rest! Welcome to the guests!' We couched our camels some yards away and set up our *taya* methodically, piling up the saddles and saddle-bags as a shelter against the prevailing wind, and laying out our canvas and sheepskins behind them. Wad az Zayadi couched the baggage camel down-wind in a place suitable for the cooking fire. Ibrahim set up the camp-bed for At Tom and later unsaddled his camel, neatly arranging his saddle-bags and his two rifles. Juma' was in charge of the camels and saw to it that they were all hobbled by the forelegs and turned into the grazing. As we were making the final touches, two little Arabs came out of the darkness to welcome us. They greeted us with an intensity that was almost obsequious, taking our hands in both of theirs and repeating, 'Welcome! Welcome to the guests!' When they had shaken hands with each one of us, they ran back into the night and reappeared dragging a fat sheep. One of the Arabs slit its throat, and at once my companions lined up and began to step over the carcass one by one, chanting '*Karama! Karama!*' I hung back, not knowing what to do, but At Tom called out, 'Come on, Omar! You must honour the hospitality of our hosts!' Soon a fire was leaping up in the hearth as Wad az Zayadi and Hamid began to cook the meat. When it was almost ready, the two Arabs appeared carrying huge platters of porridge swimming in buttermilk. When the feast was laid out before us, Hamid poured water over our hands and we began, eating first the raw liver and lights, mixed with onion and hot pepper. Then we moved on to the roasted meat and finally to the *kisri*. The food was always eaten in this order and, as if to justify it, the Arabs would sing out, 'He who is weak of brain, leaves the meat and eats the grain!' Our hosts ate with us, continually pressing us to eat more and declaring, 'By God, you eat nothing!' as one by one we sat back, replete.

To the Kababish, hospitality was a solemn duty; to refuse to honour a guest was a great disgrace. Although I knew this, it was a long time before I could accept such lavish hospitality without a pang of guilt. I knew that often our hosts were poor; while they gave us of their best, they might go hungry for a week. The Arabs associated meanness and avarice with slaves because they considered that a slave had nothing to give. The words for a freeman and a generous man were the same: *hurr*, which literally meant 'free'. It was the adjective applied to everything that was of the best quality, especially their thoroughbred livestock.

After the meal At Tom sat on his camp-bed and the others gathered around his feet and talked for hours. Now that he was out of his father's camp, he showed himself to be a powerful and authoritarian figure, already clothed in the mantle of the nazirate that he would one day inherit. The Arabs treated him with great respect, despite his age. His brother Salim was more abstemious and spartan by nature, though he had a sharp tongue and was often tactless. He was more at ease in this environment than At Tom, and could ride and shoot as well as any of the more experienced Arabs. At times it seemed to me that both brothers were worlds apart from the others. They were educated and had travelled; they knew the machinations of the great universe outside their own *dar*. They were interested in cars, aircraft and radios, and they laced their conversation with English expressions that they had learned in school. At Tom talked proudly of the truck he intended to buy, and how many camels he would sell to obtain it. Meanwhile, the Arabs at his feet talked of the things that they had always talked of: grazing, the camels, the rain.

They were excellent storytellers. That night, to please our hosts, Mahmoud recounted his adventures in the *jizzu*. He told us how he had once been dying of thirst and had come across the carcass of a dead oryx and how he had slit open its stomach and drunk its water, which had saved him. He told us that once, after four days without food, he had found an ostrich egg, which had provided so much food that he had been unable to eat it all. Afterwards old Adam took the floor, saying that he had once been responsible for tracking all the lost camels belonging to the Nurab. He told us the story of ten she-camels belonging to Sheikh Ali Wad Salim, which had been lost in the *jizzu* yet had turned up at the gap of Sheikh Ali's tent months later, having crossed two hundred miles of desert. He related the tale of the renegade bull-camel that had killed its owner and run wild in the hills, returning to the place of the killing on the same day of each year.

As I listened to these stories, I felt proud to be amongst such men, yet the feeling was soured by a note of sadness. I knew that the world they spoke of, the *jizzu* and the old patterns of migrations, was a world of the past. It was men like At Tom and Salim who spoke for the future.

The next night we made camp in a dry-wash near the foot of Jabal Hattan. At Tom wanted to press on to the mountain, but Wad Fadul argued that the pass was dangerous at night. There had been no rain here for more than a year and the ground was bone-dry, with clumps of stark thorn trees along the wadi sides.

As we ate, there were flashes of lightning across the horizon, though no one took much notice of them. Juma' and Mura'fib brought the camels in later and hobbled them by the knee and the foreleg for extra security. There had been many tales of Zayadiyya and Meidob bandits roaming in the hills.

I was woken by a clap of thunder that shook the air like an explosion. Streaks of lightning forked down to the earth, and a second later rain came surging out of the night sky, spattering across the dust in enormous droplets. Within minutes the wadi was inches deep in water, and before we could move it was up to our calves. Still heavy with sleep, we tried desperately to shift our gear, but the water rose second by second. 'Hold on to your things!' someone shouted. The water was pouring into the wash from all sides, and for a moment I wondered if we might drown. I stayed where I was, and held on grimly to my saddle-bags, praying that my camera and film would survive. Soon the water was up to my thighs, and I crouched there, trying to keep my balance as the soft sand under my feet began to melt away. I had often heard of Arabs being drowned in wadis by flash floods, and had found it difficult to believe that the water-level could rise so rapidly. I tensed my muscles and stayed without shifting for what seemed like hours as the rain slopped down the back of my shirt. Pieces of twig and tufts of grass nudged against me as they floated downstream in the torrent. I hardly noticed the rain easing off, until it had become no more than a light drizzle. Gradually the water began to subside. By morning it had disappeared completely.

The sickly grey light of dawn crept over the world to reveal a landscape transformed. Everywhere the thorn trees glinted and dripped with moisture, and the grey dust had turned into a rippled carpet of ochre mud that was plastered over the tree trunks. Masses of woody debris and uprooted bushes were piled up along the sides of the wadi. Some of the camels had been half buried in the slime, unable to move because of their hobbles. They sat there, uncomplaining, silently waiting to be released. Many of my things had been carried away. I had lost my sandals, whip, pipe, books and saddlecushions. My camera and lenses were full of muddy water and most of my film was wet. My maps looked like papier mâché and my tobacco was a pulpy mess. I watched my companions dragging their gear out of the mud, looking miserable and bedraggled. It was an irony that when rain fell in this thirsty land, it almost always brought greater hardship. None of us was in any mood to celebrate. Wad az Zayadi announced that the flour was soaked and the seasoning ruined. All our leather equipment was waterlogged and our saddles splattered with mud.

'Come on, let's pull the camels out!' At Tom said, and we went to inspect the animals. Some of them were stuck tight, where the wadi floor had melted under their weight. We had to go down on our hands and knees in the slime to unfasten their hobbles, then slither about trying to fix their headropes. In places the mud was up to our calves, and we slipped and staggered as we tried to heave the animals out of the quagmire. I hauled on Wad al 'Atiga's rope as Hamid pushed him from the rear. The beast roared and whined in confusion, and suddenly jerked back on the rope so that I plummeted into the mud-slick. Hamid began to laugh uproariously, until he too lost his footing and was sitting up to his waist in the ooze. After that he gave up and started to crawl out of the morass on his hands and knees. It took us more than an hour to drag the slime-sodden animals on to drier ground. They looked a sorry sight, their buff hide covered in slicks of red muck. Afterwards we laid our sheepskins and blankets out to dry, and Wad az Zayadi emptied the flour and seasoning on to plastic sheets. Then we began to hunt for our lost possessions. Most of them were found stuck between the split roots of bushes or covered in mud on the wadi-bed. After another hour I had found all but my pipe. I had begun to despair, when Wad Fadul held it up, grinning. I knocked a pellet of muck out of its bowl and found that it was still smokable.

We began to load the camels, but our equipment was still greasy, and as we tried to tighten our saddle-girths the saddles slipped out of position maddeningly again and again. Before long, though, the sun emerged from its membrane of cloud and started to dry us out. There was a fresh, almost spicy smell in the air. The plateau reared up before us like a colossal fortress, and as the sun climbed higher its layered orange walls shimmered in the sunlight.

The going was painfully slow that morning. The camels could not grip on the slippery surface and they tottered like drunken men. For a few metres Wad al 'Atiga walked solidly, then he would suddenly lurch forward sickeningly as he lost his grip. For a second my heart would beat wildly as I experienced the dreamlike sensation of uncontrollable falling. Each time the camel managed to jerk upright at the crucial moment and I would look behind to see the tell-tale smear of his sliding pads across the mud-slick. As he watched me, Salim burst out laughing, yelling, 'Hold his head up, or you will go down!' Just then his own camel lurched and staggered, and his grin was replaced by a grimace of instinctive fear. The others laughed loudly, but I saw that all of them were having the same problem. We inched across the wet land, alternately slipping and roaring with laughter, as the camels' feet wove a pattern of curving skidmarks across the ochre surface.

It took more than two hours to reach the hard lava base at the foot of the plateau wall. Wad Fadul told us to dismount, and we scrambled over layers of broken black detritus until we came to the entrance to the pass. On either side the cliffs rose like hand-worked masonry, and as we climbed the narrow path in single file a deep chasm opened beneath us, in which a slim ribbon of water flowed down from the mountain between ranks of *siyaal* trees. The camels hated the smooth boulders that lay in our track, and began to stagger backwards, threatening to push us into the ravine. We shouted at them hoarsely and used our whips to force them onwards. We climbed on and on as the track grew steeper, and the chasm below deepened. Suddenly it levelled out and opened into a patch of bronze-coloured gravel, beyond which was some thorn scrub and the most gigantic baobab tree I had ever seen. Its massive canopy was in full royal leaf and it had an enormous trunk, around which thirty men might have stood shoulder to shoulder. The mountain beyond looked dim and mysterious, and the great tree stood at the very apex of the pass like the guardian of a lost world.

We couched our camels under the vast canopy and sat down to drink water. 'This is where Sheikh al Murr used to hold court,' At Tom told me. 'He would camp here for days and the Arabs would visit him from miles around.'

'But the mountain was different then,' Mahmoud added. 'There was game, even lions and giraffes, and running water with wild duck and guineafowl. The trees were as thick as a forest. We used to hunt on our horses, looking for hyenas and wolves. Where are those days now? The people wiped the game out and the rest ran away, by God!'

Later I examined Wad al 'Atiga's back and found to my annoyance that the greasy saddle had rubbed against his skin, causing the beginning of a painful gall on the withers. I showed it to Juma' and he said, 'You will have to alter the shape of your saddle-cushion, or the animal will be finished.' Wad Fadul took my cushion and cut a piece off with his sharp knife, re-stitching it skilfully so that the leather would not press against the tender surface of the camel's mound.

In the afternoon we crossed the face of the plateau, riding on a hard cuticle of rock and gravel broken by the occasional thicket of acacias. There were Arabs everywhere, moving north with flocks of sheep and goats and small mobs of scrawny camels. We went on until sunset came, as grey as the sunrise that morning, the wall of cloud pierced by beams of blue light that striated the rocky desert beneath. We made camp near some Nurab who killed a goat for us, slinging the carcass in a thorn tree and butchering the animal quickly. The Nurab told us that there were rumours of Meidob raiding parties in the mountain, and advised us to stay alert during the night. The Meidob hills were only forty miles west of Hattan, and the lack of rain in their own country had sent them foraging deeper than usual into Kababish territory.

As we crossed the mountain during the next three days, the landscape seemed suddenly full of life. Green shoots were already pressing through the mud-slicks, and the air was alive with the drone of insects. Black beetles scurried underfoot and at night we were assailed by moths, flies and mosquitoes. Twice I discovered pale-green scorpions that had crept into my equipment, and often large solifugid camel-spiders wheeled around our fire and scuttled off again into the shadows. There was water in the depressions that lay at intervals across the plateau, and there were nomads with sheep and goats in every thicket. For a moment the ephemeral life of the desert had flowered.

One morning we moved through a barrier of rocky crags and came to a depression where a pool of water glittered like mercury. In the hollow hundreds of camels were moving shoulder-tight like a many-legged centipede, martialled by two Arabs who looked familiar. As we rode up to them, I recognized Ahmad Wad Ballal and Abboud. They greeted me warmly, and I noticed that Wad Ballal was carrying Dagalol's Kalashnikov. We couched our camels and sat with them for a few moments, while Abboud milked a she-camel and brought us *halib*, still warm and covered in froth. They told me that Dagalol was still in his camp at Umm Qozayn and had left Wad Ballal and the boys to bring the herd north. Wad Ballal warned us, 'We saw a party of Meidob riding west yesterday. They were carrying rifles and driving five camels with them. Watch out as you make camp tonight. The Meidob hills are very near and they are brave near to home!'

In the afternoon we crossed another treacherous mud-slick about fifteen metres wide. The mud came up to our knees and we had to dismount and haul the camels across. As they sank into the slough, they snarled and kicked, dragging us backwards through the slime. Again and again we moved forwards, helping each other to goad them on. At last the fourteen riding camels had staggered to the other side and we were waiting for the baggage animal. Wad az Zayadi led the beast and Wad Fadul prodded it from the rear. The camel took two or three faltering steps, picking his feet up high, with an expression of what looked like utter distaste. Then he rebelled, squirming back and jerking on the headrope. Wad az Zayadi tried to brace himself, but he lost his footing and went down into the mud, letting go of the headrope, which flew out of his hand. The camel tried to slither back to dry land, but his flat feet slipped sideways. His legs trembled, and for a moment he teetered uncertainly. We watched for a frozen second as he slowly keeled over into the mire, dropping sacks of flour and sugar around him. At once the Arabs plunged into the fray, shouting wildly and waving their whips. They kicked and prodded at the beast until he was upright, then heaved together on the rope until he found himself on the other side.

We made camp just before sunset in a high place overlooking the western rim of the mountain. I went with Adam and Wad Fadul to climb an escarpment littered with blue granite boulders, from the top of which Adam pointed out the misty blue hump of Jabal Meidob to the west. Behind us the familiar herds of Nas Wad Haydar were moving in their hundreds across the face of the mountain. 'We'd better keep our weapons close tonight,' Adam said. 'If these Meidob come back there will be trouble, and no doubt!' I asked him why the Kababish hated the Meidob so much. 'They have no honour,' he said. 'They will kill a man first, then steal his camels. If they find you asleep, they will bash your head in with a club or strangle you, or they will shoot you from far off. That is not bravery! If I was riding in Meidob country, I should never sleep next to my camel. I would take my rifle and lay in the bushes beyond. These people are dogs! The Arabs may steal camels, but they do it by stealth. If they cannot find a way to do so, they will leave you alone. If they are caught, they will fight, but they do not murder to steal.'

In the time of Ali Wad at Tom, the Kababish had often fought with the Meidob, and had even been reprimanded by the government for a raid on the Meidob hills. Sir Ali had occupied the Meidob hills in 1916, but had withdrawn the following year. Although the Kababish had been officially excluded from the hills in 1922, many sections continued to water at Malha and Ain Bissarro, and I had found herds of the 'Awajda in the crater at Malha when I had visited it with Donald Friend in 1981.

I remembered how we had ridden for days through the gorges and the narrow chasms of the hills, searching for the wells at Ain Bissarro, on their eastern side. We eventually ran out of water, and one afternoon came suddenly on a tiny well under an overhanging rock in the middle of a ravine. Some Meidob girls were there, watering their goats. They spoke only a few words of Arabic, so we settled down to wait until they finished their work. It was agonizingly slow, for the well only yielded a bowl of water every five minutes, and it was almost sunset before they drove their animals away. I jumped into the hole, ready to fill our skins, when an old Meidobi suddenly sprang out of the bushes with a shotgun in his hands and ordered me to get out. He said that the well belonged to his family and refused to let us use it. Expecting a fight, Don quickly seized our pistols, knowing that our lives depended on this water. Fortunately, after a long discussion the old man agreed to give us water in return for a meal from the millet flour we were carrying. He said that he had had nothing but goat's milk for months. After he ate, he told us that the last white man he remembered seeing here was Wilfred Thesiger, who had come to shoot Barbary sheep in the 1930s.

As we walked back to the camp, there was a single 'kuff' from a shotgun, and Wad Fadul said, 'That is the sound I like!' We found that At Tom had shot a young hare that he had seen skipping across the rocks near the camp.

After supper there was more talk of the Meidob. One of the 'Atawiyya told me that there was blood between his family and the Meidob, who had killed more than a hundred of the 'Atawiyya. 'There was the one called Musayid,' the Arab said. 'He was one of the Arabs who always pitched his tent in Meidob country. He was very friendly with his Meidob neighbours and they shared things and called themselves brothers. He had a daughter – a beautiful girl, by God! She was married to her cousin and was pregnant. Musayid left his camels with them and rode off to the *jizzu* to hunt oryx, as our family often do. It was winter and he was away for a long time, but the hunting was good and he shot six of the animals and dried their meat. When he arrived back at his tent, he found no one there, but he was tired and lay down to sleep. The next morning he had just made himself tea, when four of his Meidob friends came into the camp. He was pleased to see them, for he wanted to give them some dried meat, and ask for news of his daughter. They gathered around him as if to greet him, and then suddenly jumped on him and tied him up. They tied him very tight with a nylon rope, so that his arms were behind his back, lashed to his feet. Then they abused him, and took his rifle, his camels, his meat and everything they wanted. They left him there to die, thinking that no one would ever come by. No one did, but he saw the ashes of the fire were still hot, so he rolled over to them, and lay in the hot ashes. It took a long time before the rope burned through. By the time he was free the flesh was burned off his hands and his back. He took what he could and walked towards Hattan, and the same day he met some Kababish with their herds. He recognized them and asked them if they had news of his daughter. They said that his daughter had been shot dead by the Meidob days ago, and that they had taken all his camels. No one knows what happened to the girl's husband. He said that of all the burns he had received, that burned him most of all. It was a year before his hands were healed, but then he got a rifle and went back to Meidob. He shot eight of them before the devil left him!'

My companions nodded, obviously familiar with the story, muttering to themselves. Then one of the other 'Arawiyya said, 'Do you remember when the Meidob attacked the bore-well at Khitimai? I will never forget that day, by God! Forty or fifty of the slaves came out of their mountains on camels, but they found no one at the well but some womenfolk and the watchman with a boy. The watchman ran away, but they caught the boy and broke his arm. Then they stole gold from the women and told them that no Arab should use the well again, as it was theirs. But the watchman came to our camp — we were in the hills near the water-pool — and warned us. We just saddled our camels and rode out — there were about eight of us I recall. The slaves were still at the well when we got there, and we shot two of them. They sheltered behind the huts and killed two of us with their bullets. Then we just sat there. There were too many of them for us to attack them. Someone fetched the police, but they could do nothing. In the end the slaves left. But there was no settlement, and no blood money was paid. The Meidob still say that Khitimai is theirs and that they will take it when they want it.'

The next day we saw the disputed well at Khitimai. We left Hattan and rode into the valley beneath. It was carpeted in soft sand and shaded lime-green by the new growth. There were scatterings of knee-high bushes delicate as paper models, and seams of thicker trees standing out like the veins on a man's hand. Far in the distance stood a mass of granite cliffs and knolls, weathered into the shapes of pyramids and trapezoids by the winds from the desert.

Soon the vegetation thinned out and disappeared except for a few twisted *sarh* bushes with thorny leaves on the upper branches. Everywhere there were the droppings of generations of animals, and the sand was deeply imprinted with their hoofmarks. I saw the storage tower of the bore-well stuck like a black pimple on the smooth floor of the valley. It was exactly in the centre of a vast radius of dead land; not a clump of grass nor a low bush grew there. As we came nearer, I saw the two corrugated iron shacks that housed the pump engines, and a line of four concrete bunkers beneath the metal reservoir. Apart from this there were three or four broken-down shops made of grass and cane.

This was one of the wells drilled in the post-colonial period,

95

and the few *sarh* trees around it were grotesque reminders of the destruction that it had helped to bring about. I knew that this was the last permanent watering-place until one reached Wadi Howar, 200 kilometres north; these shacks and broken-down emporia were the last permanent buildings for 1,000 miles. This was where the Sudan ended. It was the last outpost of the known world, beyond which the desert lay ancient and forbidding.

The well was almost deserted. At this season the Arabs watered their animals at the water-pool that lay an hour's ride to the north. We moved on quickly and were soon sloping in under the *siyaal* trees that surrounded the pool. Hundreds of camels were being watered there. They bore the brands of the 'Atawiyya and the 'Awajda, and there were some belonging to Nas Wad Haydar, with the familiar mark of old Habjur.

The water was bright red and about a foot deep. Many Arabs stood up to their calves in the liquid as they coaxed their camels to drink, calling, 'Aw! Aw! Aw!' The animals crowded together, clustering round the mud basins that had been carefully made at the water's edge. There were many women about, slim, muscular girls with copper-bronze skin and braided black tresses smeared with butter. They wore only skirts of blue cotton and stood by the water with their flocks of goats and sheep, and donkeys carrying waterskins.

We spent the night further up the hillside, at the foot of a granite outcrop. Here we were away from the mosquitoes that always hung about these water-pools, and there was a little grazing for the camels. The next morning we rode back to the pool, to begin the work of the 'Third Requisition'; I was very curious to see how the Arabs would react to us.

At Tom made himself comfortable beneath a tree, sitting on his sheepskin with a small briefcase as a desk, and with his two rifles leaning against the trunk behind him. He looked grim and impressive with his long, unkempt hair, every inch the great-grandson of Sir Ali Wad at Tom. Throughout the morning the *ghaffirs* moved around the pool, finding out which families were there. When they found an individual whose name was on the list, they would send him to At Tom. The first arrival was an Arab of the 'Awajda, who approached us looking worried and apprehensive. He greeted us, and we stood up to return the greeting. After he had sat down on a canvas sheet that Ibrahim laid out, At Tom said, 'We are making a requisition of camels for donation to the regional government. The

96

donation is in gratitude for the hospital they have built for all the Kababish, in Hamrat ash Sheikh. Your name is on the list to donate a camel. We want a good camel, not a worn-out one. When you have chosen it, my men will value it so that your relatives can pay you their share.'

The Arab regarded him with slow incredulity, then as he realized that this was serious, he scratched his beard and said, 'Sheikh, my family gave a camel to your grandfather. Surely you would not ask another from us?' At Tom replied calmly, 'Your name is on the list. Have you anything to prove you gave a camel to my grandfather?'

'No.'

'Then we want a camel. If you do not choose it yourself, my men will, and they have very high standards.'

Taking the hint, the 'Aidi stood up and walked sadly back towards his herd.

I could not help feeling sympathetic. I knew that these Arabs hated to part with their animals and would often go hungry rather than sell them. I also realized that for most of the Kababish the hospital was useless anyway. When I mentioned this to At Tom, he replied, 'You are right, many of the Arabs do not like hospitals, and will not have anything to do with them. But most of the Kababish are uneducated and do not understand the value of a hospital. Are we to let our land stay backward just because of the people's ignorance?'

All day there was a stream of visitors in our *taya*. Occasionally the Arabs would smile and graciously agree to donate one of their best camels. Mostly though, they would look sullen and rebellious and say, 'Sheikh! My relatives will never pay me their share. They have no money, anyway' or 'Sheikh! All my animals have died, by God! I have only enough left for my family!' At Tom would listen patiently to the talk, making diplomatic answers but never allowing himself to be put off. He would reply, 'You are Arabs and you say your relations will not support you?' or 'Your camels looked fine and healthy when I collected the herd tax last year!' When the Arab had been persuaded, At Tom would send Mahmoud, Mura'fib or Adam off to inspect his camels. If they thought that the one chosen for them was of poor quality, they would select another. They would value the animal, and At Tom would present the owner with a paper declaring its value and proving that they had donated it to the

Requisition. I asked At Tom what would happen if anyone refused point-blank. 'They won't,' he said. 'We are the government here!'

At our camp that night there were many guests, Arabs of the Nurab and 'Awajda who had come to hear the news from the south. At sunset I climbed the granite knoll behind it with Juma' Wad Siniin, and we sat and looked north across the vast ranges. The land below was semi-desert, red and yellow and amber, punctuated by coarse clumps of *nissa* grass, with slabs of grey rock rising in the far distance. Beyond them lay the fabled *jizzu* pastures, and then nothing but the open wastes of the Libyan desert, on and on as far as Egypt. The distances awed and humbled me. I looked down at the fire burning in our camp, a jewel of bright orange, no bigger than a candle flame.

As I sat there, stunned by the beauty of this place, I felt once again a sense of deep sadness. I traced it back to the happenings of the day, and my conversation with At Tom about the hospital. I could not argue with his logic, yet I knew that he represented the sweeping changes that would soon come to this desert land where his ancestors had roamed wild and free for centuries.

We watched the sun slipping down through terraces of blue cloud until it reached the horizon, bathing the barren steppe in an aura of gold. Slowly it disappeared and night stole over the great plain, spangled with stars.

'What do you think the stars are?' I asked Juma'.

'They are the work of God,' he said. 'The sons of Adam should not interfere with that.'

Perhaps this was ignorance. As we climbed down the hill back to the camp, I was inclined to believe that it was not.

During the next morning some Nurab arrived on fast camels. They were messengers from the *nuggara* herds that were now grazing at Hattan, and as soon as they sat down by At Tom, one of them announced, 'Sheikh! Your father's herd has been attacked by Zayadiyya. The slaves got away with seven camels!' He told us that the bandits had come upon them at the mouth of the pass, near the place where the rain had caught us. They had come in the night and there had been a gun-battle, though no one had been shot. A pursuit party had set off the next morning, but it had not yet returned. The Nurab wanted At Tom to return with them to take charge. 'I cannot go,' At Tom said. 'Salim will go instead.' His brother agreed at once and declared angrily that he would lead another pursuit party, and take any Zayadiyya camels he saw. 'Be careful,' old Adam advised. 'This could be a trick. If you go, go well armed. Those Zayadiyya will not give up the camels. You will have to take them by force!'

Salim left the following day, while the rest of us headed north towards Jabal Umm 'Atshani. We were now driving before us the seven camels that we had acquired at Khitimai. Wad al 'Atiga was walking with them, for the gall on his withers had grown worse and At Tom had allowed me to ride one of the new acquisitions rather than founder him.

Soon we came to a herd of more than fifty camels being driven by a lad of about thirteen and his smaller brother. Both of them were dressed like miniature adults, in *jibbas*, *sirwal* and small head-cloths. As we dismounted, they greeted us with the solemnity of men, and the older boy poured us some milk. He asked At Tom why we were travelling, and when he heard about the Requisition, said, 'Sheikh, I will give you one of my she-camels.'

'Your family's name is not on the list,' At Tom replied.

'No matter,' the boy insisted. 'I will give you one of my best camels as a personal gift.'

'By God, here is a man!' At Tom declared in admiration, and old Adam smiled and nodded in agreement. I was astounded that one so young should own camels, but At Tom said, 'A father often gives his sons their birthright as soon as they are old enough to look after them.'

After we had drunk, the boy took us to see the she-camel, walking with At Tom, and conducting himself with great dignity and self-consciousness. 'Here is a man, by God!' At Tom repeated.

The little brother followed on, trying to keep up and to maintain dignity at the same time. At last we came to the camel, a four-year-old with a growth of woolly hair. 'This is my gift to you, Sheikh at Tom,' the boy said. At once the little brother let out a howl of misery, shrieking, 'That is my she-camel!' He ran at the bigger lad, crying loudly and laying into him with his tiny whip. Suddenly the mask of adulthood fell away, and the boy pushed his brother aside roughly and struck him across the head, with a look of bitter irritation.

'No, leave him,' At Tom said, with a grin spreading across his face, 'it does not matter.' The tiny Arab ran after the she-camel and hastily drove her off with his little whip. The older brother looked as if he too were about to burst into tears. 'It is not important,' At Tom added. 'But when you give something, make sure it is your own.'

99

In the afternoon we crossed a valley of baked red dust dotted with cairns of stones. The steppe here was almost devoid of trees, and clumps of *nissa* and *tomam*, the coarse grasses that grew in even the most arid of places, were the only forms of vegetation. Plain opened into plain, endless sandy ergs without feature except for the occasional tent like a dark speck on the vastness. The Arabs were camping here on their way to the *jizzu* and often we saw herds of camels, forty or fifty strong, padding on like silent flotillas. Behind the herds came the black litters, two or three or four of them, ridden by unseen women, and towing long trains of baggage camels that carried all that the nomads owned. As we passed them, At Tom would send a couple of his men out to discover who the Arabs were and to which tribe they belonged; most of them were 'Atawiyya or Awlad Sulayman.

We spent the night with some Sulayman in a dry-wash where a few acacia trees were growing. The Sulayman had arrived just before us, and their womenfolk were unpacking the litters and unfolding their tents. When we had couched our camels, two small, grizzled Arabs came to meet us. They were dressed in *sirwal* and leather slippers, their torsos wrapped in *tobes* of cloth and their necks decorated with wooden beads. At Tom found their names on the list.

'It is no good asking us for a camel, Sheikh at Tom,' one of them said. 'We gave one to the last Requisition. We cannot spare another!'

At Tom checked the list again and said, 'Your family's name is here.'

After an hour of discussion and protest, the two men went off with Wad Fadul and Mahmoud, who came back leading a worn-out *ashab* and a four-year-old calf. 'They had no good camels,' Mahmoud said, 'so we took these two poor ones. The *ashab* is old but it still has some strength.'

The next morning a strong wind blew from the north-east. 'It is the wind of *darat*,' Juma' told us. 'That means the rainy-season is over. There will be no grazing in the *jizzu* this year.'

'It is going to be a hard winter for the Arabs!' old Adam commented. 'It is seven years since the *jizzu* bloomed properly.'

That day we rode on and on across a desolate landscape, where only horns of granite relieved the emptiness. We travelled on after sunset, though the night was pitch dark and the camels stumbled over chasms filled with loose stones. In the distance we could see the feeble light of a campfire, and Wad Fadul led us towards it for two hours in the darkness. Our animals continued to stagger and slide on the shattered boulders, and at times I wondered if Wad Fadul really knew the way. 'I was born in this area,' he told me later. 'I could lead you here blindfolded.'

At last we came to the campfire and set up our *taya*. The camp belonged to Ali Wad Ibrahim, a cousin of At Tom's who had brought his camels to water at the *gelti* inside the mountain massif of Umm 'Atshani, which was hidden by the darkness. He was a massive, dark-skinned man, the son of one of Sir Ali at Tom's younger progeny, travelling light with two of his slaves. He welcomed us into his small *taya* and his servants spread out a canvas for us to sit on before bringing us a meal of meat.

In the morning we saw the double-cone peaks of Umm 'Atshani rising out of the plain, and Wad Fadul led us through a winding series of ravines until we came to the hidden *gelti*. It was a seasonal water-pool where the rainwater collected amongst the impermeable rock. Scores of Kababish were there with clusters of camels, filling waterskins from hand-dug pits. The pool itself had dried up some days ago, leaving only a patch of sodden ground where the Arabs had to dig down to the water-level.

After we had couched and unsaddled the camels in the wadi nearby, At Tom told his men to dig a new pit in order to water our animals. Wad Fadul chose a place, and we scooped out the damp earth with hands and bowls, working for several hours until we had made a pit about four feet deep, into which water began to trickle. Hamid filled a bowl with the yellowish liquid and drank some. 'It tastes like camel's piss!' he exclaimed, spitting it out. We lined the sides of the hole with grass and roots so that it would not cave in, and Mura'fib began to mould a shallow basin near its brim, to be lined with a canvas sheet, from which the camels could drink. The Arabs took turns standing in the pit and pouring water into the basin, while Juma' and Mahmoud brought the camels up one by one. No matter how brackish the water, it seemed a miracle to find it in this arid place. Wad Fadul told me that the water here was 'blessed' by the bones of a famous camel called Wad as Sihab, which had fallen into the *gelti* several years ago.

Later I climbed the cliffs around the watering-place with Juma'. From high above, the *gelti* looked tiny and impotent in the midst of the acres of black volcanic rock, with its covering of gleaming quartz, red granite and ebony lava. In the distance was a wall of sand dunes, bleached blue by the winds of *darat*. Juma' showed me the *jizzu* pastures, lying east and west of the mountain, saying, 'There will be no *jizzu* this year.' Then he pointed north, and said, 'That is the Great Desert.'

I spent the rest of the morning at the *gelti*, watching the comings and goings. Men and women crouched in bevies around the pits, waiting for them to fill up, and rows of waterskins lay around them, bulging like well-fed slugs. Much of the work was done by women. They were sensuous figures with their gaily patterned headcloths and their neatly pointed breasts, throwing back their long braided hair and smiling to display perfect white teeth, as they poured water from the water-pits or loaded their camels. I could easily have watched them all day, but I was called to our camp by At Tom to share a meal with the massive Ali Wad Ibrahim. As we were eating, Juma' came running into the camp clutching his ·303 rifle and crying, 'The slaves have taken one of the camels!' He held up a hobbling-rope and told us, 'I thought the animal had wandered off, so I went to fetch it. It was the four-year-old we got yesterday from the Awlad Sulayman. Then I found footmarks and a little further on I found this! They have taken it and no doubt!'

'Those Awlad Sulayman are not to be trusted,' Wad Fadul said. 'I saw the son of one of them at the *gelti* this morning. I tell you he is the thief. He has taken back the camel that his father gave us!'

At Tom told Juma' and Mura'fib to follow the tracks of the thief, and the two Arabs took their rifles and saddled quickly, riding south after the tracks of the stolen animal.

It was sunset when they returned, bringing with them a youth of about fifteen. He sat, frightened but unbending, in the sand before At Tom and Ali Wad Ibrahim. 'I said it was the Sulayman boy!' Wad Fadul declared. 'What do you think of him, the dirty thief!'

'A donkey!' Juma' said. 'He was too slow. If he had not stopped at his father's camp, we would never have caught him. If you are going to steal, do it properly, by God!'

Then Mura'fib told us how they had followed the tracks, trotting fast on their camels and had been led straight to the Sulayman camp where we had spent the previous afternoon. 'We only just got him, though,' he added. 'When we arrived he was saddling another camel, intending to run off into the hills.'

'His father said that the boy had a great affection for the camel,'

Juma' went on, 'and offered us another one instead. I told him that stealing was stealing.'

The boy said nothing and stared in front of him. 'He made no excuses,' Juma' added. 'He said the camel was his.'

'We will show him who that camel belongs to,' At Tom declared.

He discussed the matter with Ali. Both of them had judicial powers. Ali was magistrate for the Khitimai region and, as At Tom was officially the plaintiff, it was decided that Ali should judge the case the following morning. He told me that he had authority to deliver sentences of five years' imprisonment, a heavy fine or twenty-five lashes.

We left Umm 'Atshani the next morning before the boy was 'tried', taking the disputed evidence with us. We heard later that the thief had been given twenty-five lashes, and that the sentence was summarily carried out by one of Ali's bailiffs.

'It is the best sentence he could have got!' Wad Fadul said. 'It will be no more than sport to him. He is an Arab of the desert. Pain will not worry him, by God!'

5
Legendary Pastures

After the cloudburst the desert blossoms
like a rose, but only for a short time.
During that time, however, the nomads
can move in, graze whatever animals
they keep, and move out again when the
vegetation dries.
Maurice Burton, Deserts, *1974*

We camped at noon in some *siyaal* trees just north of the mountain. After we had eaten, At Tom called us together and told us that here the party would split up. He would take Wad Fadul, Mura'fib Mahmoud, Ibrahim and Wad az Zayadi north into the desert, while Juma', Hamid, Adam and I should ride south with the herd and the baggage camel, and meet up with the *nuggara* herd near Jabal Hattan.

I was bitterly disappointed not to be included in the desert party, but At Tom explained that this was simply because there were no spare camels that were suitable for desert conditions. The sore on Wad al 'Atiga's back made him unridable, and the only trained camels in our small herd that were not exhausted were four- and five-year-olds. I swallowed my disappointment, but when Juma' said, 'We shall find some 'Atawiyya moving south and ride with them,' I was consoled by the thought of travelling with these desert Arabs on their migrations.

We helped the others to load their camels, then lined up to shake hands. At Tom said that – God willing – he would see us near the pool at Shigil after a week. 'Go in peace,' we told him, and stood watching as the six men mounted and rode off into the sand-mist.

Then we gathered our belongings and our weapons and drove our herd south towards the steppes.

Juma' took up the guide's position on the left flank of the herd, and Adam stalked along on the right, straddling his small camel with his long legs folded easily across its neck. His craggy, clean-shaven face was shadowed by the woollen cap he wore instead of a head-

104

cloth. He carried a service-issue shotgun that hung by its strap on the rear horn of his saddle. I was riding one of the four-year-olds, fast but lacking power, and took my place at the back of the herd. Behind me came Hamid leading the baggage animal. He was about eighteen, with smooth, black skin and clean, rather obstinate features. He was inexperienced and impulsive, but as strong as an ox.

For the rest of the day we rode across an almost featureless plain of sand, and the wind from the north sprayed us with fine showers of dust. The next day we made camp with some 'Atawiyya during the afternoon. They were on their way south out of the desert pastures, and had settled for the night along a water-course where some *tundub* trees were growing. With them were about thirty camels and a mixed flock of sheep and goats, which were already feeding amongst the trees when we arrived. A group of women with long braided hair and brightly coloured dresses were busy laying out their belongings and erecting three small tents in the bushes.

As we set up our *taya* alongside them, an old man came to greet us. He was slim and very upright, with a twisted grey beard and eyes glazed with trachoma. He wore the remains of a pair of *sirwal* and was barechested except for a length of cloth looped around his back and thrown over his shoulders. His headcloth seemed moulded to his temples. He wore a black-hilted dagger on his left arm and carried a ·303 rifle. As he shook hands with us, three of his sons came up behind him. They had long hair growing in curly mops and wore torn shreds of *jibbas* that were thin and yellow with age. All of them carried rifles.

The old man inquired which family we belonged to, then sent off his sons to fetch a goat. He sat down next to us in the sand and as Hamid began to make tea, he said, 'The scouts have cheated us, by God! There will be no *jizzu* this year. There was none last year nor the year before that. I cannot remember when the *jizzu* last bloomed. Perhaps it is finished. Life is hard for the Arabs, by God!'

'They say there is *sa'adan* in the east,' Juma' commented. 'It is growing in patches around Jobul Kantosh.'

'Patches!' spat the 'Atawi in disgust. 'What good are patches? It will not be enough for all the herds. By God, I remember when the camels got so fat that they could not walk, and we had to help them to stand up. Sometimes they ate so much that they burst, by the life of the Prophet!'

105

Old Adam shook his hoary head. 'Where are those days now? Perhaps they will not come back.'

'God is generous,' Juma' said.

'Yes, God is generous,' they agreed.

Not far away from us a girl of about fifteen was trying to gather some sheep, picking up twigs and throwing them at the animals as they scampered away. She wore an underskirt of coarse blue cotton that reached down to her ankles, and above it a dress of flowery green material. Her hair, treated with butter, fell down across her shoulders in a cascade of fine braids, and she wore thick bracelets of old ivory on her wrists and silver chains around her ankles. Another girl, slightly older, was collecting firewood in the bushes. She wore only an underskirt and a scarlet *tobe* wound around her head like a turban, falling down the smooth copper skin of her back.

Several more women were working by the tents. Two of them held infants and there was a gaggle of older children. The tents were much smaller than those I had seen in the *dikka* and were set up in a line with the door-gaps facing south. Around them lay some old riding and pack saddles and the arched frame of a litter. A tree nearby was festooned with goatskins; several of them were the medium-sized *girbas* used for carrying water, and there were many smaller skins holding sour milk.

The sons soon came back with a fat black goat. Hamid slit its throat and slung the carcass in a thorn tree. The 'Atawiyya boys drew their daggers and helped him to peel the skin off. When the furry mass was free, one of them rolled it up carefully, saying that it would do for a waterskin. I watched as Hamid skilfully slit the animal's belly and cleaned out the inedible organs.

While the meat was being roasted, I walked around the camp with Adam and the old 'Atawi. The women came up to shake hands with us, removing their leather sandals as they did so. The children also shook hands, except for the infants and the very young. These we touched lightly on the head, raising our closed fists to our lips and repeating the words of greeting, which their mothers answered for them.

The old man showed me inside one of the tents. The camel-hair roof had been slung over the uprights so that the sides hung down and touched the ground. There was very little space inside, and the palm-stalk bed had been laid on the sand and covered with goat-hair rugs. From the uprights hung some saddle-bags and two basketwork jars, grey with age, which contained flour and unmilled grain. In the corner of the tent stood a carved wooden milking-vessel, called a *kabaros*, a crudely fashioned wooden mortar and two flat grindstones.

Several clay pots decorated with an intricate striated pattern lay in the dust outside, and I asked the man if these were made by the Kababish. 'Never!' he answered. 'The Kababish do not make pots. They are made by the Nuba.' Adam laughed and explained that to be a potter was considered a disgrace for an Arab.

The Arab showed us his camel herd. He was evidently proud of his animals, and with good reason: there were some superb racing dromedaries amongst them. I was careful not to ask how many camels he owned nor to praise them; I had already learned that the Arabs believed in the 'evil eye', and that if a stranger complimented livestock or children some accident would befall them. For the same reason they would never reveal to strangers the number of animals or children they had, feeling that to declare the number was to challenge fate to reduce it. Almost all the Kababish believed in this superstition, and I remembered how the nazir had insisted that it was outdated and primitive, and how the very next day, when I praised his best riding camel, he'd snapped, 'Do not put the "eye" on him!'

Later Hamid called us back to eat the ribs and the roasted meat of the goat. Juma' had ridden off to catch a young she-camel that had run away, and Hamid set a generous portion of meat aside for him; to have forgotten a travelling companion would have been a tremendous insult.

The lights of the animal had been mixed with onion and spices and made into a stew, which we ate last. Afterwards Hamid took the goat's head and buried it in the sand under the hot ashes. 'We will eat it tomorrow,' he told me. 'It will be delicious, after it has baked all night in the sand.'

It was late afternoon when Juma' came back, driving the lost she-camel before him. 'So much trouble just for a worthless three-year-old!' he grumbled. Adam went up to hobble the animal, but she screamed as if he were about to slaughter her and charged off towards the 'Atawiyya camp, where the young Arabs blocked her way. As they tried to grab her she turned tail again, shooting back towards us. Adam took a lunge at her, moving in a surprisingly sprightly way for his age, but he was too slow. Hamid managed to fix both hands on her tail and, running along behind her, suddenly heaved her off balance so that she collapsed into the dust. At once all four of us pounced on her and Adam fixed knee-hobbles on both her legs, saying, 'She won't try that again!'

Next morning we were up at first light, and Hamid dug the goat's head out of the sand. He tapped the dust from it and smashed it open with an axe, giving each of us a piece. I was given the left eyeball and part of the brain. As he had told me, it was truly delicious; I understood why the Arabs considered the head the best part of the animal.

The 'Atawiyya had already brought their baggage camels into the camp and the tents were being carefully folded and fitted on to the pack saddles. The women lashed their litters to the backs of three great bull-camels, and draped them with rugs and cloth. The litters were built on to the frames of pack saddles and fitted the camel in exactly the same way. They enclosed the woman and her infants in a capsule of shade as they moved from camp to camp. The basketwork vessels, pots, saddle-bags and even the grindstones all had a particular place below the litter, and the water and milkskins were slung from a separate camel. When everything was ready, the nomads collected their herd and flocks and moved off in a grand procession. The women climbed into their litters and took the children, who were handed up to them. The great beasts rose steadily to their feet and strode majestically after the livestock, the baggage animals trailing after them in a long caravan.

We mounted up, and followed with our herd and baggage camels. Before long several families who had spent the night nearby joined us, each with its complement of flocks, herds and litters, so that we were in the midst of a great train of men and animals that stretched more than a kilometre through the desert. We moved with solemn pageantry over the smooth desert crust that was white-washed by the ceaseless wind from the north. Here and there dead trees raised their bone-dry limbs from the sand like segments of gigantic insects. The landscape was so vast that even this magnificent cavalcade seemed no more than a trail of ants.

By mid-morning the sun was roaring like fire and the pale sand threw back its heat and light into our eyes, parching the membranes of our throats. We climbed up the gently rising side of a valley and the herds and flocks drilled themselves into ranks and files. As they climbed, the sun caught their bodies, making them glow like mirrors. On the far side the desert glistened before us in a mantle of amber, ochre and orange, shining with a blinding intensity as far as the distant darkness of the mountains. All day the procession went on and the black litters rocked silently to the rhythm of the march, hour upon hour, as the sunlight spilt down across the glaring sand and the brown shapes of the hills came steadily closer.

We stopped again before sunset where some *nissa* grass had sprouted in tufts across the sand, and the families spread out into the desert. Everywhere camels were couched in clusters, with baggage dumped in piles upon the sand. Boys dressed in tattered *sirwal* coursed along the sand on young camels, heading off flocks of sheep and goats and turning them into the grazing. Within minutes the Arabs had scooped out round holes with their daggers, setting up the tent-poles and draping the camel-hair over them. The tents sprang up like mushrooms across the landscape. We made camp alongside the same family, and after we had piled up our equipment and drunk water to ease our parched throats, I watched the same group of women breaking up firewood and lighting fires outside the skeletons of their tents. The sun hovered a few metres above the horizon; its fire burned out, and the cool of the late afternoon descended on us, bringing with it a sense of restfulness and peace.

Just before the sun set, three Arabs came walking towards our camp. Juma' said, 'Here come the 'Awajda we saw at Khitimai. Now there will be trouble!' They were narrow-boned men with ferocious, mud-dark faces, fearless and brutal. I remembered having seen them at the pool at Khitimai, when At Tom had been collecting camels there. They refused the tea we offered, and sat down in the sand nursing their rifles. Almost at once one of them said, 'We have come for the camel Sheikh at Tom took from our family at Khitimai. You have no right to take it. We gave a camel to the last Requisition and to the one before that. We must have that camel back!'

'Do you have the paper to prove it?' Adam asked.

'Paper? We have no paper. What do we need with papers? That camel is ours.'

'We cannot give you the camel back without the paper,' Juma' cut in. 'Sheikh at Tom is not here to approve it.'

'Then we will take it, sheikh or no sheikh!' the Arab declared.

Juma' grinned, but his eyes went cold. Old Adam's craggy features assumed a sour expression. Even young Hamid stopped what he was doing and glared at the three men.

109

'You shall not touch that camel,' Juma' said with chilling calmness. 'If you touch it, you will answer to the nazir himself.'

The 'Awajda glared back at us venomously, then the Arab said, 'Come, let's go. These men are but servants!' They rose slowly and with dignity, then turned and stalked away. Juma' remained where he was until they had gone, then he jumped up saying, 'They will be back! Let us get the camels in, quickly!' In a few moments all the camels had been gathered and hobbled around the camp in a tight semicircle. Juma' brought the disputed animal up close to him. I saw that it was none other than the she-camel that had run off the previous day. She squalled loudly as Juma' couched her by his bed-space. 'Like her owners!' Juma' commented. 'Plenty of noise! I should be glad to get rid of her, but it would be a disgrace to give in to such as these!'

Juma' lay down on his sheepskin with his ·303 next to him. Adam settled down a few feet away with his shotgun. I broke my weapon and pushed a cartridge into the breech. Hamid had no weapon but a curved club, so I gave him my ·22 revolver, which he put into his pocket. We lay there drowsily for two hours as darkness fell across the desert. Around us the camels shifted, groaning and belching. Beyond them the campfires of the 'Atawiyya flickered in the shadows, and there were murmurs of talk and the cries of children from the direction of their tents.

My eyes closed involuntarily and I was walking on the borders of sleep, floating off to some distant place and time, when Juma' hissed, 'They are coming!' I was awake in an instant, and my weapon was in my hand. Juma' was sitting up holding his rifle. Three shadowy forms were hovering in the shadows on the perimeter of the camp, like malevolent grey ghosts. 'Stop! Do not come any closer!' Juma' snapped.

'We come to bargain with you,' a voice came back. 'Give us our camel and we will bring you another in exchange tomorrow.'

'Who owns this wretched camel?' Juma' shouted.

'She belongs to our uncle. He is not here,' came the reply.

'You bring him at dawn tomorrow and then we will talk about it,' Juma' said. 'But we do not work in the middle of the night.'

For a second the figures stood there, unwilling to move. I saw that Adam was kneeling with his shotgun ready, covered by the wall of camels. 'One blast from his weapon would probably knock all three of them down at this range,' I thought instinctively. Then they turned abruptly and disappeared into the fold of the night.

'They are scoundrels!' Juma' declared. 'They thought that we were fools and would not do anything without the Sheikh. The Arabs of the desert are donkeys sometimes!'

We lay awake for a long time afterwards, hearing nothing but the steady breathing of the camels and occasional human sounds from the encampments beyond. I rolled over on to my back and looked at the sky. The Milky Way cut across the darkness directly above us, a mysterious gossamer path to the outer ends of the galaxy.

Not long after dawn the three men returned, bringing with them an older Arab with rheumy eyes, wearing a tattered shirt. The situation seemed to have been defused by the long night. The figures that had seemed so menacing in the darkness were stark and ordinary in the clear light of day. The old man said that the camel was his, and Juma' and Adam agreed to return her, providing the man remained with us until At Tom arrived from the desert. After a while the Arabs gave in and drove the beast away. When they had gone, Juma' told me quietly, 'Thank God they took her! That has saved us plenty of trouble!'

The 'Atawiyya had already packed their tents and belongings, and the herds and flocks were winding across the landscape in a great serpent. We saddled up and drove our camels out to join the timeless migration to the south.

A few days later we made contact with the *nuggara* herd near the pool of Shigil. There were more than 500 animals divided into groups of 100 or 150. A score of Nurab tribesmen were riding with them, some of them slaves and herdsmen and others from the nazir's family. The camels were the best to be found in *dar* Kababish, magnificent beasts descended from the herds of Sir Ali Wad at Tom. There were no women and no litters, for, like the Nas Wad Haydar, the Sheikh's people left camel herding to the men.

We found the *taya* of the chief herdsman, Sa'ad Wad Ahmad, on the rocky slopes above the pool, and made camp nearby. Sa'ad was a brawny black man with swept-back hair; Juma' was his distant relation. He welcomed us like lost brothers, embracing each of us and slapping us on the back, crying, 'Your return is blessed! Welcome in peace! Thank God for your safe coming!' With him was another *ghaffir*, a tall sinewy figure with a friendly face, called Juma'

Wad Tarabish. He was the nazir's court baillif, and I had heard often of his escapades with bandits. The Arabs made us tea, strong and black, and brought us a bowl of sour milk. 'Drink!' Wad Tarabish told us. 'The camels are in milk. There is plenty of that, by God!' As we drank, a bouncy little man with a tough-looking face came up to greet us. He wore a woollen cap that was pulled down over his ears, giving him a clownish appearance. I learned that he was Ali at Tom, the son of the late Sheikh al Murr.

The men brought us *kisri* drenched with gravy made from the meat of gazelles they had shot. After we had eaten, Ali at Tom asked us about the grazing in the north and the progress of the Requisition. He laughed freely at the stories Juma' told about the Awlad Sulayman and the 'Awajda, interjecting, 'No God but God!' and 'God protect us from the devil!' at intervals. Adam inquired about the grazing in the south and whether Salim had returned from Darfur. 'He came back with nothing!' Ali told us. 'They lost the tracks of the bandits and returned empty-handed. Now he has ridden off to the *jizzu* with the scouts, looking for pasture.'

'God willing, he will find it,' Adam said. 'For there will be no pasture in the *dar* this year!' Then the old man asked about the health of the nazir and the people who had remained in the *dikka*. Ali said that Sheikh Hassan was seriously ill again and had been moved to Omdurman.

Soon after dawn the next morning, Juma' and I rode down to the pool to choose a place for watering the herd. The water was almost finished and lay in the centre of a shallow depression surrounded by flats of scarlet mud. There was a margin of thorn trees around it, a few of them in leaf. We unsaddled our camels under the trees and tied them up. Juma' took a bowl, kicked off his shoes and waded through the mud to the water. He came back grinning and held out the bowl to me saying, 'Drink! The water is good!' It was red and very muddy, and as I raised it to my lips I saw that there were millions of mosquito larvae squirming about in it. 'Drink!' he repeated. 'Those insects will not harm you!' Realizing this was a small test, I suppressed a shudder and drank the stuff down, dimly aware of the little creatures writhing in my throat.

These annual pools were ideal breeding-grounds for the malarial mosquito, *anopheles gambiae*. Despite the aridity of this area in summer, a few females of the species managed to survive, hiding in cracks in the trees and living on the blood of passing

112

animals. When the rains came, they laid eggs by the million in any place where the rainwater might collect for a few weeks. Malaria was endemic at this time of year and many children died from it. The adults, however, were resistant to the disease, and although I knew this was a genetic immunity I wondered sometimes if I could have acquired it. I had suffered from malaria badly until 1982, when the frequent attacks abruptly ceased.

'Come on,' Juma' said. 'Let us get to work!' We stripped off our shirts and headcloths, and stepped up to our calves in the mud. Juma' explained that the camels were unable to wade out to the water, and that we would have to build a reservoir on the harder ground around the edge of the pool and construct a series of channels to feed into it. We picked up handfuls of the wet slime and began to fashion a circular basin where the solid ground met the mud-flats. When it was done, Juma' cut out an intricate system of small channels that directed the water into our small reservoir. Then we built a second basin near to the first. Juma' lined it with a canvas sheet and placed on it lumps of reddish rock salt that he produced from his saddle-bag. 'It is a long time since the camels had salt,' he told me. 'They need to have it often if they are not eating fresh grasses.' He transferred water from the reservoir to the drinking basin with a bowl and stirred the liquid with his hand. 'Tell Adam to release the first two camels,' he said. In a moment two of our herd were trotting loosely through the trees, pursued by Hamid brandishing a *mukhayyit* branch. The camels began to suck up the water with incredible speed and it was all we could do to keep the basin filled. As they drank, Juma' made the familiar noises of encouragement. 'Aw chack! Aw chack! Aw chack!' and I joined him in a kind of two-part harmony, repeating, 'Aw chack! Aw chack! Aw! Aw! Aw!' The beasts were thirsty and drank without stopping. I watched in fascination as the muscles in their necks contracted, pumping up the liquid like steam-engines, and their bellies slowly distended.

All morning we watered our animals, filling the basin again and again, until our arms ached from the pouring and our legs from the strain of balancing in the mud. It was hot and thirsty work, but often the camels dropped water from their mouths that fell on our shoulders with a pleasant cold sensation. As I watched the great square heads dip into the trough, heard the satisfied sucking and saw them trot away replete, I felt strangely fulfilled. I understood more than ever why the Arabs took such pride in their animals.

113

It was noon by the time all the animals had been watered, and we were very hungry. We made camp in the shade of the trees, and Hamid cooked a bowl of *kisri*. As we sat there, Adam pointed to the fringe of bush at the brow of the hill from which the *nuggara* herd was emerging like a brigade of cavalry, in magnificent array. They were being pushed on by many herdsmen intent on the watering-place, and I wondered idly how long it would take to water the whole herd. Suddenly two pairs of camel riders separated from the mass, one on the right and the other on the left. I saw them raise their whips, shouting wildly. 'It's a race!' Juma' declared, and stood up to watch. The four camels were bounding across the gravel in enormous strides, stretching out their necks and lifting their feet like horses. Instead of leaning forwards, the riders leaned back, perching dangerously on their backsides with their arms in the air, shouting, 'Absha! Absha!' The two pairs of riders were so close to each other that I felt sure they would collide. I watched in amazement as two of them began to push at each other with their elbows. One of the men wobbled perilously, but managed to regain his balance as his camel slowed down to a trot. The other pair shot past him, coming in through the screen of trees. As the men strained on their headropes with both hands, I saw the laughing features of Wad Tarabish and heard him shout, 'Best camels in the herd, but you cannot beat uncle Juma'!'

That night, after we had moved back to our camp on the high ground, I asked Wad Tarabish about the race. 'We call it the race of the *muhawwadin*,' he explained. 'It is the tradition amongst the Kababish at this time of year. The water in the depression is nearly finished and every herdsman wants to get the best place to build his *hawd* – his drinking trough.' He explained that this was one of the few occasions on which the tribesmen tested their camels to the full. A camel that won such races became famous and was celebrated in song and poetry. 'When a camel like that dies, the women weep as if it were a person,' he said. 'We never eat it – we just leave it for the vultures.' He went on to say that there were many famous camels amongst the *nuggara* herd. One of them was the nazir's mount, Kalash, which had once been stolen by bandits and shot in the rump by a Kalashnikov. Another famous camel was At Tom's animal, Wad as Sihar; the riding camel of Salim Wad Ali, Wad al Jaddi, was also renowned for racing. All these camels were the sons of a camel called Al Ingleez. 'Al Ingleez was the most famous camel belonging

114

to Sheikh al Murr,' Wad Tarabish said. 'It was brought from the east with a she-camel and given to him as a present by a British inspector, Mr Read. The best camels in the *dar* are the descendants of that pair. We call them Awlad al Ingleez – "the sons of the English".'

We stayed with the *nuggara* herd for more than a week in the region of Shigil. Each night after supper the men would talk for hours about the camels and their qualities. The herdsmen knew every camel by name, and its ancestry for two or three generations. Often they would dispute hotly about the relative merits of the different breeds.

One night Juma' Wad Siniin said that there was nothing to equal an *ashab*, while Sa'ad shouted that *'anafis* were always better. Wad Tarabish ended the argument by saying, 'At the races they held in Hamrat ash Sheikh a few years ago, an *'arabi* beat all the rest. You would have said he was a very ordinary camel, nothing to distinguish him at all. But he won all the same.'

The herds had found good grazing near Shigil, and by day we rarely moved far. Instead I would ride about with Wad Tarabish, learning all I could of the lore of camels. He would point out the leaders of the herds, the magnificent bulls that the Arabs called *fahal*. Each one could serve a hundred females or more during the time of rutting, which was usually in winter or the rainy season. At this time the bull's neck would swell and he would blow out the pink mouth-bladder that was a sign of his dominance.

We often watched the antics of the *fahal* with great amusement. The bull would saunter arrogantly around the females, raising his head and rolling his eyes, blowing out his bladder and burbling. He would bump the mate he had chosen on the neck, trying to force her down into a kneeling position. Usually she would run away, bursting into a full gallop and racing across the desert. The bull would give chase, turning and zigzagging as she changed direction, desperately trying to slow her down. Sometimes the male would even thrust his head between her legs and lift her back feet off the ground, and the female would flick her tail and bleat ineffectually. When he had her under his control, the bull would bump her on the neck and body until she sat down, then straddle her awkwardly with both front feet over her shoulders. The whole process would be accompanied by much growling and grunting, but despite the ferocious sounds, the male was often unable to perform without the assistance of the herdsman. If his determination wavered, the female

115

would give him a hard time, lurching to her feet suddenly, so that his legs were hooked helplessly around her neck. Then he was stuck, balancing pathetically on two rear limbs while the others were caught, unable to do anything but wail plaintively until the herdsman freed him. The nomads would often hobble the she-camel to prevent this happening. We would laugh at these tricks until the tears came, but Wad Tarabish would remind me afterwards that the bull-camel in season was a highly dangerous beast, and not to be taken lightly.

Juma' Wad Siniin told me how, when he was a boy, a bull-camel had picked him up by the back of the head, and would have killed him had another herdsman not come to his rescue. Luckily he had been saved from serious injury by his thick headcloth. Wad Tarabish said that a relation of his had been killed when a bull-camel he had been riding had rolled over on him and crushed him to death with his chest-pad. The worst injury I ever saw from a mating *fahal* was in Abu Za'ima in 1985. A Barara boy of about seventeen had been picked up by the arm and shaken like a puppet. The arm was completely shattered, a bloody mass of crushed bone and dead blood-vessels, smelling badly of gangrene. He had been carried by camel for six days to Hamrat ash Sheikh, where he had found the hospital closed; it had, in fact, never been opened.

The gestation period for a camel was about twelve months, and the females would drop their calves in autumn or winter. Several were born amongst the herd while I was at Shigil. The baby was deposited in a membrane of grey material, and was not able to move at once. The mother would lick away the material and in a few hours a fluffy calf would emerge, a delicate creature standing about four feet high, ungainly on its new-found legs.

The calf would be fed on its mother's milk for a year, though if the Arabs wanted to preserve some of the milk for themselves they would seal up the female's teats with a knot of cloth secured by a stick. The she-camel could not become pregnant again for the weaning period, which made the entire cycle a two-year one. The Kababish never used she-camels for riding, though if a camel were slaughtered for food it would always be a barren female.

A male riding camel was selected for training when it was three or four years old. Wad Tarabish was training one of the herd camels and showed me how it was done. The first thing was to separate him from the herd, hobbling both legs and tying the headrope tight around the neck so that the animal was only just able to breathe.

One morning he showed me a camel that had been left like this overnight. The animal's lips were badly swollen by the choking rope; he was spluttering and drooling at the mouth, trying to roll over, scraping his head along the ground. The Arab released him from the hobbles, holding the rope tight. Once the camel had found his feet again, he jerked sharply on the rope only to find that it strangled him more tightly. After he had been pacified a little, Wad Tarabish began to pull the headrope downwards, shouting, 'Khyaa! Khyaa!' The camel tried to strain against him again, but eventually plumped down on his knees. Wad Tarabish told me that this would be repeated for several days until the beast had learned to kneel. Afterwards he would be fitted with a saddle, and while a herdsman led him by the headrope, another would ride on his back. When the camel became accustomed to the weight, the rider would take the headrope and teach him to trot. The entire training took only three or four weeks.

Wad Tarabish told me, however, that few camels were really well trained. 'It needs an expert to train a camel well,' he said. 'The best trainers are those who make a habit of raiding. They make sure the camel learns to make little noise, and will stay in one place when he is hobbled.' I asked if he thought the camel an intelligent animal. 'He is cunning,' the Arab answered. 'But he has no real sense. His brain is full of worms. You can never trust a camel completely, no matter how long you keep him.'

I was still worried about Wad al 'Atiga. The swelling on his withers had become septic. Juma' Wad Siniin inspected him one day and told me, 'You will not ride him again, not soon anyway.' He drew his dagger and cut into the wound until the blood flowed, peeling away the infected flesh. 'At Tom or Salim will give you another camel,' he said. 'They have plenty.'

When Salim returned from his foray in the *jizzu* a few days later, he at once agreed to give me another camel. He was an *'anafi*, a slim, sturdy dromedary from the Awlad al Ingleez section, with an unusual steel-grey colour. One of the herdsmen told me that his name was Wad at Tafashan, which meant 'The Son of the One which Ran Away'. I was delighted with him. Salim said that he would keep Wad al 'Atiga in his herd until the wound healed.

Not long afterwards I had a chance to test him out, when I rode to the travelling merchant at Umm Gurfa al Himera with Wad Tarabish and two of the royal family, Mohammid Wad Ali and Salim Wad

117

Ali. The herdsmen had run out of the chewing-tobacco that they craved, and Himera was the only place nearby where it could be obtained. It was normally a full day's journey, but Wad Tarabish said that by travelling fast we could ride there and back in a day.

We set off soon after sunrise. The Arabs were all riding superb racing camels and carrying their rifles. Salim, known to everyone by the nickname Shawish, was mounted on his famous racer Wad aj Jaddi, 'The Son of the North Star'. He was a tall handsome lad, dignified and intelligent. Mohammid was a little younger, a lightly built youth with a reserved manner. Both of the men wore their hair in great uncut plumes, still in mourning for Sheikh al Murr.

After half an hour Mohammid spotted four gazelles in a grove of thorn trees and slipped silently off his camel to give chase. I watched him as he disappeared into the bushes, a slim figure with his hair sticking up like iron filings on a magnet. He carried a ·22 hunting rifle in one hand and a tripod in the other, with a thick ammunition belt lapped around his waist. A little later there was a dull report. Then the Arab came walking back disconsolately, saying, 'They were too far away. They escaped.'

We rode fast across a sandy plain and climbed a steep pass into the belly of the Umm Gurfa plateau. It was late afternoon when we came through a gap in the rock wall and saw a Hamdab camp at Himera below us. There were a score of tents, nestling under the black cliffs, and beyond them stretched a plain of semi-desert from which rose the red cliffs of plateaux like mystical islands. Around the camp was a forest of *sallam* trees. The trees were in bloom and the air was sweet with their perfume. Camels and goats browsed at the foot of the rock wall.

We were welcomed by the Hamdab, who brought us sour milk and a dish of meat. They pressed us to stay, but it was almost sunset and Wad Tarabish said that there was a storm in the air. We bought tea and the tobacco we had come for, tied up in pound bags; then we said goodbye to the Arabs and rode back quickly up the narrow path into the mountain. Darkness had already fallen, and the storm caught us at the head of the valley. The night was split by streaks of lightning and the air was filled suddenly by choking dust. A violent wind hit us from behind, threatening to hurl us from our saddles. 'Come on!' Wad Tarabish shouted. 'We will race the wind!' We rode fast, coursing forward on the wind-crest like surfers riding a wave, crashing through the screen of dust. We rode four abreast as the dust lashed against us, running ahead of the storm like wild untamed creatures, yelling excitedly as we narrowly missed a bush or a cairn of stones. We rode on regardless of the danger of being thrown or struck by the lightning that scintillated in the sky like fireworks, going faster and faster in the grip of the surging forces of nature that it was beyond us to control.

By the time we had come down into the valley on the north side of the plateau, the storm had passed. We trotted on in the calm of the night, as the pulsing silver of the stars replaced the violent whiplashes of lightning. It had been the most exhilarating ride of my life.

The following day At Tom and the others returned from the north, driving four camels that they had acquired from the Arabs of the desert. Two days later we said goodbye to the *nuggara* herdsmen and rode east with our Requisition camels, now more than twenty strong. Salim Wad Hassan had decided to stay with the *ilbil*; in his place came Juma' Wad Tarabish. The old man who had come with us as hostage was sent back to his camp.

We moved over a wild, bleak landscape where the colours were grey and white, broken only by two volcanic plugs called Tilib al Barik and Tilib al Wilayd. At noon that day we came down into Wadi Tifrig, where two Haworab tents were pitched by some puddles of muddy water. At Tom sent Wad Fadul to the tents to buy liquid butter, and I went along with him. The tents were surrounded by flocks of goats and inhabited by two women, ragged but beautiful, with braided locks. Two naked boys with curry-combs of hair rolled happily on the palm-stalk bed inside one of the tents. The women were friendly and told us that their men had gone north with the camels in search of *jizzu*. I wondered how they protected themselves in this wild land, and Wad Fadul pointed to a rifle hanging on one of the guy ropes.

'Arab women are not afraid to use it!' he told me.

The women sold us butter that we took back to our camp in a glass bottle. Afterwards At Tom said that we needed more flour, and instructed Wad Fadul to ride to Hamrat ash Sheikh, about a day's journey south. I volunteered to go with him, anxious to see this tiny settlement that had once been the headquarters of the nazir Sir Ali Wad at Tom.

It took us five days to collect the flour and find At Tom's party again. We met them at the pool at Kilagi, where scores of Kababish

119

families had gathered to enjoy the last dregs of the season's rain-water. We remained there for almost a week, watering our camels and preparing for the next stage of the journey, into the waterless pastures of the *jizzu*.

Meanwhile the work of collecting camels continued and by the end of the week our herd numbered about forty head. At Tom decided that Juma' Wad Siniin, Ibrahim and Hamid should take them east to the Wadi al Milik, while the rest of us rode north. On the 10 October we said farewell to the others and headed to a hidden *gelti* an hour's journey from the pool, where we filled our waterskins. We had ten small goatskins and the large cowskin, and as we crouched at the water's edge, scooping up the liquid in bowls and pouring it into the leather vessels, Wad Fadul said, 'Fill them well! There is not even a smell of water in the *jizzu*, and we have no she-camels with us for milk.'

That night we camped with an 'Atawiyya family in Wadi Himera, and in the morning awoke to see the desert lying like an amber carpet on all sides. As we rode north that day, the wind whipped across us, bearing a shroud of dust. We wrapped our faces in our headcloths and bent forward into it. The camels struck on into the mist of white sand, through which we could see the fangs of Jabal Shaynat, ground into stumps by the gyrating blast of the wind.

For several days we trekked on through a surreal waste of pale moon colours. The sand foamed before us and behind us, and during lulls in the storm we saw around us mysterious pinnacles like icing-sugar moulds. The vast landscape played havoc with my sense of scale and speed. At times it seemed that we moved all day but got nowhere. The horizon was dominated by the fluted hump of Jabal 'Aja, which came into bleary focus in the morning but had retreated by midday into the soupy haze of the sand like a turtle into its shell.

In some places the sand was covered with a faint emerald stain from the grass, and in others it had been roughened into ridges by the woody roots of the *tomam*. Nowhere amongst these fossils of life was there grazing for our camels, though almost everywhere the surface spoke of nomads and their animals. The sand was criss-crossed by tracks and scattered with billions of pellets of camel dung. At late afternoon the wind dropped, leaving a pure azure sky untainted by cloud. Slowly the yellow egg-yolk of the sun slipped across the ragged skyline and left the world in darkness.

We moved slowly. Our camels were exhausted after their trek of hundreds of kilometres. The baggage camel went lame, picking up one of his rear legs in a pitiful arc and stumbling haltingly after our caravan. Hunger began to pinch us. We had no firewood, and not a single tree was to be found in these wastes. The wind scoured us, and when it dropped the searing heat of the sun took its place. These endless ergs were beautiful, but they held no comfort. I asked Wad Fadul if he preferred this area or the semi-desert further south. 'If the grass grows here, this area has no equal,' he said. 'But when there is no grazing, it is a demon of a place.'

And there was no grazing. We pressed on and on, shrunken with hunger and thirst, lolloping forwards across our saddles as the sun slowly fried us, searching desperately for something to feed our camels. Anything that had grown here had been consumed long ago by herds migrating north or south. At times our quest seemed hopeless. I was aware that ahead of us there was nothing but a featureless wasteland for a thousand miles, without shade, without grazing and without water. It seemed that we were pushing far into unknown country, deep into the remote corners of an uncharted universe. But this was an illusion. Once, not long ago, the Kababish had ranged into the desert hundreds of miles north. Before that nomads of an unknown race had herded their long-horned cattle as far north as the Mediterranean coast. Some vast change had taken place here. It had turned these pastures into a desolate land. The long hours became days, and the camels bleated with hunger. Wad Fadul said grimly, 'We go on, but God alone knows what we shall find!'

Then, one morning, we spied an outcrop of white rocks far in the distance. As we came closer, the rocks resolved into a nest of about twenty camels. Soon we saw that they were couched on a wide patch of grass, *gutub* and *khishayn*. Our hungry camels saw it too, and began to trot forwards, drooling. Beyond the camels stood a single tent, like a tiny cell of cool shade in an ocean of nothingness. It was only with difficulty that we managed to drag our animals away long enough to be unloaded. As they grazed, we joined our canvas sheets together and guyed them to saddle-bags, covering the surface with blankets to protect them from the throbbing heat.

Two Arabs emerged from the tent and greeted us with solemn dignity. From inside I heard the cries of an infant and the soothing voice of a woman. The Arabs belonged to the Ribaygat. They were

121

squat, muscular men with stubbly brown faces, their hair in long, matted shags. They wore nothing but knee-length *sirwal*, torn and stained to a shade of khaki, with daggers on their left arms and rosary beads curling around their necks. They walked barefoot on the stinging-hot sand.

One of the men brought us a bowl of sour milk. As we drank in turn, I looked around at the camels on their sparse grazing, and the enormous empty vista of the desert beyond.

I asked the man, 'How do you live here? What do you eat?'

'We have only milk,' he said. 'But it is enough. What we miss most is tea. We have no sugar and little water to make it.'

'Don't you shoot game?' At Tom inquired.

'We sometimes kill a gazelle, but not often these days. The gazelle have gone west and moved farther into the desert. When I was young there was every kind of game. We shot oryx and addax, and there was addra and ostrich. The gazelle used to be in herds in the wet season. You would see them coming out of the hills, thirty or forty of them together, grazing like goats. Now you never see more than four or five, and you are lucky to see that many. We used to shoot ostrich often. They have piles of meat and you can fill a pot from the oil in their bodies. We used to find their eggs sometimes. There is plenty of food in an ostrich egg, by God!'

'Why has the game gone?' Wad Tarabish asked.

'It is the dryness,' the Ribaygi answered. 'You remember how the *jizzu* used to be? All that is gone now. The *jizzu* has not bloomed properly for years. There are patches of it, around Kantosh and Fashafish. But it is not like the old days.'

The old days in the *jizzu* were Mahmoud's favourite subject, and he explained to At Tom and I how the *jizzu* life had been the best time of the year. 'It was hard, by God!' he said. 'You might stay in the *jizzu* for three months, even four. I know men who took their camels as far as Nukheila, even 'Uwaynat, and were gone for five months or more. In all that time you hardly drank water. You slept on the cold ground shivering from the wind. If you wanted water, it was ten days' journey, by God!'

'Then why was it so good?' At Tom demanded drily.

'Because of the camels,' old Adam cut in. 'They got fatter and fatter. There was so much milk you did not know what to do with it. There was no need for water, by God! You could drink milk all day!'

We moved on in the late afternoon, and the smooth, featureless

plain of desert closed in again on all sides. During the afternoon
Adam spotted a single tree. We rode over to it together to see if there
were any firewood. Its branches were like the petrified tentacles of a
great dead octopus, and as we reached out to touch them they
broke and dissolved into powder. 'Termites!' Adam said. Any termite
colony that had lived here had become extinct long ago. We
gathered up a few shards of wood and rode back to join the
others.

We saw nothing else for the next two days, and our bodies continued to wither from lack of food. Several times Wad Fadul found
the tracks of gazelles and ran off on foot to look for them. I knew all
the arguments for conservation, but they were meaningless here. All
that mattered was the ache in my stomach and the desperate craving
for meat. I felt sure he would be successful, but always he came
back empty-handed.

We passed north of the hills of Handaliyat, riding across plains
of smooth sand bordered by peaks and knobs of rock hammered
into weird shapes by the inexorable process of erosion. Once we
discovered a thick growth of *tomam* grass. It was useless as grazing,
but Mura'fib declared that it could be used instead of firewood. We
couched our camels and the Arab instructed us to collect as much
of it as we could, while he dug a small T-shaped trench in which
he made a fire. The *tomam* burned with little heat and had to be
replenished constantly. In the end our efforts produced no more
than a pot of lukewarm tea.

As the days passed, I noticed that the Arabs became increasingly
sharp and bad-tempered. There were many lessons to be learned
in the desert. It removed complications. Its vastness pared away the
trappings of men, and reduced them to their true scale. Here A't Tom
was just another thirsty man; water and food were shared out equally
to nobleman, servant, freeman, foreigner and slave. Equality
seemed to be the natural order of the desert. The idea of aristocracy
seemed out of place here; it belonged to the Sudan. We were beyond
that world in the far off country of the Sahara.

At last we saw the black plug of Jabal Kantosh towering above
the plain, and within a few hours our camels were grazing in the lee
of the mountain. Far to the north was a scree of glinting grey stones
that turned into a herd of grazing camels, as numerous as termites.
To the east another herd came suddenly into sharp focus on the
skyline. After days of deadness the desert was suddenly full of life.

123

The amber shelf of sand was deeply grained with green, but every-where the grass was short and cropped by the thousands of animals that had crossed it in the previous weeks.

As we made camp, setting up our canvas shelter at the foot of Kantosh, several Arabs couched their camels nearby and came to greet us. They shook hands with us one by one and sat in the shade asking for the news from the south. Some of them brought us bowls of sour milk, which were cool and refreshing after our long ride.

We remained in the area of Kantosh for several days. Every morning the *ghaffirs* would ride out to the herds, claiming camels or sending the nomads to meet At Tom. Much of the day our shelter was full of ragged men who begged water and crowded elbow to elbow under the awning as the heat and dust scourged the arid plains. Many migrations passed us. Some would halt near our camp and set up their tents for the night. Now all the Arabs were moving south. 'What little grazing there was, is finished,' Wad Tarabish told me. 'The Arabs are returning to their dammering places in the south. That means the grazing there will be used up before the summer comes. By next April the Kababish will be in trouble. Then the herds will start to die.'

When our water was used up, we had to rely on the milk given to us by the nomads. My companions began to look weak and listless, drained of energy. The wind from the north blew constantly and it was worse at ground level, for it was here that the heavier dust particles were carried. At midday the heat and the wind were so savage that we could do little but wrap ourselves in shawls to pre-serve the moisture in our bodies, and lie in the shade until the heat died.

When the wind dropped in the late afternoon, the desert was breathtakingly beautiful. Then I would walk across the plain with my shotgun, losing myself in the vastness and the last white veil of the blizzard. When all the Arabs and herds were out of view, a feeling of utter loneliness descended on me. For a while I savoured its bitter-sweetness, glad to be away for an hour or two from the strain of speaking Arabic and the pressure of practising the manners and customs of a foreign culture. In those moments of relief I imagined that I could live this life for ever. I told myself that I needed nothing more, and I savoured the knowledge that I could survive in this wild land. I had been brought up in a society where everything was provided, yet here I was reduced to survival level, where the decisions a man made were always concerned with life and death. I was still an outsider; perhaps I would never be anything else. Yet already the environment I had lived in for the last few months had begun to mould me, as it had moulded these nomads for centuries. It was as if, after looking at the world through a single window for almost thirty years, a new and more illuminating one had suddenly opened up.

When I returned to the camp in the evenings, my companions would greet me, saying, 'Omar! Come and drink milk!' I would sit next to them in the sand as the camels burbled around us, and the kaleidoscope of the sunset threw a pattern of colours across the sky. I looked out across the land of emptiness and stark beauty, and felt at peace. This was what I had come to see, to feel, to be part of.

It was almost the end of October when we moved to the Wadi al Milik. We had collected more than ten camels, and now the grazing was gone and the Arabs were moving out of these desolate pastures. The wind dropped obligingly as we struck camp, but the sun came out with redoubled severity, as if in compensation. As we drove our herd on, we were riveted to our saddles and the heat braised us like boiling fat. We passed through mile upon mile of nothingness, grinding on slowly over low dunes and stunted hills. At night we camped with some Nurab in the lee of a ring of low sandhills. They were brothers, morose little men dressed in headcloths and *tobes*, who brought us bowls of sour milk as we made camp in the sand. One of them sat down with us and said, 'The *jizzu* is dead. We have been here only two weeks and there is nothing left. The news is all bad. We have nowhere to go but the south, and when the grazing there is finished, God knows what we will do!'

The next morning the Arabs gathered their few camels, and the women set up their litters. The animals looked grey and weary in the morning light. The wind started again. The men wrapped their shawls around their heads for protection against the driving sand. 'God protect you,' they told us. 'Go in peace.' They mounted up and rode south into the steppes. I watched them until they disappeared, then turned to saddle Wad at Tafashan. The tracks and marks they had made around us were already being buried under the shifting dust.

Within a few hours they would be gone for ever.

6
Arabs
of the Wadi

A rude and wilde people and in every
deade estranged from all humanitie
Leo Africanus, Travels in Bombay

Later the same morning we saw the thick tree-line of the Wadi al Milik straddling the desert like a fortress wall.

'Are those really trees?' At Tom asked, and lurched forwards on his camel as if to make sure. The wind still raged around us, and the lure of the haven of shade ahead was too much. Soon we were all trotting beside the young sheikh, extracting the last ounce of energy from our exhausted camels. We left our small herd far behind and crashed in through the first pickets of the thorn bush like cavalry charging an infantry line. It was a shock to be so suddenly out of the wind and in the cool shade, letting our eyes readjust to the unaccustomed dimness after days in the glaring sun, on a landscape bound only by the horizon. There was yellow grass growing amongst the cracked black earth, and dozens of camels were munching contentedly in the acacia thickets.

It took us only minutes to find the well-field at Al Ku', where Juma' and the others were encamped. We found them at once and couched our camels as Ibrahim, Hamid and Juma' ran out to welcome us and help unload. The first thing I noticed was how healthy and well fed they looked after the grey-faced Arabs I had grown used to seeing in the *jizzu*. Their black skin had a sheen of freshness about it; my companions seemed dry, withered and lacklustre by comparison. After Juma' had greeted me, he said, 'By God, you look as if you are half starving!'

Soon the herd arrived, driven by Mura'fib and Wad az Zayadi. Juma' and Ibrahim took the camels off to the wells at once, while Hamid produced a huge bowl of *kisri*. Some Arabs whose tent was

126

pitched nearby brought us a goat and we feasted royally for the first time in days.

Beyond our camp the well-field stretched for 500 yards in a clearing on the western rim of the wadi. Many Arabs, men and women, were at the well-heads watering sheep, goats and a few camels. The men were dressed in balloon-like *sirwal* and woollen caps, and their dark muscles stood out as they hoisted up the leather buckets to fill their mud-walled basins. The women wore coloured *tobes*, piled up on their braided hair, and whipped the flocks into order with springy sticks. A knot of camel-hair tents stood on the edge of the field, shadowed by the intertwining acacias. Through gaps in the trees, the eastern desert shone like a mirage, rising steadily from the wadi towards pillows of orange dunes and the silver-grey ghosts of the Sumi'yat mountains.

Although the nazir had chosen his camp 100 miles away at Umm Sunta, the Wadi al Milik was the real heart of the *dar*. It was a rich serpent of greenery that coiled north and then north-east, cutting the desert like a sabre and touching the Nile near Ed Debba. In heavy rains the wadi would be in flood, though it rarely happened that water filled every part of it at the same time. As it turned towards the river, the trees thinned out and became no more than brakes of bushes, low and skeletal, at intervals of many miles.

The wadi was occupied by various clans of the Kababish. One of the most numerous was the Sarajab, who were considered to be amongst the older sections of the tribe. Four-fifths of the Kababish had their dammering-places in the Wadi al Milik and their animals grazed there in the summer months.

'The Sarajab are the wildest people amongst the Kababish,' Juma' told me. 'If they have a guest, they will challenge him to a camel race. If his camel wins, they will turn him out of their camp, by God!' While I was at Al Ku', I noticed that my companions had a deprecating attitude towards the Sarajab and called them 'Arabs of the wadi' – a term that seemed to be synonymous with all that they considered ignorant and primitive. 'They know nothing of the outside world,' Wad az Zayadi commented. 'They do not understand government or rulers, they only know their animals. If you ask them who the President is, they will say, "What is the President?" '

The day after we arrived, Juma' and Wad az Zayadi brought a young Sarajabi into our camp. I noticed at once that his legs were bound by iron manacles that clanked ominously as he walked. He was short and muscular with a bullet-shaped head, his hair shaved cleanly down to the skull. He wore a stained shirt, *sirwal* and leather slippers. Juma' told him to sit as if he were talking to a dog, and when the youth hesitated, the Arab pushed him roughly down into a sitting position. As he looked around him, his eyes strafed us with hot, defensive aggression.

My two companions sat down with us and recounted what had happened. Juma' said that earlier that morning they had ridden off down the wadi to collect a camel from the boy's family. 'They were living in cabins south of the wells,' he told us, 'and there seemed to be no one around when we arrived. There were some camels and goats feeding nearby. I called out, "*As salaam 'alaykum!*" and this Arab came out. He did not answer my greeting, he just said, "What do you want?" I told him that his name was on the list for the Requisition. He just stood there. You would have said he was a half-wit and did not understand. But I knew he understood well enough! Then I told him that the Requisition was for the government. "What government?" he said. I knew there would be trouble then. I told him again that we wanted a camel. He said, "You will take no camel of mine, by God!" So I took a headrope and went to bridle one of his camels. Then he moved. "Take your hands off my camel, son of the uncircumcised!" he shouted, and ran over to me with a dagger in his hand. He would have let me have it too, but Wad az Zayadi grabbed him from behind and hit him with his club. Then we jumped on him. Wad az Zayadi got the manacles from his saddle-bag and we locked him up. "Now we will see who the government is!" I told him. He needs to learn a lesson, by God!'

I looked again at the youth who sat nearby listening. He sat cross-legged with great dignity. As I watched he spat a glob of saliva on the ground. I saw in his face an unbending, unyielding pride, a self-sufficiency that had thickened into arrogance. This Arab knew no submission and no master but the unfathomable forces of the desert; he would bow only to them.

The youth was kept in our camp for several days, and in all that time he never spoke. At Tom held a summary court and fined him fifty pounds for his offence. 'There will be no profit in lashing him,' At Tom said. 'These Arabs of the wadi lash each other as a game. Money will hurt him more.'

A few days later there was another candidate for the manacles. I had spent some hours exploring the wadi, and returned to our camp at sunset. There was a new guest in the camp, a Sarajabi with a berry-brown face and a single curl of beard. He sat cross-legged near the fire and did not rise when I greeted him. I sat down and tried to make conversation. Where had he come from? Where was he going? He ignored my questions with a rudeness uncommon amongst Arabs, and I felt irritated despite myself. As I was talking, he interrupted me, saying, 'Give me a knife!' I was surprised by the question and told him I had no spare knife. Just then the others came over with a bowl of porridge and we crouched around it to eat. The Arab remained silent throughout the meal and the others ignored him. I knew that Arabs have no luxury greater than conversation, and wondered why this man was so rude.

I slept quite near to the Arab that night and the first thing I saw when I awoke the next morning was a pair of legs bound by manacles. It was the same man, standing up for the first time. I burst out laughing involuntarily, and the Arab looked at me sharply. 'What was your crime?' I asked him.

'I refused to give them a camel!' he replied sullenly.

I learned that Juma' had again been involved. 'He is a Sarajabi of the same section as the other one,' Juma' said. 'And Sheikh At Tom sent me with Hamid and Ibrahim to collect another camel from them. One of them saw us coming and ran away, and this one came out with the rifle and cocked it, shouting, "Go back you cursed bandits!" Three more of them came running out with whips in their hands, so we jumped off our camels and cocked our rifles. I shouted to the Arab that we only wanted to talk to him, and in the end he agreed to come over to us. As soon as he was away from the others, we jumped on him and took his rifle away. Then Ibrahim clapped the chains on him. I said that he would get his rifle back if he came quietly and in the end he agreed.'

'Do you think they would dare to shoot a *ghaffir*?' I asked him.

'It has happened, I tell you!' he replied. 'A few years ago one of the nazir's men went to collect taxes near Umm Badr and disappeared. No one ever saw him again, and of course they knew someone had murdered him. Not long after that there were some Berti merchants killed while riding through the Umm Badr area. They had just taken some donkeys to Omdurman for sale and were riding back. There were nine of them, I remember. Well, they were attacked in the bush and all of them were shot dead. Later the police found out who had done it. He was a well-known Arab from the Sarajab.

129

Just before they hanged him, he told them, "Do not search for the body of the nazir's man any more. I can tell you where the body is, for I killed him. He asked me for a bribe, so I had to put an end to him!" But he was a man, by God! The Sarajab are wild men, but they do not lack in courage!' Juma' told me that the Sarajab had a reputation for attacking *dabuukas* – the camel herds that were taken to Egypt and that often followed the wadi for part of the journey, much as the one I had accompanied in 1980. 'Only two months ago a *dabuuka* came this way, being driven by Arabs from Darfur. They were Awlad Rashid or Rizayqat, I do not remember which. The Sarajab ambushed them and shot the guide dead. Then they helped themselves to the camels. It has often happened, by God! Some of these Sarajab are not just raiders – they are full-time bandits who make their living by stealing. They move around quickly and never camp in the same place for long. They only ride into the markets in late afternoon, when there is no one about to recognize them!'

These stories interested me because they showed that here was a group of Arabs, bred in the desert, who valued their freedom and independence so highly that they would be dominated by no one. It had always surprised me how easily the nomads could be persuaded to give up their animals to my companions. Here at last was a tribe that Sir Ali Wad at Tom had not succeeded in dominating.

That day At Tom shot a *kibjan*, a huge monitor lizard that we skinned and ate. Some of the Arabs would not join us, saying that the meat was forbidden. I enjoyed it, however: the flesh was not unlike chicken. In the evening I walked out in the desert to the east. I remembered how I had ridden this way with Abu Sara and my friends from the Rizayqat more than two years ago. I could hardly recognize the man I had been then. Time had reshaped and rearranged my perception of this environment. I had a vague recollection of the excitement I had felt in this remote, dangerous land. I recalled how my companions had pretended to be from another tribe, fearing that the Kababish would attack them, and how they had viewed this place as hostile territory. Now I began to understand why.

The desert here was almost as featureless as a blank page. Here and there were tussocks of *tomam*, and in the distance the shadows of solitary *tundub* trees. As I walked, I saw three riders materialize out of the sand, no bigger than flies, slowly thickening as they approached. A horde of camels came from the east, a squadron of dark warriors whose spidery legs took shape as they passed by in the distance. Another column of camels returned from the wells fat with water, travelling in file, pacing solidly, full of grace. I thought that in the desert there was nothing more beautiful than this animal, and nothing that seemed more securely at home. By one of the solitary trees I discovered the remains of a camp. There was a fireplace of three stones, a black pot with a hole in it, a torn length of goat-hair hanging from the tree, and an old waterskin, split and hard with age.

Back in the camp there was another visitor. At Tom called me over and introduced me to a Sarajabi with a twisted nose that looked as if it had been hit with a sledgehammer. The man was thin and sickly, dressed in the familiar stained desert clothes and cowskin sandals. 'This is Fadlal Mula Wad Arba'ini,' At Tom said. 'He says that his son is going to El 'Atrun soon with his own salt caravan. If you want to go with him, you have my permission. He says that his son could do with some help.'

I agreed at once, but afterwards I began to regret my decision. I had dreamt of riding to El 'Atrun for years, but now the chance was within my grasp I felt reluctant to leave these Nurab who had been such good companions over the last months. Often I had grown tired of their talk and their imperative manner, and had longed to be alone. Now the thought of leaving them made me desolate.

However, I had agreed and there was no going back; I knew that I might not find another chance. That evening At Tom gave me twenty pounds to help buy provisions. I was embarrassed but knew that I could not refuse it, especially as I had little money left. Wad Fadul told me, 'You will never make it. Your camel is too tired.'

'You cannot trust those Sarajab,' said Juma' Wad Siniin.

These were exactly the statements I needed to entrench my determination to succeed, and by the next morning I was firmly set on my course. I shook hands with my companions, saying that I should see them in the *dikka*. Then I picked up my shotgun and mounted Wad at Tafashan. I rode south with Fadlal Mula.

We rode down the wadi to the merchant's shack at Efayn where I wanted to obtain provisions. Fadlal Mula was a good companion, neither disrespectful nor obsequious, neither talkative nor silent. The merchant was a Ja'ali called Abboud, who received us like guests and brought us flat loaves of unleavened bread in a delicious gravy of onions and spices. I bought flour, sugar, oil, tea and a pound of chewing-tobacco, for my pipe had long since been redundant.

131

In the afternoon we rode west out of the wadi, and crossed the great yellow flats of desert towards the peaks of the Graynat Hills. Fadlal Mula told me that his camp was in the small oasis of Iidayn 'Aja, not far from the bore-wells at Iided Abu Sufyan. The afternoon was cool with a soft breeze blowing, and after about four hours we came to a plot of green where some Sarajab had planted sorghum. There was a single tree under which stood a shanty cabin, from which a stunningly beautiful woman flashed white teeth at us as we rested in the shade. This was the first time I had come across desert Arabs cultivating crops. I had thought that the Kababish considered cultivation a disgrace, and besides, it was illegal to cultivate in the range-lands of the *dar*. I asked the Arab whose plot it was. 'The nazir says it is illegal,' he scoffed. 'But the nazir has never been hungry. Nothing is illegal if you are hungry, and nothing is a disgrace!' He told me that this entire plot would produce only two sacks of sorghum, but that would last his family for half a year.

We rode on in the evening towards the deep orange globe of the sun, the only colour in the whole great landscape of grey sand, grey bushes, grey tufts of grass. As the sunset came, an extraordinary feeling descended on me. It was as if there were really nothing beyond this desert, which stretched to every horizon: no cities, no seas, no Britain, no place inaccessible by camel. The world seemed no more than a boxed-in garden with the great unspanned spaces of the stars above.

I asked Fadlal Mula for his opinion of the nazir. 'He holds his position by fear,' he said at once. 'You have seen it. They misuse people and cheat them. They say there is a hospital at Hamrat ash Sheikh! I have not been to Hamrat ash Sheikh since I was a boy. Nor have many of my family. I shall not start going there now. What use is a hospital to me? It will never be used, by God!' I began to realize that I should get quite a different perspective on the Kababish while riding with the Sarajab.

We rode on into the night in clear moonlight. The desert was sheer and clean without a single tree. We halted and made a tiny station on the vast platform of sand. It was perfectly quiet and peaceful. Fadlal Mula cooked a hunk of meat we had brought and afterwards, as I lay down, my head was full of thoughts of power and freedom and the complex and confusing interaction between them.

The next morning was freezing and a cold wind blew down from Jabal Dar al Humar, a flat-topped blue mass behind us. As we

132

mounted we had a view over endless miles of sand, drifting as far as the black peak of Jabal Musawwira. Below the mountain stood a rash of trees, a line of shadows standing out from the pale desert like human figures. Once we saw a group of eight camels moving across the furrowed sand. There was no one with them, and Fadlal Mula said, 'They have been lost and no doubt.' As we watched, the four leading camels stopped suddenly and gathered together with their heads touching, exactly as if they were holding a parley; then they turned and strolled superciliously by. I knew that there were no wild camels in the Sudan, and wondered if we should try to catch them and find out to whom they belonged. My companion was against it. 'They will find their own way back when they want to,' he said. 'Camels never forget directions. You could take them a thousand miles away and they would find their way back.'

The desert was the familiar colour of apricot, wind-furrowed and silent except for the crunch of camels' feet and the occasional eerie musical note, which seemed to be produced by the wind on the rocks. Fadlal Mula said it was the crying of the jinn who inhabited these lonely places. 'You cannot see them, but they are here just the same.' The breeze flowed over the bed of sand like the sea-tide, whispering like a voice in the chasm of my ear. There was little talk between us, and my mind was still and quiet, taking in the emptiness and the beauty, and the unresolved miracle of myself and this Arab riding across it.

At midday we found a patch of yellow grass and stopped to let the camels graze. Fadlal Mula made a flat loaf of bread that he called *Umm Duffan*. He mixed flour and water to make the dough, flattening it on a stone, then burying it in the sand beneath the ashes of the fire. After a while he dug it up and tapped off the ash and dust with a stick. Then he broke it up into a pan and poured oil over it. It made a change from porridge.

We rode for many hours in the afternoon, and the mountain came closer. Fadlal Mula told me, 'In Jabal Musawwira there are pictures. There are pictures of cows and men and houses. They are very old. They were made before the time of the English. They say there is a serpent living in a well there, and that the serpent guards a hidden treasure.'

'Do you think it is true?'

'Yes, I have seen the tracks of the serpent. Some Arabs have seen the serpent itself.'

133

Just before the sun set we led our camels over the rockpiles of Musawwira and came down into a grove where some gigantic boulders were covered in carvings of long-horned cows, jumping matchstick men and square huts. There seemed to be two distinct styles, but neither was of great artistic merit. I wondered who had made them, and in what era. Cows had not grazed in these pastures for millennia. The artists were certainly nomads who had ranged through these lands when they were quite different from the arid wastes of today. The Kababish had replaced them, perhaps even absorbed some of them. The cattle-nomads had disappeared, pushed south by the great changes that had taken place here. Now it was the turn of their successors.

Fadlal Mula seemed anxious to move, and I wondered unfairly if he were afraid of meeting the serpent. I chaffed him cruelly about this and he said, defensively, 'You will believe it when you see its tracks!' But the only tracks we saw that evening were those of two hyenas. There was a churned up area of sand where they had fought and few drops of blood on the surface. The fact that these animals could survive here seemed more wonderful to me than any serpent.

Soon after darkness fell, we came down into the valley and saw the dim light of a fire. 'We have arrived,' my companion said. In a few moments we were riding in amongst thick shadows of trees where woodsmoke hung on the night like a cobweb. There were several fires smouldering around us, and the soft murmur of voices in the shadows. I could smell the rich odours of camels and goats. We couched our camels by the dark shape of a tent, where a young Arab came out to greet us. He was Mohammid Wad Fadlal Mula, who was to be my companion on the long-awaited journey to El'Atrun.

Part 2
The Journey to El 'Atrun

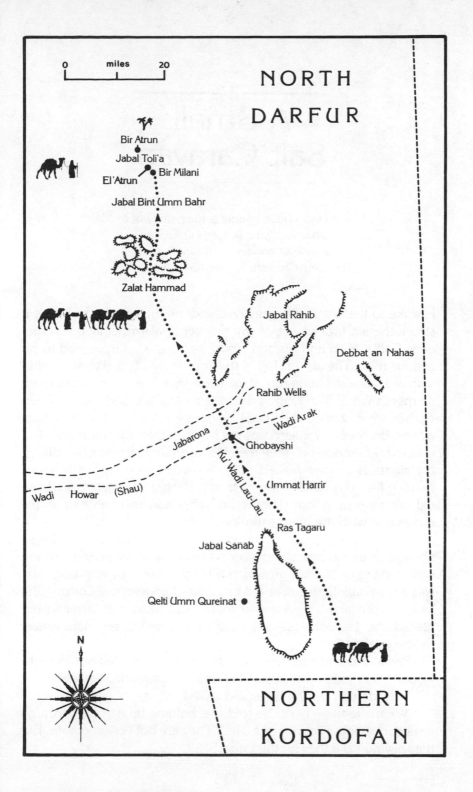

miles
0   20

NORTH
DARFUR

Bir Atrun
Jabal Toli'a
El'Atrun   Bir Milani
Jabal Bint Umm Bahr

Zalat Hammad

Jabal Rahib

Debbat an Nahas

Rahib Wells

Wadi Arak

Jabarona   Ghobayshi

Wadi   Howar   (Shau)

Ummat Harrir

Ku Wadi Lau-Lau

Ras Tagaru
Jabal Sanab

Qelti Umm Qureinat

N

NORTHERN
KORDOFAN

7
A Small
Salt Caravan

A land whose beauty is the beauty of a
moment, whose face is desolate,
whose character is strangely stern.
Winston Churchill, The River War, *1899*

I awoke to the crack of a gunshot, and the thump of a bullet as it struck the air. I rolled out of my blanket in alarm. Only a few feet away Fadlal Mula and his son stood, holding what appeared to be antique rifles. The air was full of the sour scent of cordite and a thin wisp of smoke still hung round the two Arabs. They were small men, no more than 5' 5" in height, dressed in old shirts and *sirwal*. Their clothes were stained the usual nicotine-yellow and torn in many places. Both wore woollen caps set back on their shaven skulls, and cracked skin sandals on their feet. Mohammid grinned as he noticed my alarm. His father walked up to a thorn tree a few yards away, running his bony hand along its trunk. 'Missed!' he said. 'See, these old guns are no good!' Then both father and son came to shake hands and wish me good morning.

We sat down on our canvas sheets near the tent. It was a single *shugga* of camel-hair slung over a crude frame. Nearby a woman was working over a fire on which a black kettle was vibrating. She was a lean dark figure, dressed in a skirt of coarse blue cotton. She looked worn and wrinkled and there were flashes of silver in her plaited hair. Nevertheless, she held a tiny infant to one dark breast as she worked.

Fadlal Mula handed me his rifle. It was a single-shot breech-loader, badly pitted with rust. 'My father had it made,' he said.

'How do you get the bullets?' I asked.

'We make them here,' he told me, holding up a brass cartridge case containing a flat-nosed bullet. 'They are not very accurate. But they always kill if they hit the target!'

138

Soon the woman brought a pot of tea and some dates, which she set before us. We produced our enamel mugs and Fadlal Mula poured out the thick black liquid with great ceremony. It was bitter and very hot, and we sipped it with the loud slurping sound that manners demanded. 'We have no sugar,' declared the Arab mournfully. 'But eat some dates with the tea. They will sweeten it.' As I drank, I surveyed the scene before me. The hearth area where the woman worked was enclosed on one side by a fence of thorn branches and on the other by the tent. Within those few square feet of ground lay almost everything the Arabs owned: saddles, cooking pots, saddle-bags, ropes, waterskins and grindstones.

I noticed that young Mohammid was regarding me with keen interest. I returned his stare. I guessed that he was assessing me and wondering how we should get on in the desert. He looked about twenty years old, as lightly built as his father, but with a broad head that seemed a little top-heavy on his frame. He had a wide, rather cruel smile and often broke into raucous, madcap laughter. After a while he said, 'You don't look all that strong to me. Can you lift a sack of rock salt?'

'I have never tried it.'

'It is very heavy,' he said.

'No, Omar is blest,' cut in his father. 'His coming is lucky for you. Without him you would have to go alone.'

Mohammid did not seem impressed. 'Why do you want to go to Al Ga'a?' he inquired. 'Your camel will not carry enough salt to sell in the market. Is there something else you are looking for?'

'I want to see it, that is all,' I replied, realizing that Al Ga'a was the Arabs' word for El 'Atrun.

He looked at me as if I were completely mad. 'The way is hard and dangerous,' he said. 'There are bandits of the Meidob on the way. They would slit your throat for nothing.'

'God is generous,' I said.

The young Arab grinned again and showed his yellow teeth. 'Perhaps you will be all right,' he declared.

The treasure to be found at El 'Atrun was rock salt, which the Kababish had been mining there for centuries. The mineral was essential for their herds and flocks, and could also be sold in local markets at a considerable profit. They had once carried on a lucrative trade in the stuff, though in recent years much business had been wrested from them by the owners of the great Fiat lorries that carried tons of it to distant towns every month.

Mohammid and I walked around the camp. There were half a dozen families living there and as we went from tent to tent a small crowd gathered around us. The women in their blue cotton skirts, many of them holding brown babies, stared at me and asked questions. Mohammid related my story patiently. 'He is from the *Ingleez*. He was with the nazir at Umm Sunta. Yes, that camel was given to him by the nazir's son.' From our short tour I glimpsed the hardship of life here on the edges of the great desert. The greatest problem was scarcity of water. Though there were several wells sunk into the damp grey clay on the edge of the camp, I noticed that most of them were dry. The two that produced water did so very slowly. This meant that the Arabs had to take turns filling their waterskins or watering their animals, and the wells were always surrounded by people. Peering down one of the shafts, I saw with shock the features of an Arab leering back at me from the shadows within. Mohammid smiled at my surprise and said, 'He is digging it out, but it is foolish, by God! Soon all the wells will be dry and we will have to move.'

'Why do you stay?' I asked. Mohammid pointed to the other side of the camp, beyond a grove of *siyaal* trees, where I saw a plot of green millet, standing up like rows of soldiers on parade. 'The millet,' he said. 'As soon as it is ripe, we shall go.'

'I thought cultivation was unlawful in this range-land,' I said.

'They say it is,' the Arab answered nonchalantly. 'But who is to prevent us, here in the desert?'

'But is it not a disgrace to grow crops?'

The youth laughed again. 'Of course not. If we settled down and became farmers – if we stopped moving, then we should become like the slaves. But we will never do that. The millet will feed us for a year, and we will not have to sell our camels.'

As soon as it was dark, we brought the camels into the camp and hobbled them. Campfires flickered amongst the *siyaal* groves and the night was pregnant with woodsmoke. We laid our canvas sheets near the fire, for the nights had turned cold, and Hawa, my host's wife, brought a wide dish of sorghum porridge. It was a pinkish mess drowned in sour goat's milk. Mohammid told me that they preferred camel's milk, but there were no she-camels in the oasis.

Shortly after we had eaten, a crowd of men came to visit us. They appeared out of the darkness one by one in their torn shirts and rags of headcloths. They crouched near the fire, squinting at me in the flickering light, holding their weapons out before them. After a few moments of silence they would get up, and with great consciousness of their dignity, disappear again into the night. I realized they had come just to look.

When they had all left, Mohammid, Fadlal Mula and I covered ourselves with our blankets and lay down to sleep. The fire began to die and the heavy scent of woodsmoke seemed to drench our clothes. Soon there was no sound but the rhythmic breathing of animals and men.

The only disadvantage of the sleeping-place was that it was infested with dung beetles. These small black insects were very industrious in constructing smooth round clots of dung, about the size of golf balls. They would wheelbarrow the balls with their powerful rear legs on a desperate safari across my canvas sheet. As I extended my hand to halt their progress, I would be rewarded with a handful of wet dung. I knew that in ancient Egypt the dung beetle, or scarab, had been a powerful symbol: one of the guises of Amun-Ra and the incarnation of the sun. But then, I told myself, no ancient Egyptian had been forced to sleep with them as bedfellows.

I stayed at Iidayn for three days. I was anxious to set off, but water was scarce and we had to wait to fill our skins. There was no other water source between Iidayn and Wadi Howar, about six days away. In addition the Sarajab had strong taboos about which days were propitious for journeys. They would not start on Wednesdays, Fridays or Sundays.

On the evening of the second day I discovered that I had acquired yet another set of bedfellows: lice. They seemed to lie dormant in the waist-band of my *sirwal* during the day, only to sally forth on a guerilla raid during the night. They did not bite, but were extremely irritating. I was unable to wash my clothes because of the lack of water. These Sarajab never washed anything for the same reason. They wore their clothes until they dropped into rags. The pots were left out to dry in the sterilizing sun, but clothes were never washed. The lice were the only effect of this lack of hygiene that bothered me.

We filled in some of the time hunting for hares and gazelles in the hills. Mohammid showed me how to use the gazelle traps. The trap consisted of a piece of thickly plaited straw, twisted into a wheel about six inches in diameter. From the rim of the wheel a number

141

of spokes extended inwards, leaving a small opening. The animal's leg would pass through the opening and the gazelle would be unable to withdraw it because of the sharpened spokes. The trap would be fixed over a pit and camouflaged with sand and vegetation. It seemed that the gazelles in this region were wise to the trick, for we never caught anything.

During my stay I was constantly visited by people who did not disguise the fact that they were just curious to look at me. I suppose I was the first European many of them had seen and they wondered why I had come to their remote world. 'Why are you going to Al Ga'a?' was the question they all asked, and they never seemed satisfied with my answer. One night, after I had retired, I heard one of Mohammid's cousins saying to him, 'How do you know he is not a bandit? He might kill you in the desert and steal your camels! I advise you not to go with him.' At first this seemed so ridiculous that I felt like laughing. Then I realized how real had been the fear in his voice and how serious it might be to begin the journey with such suspicion between us. It was only then that I felt how utterly remote this place was, and just how isolated these Arabs were. To them I was a nobody, from a tribe they did not know and a place they had never even heard of. I saw how lucky I had been to ride with the Nurab, who understood where I was from, simply because the nazir had been there. Yet I was proud of Mohammid when he answered, 'I am afraid of no one, not the Meidob, nor the Gur'an, nor the Zaghawa. And I am not afraid of *him*!' As I lay there, feigning sleep, I began to appreciate the real courage of this young Arab.

Life in the oasis seemed to grind on at its own pace. For the women this was literally true, for they spent much of their time grinding grain on their hand-mills. This type of mill had been used in the Sahara for thousands of years, probably with little alteration although several different types had been found in neolithic sites in the desert. I often watched Hawa as she placed a few grains at a time on the stoop of the base-stone and let them trickle down as she ground them, sweeping the flour into a bowl every few minutes. After an hour or so her little daughter, aged about nine, would take over and begin grinding furiously. It might take several hours to produce enough flour for one meal.

Every morning the women milked the goats and made liquid butter. The milk was poured into a special skin and slung on ropes from the branch of a tree. Hawa would shake the vessel briskly from

1. Mahmoud Wad Affandi, author's companion on the
journey to the jizzu

2. Ali at Tom Wad al Murr greeting wedding guests

3. Camel herd in the desert near Jabal al 'Ain

4. Salim Wad Hassan and a cousin, with cigarettes

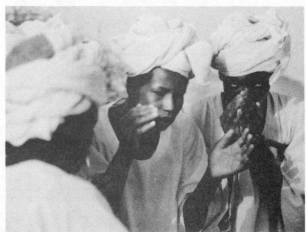

5. Men chanting
at a circumcision

6. Celebrating the circumcision at the 'Atawiyya camp

7. Juma' Wad Siniin preparing kisri in Zalat Hammad

8. Sannat, author's companion on the route to Egypt

9. Sheikh Hassan, during the author's journey in the Bahr

10. Mohammid Dudayn, the tribal scribe

11. Khamis Wad Bambidu, one of the 'Ol of Sheikh
Hassan

12. Ibrahim Wad Hassan Wad al Faki, brother of Mohammid Dudayn

13. Sharif Mohammid, Sheikh Hassan's holy man

14. Mohammid Wad
Hassan, third
son of the
nazir Hassan

15. Moving camp in the Bahr

16. Animals watering at a pool in the Bahr

17. *Slaughtering a sheep at the nazir's camp in the Bahr*

18. *Pouring tea for guests at Hassan's wedding*

19. One of Sheikh Hassan's younger sons with the **nuggara,** *the wooden drum used during migration*

20. *The market-place at Umm 'Ajayja, later wrecked by bandits during the drought*

21. *'Atawiyya drawing water by camel from a deep-well near Abu Bassama*

22. *Juma' Wad Siniin bringing back the runaway Hambarib*

23. *Kababish litters for women on migrations in the jizzu pastures*

24. *Dagalol saddling Wad al 'Atiga in the Kababish style*

25. *Ahmad Wad Ballal, Dagalol's herdsman*

26. *Dagalol*

27. *Dagalol's son, Hassan, with herdsboy Sayf ad Din*

28. *Dagalol filling his water-bottle, his Kalashnikov in the background*

29. Salim Wad Hassan riding with the nuggara herd

30. Moving north towards the jizzu

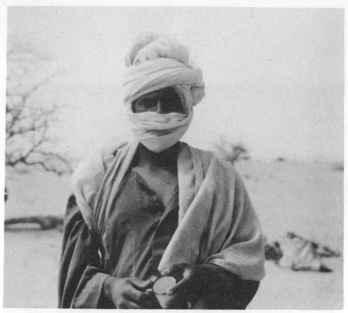

31. *Musa Adam of the Awlad Rashid, on the way to Egypt*

32. *Jabal Khitimai*

33. *Author's companion meeting camp north of Khitimai*

34. At Tom Wad Hassan, who became nazir on his
father's death in 1983

35. Nazir's party entertaining guests in the Bahr

36. Tent of the Nurab

37. Jibrin Wad Ali on author's journey to Selima

side to side until the liquid butter separated from the buttermilk. The liquid was considered a great delicacy and often stored in glass bottles held in leather pouches.

I found it strange that the children here were shy and reserved, even with each other. I thought that this reflected the bitter hardship of life here, which gave them little chance for amusement. Children were set to herd animals almost as soon as they could walk and the small boys spent most of the day herding the house camels or preventing the goats and sheep from entering the cultivated land. Mohammid had a brother, a little younger than himself, who was off with the camel herd further south.

On the afternoon of the second day Mohammid and I took two camels and rode out into the belly of the hills to collect fodder, which would be food for our caravan on the way to El 'Atrun. We climbed the steel-grey slopes of Jabal 'Aja and were rewarded by a view of Iidayn. It lay like a pool of perfect green on the pastel plain, ringed by an atoll of hills with jagged black peaks and walls of orange. We found a dry water-course that was lined with good grasses. We had a number of rope-baskets to fill. I had never imagined that there was a particular skill to pulling up grass, but I was wrong. At first I tried to pull with a twisting action, my thumb pointing downwards. Within minutes my hands were blistered and bleeding. Mohammid laughed unmercifully. 'Don't you know how to pull up grass? That is ridiculous! Every child knows how to do that! Look – like this . . .' He grasped the stalks with his thumb uppermost and jerked downwards. The grass broke off perfectly. 'Just like a camel eating!' he said. As my hands were already sore, I found the correct method difficult, and as the day wore on it became increasingly obvious that I was far behind my companion. While he was filling his second basket, my first was only half full. He said nothing more, but I guessed that he was scoffing inside. I knew enough about desert Arabs to understand that they made no allowances for outsiders.

On the third day, after sunset, Mohammid and I took our bedding down to the wells to spend the night there. We wanted to be sure of filling our waterskins. As usual there was a crowd of people there, mainly girls and young men. The girls were beautiful, with copper skin and fine-boned faces. Their braided hair was slicked with butter and fell in bunches across their shoulders. They wore skirts of the familiar blue cotton and wraps of coloured cloth across their upper bodies. Many of them wore gold nose-rings and earrings, and heavy silver bracelets on their ankles and wrists. It seemed that the wells were a social centre after dark, where young men tried to show off to the women and to each other. That evening one such young brave, rather thin and weak looking, was declaring in a loud voice his intention of riding to Libya on his camel. 'I am going to become a rich man there!' he was saying. 'I will come back with thousands of dinars!'

'Be sure and bring me a new rug,' smiled one of the coquettes.

'And, Hassan,' cut in another young lady, 'be sure to bring me a new set of cooking pots.'

'And do not forget to bring me a sheepskin,' piped up a third girl. 'A good one, mind you!'

The women burst into giggles. Hassan suddenly realized that they were mocking him and went silent. Mohammid laughed with the womenfolk. I began to realize how powerful the women were in this society, and how effectively they could dismiss any man who was over-boastful or inadequate.

The next day we began to prepare our equipment. Mohammid laid out his four pack saddles and cut lengths of wood that he fixed between the saddle-horns. These were special adaptations for the heavy salt packs we were to carry. We tested and rolled spare water-skins, and Mohammid twisted new hobbles out of wool. By mid-morning everything was laid out on the oasis floor. Our riding camels would carry riding saddles that would support all our provisions. These consisted of a bag of sorghum flour and the millet flour I had brought from Efayn, with a smaller bag of unmilled grain that Mohammid told me we should drink with our tea. We also had dates, tea, some sugar saved for the journey and a bottle of liquid butter. It seemed pathetically little for a journey of more than 400 miles in a waterless, comfortless, shadeless wasteland. I had to remind myself that for the Sarajab such meagre rations were normal. Mohammid had his rifle, and I had my shotgun and pistol. Each of us carried a dagger, a mattock, a pick and shovel for the salt, a long staff of *inderab* wood for lifting the sacks, some matches and a torch. I had my whip and Mohammid his camel-stick. Our saddle-bags held cooking pots and kettles, and we carried two full *girbas* of water. Apart from this we had our canvas sheets, sheepskins, blankets and very little else.

When everything was prepared, we drove our camels into the camp. There were five of them, including Wad at Tafashan and

Mohammid's six-year-old *'anafi*. I noticed that my camel looked thin in comparison with our pack animals. They were enormous unruly camels that seemed only half trained. They kicked and roared and spat, snapping their teeth at us as we tied their headropes. They were fully adult males, bulging with fat from months of good grazing, and powerful enough to carry tons of heavy salt for days across the desert. Mohammid told me that we should collect three more camels from the tents of his uncle, Musa, whose camp lay north of Jabal 'Aja.

Roping the camels into a caravan was even more difficult than I had imagined. Each one had to be tied by the jaw, which meant first passing the headrope behind the camel's great canine teeth. If not tied in this way, the camels would resist and break the rope.

Mohammid showed me how to tighten the loop of rope around the camel's jaw and then told me to rope in one of the pack animals. As I approached the buff-coloured monster, the camel turned his head knowingly and fixed me with a piercing stare. He snarled and a slick of foam dropped from his mouth. I inched my way up to him and tried to flick my loop of rope over his jaw. Like lightning he dodged the movement, roaring and heaving and straining on his hobble, gnashing his teeth so that I narrowly missed getting my arm crushed. I tried again and again – each time he was too quick, lurching up and snaking the massive head away from me. It took all my concerted agility and dexterity to finally clamp the rope over his mandible, and I swore to myself as I pulled it tight. As I stepped back, wiping the sweat off my brow, I saw Mohammid's big raw face creased in a grin. 'Too slow!' he announced. 'Why, my little brother could rope him faster than that!'

When all the beasts were tied, each had to be fitted with a straw mask, called a *shakima*, which resembled a surgeon's mask. It was fitted over the animal's muzzle and tied behind his ears. I thought this was to prevent the camels fighting, but my companion told me, 'It is to stop them eating the straw from the pack saddles when they become hungry.'

Finally the caravan was loaded, pack saddles fitted into place and adjusted, bags of fodder tied on, riding saddles pulled tight and fixed securely. When we were ready, Fadlal Mula called us over to share a last meal. We ate well, gorging ourselves on the thick *kisri* and the buttermilk that we should not find in the open desert. 'Eat! Eat!' urged Fadlal Mula. 'You will be hungry on the way, by God!'

After the meal the crook-faced Arab shook hands with us both. 'Go in the safe-keeping of God,' he said.

'God's blessing be upon you,' we replied, mounted our camels and led our small salt caravan out into the desert.

The caravan moved with perfect synchronicity; in motion the camels lost their aggressive savage manner and acquired the grace and power of noble creatures. We moved slowly up the incline and were soon on the volcanic underside of the mountain. The ground was rocky here, split into corries and canyons with a rubble of iron-flake crust on which the camels slipped and stumbled. Mohammid led the animals, taking the lead-rope in his right hand, while I followed on from the rear.

At about midday we found Musa's camp. His three brown tents were pitched under the rock wall of the mountain. As we ran our caravan in, he came out, shouting, 'Welcome! Welcome in peace!' He was much younger than his brother Fadlal Mula, with a broad, pleasant face and spiky whiskers. He wore a torn shirt and a thickly piled headcloth. We stayed in his camp until the sun began to sink, huddling in the shade of his tent. Musa's wife brought us more *kisri* and tea, and as we ate my host examined my camera and compass with interest. Finally he turned to Mohammid and said, 'Why is he going to Al Ga'a? What is his story?' It annoyed me, as so many times before, that they should speak as if I were not present. I said nothing, however, for I knew that this form of address was only a social convention, and not considered rude in Arab society. What irritated me more was that the Arabs continually suspected me of having some ulterior motive for my journey here, connected with material gain. They were convinced that no one would experience such hardship without some tangible profit. I denied this at the time, though now I wonder if they were right. Despite their remoteness they saw through every illusion, even those that others were not aware of in themselves.

One memory stays with me particularly from that camp: meeting Musa's old mother. She was a very ancient leather-skinned lady, who remained always in her darkened tent. 'She is almost blind,' Musa explained, and introduced me as one of the *Ingleez*. The old lady sighed and said, 'One of the government!' I told her that the Sudan had been independent for almost thirty years, but she shook her head slowly. 'I know the government!' she said. I soon saw that my words meant little to her — she had lived her entire life in these ranges

146

and deserts. Cities, countries, presidents and parties were no more than vague names in the back of her mind, something quite separate from her world, as far off as a distant star. The desert world was far off from the Sudan, far off from police or governments or armies. This was a wilderness where a man's only protection was the strength of his body and the loyalty of his companions.

We left the camp, each leading a string of camels. As we did so, I looked over the crooked canines of the hills and the wedge of yellow-green desert around them. We were like a tiny boat cast into the waves of the ocean, the boundless wilderness. As our small salt caravan climbed back into the guts of Jabal 'Aja I knew there was no possibility of turning back.

At first the going was difficult; we crossed the desert varnish of broken hard-pan that glittered with the blood-red of iron and manganese. The camels slithered down gullies, shying and breaking the lead-ropes. Each time this happened we had to dismount and rerope the caravan. At last we descended into the *jizzu*. At night we slept in the wadis where a little grazing was to be found. We would hobble our camels and allow them to shuffle about as they liked. Often they wandered several miles in spite of the restricting hobbles. This meant a long walk every night to bring them back to our camp. Mohammid was worried about bandits in the area, especially the Meidob.

As we moved, riding at a leisurely pace, we talked together. Mohammid asked me about my people and my country. How many camels did my father own? How many brothers did I have? Was the chief of my country a great sheikh and did he slaughter animals freely for guests? Were my people hospitable and would they welcome a stranger in their tents? He seemed to find my answers confusing. In return I tried to describe life in a city, since he had never seen one. I told him that there were thousands of people living in houses, not tents, and always staying in the same place. I told him that there was almost always food to be had and you could buy milk and butter everywhere. There was no thirst or scarcity of water; water came easily out of a tap. I asked him if the idea of living in a city appealed to him.

'Are there any camels there?' he inquired at once.

'No.'

'Then what would be the point of living there?' he asked.

He talked a great deal about the Meidob, referring to them as

147

'*Awwala*. Once he asked me, 'What would you do if the slaves attacked me?' I told him that no doubt I should try and protect him. Then I asked him the same question. 'I would protect you from anyone, even the Kababish!' he answered.

'Why?'

'Because if I did not and something happened to you, the women would laugh at me and I should never be able to forget it!'

Soon the *jizzu* merged with the desert, which opened before us like a silent hostile entity. Mohammid filled the great silence with the sound of his singing, like a child treading deliberately on virgin snow. The rhythm of his song seemed to fit perfectly with the flowing movement of the camels; the clear, natural beauty of the song seemed to complement the beauty of the great emptiness around us.

He was quite content to pour out the story of his life, and I was a good listener. 'Did they tell you I was once fined 300 pounds by the nazir?' he chuckled.

'Why?'

'Women!' he told me. 'I seduced a Ribaygat girl. She doesn't like her husband. He is her cousin, so she was forced to marry him. Anyway, it happened one night when her tent was pitched at Kilagi pool, and most of her family were away. In the morning her brothers found my tracks. The girl denied it, but they beat her, then they followed my tracks to a wadi. There were three of them, and when they caught up with me, I had to admit it, or they would have said I was afraid. They came at me with sticks, but two of my cousins were close by – thank God – and I called them. It was a battle, by God! I hit one of them so hard with my stick that I almost killed him! In the end they complained to the nazir, and he sent old Adam Wad ash Shaham to arrest me. He is a tough old man, that Adam!'

'You are a bandit!'

'No, I just like women.'

'We all like women.'

'But don't you try it,' he warned me grimly. 'They would kill you and no doubt!'

I told him the story of the slave-girl at Umm Sunta, and he was very interested. 'You lost your chance there!' he smirked.

'Will you see your Ribaygat girl again?'

'Yes, by God! As soon as I get back!'

We rode for about twelve hours a day, stopping for a few minutes at noon to cook a bowl of *kisri* over some firewood, which was plentiful in this part of the desert. The porridge was bitter and unpalatable, and I realized how important the buttermilk gravy had been. To my surprise Mohammid poured the dregs of the tea into the porridge with a drop of butter, saying, 'Eat! It is better than nothing!'

'God is generous,' I replied.

The morning of our third day out dawned bleak and cold, with the desert wrapped in a chiffon mantle of mist. Visibility was down to a few yards; beyond our small island of saddles and saddlery the wilderness was veiled from our sight. As I crouched by the hearth, I suddenly heard the cry of a camel, faint but distinct, from across the desert. I grabbed my shotgun immediately. Mohammid, who had been twisting a new hobble out of wool a few feet away, jumped up, whispering, 'Slaves!' and seized his rifle. There was a click as he cocked it and almost at the same moment a great grey bull-camel loomed out of the mist like an apparition. Mohammid had his rifle at the shoulder and for an instant I thought he would fire. Then a voice said, 'Peace be upon you!' in clear Arabic, and we saw that the rider was an Arab, a fresh-faced man with two little boys hanging on the back of his saddle. 'And upon you be peace!' we replied, as he couched his camel and dismounted. The two children were dressed in rags, their heads shaved except for the customary ridge of hair in the middle. The man shook hands, but eyed us suspiciously. 'Welcome! Welcome!' Mohammid said, and the visitor sat down in the hearth. He would drink no tea, but said at once, 'We are thirsty! By God's will, you will give us water.'

'Welcome!' said Mohammid again, and added, 'what is your family?'

"Atawiyya,' the Arab replied. 'We saw your fire last night, when we were with our herd.' Mohammid opened our skin and poured water into a bowl. The man drank most of it, then gave the rest to his children. Afterwards he produced a small waterskin into which my companion poured more water. 'God's blessing on you,' the 'Atawi said. 'If you are going to Al Ga'a, be careful of the Meidob. I have seen several parties of them recently. They say things are bad in Meidob country. Be on the lookout for them.' He committed us to the safe-keeping of God, mounted his camel with his two sons, and soon disappeared back into the mist. Both Mohammid and I looked at our waterskins. We knew that there had been no choice but to supply the man. By Kababish custom those travelling were

149

expected to give water to those herding. Our next source of water was still four or five days away in Wadi Howar. From now on we should drink no water, but use it only for porridge and tea.

The next day the mist cleared, and at mid-morning we halted on the top of a steep dune-slope in the centre of a vast plain. The only other feature of the plain seemed to be a single nugget of gnarled rock a few miles away. It was a strange formation, like a huge piece of unfashioned iron around which the rainbow skirts of the desert gleamed in blinding array. Suddenly Mohammid stiffened. 'A caravan!' he gasped. 'There!' He pointed across the great expanse of sand. For a few minutes my eyes scanned the landscape, until I saw what appeared to be no more than a blemish on the smooth face of the desert. 'It is a caravan of the 'Atrana – a salt caravan, that is certain,' my companion said. 'If we can pick up their tracks we will be with them by the afternoon.' He seemed very excited at the prospect of meeting more Arabs, and I could understand why. Firstly, the work of saddling and loading our caravan was difficult for two, especially with an inexperienced hand like myself. Secondly, Arabs love to talk, and though I spoke Arab fluently, there were still many things concerning nomadic culture that Mohammid could share only with someone actually brought up in it.

We soon picked up the tracks of the other caravan. Mohammid dropped from his camel to examine them. 'There are about twenty camels,' he told me. 'And three men. They are Kababish, but I do not know which family.' I asked how he knew they were Kababish, and he regarded me with the disdainful expression appropriate for my stupid question. 'It is clear from the tracks and the direction from which they come. Any child can tell!'

By late afternoon we were close on the heels of the others and when they halted briefly, we caught up with them. Three Arabs were waiting for us as we approached, standing by a mass of camels drawn up in three separate strings. Only one of the men had a rifle. He was an old, withered man with a ferret face and a feeble expression. The other men were younger.

'Salaam 'alaykum.'

''Alaykum as salaam.' We shook hands as the lingering greeting of the desert nomads was exchanged. The three men wore short jibbas of dirty white that foamed about them like skirts, above their knee-length cloth breeches. Only the old man wore a headcloth. He was called Ali, and was from the Ruwahla. His companion was a thick-set powerful Arab with a long curly beard and a shock of hair after the manner of desert Arabs. His name was Ballal, and like Ali he was a Rahli. The third Arab was no more than a youth about Mohammid's age. He was tall and ungainly with a thin body, shaven hair and an unusually aggressive expression. He was Balla Wad Ahmad, of the Hamdab tribe.

At first these Arabs treated me with suspicion, and as we rode on I felt their eyes evaluating my every move. They avoided speaking to me as much as possible, and asked my companion, 'Where is he from? What is his tribe?' in the usual way. I took a dislike to Balla very quickly. He continually mocked the way I encouraged the camels, saying, 'You do not know what you are doing!' with a leering expression, though I was riding as I always did. Once we came across the track of a young gazelle, almost obliterated by sand. 'What track is that?' he asked, his eyes gleaming malevolently.

'I don't know,' I replied.

He laughed mockingly and looked at the others. 'He does not even know the track of the *jadi*!' he declared. I saw at once that I should have trouble with this man. I had met many Arabs who were naturally suspicious of outsiders and who were exasperated by my lack of knowledge, but I had never before met one who seemed so determined to humiliate me. Now our small salt caravan had become a large one, but for the first time I began to view the way ahead with some trepidation.

That night we camped together. It was a crisp, cool evening and the black canvas above us was punctuated only by the matrix of stars and planets, a bright tapestry across the heavens. We unloaded our camels methodically, piling up the saddlery and the hay baskets into curved windbreaks to protect us from the cutting edge of the wind. Balla and I had the job of hobbling all the camels, for tonight there was no grazing for them. The job took some time, and the animals grunted miserably because of the cold and the yawning emptiness in their stomachs. After we had completed the task, we returned to the shelter of the windbreak, where the others were opening saddle-bags and laying out equipment. Mohammid found three large stones that he placed close together in the sand. Balla brought a fistful of straw from one of the baskets and laid it between the hearthstones. I sat down a few feet away and watched the thick-bodied Arab, a dim shape in the starlight, as he stooped over the stones, placing a few precious spills of firewood between them. The

151

match was struck – the straw exploded with orange fire and a crackle of sparks. For an instant the gaunt faces of my companions were illuminated, cast into grotesque bronze masks by the sudden light. Then the blaze faded to a glow of embers, and I heard Ballal blowing into the fire with long, powerful breaths. All of us waited, expectantly now, caught by the familiar yet crucial drama. The first faint tongue of flame trembled on one of the spills. Then the others caught and the flames licked up a couple of inches, creating a pool of golden light with a diameter of about two feet. All of us shuffled up close to the flames, knees and elbows forced together, holding our chilled hands up as if in adulation. No one spoke to break the spell of this miracle. For us, this spot in the desert had become the centre of the universe. The five of us sat entrenched by that tiny flicker of power, with our backs turned away from the great void that surrounded us.

This was how it began, I thought, a million years ago, when the first flame trembled on the first twig. That had been the beginning of man's conquest of the environment. From those hearthstones, the simplest of all architecture, had grown up villages and cities. From the closeness of those hearth companions had grown up the tales and myths that had become history and literature. In my world the process that began with fire had ended in electricity and engines, computers, space-craft, microchips and atomic fission. Here, though, there had been no such progress. The ancestors of these men had broken away from those who had become city dwellers at a very early stage; they had adapted themselves well to life in this wilderness. For millennia they had needed nothing more than the simple technology required to live here. But already the world of the city dwellers was encroaching upon them. Already the fume-spewing motor-vehicles were crossing this desert, taking away the salt that had been theirs for centuries. Already great climatic changes beyond their control were biting into the life they and their forefathers had known since ancient times.

After eating, the Arabs talked, getting to know each other. Mohammid and Balla discovered that they were distantly related on their mothers' side. Much of Arab conversation was designed to discover such relationships, so that each man could fit the other into the greater world of tribal and family links. I knew that one of the reasons I would remain an outsider was because I did not fit into this intricate system.

Later the conversation turned to the subject of lorries. 'These lorry-people are taking away all the salt from Al Ga'a!' declared Balla. 'By God, we should attack and kill every one of them, then they will not come back!'

'What about the government?' I said. 'I do not think they would let you get away with it.'

'Hah! What is the government!' stormed the youth, lifting up Mohammid's old rifle. 'This is the government, by God!'

'Yes,' Mohammid agreed. 'The Kababish rule here. We will not let slaves rule us. The Arabs have no government, by God!'

It was freezing that night, as we curled up in our blankets. We had a single blanket each, except for Balla, who slept in a thin prayer mat. It was too cold for any of us to sleep except in snatches. I knew that I could have brought a sleeping-bag, as I had on my earlier journeys, but told myself that I had no wish to sleep in comfort while my companions shivered a few feet away. If there was any chance of being accepted by these Arabs, it would only be by sharing hard-ships. If I had brought with me foreign luxuries, then why not travel by motor-vehicle? I could have reached El 'Atrun much more efficiently in one of the salt lorries, as many European tourists had done. But El 'Atrun was only a goal, a place on which to set my sights. The real secrets I had come in search of lay here in the open desert with these desert peoples. Without them I should have been just another tourist, and my journey would have been no more than a sight-seeing trip.

The next morning we were assailed by a biting wind from the north-east, and we wrapped ourselves in blankets before setting off. The camels now moved close together in four parallel strings, and we took turns leading them. They paced on over the sand and rock, stalwart and impassive. The plain looked like a sheet of polished bronze, crusted with a dark patina of iron. At intervals there were rock towers with sharp, angular faces. Pieces of rock had cracked and fragmented; they lay across the desert in nests of debris. To our west lay the faint outline of Tagaru, the massive inselberg that extended eighty miles north towards Wadi Howar. I had heard that the plateau had some interesting rock pictures, and I asked Moham-mid if he had seen them. He replied that he had not, and that only the 'Atawiyya really knew the inside of the mountain. 'They say that there are caves there where the whole of the Kababish could hide, and no one would ever find them,' he told me. 'There is plenty of treasure buried there too, by God!' I knew there was no chance of exploring the plateau on my present journey, but I hoped that one day I should find a chance to return.

As the days passed, I got to know my companions better. Old Ali was treated a little mockingly by the others. He was unmarried, which was unusual for a man of his age. As he had no sons to help him, he was forced to make the arduous journey to El 'Atrun several times a year. Ballal was a tough, hardy Arab, inclined to be gruff and moody. He spoke as little as possible. My liking for Balla did not increase, for he was a merciless critic of everything I did. Often we would go off to bring back the camels in the morning, if they had been left out to graze all night. I was still unaccustomed to the vicious animals and several times I was almost bitten or kicked as I stooped to untie the hobbles. On one occasion I was wrestling with the hobble of my old friend of the jaw-tying incident, a huge camel called Girish. Someone had pulled the hobble tight, and as I struggled with chilled hands the animal lowered his head and snapped at my skull. I noticed the movement, which could have broken my neck, only a second before the jaws champed together, and thrust myself backwards into the sand. As I picked myself up, I saw Balla standing a few yards away and laughing loudly. 'You are a fool if you cannot even untie a hobble!' he said.

As we rode on that afternoon, Balla leaned over and said to me, 'What can you do? It seems that you know nothing!' I thought of trying to explain that I was here, speaking in a language that I had first heard less than four years previously, riding an animal that I had formerly seen only in a zoo, travelling with an alien people in a foreign land. Yet I knew that these were excuses that would have no meaning for him. He was totally unaware of the world outside this desert. 'What can *you* do?' I asked in return.

'I can tie ropes and hobble camels, I can make hobbles and waterskins, I can ride and shoot and hunt, herd camels and dig wells. I know all the names of the trees and the grasses, the birds and the animals and the meaning of the tracks. That is what is needed for living here. If you do not know these things, then you know nothing!'

And I was forced to admit that he was right.

Over those days I became increasingly worried about my camel, Wad at Tafashan. It seemed that Wad Fadul had been right when he predicted that the animal was too worn out to make El 'Atrun. He began to stumble and his head sagged. It became more and more difficult for him to keep up with the others. Finally, one afternoon, he sat down and refused to get up again. We kicked and pulled at him until he responded. I remembered the she-camel I had seen with Dagalol; those that could not keep up were left or slaughtered. Mohammid said, 'It is not just tiredness. He has a saddle-sore for certain.' Later, after we had made camp, I found that the Arab had been right. Beneath the rear saddle-pad was a neat red sore that was badly swollen. When the fire was lit, Mohammid heated an iron and cauterized the swelling. 'So that the poison will not spread,' he told me. We all knew that the camel would be unridable for days. 'You will not make it even to Wadi Howar if you ride him,' Mohammid said. That night, when I went out alone in the darkness to bring back the camels from the little grazing they had found, I felt deeply disappointed. Without my camel I felt that my independence had been lost. But far more serious was the lack of trust between myself and Balla, which in this vast environment felt unnatural and destructive.

When next morning came and Mohammid told me to saddle my old friend Girish, I could not suppress a laugh. He was far more comfortable to ride, and far more manageable than I could ever have imagined. During the next few days we crossed valleys thick with red sand piled into drifts and shallow crescents. The desert surface was a constantly changing pattern of colours and textures – the deep ochre of the sand-sheets, the steel-grey of the gravel plains, packed as hard as asphalt. In the mornings the wind drove runnels of dust across the ground, sawing against the clusters of blue basalt boulders that stood like nests of giant eggs in the sand.

Once we came across an 'Atawiyya camp. Two brown tents were pitched in the very centre of a sand-sheet. Mohammid and Balla rode off to investigate them, and returned saying that there was no one there but an old lady and her dog, and that she had given them a little buttermilk. I was astounded that anyone lived in this almost sterile desolation, yet I knew that many Kababish, particularly the 'Atawiyya, the Awlad Huwal and the Sulayman, had adapted to this harsh world. They had survived here because of their skills, their ability to shape things with their hands. They survived by their understanding of the camel that provided them with milk and wool and enabled them to carry their shelters and water-supply over large distances.

I soon began to see that what I had thought a sterile world was actually teeming with life. As my eyes trailed along the surface, I learned to take in the tell-tale signs that my companions saw. I noticed the hardy desert grasses and lichens, the tracks of insects and arthropods, lizards of all sizes, hares and foxes, ostriches, gazelles and Barbary sheep. Much of the life here was not on the surface, where the stinging tongue of the sun sucked away all life-giving moisture. It dwelt in the cool, dark womb of the earth below, where it had been woven into many forms, exotic and beautiful – the delicate structures of the ants and beetles, the glittering scales of the lizards and snakes, the shimmering silver of the fennec fox. Each of these creatures survived here by developing some special mechanism that enabled them to adapt to the hard dictates of the environment. Only man had no such mechanism, but depended for his life on his culture, his behaviour and his social organization.

After sunset on these days we would ride for hours. I began to feel the first pinch of real hunger. It was a gnawing, acid ache that seemed to dissolve the stomach lining, lingering all day, even after eating. Our meals were even more frugal now there were five of us, but the rations all came from the stocks of Mohammid and myself. The Ruwahla in particular seemed reluctant to share their food, though they ate ours with gusto. Mohammid and I both noticed this, but said nothing.

Balla continued to criticize me, and I began to wonder if I could do anything right. One day as we were crouching to eat, he said, 'You do not eat properly. You waste too much. That is forbidden here in the desert!' He went on to explain in great detail how the globs of porridge that remained on my hand after eating should be slopped back into the pot and not allowed to fall on the ground.

The Arabs talked at great length about sex, and were very explicit in their descriptions. They questioned me in detail about the sexual practices amongst my tribe. I tried to answer as truthfully, but was met by either horror or amusement. The idea that our women were not circumcised, for example, struck them as disgusting and filthy, while my description of kissing brought peals of hilarious laughter. I gathered that their sex lives were very surreptitious affairs. Because of the lack of privacy men and women neither undressed nor indulged in any foreplay during their love-making.

One night as I knelt down to relieve myself, Balla cried, 'God! That is not how to do it! You do not know anything! You should not kneel, but squat down as we do!' This was humiliating to the point of provocation, but I refused to be provoked. I told myself that Balla was right – there was only one way to do things in the desert – the way tried and tested by time. However, there were further humiliations to come. Once, Balla noticed that I was uncircumcised. This was considered by the Arabs to be a kind of deformity, for to them circumcision signified the passage from childhood to manhood. Anyone who had not been through this ritual could not properly be considered a man. The new revelation provoked massive contro-versy and a whole day of discussion. In general, they were very anxious that the situation be put right. When we made camp, Ballal offered to perform the operation there and then. He began to sharpen his knife on a stone, saying, 'It will not hurt at all. We will tie a piece of string round the end. Look how sharp my knife is, by God! We will have it off in a moment!' I actually considered permitting the operation, but I knew it could cause serious bleeding and might attract an infection that would be fatal here. I had a tremendous struggle to dissuade him from the idea without being aggressive or seeming to be afraid.

We remained with Tagaru for three days. On 2 November how-ever, we saw the head of the plateau, Ras Tagaru, looming out of the desert like the bow of a battered submarine. We moved into a vast area of volcanic rubble, like a geological rubbish-tip. Our cara-van passed over shelves of gravel scattered with hard flint boulders, cut by narrow channels that were carpeted with soft sand. Soon the rocky ground gave way to a great sand-sheet stretching as far as the eye could see, broken only by the peaks of Ummat Harrir like a strange, fairy-tale castle.

About two hours before sunset Balla spotted a group of camel riders. They were as small and black as mosquitoes, moving on the extreme periphery of our vision. 'Meidob!' Mohammid cried. 'They must be. They are moving from the west, out of Wadi Majrur, by God!'

'The slaves had better not come near us,' growled Balla, threat-eningly.

'We will be in Wadi Howar tomorrow,' old Ali said. 'They will not touch us there. The 'Atawiyya will not let the slaves get away with anything!' Despite the talk, though, a palpable sense of tension seemed to grip the party as we drove the camels on. While Moham-mid, Ali and I led the strings from the front, Balla and Ballal pushed them from the rear. Occasionally one of us looked back to check

157

on the movements of the other party. They remained at a distance, pursuing their own oblique course north-east.

After sunset we camped at Ummat Harrir. It was again bitterly cold and the camels shivered wretchedly as we unloaded them. None of us mentioned the riders we had seen, but there was an unspoken agreement tonight that the animals should be hobbled and not left to find grazing. The Arabs built up their saddles and baskets into a semicircular fortress, laying the hearth in its centre. We piled up all our remaining firewood and lit a blazing fire against the cold. It seemed to hold back the gloomy curtain of the night, beyond which unknown primeval horrors seemed to lurk, as real for us as for our remote ancestors.

I went to sleep early, but the Arabs sat up for what seemed like hours, and I was dimly aware of their voices until the middle of the night. I awoke suddenly, shivering with cold and saw that the fire was still burning with a desultory flame. Old Ali was sitting by it, hunched up and wrapped in a blanket, shawl and headcloth. His old rifle was clasped over his knees and a grim expression set on his features. I rose to join him, throwing the blanket over my shoulder and taking my shotgun. The fire gave out little warmth, but both of us sat staring into its flickering flames without speaking. I felt an almost hypnotic sense of calm, sitting there in the acute silence and the impenetrable darkness. Above us several constellations glittered through the night sky, but I recognized none of them. We sat there almost motionless until the first red glow of the morning crept over the horizon. The others soon uncurled from their sleeping-places and began to perform their morning prayers. Ali and I joined them, still wrapped in our blankets.

The waterskins were empty and the firewood all gone. We wasted no time on tea, but began loading and saddling almost at once. The camels seemed frozen and exhausted; Wad at Tafashan was reluctant to get up from the pit of sand he had excavated during the night. I noticed how tight the skin was stretched over his ribs and how his legs trembed as he finally stood up.

We were on our way before sunrise, two of us leading the camels and the others driving from behind. We were thirsty, hungry and exhausted, and our camels seemed to know it. Before we had been travelling for half an hour, one of Balla's animals shied and jostled, breaking the lead-rope as if it were a thread of cotton. The other animals roared and spat in agitation, writhing and cavorting on their ropes until they also snapped. There were crashes as several of them cast off their saddles. We had to halt the caravan, dismount and carefully reload and rerope the miscreant animals. We set off once again, but before long the same camel, the third in Balla's string, roared and skipped once more, pulling the lead-rope apart and causing a commotion. The Arabs dismounted, cursing and shouting in desperation. Balla seized the trouble-maker by the nostrils and lips, and Ballal got out a long packing needle. While the camel gnashed his teeth, growling and bellowing, the Arab made an incision through the nostril until the blood ran down the creature's jaws. He then strung a piece of thin cord through the hole and tied it to a headrope. 'Now break that, my friend!' he said. For a time the caravan went smoothly, but suddenly one of Ali's camels tore the headrope from the tail of the beast before him and threw off his saddle, shaking and bleating in anger. The other camels rushed forwards, startled by the sudden noise, and we narrowly prevented them from stampeding. This meant another exasperating delay.

As we drove on, the desert seemed interminable. Our eyes scanned the horizon for the faintest shadow of grey that would mark the wadi. Several times we imagined that we had seen it, but it always proved to be an illusion – a core of grey rocks or a patch of dark sand on the desert's crust. Ali and I had the lead, when suddenly Ballal came trotting up from the rear. 'The slaves are with us!' he shouted. We looked back, straining to make out the nest of grey-black figures riding behind us, still far away but closer than on the previous day. It was at that moment that Ali saw the peak of Jabal Rahib and the greyish line of the wadi at its base. We drove the camels on now in desperate haste, hoping to God that the lead-ropes would not break again. Slowly the ghost-thin line thickened into the recognizable form of trees, yet still it seemed an age before we came near them; then all at once we were amongst the groves of *siyaal* and *arak*. There was an oval hill that marked the well of Ghobayshi, and the well itself lay in the bed of the wadi below. The wadi was an expanse of sand bars covered in thorn trees, between which ran numerous channels cut by the passage of water some time in the past. Half of the trees were in leaf, and the perfume of their flowers was thick in the air. Others were brittle, dead and broken, with their branches lying like dry splinters around them. The ground was disturbed by the footprints of hundreds of camels, and littered by their droppings.

There was no sign of human life, apart from an old wooden scaffolding over the well-shaft. In this season most of the Arabs who lived in this area were away on their migrations to the south. We unloaded in a copse of *arak* trees, and turned the camels loose to graze. It was good to see them eating voraciously at last. After the equipment had been dumped, Mohammid and Balla rode down to the wells to fill our skins. The camels scattered along the wadi. Ballal and I took the weapons and went to guard them. I climbed to the top of a sand-bar and scanned the desert to the south for riders. The party that had been pursuing us had disappeared as completely as if the sands had opened up and swallowed it whole.

Late that afternoon we climbed out of the wadi into another great sand-sea bordered by the hills of Rahib. I was mesmerized by the strangeness of the world in which I found myself. It was almost as if we were no longer on earth, so strange were the shades and colours of the desolation. Later we passed through a gorge of rock and came into a gravel plain bordered by a long wall of basalt to the east, and that evening we moved into the weathered rock massif of Zalat Hammad.

The next morning I woke to find myself in a fascinating world of rock and gravel. It was a mysterious primitive world, a world of greys and blacks; a blue carpet of tight stones, scarred with fallen flakes glimmering manganese-red, blocks of sandstone, deep ranks of cliffs where amber sand lay in sloping piles. Mohammid went off early, and came back saying that there was plenty of grass growing between the rocks. After a discussion it was decided that we should remain here for the rest of the day so that the camels could graze. El 'Atrun was no more than a day's journey north, and Mohammid and Ballal would ride to the oasis to prepare the way. Mohammid said that he would see us the next morning at Bir Milani, the southernmost well in the El 'Atrun oasis.

There was little to occupy me all day, so I took my shotgun and went off to explore the sand drifts, dunes, and rock chimneys. After about an hour I returned to the camp. On the way I came across another set of prints that had followed my own before turning back. The prints were shoeless and long in step; they could only belong to Balla. I wondered why the Arab had followed me so mysteriously. I did not question him when I arrived in camp, but the thought worried me for the rest of the day.

Just before sunset Balla and I went to collect the camels. I still carried my shotgun and he took his long-shafted axe. We walked for about twenty minutes before we came across the animals, gathered in the lee of a ridge of shattered rocks and sandstone fragments. Many of the camels had sat down, for the grazing was very sparse, and they were tired after the long trek. As we reached the ridge, Balla walked forward slightly and suddenly I saw him stiffen. He inched further cautiously and dropped, crouching by a boulder. I watched him, mystified, wondering why he was performing this strange act. Then he beckoned to me and motioned me to keep quiet. As I crouched by him, I saw what he had seen first. About a hundred metres away a group of men were unsaddling their camels amongst the rocks. The men were short and negroid, wearing long shirts and skull-caps. 'Slaves!' Balla hissed. 'Meidob! They are the bandits who chased us. They will steal our camels.'

I looked at the men carefully. They certainly looked like Meidob, but I saw no sign of weapons, neither did there seem anything overtly sinister about them. Their camels were strung like a caravan, and were not riding animals. I was convinced that they could not be the men who had followed us. 'You have got a gun,' Balla said. 'Kill them! Go around this ridge and shoot them from behind! If you do not, they will put an end to us all!' At first I thought he was joking. Then I noticed that his hands were shaking and his breath was coming in short pants. For a second I wavered. In that moment my thoughts travelled through an entire gamut of ideas and images: fear, suspicion, amusement, loathing, pity, courage and cowardice. I had wanted to be accepted by these Arabs. Now I had been asked to pay a price that I could not pay. These men could well have been enemies, and to kill an enemy and take his camels was acceptable to these Arabs. Yet I knew I was not prepared to kill anyone, even bandits. To fight in defence of my companions was one thing – but to initiate the attack was something quite different. 'I am not going to kill anybody unless they attack me first!' I said. Balla stared at me with eyes full of hate. I realized that I suspected his motives. Was he merely trying to test my loyalty? If so, how far would he push it? Was he trying to gauge my gullibility? Or could he be intent on stealing Meidob camels with my assistance? Could it be my camel and possessions he was after? Was he just stark-staring crazy? 'You bastard! Son of the forbidden!' he swore. 'You are a disgrace! Give me the gun and I will do it!' This was even more frightening. Once he had possession of the shotgun, there was no telling what might happen.

161

'No one is doing any killing with this gun!' I told him. Then I walked away with as much dignity as I could muster, feeling his eyes boring with hot anger into my back. I was stunned and numb as I walked back to our camp — out of my depth, lost and farther from home than ever before. Worse than the fear was a sense of confusion that was enhanced a thousand-fold by the loneliness and desolation around me.

He brought the camels back alone later. After dark we lit a fire and made some *kisri*. Old Ali seemed quite unaware of the incident, though he knew the Meidob were encamped not far away. This strengthened my conviction that something strange was going on in Balla's mind. We sat apart from each other and treated one another with polite forbearance. I felt that the root of the problem was that we did not understand each other; we were men from different worlds, too far apart to touch without willingness on both sides. Balla had no such willingness, nor the obligation for it. By far the most frightening aspect was the fact that we were 200 miles from the nearest settlement, outside any kind of jurisdiction in the hard, raw face of the real world where personalities counted more than laws. I knew now why St Exupéry had called the desert 'the land of men'. Yet I was determined not to lose control, and was proud that I had mastered my emotions. I was afraid, but I would not give in an inch to fear. Danger was always to be expected in the desert and could come from any quarter, but I had never expected it to come from within.

That night I lay down with my shotgun near me and my pistol in the pocket of my *jibba*. It was the most terrifying night of my life, fraught with fears and confusion, but it was a night in which I learned something of myself and of these desert people. I awoke the next day to the realization that if I had ever regarded my travels in the desert as a game, that game was now over. Only the cold, desperate realities of survival were left for me to pursue.

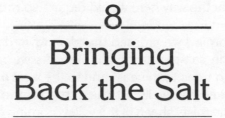

8
Bringing
Back the Salt

A desolation of desolations. An infernal
region. I have passed through it and
now have no fear of the hereafter.
Ewart Grogan, quoted in The Sudan
Today, *1970*

It took until sunset the next day to reach Bir Milani. Wad at Tafashan collapsed twice in the afternoon. Both times we managed to pound him into life again, but though he staggered to his feet there was a glazed look in his eyes that told me death was not far away. I knew that a camel would continue until the point of utter exhaustion, then just sit down and die. Wad at Tafashan had already gone beyond his physical limit, and would survive now only on the power of the will. Ironically, I thought, the same applied to myself; this harsh land had no mercy on man or beast.

We moved slowly, dropping from hunger and fatigue. The plain seemed to go on and on. To the east was the massive hogsback of Jabal Bint Umm Bahr ('Daughter of the Sea'). It seemed a ludicrous name for a hill in this arid place. We were moving towards what looked like a white cliff, under which was a seam of black rocks. As the hours passed, the rocks took on a soft and fuzzy aspect, but it was not until we were almost upon them that I realized they were trees. They were growing out of a mass of steep dunes. As the sun cast long grey shadows across the sand beside us, we stalked in amongst them. Here in the midst of nothing was an island of life.

We found a place between the dunes and began to unload. Before it was quite dark, Mohammid and Ballal found us. We made porridge and afterwards I flopped down on my sheepskin. I knew that there was a chance now for my camel to survive, and at least I had reached El 'Atrun, which had been my goal for so long. I had

163

never dreamt that the way here would require so much in tears, toil and sweat.

The next morning we crossed the plain towards the limestone ridge that hid the salt-pan from our view. As we moved closer, I noticed two palm trees to the east and to the west a small grove of palms that marked the wells. At the same time a great caravan emerged from the misty sheen of the valley, coming directly towards us. The camels were dark spectres on the dust flats, striding on unswervingly like robots. Each animal carried two bloated leather bags of salt and was strapped to the beast in front by a leather rope. Four men walked with the caravan. They were Arabs of Darfur with dark and hooded faces; they passed without waving or turning aside, stalking on south as if mesmerized by some great power.

Under the palm trees there were no permanent wells. Instead there was a wet area where the surface was covered with a growth of spiky *hallif* grass, where pits had been dug out for generations. We spent most of the morning digging out one of these pits with shovel and mattock. It was hard work, for we were still weak with hunger. Slowly the pit filled up with green water. It smelt of sulphur, and tasted slightly brackish. Mohammid said, 'You will be running to the wadi when you drink this stuff!' His prediction proved correct, and later in the day when I was attacked by severe stomach cramps I found for the first time amongst the Kababish that I had developed diarrhoea.

Our camels kicked and fought to get near the water, and we had to keep them off with sticks and whips. Wad at Tafashan was the last to drink. As I watched him sucking up the liquid, I felt a deep sense of relief — his chances of survival were steadily becoming greater.

When all the camels had drunk, we resaddled them and led them on to the salt-pans beyond the ridge. The salty crust of the earth glistened white in the sun. The place was dotted with nests of sacks and ranks of miniature slag heaps that had been thrown up over the years. Lines of camels were couched across it, and there was the sound of picks and shovels as a score of men worked on the salt. To the west stood the glittering hulk of a Fiat truck. To the east was the humpback spur of Jabal Toli'a, squatting like a watch-tower over the workings. On the rim of the salt-pan was a ragged line of shacks that housed the oasis's population of salt diggers.

There was nothing here but the severe and comfortless panorama of the desert.

We settled our camels, calling out a greeting to the men nearby. They called back, but did not stop work. We dropped our equipment and Mohammid and Ballal drove the camels off to the dunes below Toli'a where there were some *sallam* trees in leaf. Before he left, Mohammid said, 'Tomorrow you can go and look after the camels. You will be no good at digging the salt so you may as well do something useful!'

The surface of the salt-sheet was scarred and blistered by the workings of nomads over hundreds of years and smothered by the droppings of their camels. After we had eaten, we laid out our tools and stripped down to the waist, ready to work on the salt. The ground was soft and easy to break with a pick, and the salt-seam lay about eighteen inches below the surface. I swung the axe, delighting in the chance to exercise some different muscles. Again and again I attacked the ground, splitting the soft calcium crust and sending up showers of dust, totally lost in the new frenzy of activity. When I stopped to rest for a moment, I noticed old Ali and Balla digging a few yards away. They wielded their tools feebly, with ineffectual movements of the forearms that produced poor results. I saw at once that neither had a clue about using a pick and shovel. I had been afraid that I should be embarrassed once more by their superlative skill, and this turn of events amused me so much that I began to laugh. Both of them stopped work and looked at me.

'What's wrong with you?' Ali asked.

'Nothing!' I replied, grinning maliciously. I remembered then that nomads hate manual work. The look of utter distaste on their faces was hilarious. I had been schooled well in the art of entrenching in the army, and knew the technique inside out. There was a right and a wrong way. It was childish, but incomparably sweet to wreak a little vengeance on them at their own game.

The chunks of pinkish crystal we turned up were natron –sodium carbonate. Such deposits were probably the residue left from ancient seas that had long ago evaporated. This rock salt had been in use for at least 2,000 years and was one of the crucial secrets of the embalming process in ancient Egypt. There were several such salt oases in the Libyan desert and Herodotus told of a caravan route that united them all. El 'Atrun was the most renowned, as it was the first main station on the Darb al 'Arba'in – the ancient trade route

165

from Darfur to Egypt. The first European known to have visited it was W. G. Browne, who had come here in 1793 and found the Kababish Arabs with their camels. Douglas Newbold and William Shaw, the first men to explore the south Libyan desert, had been here in 1927 and found Kababish of the Umm Mattu and 'Atawiyya with 300 camels. Eleven years later Wilfred Thesiger had been here on his first desert journey, and had caused a scare, his party being mistaken for an Italian invasion force.

In the past the oasis had often been threatened by raiders of the Gur'an from the nearby Ennedi mountains in Chad. The British had stationed a detachment of camel corps at Jabal Toli'a, then known as Jabal Kashafa, and the sangar that they had built still stood on the sugarloaf summit of the hill. The salt-pans had been raided by Sir Ali Wad at Tom's men in 1911, and they had returned with a small herd of stolen camels.

When Mohammid and Ballal returned, they were surprised to see the piles of the red mineral that had appeared in their absence. Mohammid examined my pile and weeded out some of the lumps, which he said were too diluted with earth. Then the two of them stripped down and we worked together solidly until sunset. By this time we were knee-deep in the salt, and our hands were blistered and raw from digging. The salt entered our cuts, bursting blisters and making them sting badly. After dark a cold wind dragged across the workings; we made a fire, sheltered by our saddlery. As we sat around it, Balla said, 'Of course, cutting salt is really the work of slaves.' The others snickered at his obvious meaning, but I said nothing. I noticed with secret satisfaction that nothing more was said about my looking after the camels. The next morning Mohammid went off to them without a word.

It was pleasant to flex my muscles in the cool of the morning, but as the sun climbed higher the effort became harder. Gusts of wind blew the caustic salt-dust into my eyes, ears and mouth; the sun baked my skin from above. My movements grew steadily weaker as the lack of nutrition took effect. This back-breaking laborious work required steak to sustain it. Around noon Mohammid returned from the east, and I decided I could continue no longer. I had already piled up twice as much as the others, and I could see that my companion was pleased. I put on my shirt and went with him to visit the tiny settlement.

The huts were crudely made of timber and sacking. The place

was almost deserted, for the workers who lived here were all on the salt-pans, where they filled sacks for the large trucks, at £S3 a sack. Many of them were former slaves of Kababish families who had found a lucrative yet hardly comfortable trade here in El 'Atrun. As we walked between the shacks, we were called over by a group of youths. They were not Arabs, but had the broad, black faces of townsmen and wore long Arab shirts that looked clean and white beside our mould-yellow garments. They greeted us with the short townsman's greeting, which seemed very abrupt now I had become familiar with that of the nomads.

The men told us that they had come from Darfur by truck and were travelling to Libya. They would complete the journey on camels, which they had already bought from passing salt caravans. They were waiting for a guide to reach the oasis with the main party. The border between Libya and the Sudan was officially closed for diplomatic reasons, though the Libyans often welcomed workers from the Sudan to augment their tiny workforce. Hundreds of Sudanese migrated there every year, many of them by camel. But the way was dangerous between El 'Atrun and Kufra and many townsmen, unaccustomed to the desert, had died on the way. Many others had been turned away at the border post at 'Uwaynat, and had been forced to return to the Sudan on exhausted camels.

The youths were bright and optimistic, and talked about schools and jobs, about the government politics. They were educated and informed and knew the workings of the world. Mohammid leaned against the hut, bored by the talk, which meant nothing to him. It occurred to me suddenly and very clearly that these men and I were from the same culture, the same environment. They were black and spoke Arabic, yet they lived in the same dimension as myself. It was a dimension from which Mohammid and my other companions were excluded. Later, though, the tables were turned when one of the youths asked Mohammid, 'Don't you have any camel's milk for us?' Mohammid looked at him incredulously and replied, 'Are you mad? Is this the place to find camel's milk?' Then he got up and said, 'Come Omar, let us find some sacks for our salt.'

As we walked away, he muttered, 'Slaves! They are all talk but they know nothing, by God!'

We bought some sacks from a huge fat negro who sold food to the salt workers. He told us that he had originally come here as a

worker and had used the profit he had made to set up as a small trader. He had originally belonged to the *'Ol* of Sheikh Hassan himself.

We returned to the digging in the early afternoon. The others
had stopped for a rest and were sitting in the shade of a canvas
sheet. Mohammid and I had brought eight camels with us. Each
one, except for Wad at Tafashan, would carry two bags of salt each
weighing about three *gontar*. This meant that each camel would
be shifting almost 600 pounds, which was maximum capacity even
for such camels as these. Only Mohammid's riding camel would be
spared this weight, and would carry lighter bags. As I worked in my
pit, Mohammid sorted the natron into piles, throwing away the dross
and preparing the stuff ready for sacking. By the end of the afternoon
we had enough to fill ten bags.

That night Mohammid and Balla slept with the camels at Toli'a.
Mohammid had spotted some gazelles there and hoped to shoot
one at first light when they came to feed. As we sat drinking tea
the next morning, there was a muffled report and Ali said, 'That is
Mohammid! God willing, he bagged something!'

The two Arabs did not return until noon, but they brought with
them the carcass of a gazelle hidden in a saddle-bag. 'We will eat it
tonight,' Mohammid told me. 'Or everyone will invite themselves!' I
had already piled up enough salt for the remaining four bags. We
spent the rest of the afternoon filling sacks, which Mohammid stitched
up with rough thread. Afterwards I walked to the base of Toli'a
and climbed up through the rippled sand on its western side. I sat
down in the old camel-corps sangar and looked around me. The
sun was still hovering just above the skyline and the desert was
bathed in soft gold. To the south I could see the dunes of Bir Milani
and to the north a barrier of jagged hills that guarded the route of
the ancient Darb al 'Araba'in. I felt exhausted, yet satisfied. I had
achieved my ambition of reaching El 'Atrun by caravan with the
desert nomads. If I had come by lorry I should have learned little,
and the desert would have flashed past as if on a cinema screen. I
knew that to really understand the vastness of this land, it had to be
crossed by camel. Just then, as if in answer to my thoughts, there
came the penetrating roar of an engine. I looked down and saw a
Fiat lumbering across the salt-pan, leaving a tail of dust in its wake. It
seemed to dwarf everything with its booming motor and its choking
fumes. Ten years previously there had been no trucks at El 'Atrun.
Ten years hence there would probably be no more caravans.

As soon as I arrived back at the workings, Mohammid took me aside and said in a quiet voice, 'We are ready to leave. We will load in the morning and spend the night at Bir Milani.'

'Ballal and Ali are not yet finished,' I said.

'We do not need to wait for them. We shall go without them, you, me and Balla. It is better to have three men to lift the salt. Two can do it, but it is more difficult. Anyway, they are not good companions. See how they ate our food. Do not tell them that we are leaving.'

I was too confused by this new revelation to argue or ask questions. It was unusual for Arabs to abandon travelling companions in this way, but I told myself that this was Mohammid's business. Anyway, I was starving and could think only of the gazelle.

We ate it after sunset, cooked in a little oil over our wood fire. After so long without it, the meat was indescribably delicious, the most succulent of flesh. We dipped our hands into the pot again and again until the grease ran down our chins, and when there was no meat left we scraped out the pan greedily with our fingers.

The next day we laid out our fourteen sacks on the surface of the salt-pan, two by two. Mohammid and Balla brought up the camels for loading. With Balla's camels we had fourteen between us, and a total of twenty-six bags of salt. Only Wad at Tafashan carried no load, and I was pleased to see that he looked much better after his rest. The dull sheen in his eye had been replaced by a brighter light, and he looked more alert. I hoped that he would remain like this, for I knew that the return journey might prove even harder than the outward one.

First, we saddled each camel carefully with the specially modified saddles, then each camel was brought up individually and couched between two of the sacks. Two men would lift the first sack, using the *inderab* pole to help take the weight. A third man would hold it in place against the saddle, while the other two ran around and lifted the second bag. The two sacks acted as counter-weights, and were secured over the bar of the saddle by two wooden pegs. The bar between the saddle-horns was designed to keep the load high, for if it rubbed against the camel's hide a sore would appear in hours and a septic wound in days. This would mean the loss of a load.

Just after noon we moved the caravan towards Bir Milani, walking and leading the camels in two strings behind us. Mohammid told Ali and Ballal that we should meet them at Bir Milani. I still could not guess what this deception was really about, but I had little choice but to go along with it.

It was a freezing night and the cold would not let us sleep, even in the shelter of the high sand dunes. I was up with the red glow of dawn, collecting firewood with the help of my torch. I shivered desperately with the cold, dressed only in my thin cotton *jibba*. Soon the fire was roaring in the hearth and Mohammid made tea. After I had thawed out, I took two skins down to the nearest well to get water. It was still very cold. The well was about seven feet deep and had a bucket made out of a broken plastic oil can. I hoisted one bucketful to the lip of the well and tried to pour the liquid into my first skin. The bucket was heavy and required two hands for pouring, and the freezing water splashed over my fingers, making them smart. I realized then that the waterskin also needed two hands in order to hold it open. The task was impossible for one person. I managed to pour a little water into the skin, and to stand it up against a stone. Smiling at my ingenuity, I hoisted up another bucketful. I gripped the bucket in both hands and took the rope in my mouth, pouring carefully, not spilling a drop. The skin bulged out as the liquid went in. I turned to draw another bucketful and at that moment the skin tipped over slowly into the sand, and all the water ran out. Livid with rage I hurled the bucket into the well, but forgot to grip the well-rope in my frozen hands. At the last moment I realized, but too late. The bucket and rope had fallen into the well, seven feet below me.

I felt like running away or jumping up and down in desperation. Suddenly a figure appeared. He was an Arab of middle age, dressed in a black overcoat and a tightly bound *'imma*. He chuckled to himself as he greeted me, and I got the feeling he had watched the entire performance. 'You dropped the bucket!' he commented, smiling. 'That is not good, by God, not good at all!' Then he walked calmly over to a bush and came back with a long thin branch of *sallam*. He knelt at the edge of the well and fished beneath with the branch, as if it had been the easiest task in the world. In a moment he had the rope in his hand. Afterwards he held my waterskin open as I drew the water up, carefully winding the rope around my hand.

This was no more than the overture to the day. When I returned to camp, we set out at once to collect our camels, which had wandered off in the night. Some of them had walked almost as far as Bint Umm Bahr, and it took two hours to gather them all. I drove a group of five back towards the camp, but I could not keep them going in a straight line. One would waddle off west, making a beeline for a bush, and as I went to chase him back another would turn sharply east. They seemed to know what lay ahead of them, and were being deliberately exasperating. When we finally got them all together, each one had to be tied by the jaw and roped into the caravan. When this performance was completed, they all had to be saddled; then came the loading.

It was an excruciatingly hard job even for three men. The bags seemed dauntingly heavy on an empty stomach, and we had twenty-six of them to lift. At first I had the job of steadying the bags while the others lifted. I imagined that it was the easier job, but I was wrong. The lifting involved two quick efforts, but the holding involved one protracted one. The entire weight of the bag, almost 300 pounds, rested on my arms for several minutes, while the others lifted the counter-weight and wrestled with the pegs. The camels were no help. As I strained to balance the enormous weight, they would try to rise and throw off the load. They lurched and roared, turning their heads back as if to bite. Once I dropped the bag completely, hopping madly out of the way, afraid of being crushed. The bag split open and had to be restitched. 'You fool!' Balla said. 'You are too weak to hold the bags!' Five minutes later the two of them dropped a bag as they brought it up to the saddle. I grinned at them silently. 'Why don't we take it in turns?' I suggested. Mohammid agreed, and for a while I lifted with them, while Balla secured the sacks. However, none of us dropped one again, and we let the matter rest at one-all.

Once the load was on, we had to help the camel to its feet. The beast would stand in the queue with its legs trembling from the tremendous weight. We had to be very alert to make sure the camel did not sit down again, for once on his knees he could not bear the weight and would roll over and split the sacks or smash the saddle. I had never realized that the organization of a caravan was so complex.

It was mid-morning by the time all the animals had been loaded, and we set off, walking at the head of the strings in order to preserve the strength of the camels. We paced on towards the grey weathered mass of Zalat Hammad, until the biting wind dropped and the hot sun came out. We could no longer afford to stop at midday as we had done previously. Once the caravan halted for more than a few minutes, the camels would sit down. This meant that the loads would have to be dropped to prevent the animals from wrecking the saddles; then the bags would have to be lifted again. We could barely manage to lift them once a day on our meagre rations: twice would have been an impossible effort. We had to keep the camels moving all day from sunrise to sunset.

Every few kilometres something would go wrong. A camel would cast its load. A bag would come undone, and lumps of natron would be scattered across the desert. One of us would notice a potential sore, and the load would have to be shifted higher. The saddle-bags would come loose. A camel would sit down and break the lead-rope. We moved in fits and starts all day and seemed to get nowhere. Each time we stopped, we had to work with feverish speed in case the animals sat down. I began to understand why the Arabs said that the return from El 'Atrun was the most difficult journey of all.

Each small drama was acted out against the background of the empty plain of steel-grey gravel, with its spattering of volcanic chunks, blue, black and russet-red. I picked up a boulder as we walked. It was the size of a billiard ball and felt as heavy as iron. Yet it was hollow inside, a volcanic bubble that had shot out of some hot cone two million years ago.

We mounted our camels in the afternoon and rode on until the heat was again replaced by the chilling cold of the night. Sunset came, and we travelled into the blackness for two hours until we came across a lone *siyaal* tree that had somehow pushed its way through the hammada. We made camp there. The camels sat down, grumbling, and we ran along the lines pulling out the wooden pegs and jumping clear as the loads crashed to the ground. Afterwards we left the saddles on for another hour to prevent the animals' backs from swelling while we made tea. There was a little firewood under the tree and I climbed into its branches with our axe, cutting off any branches that seemed dry enough to burn. After we drank the tea, we unsaddled the camels and hobbled them. Balla chased them out into the night to find whatever poor forage they could. As I sat down wearily by the glowing spills of our fire, my blanket wrapped about me, I reflected that this had been one of the most exhausting days of my life.

But the hardship was not yet over. Eating our porridge was an ordeal in itself, despite our hunger. The flour, from Balla's stock, was bad and tasted bitter. We had no seasoning to smother the bitterness, and to cap it all there was insufficient food to alleviate our hunger. After we ate, Balla said, 'Omar, you can lift salt and you can

172

dig it out, but you are not a man. Men are circumcised, and anyway, you have no scars!' I looked at his gloating face in the poor light and sighed. He and Mohammid had often showed me the deep whip scars they bore on their backs. The scars were a source of great pride. I knew how they were obtained. It was the custom amongst the Kababish for the young braves of the tribe to submit to being lashed on occasions such as weddings. The youth who wished to display his strength and endurance would call out a rival – usually someone known to have a grudge against him. He would hand the man his rawhide whip and doff his shirt. The women would gather around to watch, singing and clapping, as the youth turned his back to them. The rival would lash him viciously from shoulder to kidneys. Crying out was permitted, but not flinching. The youth who flinched would be mocked by the watching women, while the man who stood firm would establish a solid reputation as a strong and brave warrior. Juma' Wad Siniin had once told me, 'If you can take the first two strokes it is easy. Those are like fire, but after that you don't feel much!'

I had often scoffed at the idea that whip scars made a man, but I now reminded myself that this was their world, not mine. My views had been nurtured in an effete culture where men used machines to do the real work. Here, physical strength and prowess were the measure of a man. No matter how objectionable their views might seem, I had to remember that my own ideas were firmly rooted in a culture that was vastly different.

It was two days before we reached Wadi Howar. They were days of unending toil. We were always up well before dawn, shivering on the freezing sand. The camels always wandered off in the night, and scattered far and wide; we had to walk for at least an hour to find them all, and bringing them back to camp took even longer. Then came the ritual of jaw-tying and fitting the *shakima* masks. When this was done, we would drink tea with a little unground millet to prepare ourselves for the task that we always viewed with trepidation: loading the salt. Each day it became harder, and I looked on it as an exacting test that had to be performed every morning. To have failed would have invited humiliating mockery from the Arabs. When everything was ready we would lead the caravan off across the desert, striding on barefoot over the cold surface for hour upon hour with our blankets clutched around us to ward off the icy grip of the wind.

173

Always there were delays, and as we grew more tired and hungry such small stoppages seemed disproportionately irritating. Sacks split, utensils dropped, the axe was lost and I had to run back to find it. We were all bad tempered and the Arabs continued their mocking jests, which I found more difficult to laugh off as time went on. Balla continued with the theme, 'you are not a real man', which he knew irked me, and occasionally Mohammid joined in.

We moved through the massif of Zalat Hammad. If I had not been so tired, I should have delighted in exploring this ancient rock maze, with its monoliths of sandstone perched on plinths of harder rock, and its great cliffs of shattered blocks, looking as if they had been hit with a gigantic sledgehammer. We walked out of the *zalat* on to a smooth plain of grey dust, the camels tramping on like automatons, knowing they were heading for home.

We would mount around noon, swinging up into the saddle. Mohammid was always first to mount, and I would follow about half an hour later. Balla mounted last, trudging on across the nothingness with a grim look on his face, his pathetic prayer mat wrapped around his gaunt body.

Wad at Tafashan went well for a time, but soon a flow of green slime replaced his solid black droppings. 'There is something wrong in his belly!' Mohammid told me. 'But it may not be serious. Anyway, there is no other camel to ride, so you will have to go on as you are. God is generous!' My companion was also having trouble with his riding camel. It was badly trained and objected to carrying the salt bags. When he mounted, it would spin and buck, sitting down and rubbing its neck on the sand petulantly. Once he gave it a tremendous thrashing with my whip. The camel behaved for a time, but was soon back to its old tricks.

We descended into the wadi in the middle of the afternoon. Mohammid led the caravan, weaving a tortuous path through the sand bars with their topping of thorn bush. Suddenly we saw the dark shapes of grazing camels and with them the unmistakable figure of a woman. As soon as they saw her, the youths' mouths fell open and both of them said, 'Omar, take my rope!' Then they charged off madly towards the girl on their camels. I had no idea what they hoped to achieve, nor why they had become so excited. Certainly sex was the last thing on my own mind. I was left to lead the camels through the labyrinth of dunes. There was no easy path. In the end I was forced to climb over one of the steep ridges of sand.

174

As I approached the top, Wad at Tafashan bolted suddenly. At once the lead-rope twanged. The camels, half-way up the slope, began to turn back. There were struggles as the animals pulled briefly against each other, then the ropes snapped. Some camels sat down and others began to scatter into the wadi. I couched my camel and ran around in desperate confusion, shouting for Mohammid and hoping that he would hear me far across the dunes.

In a few minutes he and Balla appeared and together we managed to gather all the beasts and rerope them. As we set off again, Mohammid said. 'It was stupid to try and climb that ridge with a caravan.' I was suddenly livid with anger. 'It's your damned fault!' I shouted. 'Whose salt is this, mine or yours? What would your father say if I told him you left me to find my own way while you went running after some girl? You say I am not a man, but you two are just children who have not yet grown up!' Mohammid was silent for a moment, then he said. 'You are right. It was wrong to leave you.' It was the first time he had admitted that he might be in the wrong.

That night we camped near the wells at Ghobayshi. After dark we had to fill our skins from the well, and took turns hauling up the heavy buckets. I was amazed that any of us had the strength left for this task.

The next day my face turned to a raw red mass and my skin itched so much that I scratched at it violently. I saw that my companions' skin was covered in brown blotches where it was peeling. 'It is the salt,' Mohammid said. 'It gets under the skin. There is nothing you can do about it. It will go in a few days.'

We left the wadi behind and headed for the outcrops of Ummat Harrir, where we had spent the night on the outward journey. I remembered the Meidob bandits we had seen on our way, and sincerely hoped we would not be attacked now. I doubted if we would have been able to put up much resistance. Perhaps our ravaged faces would have been enough to scare them off! The only people we saw were some 'Atawiyya who had been herding camels in Tagaru. They begged water from us, and we were obliged to give them as much as we could spare. We had filled only two skins at Ghobayshi, one large and the other small. I doubted that the water we had left would last us until we reached Iidayn, but I said nothing. It would have been considered rude to refuse water to those who asked for it, and the Arabs were by nature improvident, trusting always to the will of God for preservation.

The oval shadow of Ras Tagaru loomed up beyond the horizon; after sunset we camped to the east of the inselberg. We ate another miserable meal, and retired unsatisfied. The same gnawing pinch of hunger kept me awake all night, and in the morning we were up again before the sun rose, working frantically. Now there seemed nothing so important in the world as getting this salt back home. It was not my salt, but these Arabs had thrown down the gauntlet to me with their mockery, and I was determined that I should neither weaken nor fail. Some astonishing atavistic instinct seemed to have me in its grip. I was utterly drained of energy, yet I suddenly seemed to be able to call upon new sources of power that I had scarcely known existed. I was working on the level of instinct. I was pure aggression, pure survival. My companions growled at me and I growled back. I could have eaten anything, hunted and destroyed. I could have killed. Only survival seemed to matter, and bringing back the salt. I no longer felt fear: that was behind me now. I did not understand's Balla's hostility, but I no longer cared. I was a desperate predatory animal, longing for the pain and the hunger to end; yet something inside me wanted it to continue for ever, so intense had the experience become.

The next time Balla said, 'You are not a real man!' I was ready for him. I stopped abruptly and fixed him with a piercing stare. He stopped walking, thinking that I would strike him. Instead I thrust my whip into his hand and said. 'If you think you are such a man, strike, by God!' Then I turned my back on him and stripped off my *jibba* in a single movement. The cold wind touched my bare flesh and turned it to goose bumps. 'You asked for it!' I heard him say. I stood tensing myself for the blow. I told myself that whatever happened I must not flinch or cry out. I remembered Juma' saying, 'The first lash is like fire! It is harder than the knife!' I heard the faint swish as the whip came down. Then there was a thump as the lash struck the sand beside me. I turned back and saw Balla giggling sheepishly. I put out my hand for the whip and he returned it carefully. 'You could not endure it!' he blustered.

'You had your chance!' I snarled back.

'Come on, you fools!' Mohammid said. 'Or the camels will sit down. Then we shall be stuck!'

All day I was unable to get the thought of food off my mind. No matter how I tried to redirect my thoughts, I always ended up imagining a feast. I thought longingly of some dates I had once given away, and about the lizard we had eaten at Al Ku'. I thought of the goat-milk sauce we had had at Iidayn, and even of the wildcat Wad Ballal had killed in Darfur. Only my chewing-tobacco kept me going, and that had now dwindled to almost nothing. I was obliged to follow the Arab practice, spitting out the chewed lump into a container so that it could be chewed again.

That afternoon we were back in the *jizzu*. Mohammid told me that there had been good pastures east of Tagaru in past years, though now there was little but a few clumps of *nissa*. Occasional rings of camel droppings were a reminder of those more prosperous times. Once, we passed two fennec foxes that dashed for their earth as we went by. 'Supper!' Balla said, and he and Mohammid went off to hunt them while I took the caravan on. I did not object this time. They came back with the foxes half an hour later. Mohammid described how they had dug them out of the earth and strangled them. One of them had bitten Balla badly on the hand.

That evening, after we stopped and unloaded, we sat down to cook the foxes. There was no firewood, but Mohammid suggested that we should collect all the dried camel dung that we could find. There was plenty of it scattered about, and Balla and I emptied two saddle-bags and went off to collect it with our torches. The dung was in flat, brown pats, which was the best type for burning. It was as hard and brittle as wood. Mohammid piled it up in the hearth and set light to it, crouching and blowing hard for many minutes, until it began to smoke and glow. It gave out little heat. Balla skinned the two animals. They looked very small and fragile. I helped him to cut up the carcasses, already licking my lips. I could have eaten them raw, so hungry for meat had I become. Soon the enticing smell of cooking flesh filled the air. When it was ready, we ate ravenously, dipping our hands into the pot and tearing at the gristly joints with our teeth. I hardly noticed the taste. It was meat – that was all that mattered.

Afterwards we sat by the smoky ashes. I still felt hungry, but the meat had dulled the acuteness of the hunger. Mohammid began to sing, the same haunting camel-song that he always sang. Above us the stars were very bright, and there were some familiar constellations – Taurus, Orion and the Pleiades. The camels chattered and spluttered somewhere in the darkness. Mohammid's melody seemed to hold back the yawning emptiness that assaulted us from without and within.

177

When we loaded at dawn, I felt dizzy. As I lifted the sacks, the surroundings went out of focus and a heavy weight seemed to swim in my head. I shook myself sharply to get rid of the feeling, but it recurred several times. The sun was hot that morning, and we had three weary stops to pick up fallen loads. Just as everything seemed to be going smoothly at last, one of Balla's camels cast both sacks, which burst and threw chunks of salt across the sand. 'Now we shall have to stop!' Balla declared. It was afternoon, the hottest part of the day, and the sun was fiercer than usual. We couched the camels one by one and dropped the bags. We had to empty out the broken sacks, careful not to waste anything, even the salt-dust, before Balla restitched them with his packing needle. Meanwhile Mohammid and I tried to make a shelter. We had no uprights on which to sling our canvas, so we buried our rifles up to the stocks and threw the sheet over them. When the work was finished we all crowded into the shade, curling up side by side and trying to keep our limbs out of the sunlight.

I must have fallen asleep, for I awoke to find an Arab standing over us. He was a Kabbashi wearing a *jibba* and a long headcloth furled around his head and neck. He carried a dagger but no rifle. Mohammid and Balla did not get up, but blinked at him lazily. 'I need some water,' he told us. 'I have got some goats here, but my water has run out.' He held up a goatskin. Mohammid shifted himself resentfully, and half asleep poured half of the contents of our skin into the Arab's vessel. The Arab thanked us. When he had walked away, our eyes turned instinctively back to the waterskin. There was only enough water left to make tea.

After it had been made and drunk, Mohammid said, 'That is the last we have to drink. Now we will see who the real men are!'

Somehow we managed to load for the second time that day. Then we set off, going slightly east of south, towards the blank horizon beyond which, still miles away, Jabal 'Aja stood. It was desperate going now. The camels lurched on, shattered by the weight of the salt. We were too thirsty to talk, and as the cold night fell we went on silently. The first quarter moon came out, misted by the dust. At midnight we made camp. As soon as the camels were unloaded, we curled up in our blankets, protected from the wind by our saddlery. There was to be no meal tonight, no tea, not even a sip of water. We had not eaten since the previous evening, and my stomach felt as if it had been twisted and strained by an invisible hand. As I lay down to sleep, I thought, 'So this is what hunger is really like!' I nursed my aching stomach all night, and no sleep came.

The next day thirst took over. Until then I had thought of little but food. Now my mind seemed to hunt down images of succulent fruit, long, cool drinks and cascading water – vivid, detailed pictures drawn from deep within my memory. My mouth and throat felt scarred and pitted as if they had been cleaned with a wire brush, and a stinging pain in the kidneys had me doubled over the saddle. The camels limped on, near to the point of collapse. The sun came up like a beacon and rained its streams of fire, but I knew that we were lucky. In summer we should have been seriously ill by now.

We were hoping to see the outline of Jabal 'Aja that morning, but we crested horizon after horizon without spotting it. Every inch of ground seemed agony. When I tried to speak, my words came out in a drunken drawl. Mohammid and Balla complained of headaches, and there were slicks of dry white saliva on their lips. My own head seemed to roar like a furnace.

I had the familiar feeling that we were getting nowhere. The horizon was continually blank, and only the sun moved to show that the time was passing. It seemed that we were doing no more than marking time, marching on the same spot as the temperature shifted from cold to hot and then to cold again. At last Mohammid said, 'There must be a migration nearby. I am going to get some water.' Balla and I took the camels on, watching the youth as he trotted off into the distance.

We did not speak. We were both bent over our pommels and rocked steadily back and forth to the hypnotic rhythm of the camels' tread. I hardly dared hope that Mohammid would be successful. Within an hour, though, we watched him trotting back. 'He has found some!' Balla said, and at once my eyes sought out the comforting bulge of the waterskin slung from his saddle. As he came nearer, the sound of swishing water seemed to fill the air.

'Thank God, I found some Hamdab!' Mohammid said as he came up. I was about to couch my camel to drink when I noticed that the others made no attempt to do so. I realized that we would press on as normal. We rode for another three thirsty hours, and halted after sunset near some acacia trees. We went through the drills of unloading and setting up camp. Mohammid made a fire and we sat down next to it. 'Now we must drink,' I thought. To my dismay, however, Mohammid filled our two kettles and hung the waterskin

179

in a tree. He set them on the fire and we sat with our eyes glued to them. No one commented. When the water boiled, Mohammid performed the customary rituals. He filled the teapot and set it on a bed of ashes. Then he poured out a cup, tasted it, and poured it back in. 'Where are your cups?' he asked in the usual way. We produced them and he lifted the pot with exaggerated dignity and filled them. We waited until he had filled his own cup, then we raised them, whispering, 'In the name of God!' as if it were a toast. The first mouthful of tea was scalding hot and ate through the thick layer that had formed on my tongue. Undeterred, I drank it down in long gulps until it was gone. Never before or since have I tasted such wonderful tea.

We awoke to find ourselves under the wall of 'Aja. I was still thirsty, but the wind from the desert was cool, and I knew now that we were almost home. The camels perked up, and we rode instead of walking. Within two hours the lidayn was in sight, a circle of inviting green in the pastel plain. Suddenly Balla said, 'I shall leave you here.' We exchanged glances once. There was no goodbye or shaking of hands. The youth just took his lead-rope and led his camels away, going west towards a nugget of black cliffs. I turned to watch as he rode. He seemed a lonely, almost tragic figure in his wretched shirt as his spare body rocked slightly and the camels plodded on behind him. I watched him until the tiny caravan had become a string of beads on the landscape. Then Mohammid said, 'That Balla is a bad lot. We should not have travelled with him. You cannot trust him at all!'

Suddenly the trees of lidayn were all around us, and Arabs were running out and shouting welcome. In moments we were couching our camels by Fadlal Mula's tent. The broken-faced Arab came out and shook us by the hands, embracing us and clapping us on the back, saying, 'Your return is blest! Thank God for your safe return!' Other hands than ours unloaded and unsaddled our camels for the first time. We were led off to the small tent where we sat in a daze, waiting for someone to give us water. Instead Fadlal Mula presented us with some dwarf melons that had grown in his millet plot. As I bit into the juicy fruit, I thought that there could be no more fitting reward for such a journey.

I rested for the remainder of the day, and in the evening Fadlal Mula sent his youngest son to massage my feet with a bottle of liquid butter. As the boy rubbed the stuff in and gently massaged them, I thought that this act spoke more than words could ever do. It was, I knew, a singular honour.

After dark Fadlal Mula said, 'We had better slaughter a goat.' He went to fetch one. Mohammid cut its throat, and hung the carcass from a pole outside the tent. A host of uncles and cousins came to join us and to ask about our journey. 'What did Omar do?' was the question they always asked. 'Omar did plenty,' Mohammid said. 'He dug out the salt for all the camels almost single-handed.' Then I warmed to my companion, and felt ashamed for some of the differences we had had. The meat did not go far, but for once I was satisfied. After the meal Fadlal Mula called Mohammid and said, 'The camels need watering, and we need water for the tent. You had better go to the wells. Take your blanket because they are almost dry. You will be there all night.' Mohammid took a skin and went off without a word.

I watched Mohammid as he collected the camels. This was his welcome home, after the most arduous of journeys. For the Arabs the necessity of survival never ceased. The life they lived was one of bitter hardship: digging through twelve feet of clay to find water, killing one of the last goats to feed a stranger, staying up all the freezing night to water camels, travelling 400 miles through cold, heat and burning hunger to bring back salt. It meant living in these squalid conditions, with no shade, no room, no privacy, only lice and dirt and discomfort. It was this that produced the whip scars and the talk of killing, the surreptitious sex and the refusal to make a single sound of pain.

Yet the Kababish lived this life out of choice. At almost any time in their history they could have moved to the palm groves of the Nile and become river farmers. They could have dispossessed the cultivators in the green belt and settled there. They preferred the harsher world of the desert because it defined them and gave them a unique identity. They did not hate the desert. To them it was everything.

9
Legend
of the Drums

These Kababish are the perfect devil.
*British military staff officer, personal
letter, 1902*

For the second time in the Sarajab camp I was woken up roughly,
this time by someone shouting, '*Gom!* See the *gom!*' I opened my
eyes lazily and saw Fadlal Mula standing at the gap of his tent,
with his old rifle in one hand, gesticulating towards the desert. As I
staggered to my feet, bleary-eyed, I saw that the landscape was full
of camels and camel riders. There were at least 200 of them, seeming to straddle the desert, winding back towards the southern skyline.
They marched doggedly forwards like soldier-ants, intent on our tiny
island of green.

'Meidob!' shouted Mohammid's cousin, running up from his
tent. 'They mean to put an end to us, by God Almighty!'

'No,' Fadlal Mula said. 'They are Dar Hamid.'

Mohammid came bounding across the tribulus from the direction of the wells. Five or six Arabs ran after him, all carrying their
rifles. I watched them as they scattered into the thorn trees along the
edge of the oasis. One of them raised his rifle as if to fire at the men
tramping towards us on their camels. 'Stop!' Fadlal Mula shouted.
'Let us see who they are!' The three of us trotted down to join the
other Sarajab.

The leading riders were about 200 metres away when suddenly
a rider detached himself from the multitude and rode towards us at
a trot. The camels following him stopped. As he came into easy
range, I saw the Arabs stiffen, facing the horde like grim little hornets
defending their nest. Within forty metres the man swung down from
his saddle and crossed the rest of the distance on foot. He was a
weedy black man who wore a pair of spectacles and what looked

182

like a ragged tweed jacket over his *jibba*. He carried no weapon except a camel-whip.

'Peace be on you!' he shouted.

'And on you be peace!' Fadlal Mula replied. 'Come forward.'

The men shook hands and exchanged a greeting. 'What is your family and where are you going?' the Sarajabi demanded in the imperative Arab manner.

'My family is Dar Hamid, and I am guide for these men. They are mostly from El Obeid – Dar Hamid, Jawa'ama, Bedariyya – I am taking them to Libya. This oasis has the only decent grazing south of Wadi Howar. You would not refuse to receive travellers in your land?'

'Grazing is one thing,' Fadlal Mula growled. 'But we have ripe millet. You will find good grass on the north side of the oasis, but if a single camel gets into the millet there will be trouble!'

The man smiled and beckoned to his followers. Within moments they were passing us in a great procession. The riders were broad-faced city men, like those I had met at El 'Atrun. Their eyes were full of fatigue and many of them clung to their camels awkwardly, obviously unaccustomed to riding. Their camels were big, healthy animals carrying brand-new pack saddles, bulging waterskins and nylon sacks of flour. None of them had any proper saddle gear. After the riders came the infantry – more than a hundred men on foot. They staggered rather than walked, drumming onwards with nerv-ous, spasmodic movements. They passed us looking neither right nor left, following the men in front as if they were blind or mesmer-ized.

Soon they had unloaded their camels on the outer rim of the oasis. The camels were hobbled and shuffled about cropping the grass, while some of the men began to fill net baskets with the taller grasses. Moments later cooking fires had been lit, and the camp was full of smoke and the babble of voices. The men had divided themselves into messes for feeding, and the guide called myself and Fadlal Mula over to join them. We ate the porridge they pre-sented, and I looked at the black faces around me, which seemed as incongruous in this arid environment as my own must have done. One of them asked if I was a Libyan, and his question showed just how remote these people thought themselves to be: to them this place was beyond the borders of the known world. For them, as for me, this was not the Sudan, but the wild and incomprehensible no man's land of the desert.

The guide told us that his route led through El 'Atrun and to the oasis of Nukheila beyond. From there it was another eight days to the border post at 'Uwaynat and another six to Kufra. I asked the men why they wanted to go to Libya. They replied that they were after work, any kind of work. They would work as butchers, waiters, labourers. They would stay there for three or four years and then return to their own country to marry and settle down. 'You cannot get enough money even to marry in the Sudan,' someone said. 'In the town you have to pay 2,000 pounds for a respectable girl!'

The guide asked us for news of police patrols in the El 'Atrun region: this kind of emigration through the back door was illegal. I asked if they had heard the stories about immigrants being drafted into Colonel Gadaffi's 'Islamic Foreign Legion'. 'It is not so bad!' the guide cut in defensively. 'They get paid well, and every recruit gets a Libyan wife!'

Many townsmen like these had died on the road to Libya. They were improvident and had little idea how much food and water was needed. They could buy one camel between three or four men, taking turns to ride and thinking that the animal could carry limitless provisions. Several years earlier a caravan of men from Darfur had been lost north of Nukheila. Out of forty men only two had survived. The same happened again in 1985 when more than fifty men from the El Obeid region died of thirst in the desert. Their bodies were found by a truck driver en route from Kufra to Darfur.

After the meal the men began to pack up. Half an hour later we watched the column as it marched off northwards and disappeared into the desert sands.

Rest, rest, rest, was all my body craved. For most of the day I sought out the shade and left it only to eat and drink: porridge, goat's milk, dates, tea, the remainder of the goat. As the hours passed, the familiar ache of hunger receded. I had never expected the meagre fare of this place to seem so opulent. Over the three days I remained at Iidayn my body recovered some of its vitality. It was much needed, for the journey was by no means over: we still had two hundred kilometres to cover between Iidayn and Sawanat al Haworab, where the natron would be sold. On the second day Mohammid disappeared, and I was pleased when his mother asked me to perform some of the household tasks in his stead: filling waterskins, watering goats and collecting camels.

Watering was always a difficult task here. Many of the Arabs spent days digging through the blue clay to be rewarded with only a few skins of water. Some of the wells were dry, and the others were in constant demand; this meant a long wait in the biting winds that seared down from the hills. Often the Arabs were reluctant to hand over the well bucket and occasionally I quarrelled with them. Often I wondered just how enduring a man had to be to live in this place.

On the morning of the third day Mohammid woke me from a deep sleep, saying, 'We had better get moving. I have been to see my Ribaygat girl again!'

'Did they catch you?'

'No, but they will find my tracks.'

'They will kill you this time!'

'Let them try! I am not afraid of them. But I cannot pay another fine to the nazir!'

It took us only a few hours to sort out the salt. We made up new loads, about half the weight of those we had brought from El 'Atrun, so that we could manage them more easily between the two of us. Mohammid said that we should meet one of his cousins further south, who would help us.

Before we loaded, Fadlal Mula came up and said, 'Omar, why not sell me your shotgun? You will not need it again – I will give you money for it.' I looked at the old weapon, remembering the dreadful scene with Balla in Zalat Hammad. I was not superstitious, but it seemed to me that the thing had brought me nothing but trouble. I remembered how, years ago, I had put away the pistol I had carried in Northern Ireland, vowing that I should never carry firearms again. I had not kept that vow, but firearms had always led to trouble. I handed him the gun and the cartridges, saying, 'Take it!' As he took the weapon, I suddenly felt pounds lighter; but this was not the last I was to hear of it. I still had my ·22 revolver, which I had carried on many journeys. Now I no longer needed that either. I had a good idea what I should do with it.

Fadlal Mula and his wife came to see us off, but there was no ceremony. Within moments Mohammid and I had left the oasis and were leading our camels back into the bleak winter landscape of the desert. As we walked, Mohammid said, 'I told you I should see her again. They will not make me give her up, by God!'

185

'Will you ever be able to marry her?'

'Not unless the husband divorces her.'

'Is that possible?'

'Only if she runs away from his tent or refuses to sleep with him.'

'Do you think they will follow you?'

'Yes. If they catch us will you fight?'

I knew that it was incumbent upon me to defend my companion, but my body had suffered much in the thousands of miles I had ridden in the past few months. I said, 'Of course!' but I wondered wearily how much more fight I had in me.

We spent the night under the cold ramparts of Shaynat mountain. In the middle of the night I was woken from a doze by my companion saying, 'Look, here they are!' Mohammid pointed out four dusky forms riding along the base of the mountain. They were going south. As they disappeared into the night, Mohammid whispered, 'They did not see us. I am certain they were Ribaygat, by God!'

A strong wind was blowing as we led the caravan down into the valley the next morning. Sand sifted like snow through the bony battalions of the thorn trees. Within minutes the tracks of the nightriders were covered, and it was comforting to know that ours too would soon be lost under the spindrift. We had only five camels with us now. Wad at Tafashan looked thin and ravaged, though the knowledge that he was returning to his own pastures probably kept him going. Still our animals played up, casting loads and snapping ropes. Even though the animals were fewer and the packs much lighter, each stoppage drained a little more from the small reservoir of energy I had built up.

In the afternoon we came upon a rich vein of grazing. We stopped and turned the camels loose. Mohammid's cousin found us there. He was a well-groomed Arab named Sulayman with a faintly menacing manner; he wore a Webley ·45 in his belt like a cowboy. I discovered that he had just been released from prison, where he had been sentenced to death for murder. 'It was all over a woman!' Sulayman told me. 'Her husband caught us, and I stabbed him to death. Then the nazir's men tracked me down and I was handed over to the police.' He described how the judge had sentenced him to death and how he had waited in his cell for the day of the hanging. 'The day before they were going to string me up, they said that I had been reprieved. I got five years instead!'

'Weren't you afraid?'

'Not me!' he scoffed. 'We all die when our time is up. But I hated being in that prison! You are cooped up worse than a goat!'

'Do you leave women alone now?'

'No, by God! I shall never leave women alone!'

And as if to demonstrate this beyond doubt, he said to Mohammid, 'There is a Ruwahla camp near here. The men are away, but the women are there.'

'Why don't we try them?' Mohammid said.

They prepared for the excursion by burning a flake of incense and inhaling the smoke deeply beneath their blankets. Mohammid told me that it was a potent aphrodisiac. I agreed to stay and look after the camels, and the two of them rode off into the night.

It was sunrise when they returned, saying, 'Come on Omar! Let's get out of here!' When the camels were packed, we moved off into the bushland. By now the desert steppe had fallen away and we were in more wooded country. All day the Arabs discussed their new conquests, and boasted about how easy it had been. 'I cheated her!' Mohammid announced. 'I said I would just sleep next to her, and not touch her. But I did!'

It was another four days before we reached Sawani. No irate brothers or husbands caught up with us, yet for me those last days were torture. We had little food left and still we shivered at night, praying for sleep. My small colony of lice had undergone a popu-lation explosion and was viciously irritating after dark. But I was most worried about my camel. The gall on his back had gone septic, and one morning, as I mounted, he snapped at me for the first time. I realized he must be in pain, and would not carry me much further. I felt black inside, and thought only of journey's end.

Eventually I had to dismount and walk. We passed close to the pool at Kilagi from where I had set off into the *jizzu* with At Tom and the others. There were no Arabs there now. The pool was dry and its bed baked hard. Gone was the hustle, the life that had bloomed here like a brief flower. We travelled around the hard-packed rim of the pool. There were broken trees and the discarded artifacts of the nomads – lengths of torn *shugga*, pieces of hob-bling-ropes, the frame of a cabin eaten by termites. Everywhere there were the mangy white bones of camels, some of them set hard in the dry mud. Desiccation had come here like an avenger, leaving only a graveyard of hopes. I remembered how the Nurab had ridden forth from their summer-camps, moving joyously towards these rain-pools. Their joy had turned to despair when the rains failed and the *jizzu* had fizzled out.

There were many families moving south of Kilagi, going back to their camps in Hamrat ash Sheikh. The goats – black, white and brown – looked thin and lacking in milk. The sheep were small and underdeveloped, and the camels were blighted with grey-black patches of mange. As we moved past them, Mohammid said, 'Those camels will soon be dead too!'

I wondered grimly what would happen next summer, when the Kababish had to swelter again in their camps, surrounded by animals for which there was no pasture. I doubted if there was any alternative for them, but to move south into Central Kordofan or South Darfur; but if they did so there would undoubtedly be conflict with other tribes.

Now I had been denied the comfort of riding, the days seemed interminable. I stumped on through the acacias and the *mukhayyit*, too weary to think or talk. Sleep eluded me at night, and hunger became sharper as our supply of flour ran out. When it had gone, Sulayman proudly produced a bag of dried gazelle meat that was very wizened and very old. We ate it raw as we had no oil to cook it in. After we ate, I quickly had a resurgence of the diarrhoea I had suffered at El 'Atrun; Mohammid vomited vilely, and lay groaning all night.

At last we saw the peaked roofs of Sawani peering over miles of scrub. I mounted Wad at Tafashan for the final effort: the last leg of any journey always seems the longest. We lurched and rocked forwards, weaving around the trees for what seemed like hours – then suddenly we were couching our camels in front of one of the straw shops. Across the convex slope of grass I could see the small court-house where I should find Ali at Tom's brother, the magistrate of this area. This, and the five or six rambling structures of cane and mud, were the first buildings I had seen for months; this was civilization.

It was a tremendous anticlimax. I felt hollow and emotionless as I dismounted. One of the fat merchants came out to greet us and brought us a melon, which he bounced once on the ground so that it split in half. The juicy maroon flesh was irresistible. As we crouched down to eat, I realized that this was our last meal together. The dream was over.

Afterwards Mohammid said that he and Sulayman would take

the camels off to browse in the wadi. Before they left I reached into my saddle-bag and brought out my ·22 pistol. It was scarred and battered, the victim of many journeys. When I handed it to him, his face lit up with surprise and delight. He put the gun away in his pocket and we embraced, touching each other lightly on the shoulder with our right hands.

'By God's will, we shall meet again,' he said.

'Amen.'

I watched the cousins leading their minute salt caravan to the wadi, then I roused my camel and limped off towards the court-house.

I arrived in Hamrat ash Sheikh the following day. I led Wad at Tafashan up to the two corrugated iron shacks that formed the centre of the market. We were on the verge of collapse, both mental and physical. Just then a voice said, 'As salaam 'alaykum!' It was Juma' Wad Tarabish, mounted on his camel. With him were Mahmoud and Mura'fib. They jumped down from their mounts and embraced me with real warmth. 'Omar! By God Almighty, you have got weak!' they shouted, slapping me on the back. They took me up to the nazir's old house that stood on the crest of a hill. It was a delapidated collection of mud huts and straw dwellings in a yard that had once been encircled by a stockade. There was a single tree in the yard, and I tied Wad at Tafashan to it. As he sat down, his neck drooped and his head sagged, he was too exhausted even to sniff the fresh leaves. The door of one of the huts flew open, and out came Wad az Ziyadi and Hamid with a white-haired old man. 'Omar! Thanks to God for your safe arrival!'

It was another bitterly cold night, but for once I was protected from the wind by thick mud walls. The old man, Khalifa, who was the watchman of the house, made us tea; Wad Tarabish came back from the bakery with a pile of fresh loaves and some slivers of roasted meat, and Wad az Ziyadi brought out some handfuls of dates. We ate with gusto. Khalifa lit an oil lamp that spluttered as a chilling blast rattled the rafters and pierced the cracks in the boarded-up window. We sat on our sheepskins on the mud floor. After we ate, Wad az Ziyadi explained that they had just arrived from Sodari, the administrative capital of the *dar*, where they had presented the Requisition camels to the local officer. 'We got ninety-four camels in the end,' he told me. I thought of the Sarajab, and could work up no enthusiasm for the Requisition: it seemed futile. I knew that even if the hospital opened here, the Arabs who needed it most would never use it.

I asked after At Tom. Hamid said, 'He has returned to the *dikka*. The nazir is still very ill, and At Tom is now head of the tribe until his father recovers. The *dikka* is no longer at Umm Sunta. It has been moved to the wintering ground at Umm Qozayn.'

They asked about the Sarajab and my experiences with them, but I was not prepared to go into the details of the journey to El 'Atrun. 'They are bandits!' Wad az Ziyadi commented. 'You found they could not be trusted and no doubt!'

'They are bandits, but they are brave men,' I said. 'Their life is hard. They are strong and not afraid.'

'Anyone who goes to Al Ga'a is strong!' Wad az Ziyadi answered.

It was an obvious compliment, but I was too weary to rise to it. I was grey and washed out. I did not feel proud of my journey to El 'Atrun, only humbled by the endurance of my companions. I knew that I had learned some shattering lessons on the way there, but tonight I was too confused to know what they were. I could only think about the salt, and reflect with bewilderment and relief that I would never again have to load those sacks of natron. It was not until much later that I realized how welcoming these Nurab had been, and how this reception had made my return a real homecoming.

Next morning the *ghaffirs* rode off to the *nuggara* herds that were grazing near Umm Qozayn. They took Wad at Tafashan with them, and as they led him off I wondered if he would survive the tremendous shock his body had sustained.

After they had gone, I sat in the hut with Khalifa. He was thin and sickly, and his eyesight poor. 'Why do you stay here?' I asked him. 'No one uses this place any more, do they?'

'No,' he answered. 'It was built by Sir Ali Wad at Tom. But the present nazir never uses it now.'

'Then why are you here?'

'There is a good reason,' he drawled. 'A very good reason.' He waved a bony hand towards the back of the hut. There was an iron bedstead standing against the wall, rusty with age. It supported something lumpy and thick covered with a mouldy canvas sheet. 'That!' he said mysteriously. 'That is why I am here!'

He pulled at the canvas sheet weakly until it slipped off: I was astonished to see five brightly polished copper kettle drums. A single ray of light from the boarded window struck the burnished skins, and they threw the light back brilliantly. They looked very valuable. I was astonished that they should be here in the midst of such delapidation; it was like finding the crown jewels of England on a building site. 'There they are!' the old man gloated. 'These are the *nahas* – the war drums of the tribe. I am their guardian.'

I could not resist touching the red copper skin: my hand left a dirty mark on the shining metal. I saw that there were two large drums and three smaller ones. 'They all have names,' Khalifa told me. 'The biggest is called "Bull" and the second biggest "Cow" – the other three are "Calves".'

'Where did they come from?' I asked.

'These drums were given to the nazir Fadlallah Wad Salim. That was long ago, before the English came. They are old, these drums, older than anyone alive now. They were given to Fadlallah Wad Salim by the Khedive of Egypt, Mohammid Ali Basha. They have been handed down for generations. No one is truly nazir unless he has the *nahas*.'

'When was this?' I inquired.

'Fadlallah Wad Salim was the grandfather of Sheikh Hassan's grandfather, that is the grandfather of Sir Ali at Tom. He passed the drums on to his son, At Tom Wad Fadlallah, at the beginning of the Mahdi's revolution. Most of the tribes joined the Mahdi, but At Tom Wad Fadlallah refused. He knew that it would not be long before the Mahdi's men captured him, so he sent the drums to his brother, Salih al Bey, who was hiding in the desert. Salih rode out of his camp one night with his slave. They took the drums with them – there were only four of them then, "Bull", "Cow" and two "Calves". They took them to the foot of Jabal Aw Dun and buried them in pits. Before they had finished, Salih drew his sword and *shshickck!* – he cut the slave's head clean off! Those were hard days, by God! Salih knew that dead men tell no secrets. He was the only man alive who knew where the drums were hidden. Not long after that At Tom was killed by the Mahdi, and Salih became nazir of the Kababish.'

'What happened to him?'

'They killed him in the end. He stayed a rebel and attacked the Mahdi's army. By that time the Mahdi himself was dead, and in his place was the Khalifa Abdallahi. Abdallahi hated Salih and sent an army to capture him, led by a man called Jarayjir. Jarayjir was from the Bani Jarrar and there was a blood feud between him and Salih. Salih had killed his father and his cousin.'

191

'How did he die?'

'They fought him at Umm Badr and chased him into the desert again. Then they killed most of his family. In the end he had no wish to carry on living. He just spread his sheepskin on the ground and waited for death. The enemy surrounded him and said, "Come with us to the Khalifa!" "I will die here!" he answered. Then Jarayjir came forward and cut his head off! By Almighty God, what men they were in those days! They put his head on a spike in Omdurman. It was there for thirty days!'

'But if the secret of the drums died with Salih,' I asked, 'how did they come to be here?'

'Hah, that is a story of its own,' the old man answered. 'You must ask Sheikh Musa about it, for I will tell you no more!'

Try as I might, I could get nothing further out of him.

Part 3
The Trek to Egypt

_____10_____
Interlude
in the Damar

They are nomads as their fathers and their
fathers' fathers . . . and the nomad has
changed but little since Joseph watered
the flocks of Laban at Harran.
Sir Harold MacMichael, Tribes of
Northern and Central Kordofan, _1912_

I had almost forgotten the war with the Zayadiyya, but in the _dikka_
it was still on everyone's lips. In January a boy from the 'Awajda was
shot dead as he herded his family's flocks near Umm Qozayn; the
Zayadiyya were suspected. Not long afterwards three camels were
stolen from the _nuggara_ herd, and the bouncy little Arab we had
met at Shigil, Ali at Tom Wad al Murr, led a pursuit party into Zayadiyya country. Eleven of the twelve Kababish who had been
arrested for the murder of Tahir were still languishing in a Darfur
prison; the twelfth had died of an illness contracted there.

In February I visited Sheikh Hassan in Omdurman. He lay bed-
ridden in the house of the Kababish guarantor, Sheikh Jami', para-
lysed on the left side of his body. It was distressing to see him in this
state when I remembered how, the year before, I had ridden with
him in the ranges of the Bahr. This was to be our last meeting.

The _dikka_ was pitched at Umm Qozayn so that the goats and
sheep could be watered at the pool there. It was a cold winter, and
the sense of depression I had sensed during the summer had
returned. For the Nurab in particular, it had been a desolate year. Al
Murr was dead and Hassan was dying. The royal family was in
mourning, and the herds had returned from the north earlier than
ever. Many cows had died already, and more animals would die if
the conditions did not improve. The _dar_ was wasting away, as if an
evil spirit had moved across it, withering the trees and the grasses,
blighting the sheep and the cattle.

195

At Tom had taken over the effective leadership of the tribe. He was a strong character, but young and inexperienced. The local government was pressing for a solution to the continuing hostilities with the Zayadiyya, and in February the sheikhs of the tribe gathered to meet the chiefs of their rivals in the Darfur town of Umm Kaddada.

Meanwhile I stayed in the *dikka* in Umm Qozayn, and in Umm Sunta when it was moved back there. I saw much of Salim Wad Musa and his friend Ibrahim Wad Hassan, a very dignified young man, who was one of the small corps of educated Kababish. The nazir's people were very hospitable and generous, yet now the *dikka* seemed as formal as a royal palace in contrast with the austerity of the desert. I yearned for the bitter-sweet life I had tasted amongst the 'Atawiyya and the Sarajab, and my thoughts turned constantly to the desert.

I wanted to complete the journey I had set out to make with the Rizayqat, the journey to Egypt. It was the longest of the nomadic treks – almost a thousand miles – taking camel herds to be sold in the Cairo market; with my Rizayqat I had covered only two-thirds of the route. I was certain that with my powerful friends amongst the Kababish I should now be able to find someone willing to take me the whole way. Salim told me that there were several Kababish merchants in the area gathering camels for export, and that he would keep an eye out for any herds that might be leaving in the near future.

The days went by with featureless calm. I spent my time walking around the market in the village, talking with the traders and the nomads who rode in from the surrounding deserts to obtain their few needs. One thing that became clear was that the traditional economy of the nomads was dying. Despite their antipathy nomads and farmers had always lived in symbiosis. To the Kababish grain was essential. Without it the families could not separate for part of the year. The farmers relied on the nomads for meat and for draft animals, which they could not produce in large enough numbers. In 1979 a sack of sorghum flour had cost only £S10, while a camel might fetch £S300. Now, three years later, the price of sorghum had risen to £S50, and livestock prices were falling. This meant that the Kababish were obliged to sell more animals than previously in order to maintain the same standard of living. They were reluctant to sell, for tradition dictated that they keep as large a herd as possible. This made sense, for their herds were their capital, and it was logical to preserve that capital and live only on the interest. If they were forced to sell their livestock faster than the animals could reproduce, it meant the eventual loss of their herds and flocks. Without them the nomads had nothing.

In the past the Kababish had bought grain from the farming tribes in Central Kordofan and had transported it themselves by camel; now almost all of their supplies came from Omdurman by lorry. If the farmers had been able to keep grain prices down, the Omdurman supplies might eventually have been cheaper, but rising prices were added to by transport and fuel costs. A clique of truck owners had grown fat as middle-men in the trade. It seemed, as so often before, that new technology was interfering with the traditional ways, concentrating power in few hands.

Often I visited the bore-well in Umm Sunta, sitting in the shade of the two black iron water-towers and looking out across the mounds of bone-dry ordure that surrounded the iron troughs. The Kababish herds were being watered here every sixteen days, and every day men and women came to fill waterskins and plastic containers. Some of them were professional water-carriers, while others drew water for their families only. The well supervisor was Sheikh Hassan's brother-in-law Mohammid Reyd, and I frequently chatted to him as I sat there. Here too I saw the same pattern of decline, brought about partly by reliance on modern technology. 'The bore-well used to work efficiently,' he told me. 'But lately the fuel has been so expensive and difficult to get that the pumps are idle. Then the herds have to wait for days, or go back to Hamrat ash Sheikh where there are deep-wells. It was better in the old days. There were fewer camels and sheep, but the Arabs watered in the hand-dug wells and did not rely on fuel.'

One of the water-carriers, a Nurabi called Ismael, became a particular friend. He was never in a hurry to fill his great double-sided waterskin, and was quite ready to talk about his life. 'When I was young our condition was fine,' he told me. 'My father had plenty of livestock and I was the only adult son. We were happy. Then he got married to a second wife and moved to Omdurman. We never saw him after that. He had many children, and when he died the animals were divided. Over the years we ate what was left of them. Now I only have a few goats, such as the poor have, but God knows, animals can be devils anyway! Take my uncle – he had plenty of cattle. Last year he sold ten bullocks to a merchant for 350 each. Then, just as

197

he went to get on his donkey, my uncle regretted it. "Here, keep your money!" he said. "My cattle are too good to sell!" The same year he was hit by disease and nine of the ten died. Stupidity, you see! Animals can drive you mad, by God!'

In the evenings I sometimes sat in the room of the school-house with Salim, Ibrahim and an old Arab called Marghani. We would sit around a smoky oil lamp, and someone would bring a bowl of seasoning and some round, flat loaves. Marghani was another of the few educated Arabs. He had been a pupil of the famous Hassan Najila, the tutor of Sir Ali at Tom's children, and the first teacher to work in the *dar*. I had read Najila's account of his work and experiences, *Memories of the Desert*, and was fascinated to meet one of his students. I asked the old man about the changes he had seen in the area. 'The Kababish were rich once,' he told me. 'They were the richest tribe in the Sudan. A Kabbashi would look down on a farmer, not because he was a slave, but because he was poor. The nomads had everything. Now we have no future as nomads. We must make livestock breeding more commercial, even if it means cutting down on the numbers and improving the strain. We need to buy lorries and start trading. If the Arabs cannot adapt to the new conditions, they will die, by God!'

There was much in what he said, but I could not forget that Marghani belonged to the élite of the tribe. The nazir's people were in every way atypical; they were a tiny minority amongst the Kababish – less than a hundred households. Outside this clan few Arabs could even read or write. I remembered how Mohammid Wad Fadlal Mula had scorned the idea of living in a city, and how the other Sarajab in the Wadi al Milik had scoffed at the notion that they had any duty to the government. There were several schools in the *dar*, but their pupils were mainly from the Nurab. This was not intentional policy; when they had first been opened, there had been a proportional number of places set aside for each tribe, but the Arabs of the desert would have nothing to do with them.

I slowly built up a picture of this land as it had been in previous years. I started to see and understand the matrix of factors that was already crushing the life from these people. Much of the grazing had simply disappeared. Over twenty species of grass had gone from their normal places in the previous ten years, and several species of trees no longer grew. With them had gone the wildlife that once flourished here. If conditions did not improve, the nomads would have no choice but to move south. I asked one old man of the Nurab if he would move to the city. 'What should I do in the city?' he asked me. 'I went to the city once. So much noise, and such smells, and people I didn't know. No one invited me, by God! One day was enough for me! The next ten years will see the end!'

As I was buying cloth in the market one day, a decrepit old Arab touched me on the arm. He was bowed and wizened and wore a dirty, dishevelled *jibba*, and a headcloth that was full of holes. 'You are a *nasrani!*' he said. 'You are like the *nasrani* I went with in the desert!'

I could hardly make out what he was saying. Though I knew that *nasrani* meant 'Christian', it was a word not normally used by the Arabs, who referred to Europeans as *'Ajam*. 'I went with the *nasrani* looking for Zarzura,' he continued. 'It was beyond Al Ga'a and beyond Nukheila. We were riding for days and we thought we should die. Then the *nasrani* took us to an oasis. It wasn't Zarzura. It was Selima. From there we went to the river!'

Just then Salim came up and hustled the old man away, saying, 'He is half crazy! Don't listen to his talk!'

If I had done more research into the early exploration of the area then, I should have realized at once that the old man was by no means mad. He was referring to the expedition, completed by Douglas Newbold and William Shaw in the south Libyan desert in 1928. One of their objects had been to locate the site of the lost oasis of Zarzura.

I was diverted, however, by Salim's news. He told me that a herd raised by an Arab of the Barara, Abdal Karim Wad al Ghaybish, was due to leave for Egypt shortly. I decided to collect Wad at Tafashan from the bore-well at Umm Sunta the following day, when the *nuggara* camels were being watered, and ride to Abdal Karim's camp.

But before I left I was determined to hear the conclusion of the story of the Kababish drums. Salim told me that his father, Sheikh Musa, was the leading authority on tribal history and advised me to ask him. His tent was the last in the straggling cluster of the *dikka*. As I approached it, a pack of snarling dogs broke from under its eaves, baring their yellow fangs as they dashed towards me. At the crucial moment the Sheikh appeared in the door-gap and shouted to them, halting them in their tracks. 'You should always carry a stick with you!' he told me. 'These animals are dangerous!'

Inside his tent there were two rope-beds, and the ground was covered by a thick woven carpet. A number of decorated saddle-bags hung on the wall. The Sheikh's servant brought me tea, and as I drank he said, 'Salim tells me you are interested in the *nahas*.'

I explained that I should like to know how the lost drums came to be found.

'You know that Salih al Bey was killed by the Khalifa's men,' Sheikh Musa said. 'And that afterwards no one knew where the *nahas* was buried. They searched for it in Jabal Aw Dun, but it was not found. In those days there was some pasture in the mountain, and the Ghilayan used to graze their camels there. Often on windy nights they would hear a great drum booming in the hills. They said it was the jinn who live in the wild places. The Arabs always blame the jinn! Others said that it was the lost drums of Salih al Bey. One day a Ghilayani called Abdallah Dugushayn was riding along the foot of the mountain, when he saw something big and shiny in a thorn tree. It was a copper vessel with handles. He did not know what it was, so he took it to his sheikh. The sheikh knew it at once. "Almighty God!" he said. "It is the 'Bull' – one of the lost drums of Salih al Bey." He advised Abdallah to take it to the nazir, who was my father, Ali Wad at Tom. The *dikka* was at Haraz then. He was a tricky one, that Abdallah. Before he gave the drum to my father, he said, "Sheikh Ali, I have brought you the 'Bull' – what will you give me in return?" My father asked him what reward he wished, and Abdallah said, "I want freedom from taxes!" My father said, "That I cannot grant you, for taxes belong to the government, not to me. But you will have your reward." Then the "Bull" was brought in and there was a great celebration in the *dikka*. They slaughtered an ox, and there was dancing and singing. Soon they reskinned the drum and its voice was heard for miles. All the Arabs around Haraz heard it and hurried to the *dikka*. They said, "The 'Bull' has returned. Now Ali Wad at Tom is really chief of the Kababish!" They said the *nahas* would bring them luck, and it did, for the nazirate of my father was the best time of all for the Kababish!'

'What about the other drums?' I asked him. 'I saw five in Hamrat ash Sheikh.'

'My father asked the government to supply him with three smaller drums to make up the set. There were always four *nahas* amongst the Kababish.'

'What about the fifth?'

'Aah! That is my part of the story. The fifth drum is the one called

"Cow". I found it being used by some Ghilayan to water their goats. It was in 1952 in Marikh, exactly fifty years after the "Bull" returned. It was filthy and green with age. The Arabs did not know where it had come from, but I knew it was the "Cow". I took it to the camp of my brother, Mohammid al Murr, and the old men remembered it. We reskinned it and put it with the rest. But it brought us no luck. The fortunes of the Kababish died with my father. Now look at us! If the rains don't get better, we will be finished!'

That evening I wished farewell to my friends amongst the nazir's people. At Tom told me that he had concluded a truce with the Zayadiyya, and that blood money would be paid by both sides. 'The Arabs who were in prison will be released,' he told me. 'But it will not make much difference. The feelings between the tribes run too deep.' Ali at Tom had just returned from his foray into Darfur. 'We got the camels back,' he said. 'It was a lucky chance though. We the trail and we were in Mellit. There was a wedding feast for one of the rich Zayadiyya, so of course we joined in with the eating and drinking. A Saudi Arabian minister was guest of honour. Right in the middle of the feasting I saw a "Son of the Forbidden" riding one of my camels! I grabbed hold of the rope and told him, "If you come down I will break your head open!" Then we dragged him down and took him to the police. He soon told us where the other camels were. It caused a stir all right! You should have seen the look on the Saudi's face! That was the best thing of all, by God!'

I told Salim Wad Musa that I should return later in the year. He warned me, 'Watch out for the Egyptian border police. They are not very hospitable!' Then we shook hands and embraced. 'Go in peace,' Salim said.

I was at the bore-well very early. It was a bright morning, and the camels were already crowding around the troughs when I arrived, a legion of reflecting shapes against the silver-grey background of the well-field. Many of the nazir's people were there, standing like a picket of generals about to review a parade. Amongst them were Mohammid Dudayn, Ibrahim Wad Hassan and Salim Wad Hassan. The herdsmen drove the camels into the troughs, rank after towering rank; they were now sixteen days without water. The animals shoved and squeezed their way to where the liquid flowed from the funnels, warm and clear. After some time I spotted Wad at Tafashan. He recognized me as I approached him and shuffled away, perhaps remembering the torture of the journey to El 'Atrun. He had become

201

a little fatter in the two months since I had seen him, and his winter coat had grown, giving him a bluish colour. One of the men bridled him and I led him away to prepare for the journey.

As I rode off towards Umm Batatikha, I was glad to be alone, to have a short breathing-space; so many impressions crowded into my mind, and I had not yet been able to get them into perspective. As the temperature rose, the sun baked the pale sand beneath the graveyards of the trees. I passed through the old site of the *dikka* where I had spent the last hot month of summer with Sheikh Hassan. I saw the frame of the tent where I had first got to know his family. I was again beset by a feeling of sadness as I looked at the ruins of the camp, the skeletons of the tents now bleak and desolate, where there had once been life. It was the sense of transitoriness that affected me – a townsman's emotion, which had little place in the lives of the nomads, whose sense of home was built around people rather than places.

In the afternoon I came to some tents of another branch of the nazir's family. They belonged to one of Sir Ali at Tom's widows, and I was welcomed by a powerful-looking man called Faraj whom I had once met in Umm Sunta. Inside the tent the old lady sat on her rug, looking stately and aristocratic. She told the servants to bring me tea and mutton. As I ate, Faraj told me, 'These tents are permanent. The lady cannot ride in a litter any more. So the herds move and she stays here.'

'But we are affected by it,' said the old duchess. 'We are used to the milk and meat and having a change of air.' I guessed that it was the last that affected her the most. It was difficult for a nomad to get used to the settled life after years of perpetual motion. I wondered how old she was. She had almost certainly been born in the age of Salih al Bey, the age before the engine, when camels were everything and when her husband, Ali Wad at Tom, had been the brightest rising star in the Kababish firmament. Now she was old and feeble, unable to stand the rigours of the migrations. I saw in the corner of the tent the frame of her litter. It was no ordinary litter. Its carefully carved and decorated laths of black wood were still brightly polished, a tribute to those far-off times when she had taken her place in the caravan of the nazir.

Faraj suggested that he should ride with me to the camp of Abdal Karim, and I agreed. He rode a white donkey and together we crossed a wasteland where the sand lay as clean as if it had been brushed, and only a thin rash of *siyaal* trees stood as sentinels of the changing environment. Two hours later we came upon a camp of five tents. Their thick roofs of camel-hair, grey, white and brown, blended in the pastel hues of the winter desert. As I couched my camel, a woman came out to welcome us. She was Abdal Karim's 'number-one' wife, deep bronze with flowing braids of black hair, wrapped in layers of colourful cloth. As I shook hands with her, I saw that though not young, she had impressive poise and dignity. Life in these deserts had matured but not marred her beauty. Behind her hid a troupe of shaven-headed little boys and a strikingly beautiful girl, as slim as a camel-whip. The woman called to some herdsmen who dragged rope-beds out of the tent and showed us a place to sleep, sheltered from the winds by a wooden *tukul*. The men hobbled Wad at Tafashan for me and led him off to pasture with the household animals. The woman said that Abdal Karim would not be back until late, and would meet us in the morning.

At dawn I was woken by the shouts of the little boys who came tumbling out of the tent and staged a noisy mock-battle outside. They were all very alike, almost naked and wearing the traditional curry-combs that showed them to be uncircumcised. The house camels, which had crept into the shelter of the *tukul* by night, were already on their feet and shambling off towards the nearest grazing, accompanied only by their gigantic shadows. A nest of goats was curled up under my bed, and behind me, through the bars of the *tukul*, I saw an old slave-woman lighting a fire. One of the herdsmen brought in a superb off-white riding camel from the eastern side of the camp and covered its snout with a nose-bag of grain. The animal tossed the bag impatiently as it munched the stuff. Another Arab climbed into the branches of a tree and brought down a sheaf of hay for the donkeys tethered beneath. All over the *dar* at this hour, the scene would be the same, as the immemorial life of the nomads went on.

After we had drunk tea, Abdal Karim came out to greet us. He was a big man with a face both young and old, shrouded in a white *tobe* against the cold. His hooked nose and curving moustache, and the copper skin braised by years of desert sun, gave him the look of a veteran camel-man. 'I received a message from Salim Wad Musa,' he told me. 'He said that you wish to travel to Egypt with my herd.'

I replied that I had once ridden as far as Dongola with a

203

dabuuka. 'Have you got permission to enter Egypt?' he inquired. I shook my head.

'Then you will have to be very careful,' he said. 'The Egyptians are not very welcoming to strangers.'

After we had eaten our breakfast of *kisri*, Abdal Karim introduced me to a thin, sick-looking negro who wore a red cap and faded blue overalls; his name was Khamis. 'I am building a deep-well here,' my host said proudly. 'And Khamis is the engineer who is helping me. Come over and look at it.' The well had been sunk into the bed of a wadi nearby and was about fifteen metres deep. The Kababish measured wells in 'men' – the height of a man with one arm held vertically above his head. Khamis told me that this well measured about five 'men'. Several of Abdal Karim's herdsmen were working inside it, scraping earth into leather pouches that were hoisted up from above. I remembered the hardship of the Sarajab, with their tiny, unproductive wells. There would be no such hardship for these Barara. 'When the well is ready I will never use the bore-well at Umm Batatikha,' Abdal Karim told me. 'I will water all the herds here. There is no talk of fuel shortage with a deep-well. This place will be my *damar* then, and I might even put up some mud buildings.'

Later Abdal Karim rode off to the village of Umm Batatikha and did not return till sunset. He told me then that the *dabuuka* was complete and ready to leave, but that the guide had not yet arrived from Umm Badr. As soon as he came, we would depart. He had a good look at Wad at Tafashan and commented, 'That camel is very weak. You have driven him too far. It takes a camel six months to recover from a long journey. He will have difficulty on the road to Egypt.'

As we sat talking outside the tents, he explained that he had first travelled to Egypt as a young herdsboy. 'I went there twice when I was just a boy,' he said. 'We crossed the Jabal Abyad rather than going up the river as they do now. It was easier then because there was grazing in the desert and you would always find Kababish herds. Now it is clean desert, and you will find nothing. After my first two trips, I went as guide. I would take thirty or forty camels, and for each 100 pounds they made I got ten. It was not much, but I made a profit by bringing back guns. I would buy them in the market at Isna. There were British rifles, 'Mother of Ten Shots' and FN pistols and sometimes those old Martini carbines. We would load them on our camels and disappear into the desert. We crossed a mountain called Abu Sinn and brought them down to the Ga'ab oasis near Dongola. Often the Egyptian police would come after us in their trucks. We would stop and fight them until we drove them off. It was kill or be killed then! The Egyptians had no guts. They would not stand up to the Arabs, by God! I have been to Egypt many times and I know the desert well. I was taking camels there long before you could load them on to the trains at Isna. We took them all the way to the market at Umm Baba in Giza. It was a hard route, though. Later the gun-running got more difficult and the borders were carefully watched. We started to come back on the steamer then, and brought ordinary goods instead. You know, I have not been to Egypt for twenty years, but I still know it better than most!'

Egypt was the main market for camels raised in Kordofan and Darfur. The Egyptians ate a great deal of camel meat, which was generally unpopular in the Sudan. For centuries the Egyptians obtained their camel meat from the bedouin tribes of Jordan, Syria, Iraq and the Arabian Peninsula, but during the past fifty years import of camels from those sources had virtually dried up. Instead Egypt imported almost all her camels from the Sudan. The number of camels in the Middle East had declined drastically during that time. In Syria alone the camel population had decreased by 90 per cent. The ancient masters of camel breeding – the Arabian bedouins – could no longer compete with the African countries in their tradi-tional expertise. Many of them had left the wandering life and settled in or near cities. Even those who stayed in the desert used lorries to bring water and grass to their herds. The Saudi Arabian government paid its nomads a subsidy for their livestock, but this made little difference when the Saudis themselves could afford to import camels from the Sudan and Somalia. It was the persistence of the old ways in these countries that had, until now, made them the most efficient producers of camels.

It was another five days before the guide arrived. I spent much of that time exploring the area, talking to the herdsmen and visiting the camps of other Barara. I found one family living in a tent of camel-hair that was grey and threadbare with age. They possessed nothing but a broken rope-bed, a thin donkey and some much-patched waterskins. The old man and his wife who lived there were friendly, and would not hear of me parting without eating porridge with them. 'As the house gets bigger, the herds get smaller, that is what the Arabs say,' the old man told me. 'I used to have two good herds of camels. We had cows and even horses. The cows died of disease and the camels stopped giving birth when the grazing failed. We ate the remainder one by one. Now I have nothing but this old donkey and a few goats. I have a son in Omdurman who is doing well. Every year I mean to go there, but somehow I never manage it.' I watched his wife as she tipped out a sackful of sorghum bit by bit into a metal sieve. 'The grain is always full of dirt these days!' she complained. 'And at fifty pounds a sack too!'

Once I rode with Abdal Karim to inspect the herd at Umm Batati-kha. We trotted across a tableland of parched bush with deadfall lying broken in the sand. The trees were as grey as corpses, though climbing up a gentle rise we came to a spiky mass of *tundub* that was still green. 'My brother lies buried under those trees,' my companion told me. 'He was a better guide than I. He was one of the Arabs who first opened up the modern trade route to Egypt.' Not long afterwards the settlement appeared suddenly out of the wasteland. It was a ramshackle camel-town of grass huts and cabins of the usual deadfall, grey and termite-infested. Like other dammer-ing centres in the *dar* it was peopled by small traders of the Berti and Mima tribes.

The sky over the bore-well was full of dust. Groups of Abdal Karim's camels pressed themselves to the troughs, and were held in place by fierce black men armed with whips. Abdal Karim and I dismounted, and two of the men came over to greet us. One was an Arab of the 'Awajda called Sannat. He had protuberant yellow teeth and curious, menacing slitlike eyes. The second man was even more piratical. His left eye was grey with a slick of trachoma and he had no teeth except a single wedge-shaped gold incisor. After greeting me, he asked, 'Did I not see you in Omdurman prison?' which did not bode well for the future. As Abdal Karim walked away, the one-eyed man said, 'I *will* go as guide on this journey. You will see!'

As we rode back to the camp, I said to Abdal Karim, 'I thought the guide was still to come.'

'He is,' the Bari answered. 'In fact, I have just sent that man Sannat off with a camel and a rifle to escort him here. He is carrying the money from the sale of the last *dabuuka* he took, 50,000 pounds.'

'Then what about the one-eyed man?'

Abdal Karim laughed uproariously. 'You mean Kurkur!' he grinned. 'It is true, he was going to be guide, but I couldn't employ him after what he did. I had to get rid of him!'

'What did he do?'

The Arab burst out laughing again. 'He had intercourse with a she-donkey!' he said. 'Yes, it is true, by God! One day he got drunk on 'aragi and he found a she-donkey hobbled near the hut. He started to have intercourse with it. Then the owner came out and caught him and hit him a whack with his stick. He dragged him off to the police. The magistrate fined him 200 pounds. It was very funny in court. When the judge announced the fine, someone shouted, "Two hundred pounds! He could have bought it for that!" and another Arab answered, "What do you mean bought it? He could have married it!" Anyway, he had no money, so I paid the fine for him. But I could not have him as a guide after that!'

I laughed with him, but a year later I heard the story of Kurkur's tragedy, which began that very day. While Abdal Karim and I were riding back to camp, Kurkur was busy stealing a waterskin from the gear. He sold the skin and with the money bought a lorry ticket to Omdurman, where he found work as a herdsman with another herd being taken to Egypt. On his way back he had been aboard the ill-fated Nile steamer *Ramadan 'Ashara*, which had sunk in Lake Nasser with the loss of 300 Sudanese. Like most Arabs Kurkur could not swim.

Back in camp we found that two Zaghawa gunsmiths had arrived. They were father and son, and they travelled by camel with their mobile workshop of vices and anvils. The father told me that his ancestor had been the gunsmith of Ali Dinar, the last of the independent Darfur sultans. Abdal Karim brought out his small arsenal of weapons – a five-shot Churchill rifle, a revolver and a Soviet-made shotgun. The smiths began work at once. It was fascinating to see how this trade had become traditional and esoteric within a few generations. The Zaghawa were renowned as potters and smiths, though the Arabs considered such work beneath them and had few smiths of their own. Throughout Africa those who worked with metal and fire were considered unclean, and even amongst the Zaghawa they formed a distinct caste and were unable to marry outside their own group. I often wondered why this was so. In medieval Europe smiths were almost an aristocracy, whereas in Africa they were feared and isolated. Perhaps this was due to their control over the production of weapons, and was connected with superstitions about fire.

The smithy's son was a mercurial lad with a broad grin and intelligent eyes. 'We can repair any firearms, even the modern ones,' he told me. 'In fact, the modern ones are easier, because they are built to a pattern. The home-made ones are all different and are more difficult to fix.' The smiths also made weapons of their own. 'Ours are better than most,' the boy said. 'We can make them even here in the desert. Only the barrels are imported. We can even make pump-action shotguns. We charge about 200 pounds.'

During the next morning Sannat arrived with the guide. He was far more impressive than Kurkur. He was a bear of a man, as powerful as a rhino, his face basalt-black and his eyes shaded with pickled folds of skin. He wore an old check overcoat and walked with the ambling stride of a camel, his feet split and calloused like oxhide. His name was Bakheit, and he belonged to the Duwayih.

When he heard that I was to travel with him, he looked me up and down and said, 'I hope you are strong. It needs a strong man to ride to Egypt.'

'How many days' journey is it?' I asked.

'As far as Isna, where we load the camels on to lorries, it is thirty-five days. It is twenty-five to the border of Egypt.'

'Are there police patrols on the border?'

'Yes, but if we have no permission we go by the hidden ways of the desert and avoid them. Still, we may run into a patrol whichever way we go.'

'Do they look at your papers?'

'Yes, and they often search the camels, looking for hashish or ostrich feathers.'

'They say that only the Sudanese are allowed to cross the border.'

'Then you must tell them you are Sudanese!'

That evening Abdal Karim slaughtered a goat in our honour, and after we had eaten we sat quietly together enjoying the last chance of repose before the long journey. It was a world of animals and simple men, close to the rhythms of nature. Above us the stars and planets ticked by in their own eternal rhythms. The night was crisp with cold and a chill wind battered the tents, shivering the wooden frames. We draped ourselves in blankets and huddled up by the cheering warmth of the fire. Beyond the firelight and the brave little city of tents the night hid the bleak, savage mystery of the desert.

11
A Camel
Race to Egypt

In the rough wastes of north-west
Kordofan are the two strongest and
richest camel-owning tribes of the Sudan,
the Kababish and the Kawahla, age-
long rivals, who graze their herds over an
area extending west to Darfur.
C. G. Seligman, Races of Africa, *1930*

Next morning we rode out to the herd as it grazed in the bush east
of Umm Batatikha. The camels were a superb sight, moving in open
order through the sparse acacias. All of them were fat beasts in prime
condition, including rutting bulls, she-camels with finlike humps and
heavy, castrated males. Beyond them the landscape extended to the
north, unbelievably vast and arid, its flatness interrupted only by the
blue ridge of Jabal Azraq stretching across the horizon.

Two more herdsmen rode out to meet us as we arrived. One
was a black youth called Musa, a Meidobi who had been raised by
the Kababish. The other was a man bordering on old age, with a lick
of grey whisker and a stringy body. He was a freeman of the Bani
Jarrar, named Mohammld. After we had saluted them, Bakhelt gave
the order to draw in the flanks of the herd. He took up the familiar
guide's position on the left forward side while the rest of us trotted
around the grazing camels, gradually forcing them into tight formation. Wad at Tafashan was still fresh and moved easily beneath me.
I was filled with a new confidence that came from the knowledge
that I was no longer an ignorant outsider. The doubt I had felt after
my return from El 'Atrun had somehow evaporated, and I began to
understand how much I had learned from that ordeal. I knew these
men. I understood their customs and their language. I knew how to
ride and how to herd camels. It gave me a thrill of pleasure to know
that I could perform the simple tasks of the herdsman; at its most
basic level this was what nomadic life was about.

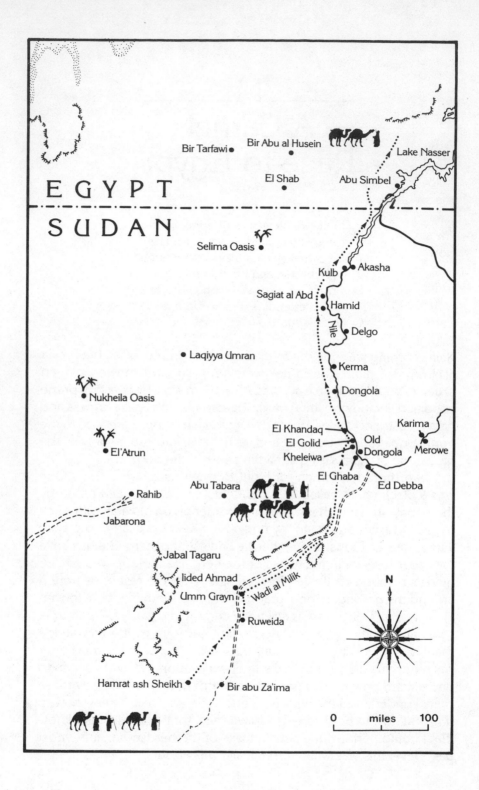

EGYPT

SUDAN

Bir Tarfawi •   • Bir Abu al Husein

• El Shab   Abu Simbel

→ Lake Nasser

Selima Oasis •

Kulb •   • Akasha

Sagiat al Abd •
•   • Hamid

Nile

• Delgo

• Laqiyya Umran

• Kerma

Nukheila Oasis •

• Dongola

Karima •

El Khandaq •   • Old
El Golid •   Dongola   • Merowe
Kheleiwa •

El Ghaba •   • Ed Debba

• Rahib

Abu Tabara •

Jabarona

Jabal Tagaru

lided Ahmad

Umm Grayn •   Wadi al Milik

• Ruweida

N

Hamrat ash Sheikh •   • Bir abu Za'ima

0   miles   100

All day we pushed the camels on through the dead brush towards Umm Sunta. The sunlight played across the rippling backs of the great beasts, which pounded on, brimming with power and oozing vitality. We passed the tents of the nazir's people, brown and dirty-white along the wadis. There were lumps of humanity around the deep-wells where camels hoisted up the great buckets from far below, the rawhide cables creaking audibly with the strain. Below us the sand was blemished by the patterns of a million tracks: the thick, elliptical pads of running camels winding through the thorn trees, the scuffled dragmarks where an armada of sheep had been brought down to the wells, the neat hoofclips of a donkey, the flowerlike pads of a hunting saluki, the almost invisible filigree patterns of a lizard, the double hopmarks of a gerbil. By evening we had reached the wadi of Umm Sunta, crossed the wall of trees and couched our camels in the marrow of white sand within. The lowering sun cast gilt fingers across the smooth surface. We set up our camp under a *siyaal* tree and turned the camels into the wadi to browse for the night.

Musa the Meidobi unloaded a sack of ground millet from the pack camel and began to make *kisri*. Abdal Karim rode off to the market in Umm Sunta and came back with a goat slung from his saddle in a canvas sheet. Sannat slaughtered the animal, and within an hour we were ready to eat. It was just after sunset. Drops of light hung like baubles in the clean grey sky. We heard the sound of several camels being couched in the bushes nearby, and shortly afterwards two Arabs came walking into our camp. They were men of the Awlad Rashid from Darfur, impressive and mysterious in dark, hooded cloaks and high-furled headcloths. The Rashid were orig- inally a cattle-owning tribe who had turned to rearing camels in recent years. There was no love lost between them and the Kababish, though they were not in open hostility. I had met many Rashid in my days in Darfur, and the two Arabs obviously recognized me for they shouted exuberantly, 'Omar! Where have you been? Only last year I saw you buying camels in Gineina market!' After they had greeted us all, they sat down and began to talk to the guide and Abdal Karim, while the rest of us gathered around to hear what was said.

The Rashid were called Musa Adam and Bakkour, and they had just bought eighteen camels from my old companion Dagalol. 'It is a small *dabuuka*,' Musa Adam said. 'And we want to take it to Egypt.

211

But we need companions to pass through your territory. Those Sara-jab bandits along the wadi will eat us!'

'The Sarajab have no mercy for anyone, not even the Sarajab,' old Bakheit growled. 'They know that *dabuukas* don't carry fire-arms. They respect no one. But you are welcome to travel with us. From tomorrow morning we shall go together.'

I knew that this was no light matter. To accept travelling com-panions was to accept a contract of mutual loyalty in any predica-ment. If we were attacked by Awlad Rashid, for example, even if they happened to be Musa Adam's own cousins, then he and his friend would be obliged to defend us. These Arabs, of two distinct tribes, were now obliged to defend each other with their lives; to fail in this would be to invite stigma for the rest of their days.

After we had eaten, the Rashid made camp amongst their own camels, screened by the bush about fifty metres away. As I lay down to sleep, I heard a strange chanting, like a meditation mantra, repeated over and over many times in a compelling and hypnotic rhythm. 'What is it?' I asked Sannat.

'They must be Tijanis,' he replied. 'They repeat holy words, and it brings them blessing from heaven.'

When I asked Bakkour about it, he explained, 'We are members of the Tijani brotherhood. There are Arabs all over the desert who belong to it.'

'What is the point of the chanting?'

'It is called *zikra*. The more you do, the more profit you get in heaven. It is like your saddle-cushion. At first it is flat, but the more you fill it with wool, the more it rises.'

'I never had much use for a saddle-cushion that was too full,' Bakheit commented dourly.

The next morning we mustered the herd before dawn. The Rashid brought their eighteen camels into our camp and let them mix with the others. We drove them out of the wadi and through a bottle-neck so that they could be counted. Abdal Karim stood on one side, with old Bakheit on the other; two stark, primitive figures in their thick overcoats and furled *tobes*. As the camels ambled past them in ones and twos, they counted them out loud, moving their right hands, two fingers held aloft like priests giving absolution. There were about 160 animals in the *dabuuka*, which was slightly over optimum size. Apart from the guide, Bakheit, there were the three Kababish herdsmen, Sannat, Musa and Mohammid, the two

Rashid and myself, a total of seven men. Abdal Karim did not intend to ride further with us.

After the herd had been counted he strode over to me and said, 'Your camel will never make Egypt. But don't worry. I have told Bakheit to give you a replacement from the herd when he weakens. If necessary you could sell him in Dongola.' Then he gave me ten pounds as a parting present. As always I disliked accepting a gift, but I knew now that my host would have been deeply wounded if I had refused. I took the note and thanked him, saying, 'If God wills, I shall be back later in the year.'

'Go in peace.'

Within a few moments we were all mounted and moving the great herd out, north-east to the Wadi al Milik, singing camel-songs and hooting with the familiar cries. We moved through the pale vestige of the greenery I had seen here the previous year. There was now no trace of grass underfoot, and the leaves of the *siyaal* trees had withered, leaving only the silver-grey branches. There was no green at all except the bitter, hollylike leaves of the *mukhayyit*, shrivelled and covered in a fine layer of dust. The sky was dark and filled with fleecy cloudlets, suggesting eerie elfish faces. A wing of soft grey fluff surrounded the molten sun. Beneath the shuffling pads of the *ilbil* the ground was mudpack hard. Away in the distance I could make out the glowering line of the Hattan plateau, and beyond it a patch of orange desert. Everywhere the land seemed deserted and dead.

We halted for a few minutes at noon for a meal, then pressed on into the second half of the day. In winter the Arabs preferred to move in one continuous drag, from sunrise to sunset, for the camels would not travel into the night during cold weather. On warmer days they would rest for most of the afternoon and travel perhaps to the early hours of the next morning. In the afternoon we walked for hours, following the camels. The idea was to preserve their strength for as long as possible, for soon we should be out of the desert steppes and into the desert proper where there would be no grazing. Many camels died on the journey to Egypt, and the desert was littered with the bones of animals that had died from hunger or exhaustion.

Walking at ground level had its advantages in the winter, for the camels shielded us from the bitter winds that blew in the morning and evening. The pace was brisk and required a steady, unfaltering stride, for the herd moved with surprising speed. If we had to stop, even for a few minutes, we could only catch up with a jogging run; the idea of being left behind was a sobering one in this bleakness. The Arabs would mount their camels as the fancy took them, so that there were always some of us walking and others riding. To mount they would run into the herd, scattering some of the beasts and singling out their own animal. They would catch his headrope, which was tied to the saddle, and bring his head down, clambering up on the neck and swinging back into the saddle. When they wished to walk, they would just leap down from the camel's back and tie the headrope up so that it did not restrict his movement. Walking with the camels, one could sense the herd compulsion that seemed to hypnotize them. When moving fast, camels hated to be separated from their fellows, though when they were grazing some animals would always wander off.

As we moved further east, we passed through wadis where lines of *siyaals* perched lifelessly above the sand, and where the trunks of *kitir* lay twisted and dead, turned over by the wind. As we walked, I saw that not all was lifeless here. I caught the brilliant yellow flash of tiny bee-eaters in the dead trees, and once Sannat pointed out a big hare that dodged through the husks of the bushes. 'You would not die of hunger here, even today,' the big man said. 'Not if you know the secrets of the desert.'

Later the sun came out of its covering of cloud and, taking off our cloaks and overcoats, we mounted. It was blissfully comfortable in the saddle after miles on foot, and the herd seemed to bowl along, gliding over the flat ground. There was often silence, broken only by the electronic burbling of the stud-bulls that walked at the back of the herd or led from the front. They were enormous animals, their drooling maws and swollen necks showing that they were still in season. Occasionally they would quarrel, testing each other with their canine fangs and butting each other's heads, belching forth their revolting mouth-bladders and roaring like lions.

At sunset we would make camp. As it was continually cold by night, we would find a place sheltered by rocks or *tundub* trees; the saddles and saddle-bags piled up together made a good windbreak. The ritual of hobbling took about an hour. When this was completed, each man retired to his own space to perform his prayers. Those were the most delicious moments of the day. The work was over, and for half an hour no one moved. The Rashid recited their *zikra* in quiet meditation, while the others sat with their rosaries of wooden beads, staring into the depths of the desert night and repeating, 'The lord be praised! The praise be to God!' as they counted the beads between finger and thumb. Often in those moments my mind was filled with tranquillity. The desert wind, drawing its breath across the sandy floor, seemed to merge with my own breathing, so that the internal and external became one. For almost the first time I felt completely at ease and at home in this land.

After we had eaten porridge and drunk tea, we would sit around the fire, completely swathed in our blankets. With the low flames curling up from the hearth and the freezing night around us, this was the time for tales. Almost all nomads were good storytellers, but Sannat was a prince amongst them. While most Arabs recounted their own adventures, Sannat's tales were of a different calibre. He told of the days of heroes like 'Antara Ibn Shaddad and Abu Zayyid al Hilali: magical stories that had been told for generations amongst the Arabs and that pre-dated Islam by a long way. 'Abu Zayyid al Hilali lived in the far-off time,' he told us. 'And once he said to an old woman, "I was born without fear and no one can throw me!" She said, "Go to the Great Wadi that lies to the north and you will find an old man called Jalajil. He will throw you!" So Abu Zayyid rode off on his camel to the wadi where he found an old man with a cowskin of water. He took his spear and threw it at the old man so that it stuck in his body. But the man paid no more attention to it than if it had been a splinter. He pulled it out and, seeing a lion in the wadi, went and killed it with the spear. He carried the lion back and said to Abu Zayyid, "You shall eat half and I shall eat the other half!" They sat down to eat, and the old man ate skin, bones and all, but a little was left to Abu Zayyid. Then the old man picked up the cowskin and said, "You shall drink half and I shall drink the other half!" The old man drank a good half of the skin, but a little was left to Abu Zayyid. Then the old man said, "Now, my son, what is it?"

"I have come to wrestle you!" said Abu Zayyid.

"I will wrestle you with pleasure on the condition that he who throws the other shall have the right to slaughter him."

Abu Zayyid agreed and they struggled together. Then, tub! Abu Zayyid was thrown. "Let us decide on the best out of three throws!" the old man said. They struggled again, and tub! Abu Zayyid was thrown twice more. "You had better slaughter me!" said Abu Zayyid, lying on the ground beneath the old man. Then suddenly he burst

215

out laughing. He saw that beneath the old man's loincloth his groin was covered in camel ticks like an old bull-camel. He laughed until he cried. "Why do you laugh?" the old man asked him. "Nothing. You had better slaughter me!"

"Not until you tell me what made you laugh!"

"It is because you have camel ticks on your groin like an old bull-camel!"

Then the old man said, "If you think that is funny, then you are no more than a child. And I cannot kill a child!" So he let Abu Zayyid go. He rode off on his camel and they never met again. The old man was the only one who could throw Abu Zayyid al Hilali.'

I was fascinated by the story. 'Where did you hear it?' I asked him. 'From people,' he told me. Like all the other Arabs with me, Sannat was illiterate. It was thrilling to think that this tale, perhaps a thousand years old, had been passed from mouth to mouth since the Bani Hillal Arabs had first come to the Sudan. 'It is an old tale,' he said. 'But the story of 'Antara is even older. 'Antara Ibn Shaddad was an Arab, but he was black, like me. His father was a free Arab but his mother was a slave from Habesh. 'Antara took after his mother. When he was young, his father called him a slave and set him to work as a herdsman guarding his herds. But 'Antara secretly sold some of the camels and bought a fine horse. Then he bought a helmet and a breastplate and a shield and spear. He buried them in the desert so that his father would not know, and he spent his time always with the herds. One day raiders came and carried off all the camels. His father said, "I trusted that slave 'Antara and now I have nothing!" Then 'Antara saddled his horse and rode out into the desert. He dug up his armour and his spear and shield. Then he rode out to fight the bandits. He followed their tracks until he found their camp. There were fifty of them, a whole tribe! "I have come to take back my father's camels!" he said. Then he charged at them and killed them all. He collected his father's camels and drove them back to his father's camp. Then all the women cried with joy and his father said, "From now on, 'Antara, you are my son!" What a man he was that 'Antara! You know he had a house built of stone with a door that only he could open. He built the house out of a cave, with his own hands. Many people came to try the door, but only he could open it. He was the strongest man in the world, by God!'

In those first few days I had warmed considerably to Sannat. I had been quite misled by his rascally exterior. He was a man of great and sincere warmth, with a generous heart. He would have shared his last crust even if he were on the edge of starvation. He had travelled to Egypt many times and had worked as a guide. I noticed that occasionally Bakheit deferred to him.

Mohammid was a quiet man who did his job well but rarely joined in the conversation. This was unusual for an Arab and I guessed that he was one of those unmarried old men whom the Arabs despised so much. Musa was no more than a boy and this was his first trip on the route, which put me in the strange position of being more experienced than him in this instance. He was an excellent herdsman, like so many of the 'Awwala boys who had been brought up amongst the herds.

The Rashid were bright, intelligent and alive, constantly talking and telling stories. Bakkour was unusual in that he had been outside the country to work. He had been employed as a labourer in Iraq. He told me how he had seen herds of the Ruwala bedouin coming across the country's southern borders, with their womenfolk in litters similar to those of the Kababish. It was soon clear, however, that the Rashid regarded themselves as superior to my other companions. 'These men are not true Arabs,' Musa Adam once told me. 'Even the guide is a slave!' At meal times they would scoff a little at the Kababish porridge, saying, 'Your *kisri* is not ground properly. It is only crushed in a mortar. Ours is properly ground in a mill, it is far better than this!'

Like Sannat, Bakkour was an excellent storyteller. He had been brought up in the savannah lands of South Darfur, along the Barh al 'Arab, where there were elephants and giraffes, and his hunting tales were enthralling. 'The cattle-Arabs have a special way of hunting elephant,' he told me. 'Often they use big, heavy spears because bullets have no effect. They hunt on horses. One man rides out to distract the elephant – they usually choose the bull – and when the beast is chasing him, the others ride out from behind and stab him with their spears. He has to be a brave man, that one! Sometimes they make a platform in a tree near to the track where the elephants come down to the watering-place. The outside track always belongs to the bull, because he escorts the cows and the young down to drink, just as the *fahal* camel does. The men have to use a special scent to disguise their smell. The elephants have a good sense of smell and they can pull up a tree like a bunch of grass. They come at sunset. As the bull passes under the tree, they drop their spear on his neck! There is plenty of meat on an elephant, by God! They have enough meat for seven camel-loads. Of course, their tusks bring a great deal of money. The Mahriyya and the Awlad Janub are the best hunters. They will stay in the bush for three months. They kill elephants and giraffes too, and take the ivory as far south as Juba. They have an injection against tsetse fly that they give their camels so that they can enter the wet areas. But it is expensive and the camels have to be injected every day. The Arabs hunt giraffes as well, because the women like the skin as an ornament, but many Arabs are killed in the hunting. Elephants are dangerous. They can destroy a village easily. I once knew a man who saw a cow-elephant giving birth and he killed the baby out of badness. The elephants came after him like a swarm of bees. He hid in a village, but the elephants just knocked it down until they found him. They picked him up and smashed him to pieces!'

In the morning we would saddle up and move the herd out early. There were many families of Kababish moving across the dusty plains towards the Wadi al Milik. They were men and women of tribes like the Ribaygat, Ruwahla and Sarajab, usually driving with them a straggle of camels or a knot of goats or sheep. The camels looked thin and exhausted, and the men told us they were still moving back from the north, where the ranges had not bloomed. One evening we spotted a circlet of vultures in the azure sky, and by the forks of two thorn trees we found a father and son of the Ruwahla slaughtering a bull-camel. Four other camels carrying pack saddles and a mass of leather bags and equipment were couched nearby. Further on two little girls with brown faces and butter-smeared hair were watching six milch camels and a flock of bony goats. A woman in a blue cotton shawl sat in the shade.

The camel had been trussed up in a kneeling position by its front legs. Sannat and I stood by as the Arab told his son to stretch the animal's head backwards. The camel growled its last protest and the Arab drove his dagger into its chest, just below the neck. The blood gushed out, welling across the sand. The light went out of the camel's eyes, the head sagged, and the boy laid it gingerly on the ground. It was all over very quickly.

Then, like the superb predators they were, the Arabs set about skinning and butchering the animal, severing the back of the neck and uncovering the jelly of the hump. They cut out the entrails and stripped off hunks of meat that they dropped into saddle-bags. The

Rahli invited us to eat the raw liver with him and his son. It was cut up into chunks that we ate from a wide dish. As we squatted down, I saw the hollow carcass still kneeling by the trees where it would mark the way for decades. About fifty metres away four gigantic Nubian vultures perched on some rocks, and two more came gliding down on their great wings; a few yellow-headed Egyptian vultures settled in the sand, and several ravens. I knew that they would close in as soon as we moved off. After dark the jackals would be out to finish off the feast.

'Why did you slaughter him?' I asked the Arab. It was rare for the Kababish to butcher a camel. 'He was about to die,' the Rahli said. 'He would never have made it to the wadi. He was too hungry and tired. When the spirit has gone, the camel will never live, even if you feed him. He is beyond the limit. It is the same with all things, even the sons of Adam. This has been a bad year for the Arabs. There is no grazing anywhere. Grain is too expensive to buy. If this goes on, we shall soon lose everything!'

Sannat and I caught up with the herd just after sunset. They had camped in the lee of some bare, rocky hills. For supper that night we ate fresh camel meat – the gift of the Rahli and his son.

It was eight days before we came out of the lava plains and sighted the Wadi al Milik. We made camp one afternoon under the flinty blue oval of Jabal Ruweiba, across the wadi from the merchant at Affan, where Fadlal Mula and I had bought provisions the previous October. Our camels fell greedily upon the *siyaal* trees, amongst which stood a tiny cabin. An old crone came hobbling out of it followed by a snappy little dog, and tried to drive the camels away, complaining bitterly that the trees were hers. By Arab law the trees in the vicinity of a camp, especially *siyaal*, belonged to the owner. The *siyaal* were particularly valuable in summer, for at that time their seeds provided the sole grazing for goats. The guide told us to drive the camels a bit further up the wadi. I shook hands with the old lady, now a little soothed, and she told me that she had seen me here previously with Fadlal Mula.

The next day we moved the *dabuuka* across the wadi where it twisted west to east, and emerged into the rippling sands on the east bank; from there we could see the bluish glow of the Sumi'yaat hills on the skyline. As the herd moved through the day, Bakheit, Musa Adam and I rode to the wells at Al Ku'. Some Sarajab were watering their little herds of camels there and greeted us with rather cold, fearful glances. I asked for details of Fadlal Mula and his people, and heard that they had moved south into their *damar* at Umm Gurfa. There were some Ribaygat washing their red sheep, forcing the animals' heads between a forked stake and dousing them with water. Bakheit had decided to invest some of his savings in buying two camels, which he could sell at a profit in Egypt. He purchased two small she-camels from the Sarajab. One was a very wild little beast that scrambled off into the trees as soon as we tried to bridle her. She raced backwards and forwards, whining in a shrill voice; eventually it took five Arabs to restrain her. I tried to catch her by the nostrils as I had seen the Arabs do, but as I approached she dropped about four litres of her disgusting bile in my face. I was completely soaked in it, and the smell remained with me for days afterwards. Old Bakheit told me, 'Next time you try to catch a camel, approach him from the side. If you come from the front, you will always get the cud in your face!'

'By God, but she is a wild one!' Musa Adam commented.

'She is like her owners,' Bakheit replied. 'Let us be careful tonight. I should not be surprised if these Sarajab come and tell me that I have not paid for her!'

That evening we made camp on the flat shelf of the desert north of the Sumi'yaat hills. A freezing squall blew across from the north, and the margin of the wadi was a dark line to the west. 'We must not sleep tonight,' Bakheit said. 'I do not trust those Sarajab. Only a few months ago they attacked a *dabuuka* near here. It was after sunset and the herd was travelling outside the wadi just as we are. The Sarajab opened fire from hidden places in the trees and shot the guide and two others. Then they drove off plenty of the stock.'

We took turns to stay awake, sitting wrapped in our blankets and gazing out across the dark desert. I was very tired and found it almost impossible to stay awake when my turn came. I tried forcing my eyes open, knitting my brows in determination, but within moments I was seeing strange apparitions, men in white medical overalls and frightening insect creatures gliding across the sand in front of me. I realized that I was dreaming with my eyes open, and shook my head violently to get rid of these visions. For a few minutes my head would remain clear, then the apparitions would begin again. I was very glad when Sannat touched my arm and told me to get some sleep.

The day after, we walked for three hours, moving slowly north, still keeping the wadi on our left. I walked barefoot, feeling the cold sand refreshing my feet, on and on through yellow desert, through stones, sand, camel tracks, camel droppings, camels' shadows on the earth. Time was an undivided stream, mixed in with the cries of the drivers, the unflinching green line of the wadi, the *markh* bushes like enormous feathers, the blue mystic mountains and the grey sky.

That night we camped at the wells at Umm Grayn with some Hamdab, hoping to water the herd there the next day. The Arabs were small men with foxy faces. They shared our *kisri* with relish, complaining that the hunting was no good these days. 'Where is the meat of yesteryear?' one of them said, so mournfully that I almost laughed. 'The hunt is not what it was! My father kept two salukis just for hunting. They could outrun any gazelle, by God!'

Bakheit was anxious for news of other *dabuukas*, most of which were obliged to water here or at Iided Ahmad a little further north. These were virtually the only accessible watering-places before the open desert, which stretched from here to the Nile. 'The last *dabuuka* watered here days ago,' the Hamdab said. 'There is no competition unless there is anything close behind you. You will have the market to yourselves.'

Just after dawn we watered the herds from a mud-basin between two hand-dug wells. The Hamdab filled the basin with leather buckets while we drove the camels up in small groups. The work was over quickly, for the cold prevented the camels from drinking. We breakfasted on *kisri*, and the Hamdab talked about the grazing. 'It is terrible this year,' they said. 'Camels have died as well as sheep and goats. There is no grass at all in the wadi now and only a few patches outside.'

'Why don't you move south?' I asked them.

'Is the south any better?' one of them said. 'We are better off here, at least we are near the salt.' I realized that this was an excuse. The Hamdab had lived in this remote part of the wadi for generations. Before that they had ranged far into the deserts beyond. They had been moving south for decades and they would not move any further. Yet I knew that if the rains failed this year then they would have little choice. It had not rained properly at Umm Grayn for five years.

Before we set off, Bakheit examined Wad at Tafashan and said, 'It would be wrong to ride him further. See, he has grown weak. His legs are affected by *zabata*.' He pointed to the tell-tale scars on the inside of the camel's forelegs, near the elbow pad. I had always

221

thought that this defect, caused by the rubbing of the legs against the pedestal chest-pad, was congenital. 'Any camel can be affected by *zabata* when it grows weak,' the guide told me. He singled out for me a strong bull-camel, ideal for the long dry trek to Egypt, and Wad at Tafashan was allowed to run with the herd.

When the Arabs were ready, we moved out through the swath of *markh* bushes and into the open desert. All day we travelled around the foot of the sweeping black downs of Jabal Abu Fas. The line of the wadi faded behind us and dissolved into the desert. We were going north-east towards the Al 'Ain plateau, which was still below the skyline. The desert to the north was dimmed by a scurry of dust that grew thicker towards evening. At the end of the afternoon we found some clumps of *hadd* and let the camels graze as they moved. The sun had cooled and become a silver disc, scored by blue muslin streaks. As I walked behind the herd in the half-light, I felt as if I could go on for ever. Nothing seemed to matter, neither the past nor the future, not even the Arabs of the desert. The vastness of the landscape and the unreal aura of twilight dwarfed all emotions.

After dark a savage sand-storm punched into us with hammer force. We made camp at once by a single bush, a tiny island in the void. As we piled up our equipment, the wind screamed past us, pouring liquid sand into everything. The storm was as thick as a blizzard. It was a struggle to cook up our *kisri*, to build up a fortress of saddle-bags around the fire, which flickered and trembled in the wind. The porridge was covered with sand as soon as we tried to eat it. After we had eaten what we could, we had no alternative but to disappear under our blankets. Sand piled up into drifts around us, and as the night grew colder and the wind more icy, we shivered at the base of our lone bush.

In the morning we were half buried in a drift of sand. The wind was still so bitterly cold that we huddled close to the fire, wrapped up tightly, until the sun came up. We watched its pale glow turning the desert luminescent, the horizons fuzzy and insubstantial. The flat plain, embossed with the shining lumps of low dunes, was licked by slip-streams of sand that streaked across the surface like currents of electricity.

We drove the herd out into the eye of the wind, all of us walking in the shelter of the great animal bodies. The wind showed no sign of dropping and all day the storm raged over us, white-out on all sides. The camels were reluctant to travel into the squall and we had to force them on with our whips.

Often we came upon tall clumps of *nissa* grass and tangled masses of *tundub* trees, and the hungry camels broke formation to graze, disappearing into the veil of dust. When this happened it took many minutes to reassemble them. The entire day we moved in short bursts with little progress. 'We are going badly!' Musa Adam shouted at me through his furled headcloth. 'At this rate it will be another twenty-six days to Isna. I don't know what the guide is doing. We keep turning and circling, but we should go on straight. Moving is better than grazing for these camels now!' I thought the comment unfair, and I checked the compass-bearing I had taken the previous day at Umm Grayn. It was no more than two degrees out.

At mid-morning we stopped amongst some rocks and made porridge, our faces still covered in our headcloths. As Sannat and I lay in the shelter of the rocks, he told me, 'The Arabs hate sand-storms more than anything. How many people have lost their way in them and died! Even experienced desert-men can die in a storm like this. Don't listen to anyone who tells you anything different. There is no Arab alive who can navigate in these storms unless he has travelled the route scores of times. Only last year a guide was taking a *dabuuka* past Jabal al 'Ain when he ran out of water in a storm like this. He tried to make for the spring in Al 'Ain but he lost the way and all his men died. It is a good thing old Bakheit and I know the way!'

That afternoon the desert was at its wildest. We lapped ourselves around with blankets and headcloths and bent forward into the wind as we walked, plodding on in the soft sand. We wound through great fields of boulders that channelled the streams of dust into flying eddies, and after them came more patches of sand, red and amber, hard dunes littered with basalt, and a narrow pass that was converted by the dust into a long tunnel with neither entrance nor exit.

The storm went on for three days. It was a grim time, yet solid old Bakheit never wavered. He was a silent man, not given to bursts of excitement as most Arabs were. He rarely walked like the rest of us, but rode his gigantic camel on and on, unperturbed by the wind or the sand, the cold or the heat, never irritated by the nagging stoppages nor the criticisms of the others. He and Sannat belonged to a different breed from the Sarajab I had travelled with. They were certainly of slave stock, yet they were huge, massively powerful men who seemed to be hewn from the granite of the desert itself.

On the evening of the third day the storm dropped suddenly. The sky cleared, and the golden beams of the dwindling sun spread out across it like the arms of a giant starfish. The sea-spray hiss of the wind stopped abruptly; there was silence. Far to the north we saw the solid sandstone citadel of Jabal al 'Ain springing up from the void of orange sand.

We spent a peaceful night and in the morning drove the camels across the almost featureless sand-sheet, smoothed and rolled flat by the storm. Sannat was walking on the right flank of the herd, a bulky black figure with a whip in his hand. Suddenly he stopped and shouted, 'Hey, brothers, look at this!' Several of us ran over to where he stood, and saw a broad swath of camel tracks, thousands upon thousands of them swelling over each other and spreading out thirty metres across the sand.

'It is a *dabuuka*,' he said. 'And it is not far ahead. They must have passed us in the night. Now they will be before us to market in Cairo.'

'Not if we catch them first!' Bakkour said.

For the rest of the day we drove the herd on with ferocious determination, but though we strained our eyes to the distant horizon we saw nothing ahead but rocks, sand and the occasional tree. We worked together as a close team, covering the flanks and the rear and whipping the animals into line like janissaries. Bakheit followed the tracks of the other herd and we rode fast across patches of rippling sand, its smooth skin shattered by cairns of rock and high sugarloaf hills that reared up like toothless gums. The next day passed in the same way, and the day after that we came to the undulating terrain beyond Al 'Ain—Aw Dun pass, where the rocky hammada made it impossible to find tracks. In any case my companions were diverted by watching out for tribesmen of the Umm Mattu Kababish who inhabited this part of the desert. 'They are in resistance to the government,' Sannat told me. 'They refused to pay their taxes. The government sent police down from Dongola, but the Umm Mattu shot them. They are as wild as the Sarajab. No *dabuuka* is safe from them. Either they will stop a herd and demand a number of animals or they will attack you at night. Two years ago there was a *dabuuka* that ran out of water here. The guide and one of the herdsmen went off to the nearest well to get water. There were some Umm Mattu there, and they asked them for help. The Umm Mattu shot them both. Then they rode out to the herd and helped themselves to any camel they wanted!'

Two days later we were watering at the wells of Ma'atul in the Wadi al Milik. There were some Umm Mattu living there in squat cabins of straw and brushwood amongst the great dunes topped with groves of thick thorn trees. They seemed harmless enough to me, earning a little money by helping to water *dabuukas* bound for Egypt. Ed Debba was only two days' journey to the east, and the Umm Mattu had a ready market for their animals there.

Umm Mattu were Kababish, but were not traditionally under the authority of the nazir, though they acknowledged him as their titular overlord. There had always been Kababish in the Northern Province of the Sudan, though in past centuries many of them had forsaken the wandering life and become date farmers. These tribes included the Gungonab and the Bayudab, whom the desert Arabs despised and refused to acknowledge as true Kababish. The Umm Mattu, though, were still largely nomadic, and their number included some famous desert guides.

After we had watered, Bakheit asked them for news of other *dabuukas*. 'There is a herd in front of you,' one of the Arabs told us. 'There are six men and about 150 camels. They are Kawahla, and they are almost a day ahead.'

The knowledge that our rivals were Kawahla gave fuel to the sense of competition my companions felt. The Kawahla had been rivals of the Kababish for centuries. The second most powerful nomads in Kordofan, they had fought on the side of the Khalifa Abdallahi at the battle of Omdurman and many had been killed by the British. After the Kababish renaissance Sir Ali Wad at Tom's men had pillaged the Kawahla herds and driven them further south. 'We will catch them and no doubt!' Bakheit commented.

We collected a load of firewood, and set out that evening into the gravel plains north of the wadi. The next morning, quite early, we came on the remains of a camp. The sand had been churned and scattered by scores of camels and was thick with their droppings. We saw the places where men had lain down to sleep, and the remains of a fire that was still warm. 'There are six of them,' Sannat said. 'And they must be close now. They would not set off before dawn.' Sunrise had been about six. Presuming they had left at that time, they could not be more than three hours ahead. The Arabs at once grew very

225

excited and pushed the herd on fiercely all day, pausing only briefly for a meal at midday. 'We will have them, by Almighty God!' Sannat declared regularly.

It was just after sunset, and we had begun to give up all hope, when we saw ahead of us and to the east a sprawling dark spot on the sand. 'That's it!' Sannat yelled at once, and as we moved closer I made out the faint yet familiar shape of massed camels. 'Come on, brothers!' someone shouted, but no exhortation was needed. Already the air resounded with our cries and the crack of our whips. The *dabuuka* moved faster and faster, but seemed to gain no ground. We shouted until we were hoarse, twisting our riding beasts left and right along the herd so that none of the camels could fall behind. But still it seemed that we were making no progress. I guessed that the other herdsmen had seen us and had no intention of letting us pass. I was suddenly and irrepressibly reminded of the Oxford and Cambridge boat race. Gradually we drew abreast of the other herd. After what seemed like ages we pulled ahead. Suddenly we were a length ahead, then two lengths and pulling away. Sannat let out a whoop of glee, and we all cheered instinctively. As we drew further away, the light faded, hiding the Kawahla from our sight. After we had made camp later, however, we heard the growl of camels from far across the sands and saw the blinking orange eye of a fire somewhere to the south.

As soon as the first rays of light were in the sky next morning, the Arabs were anxious to be off. Our watering-place at Khileiwa on the Nile, was only a day's journey away and we were determined to be the first there. Old Bakheit, less excitable than the others, tried to calm them down, saying that everything was in the hands of God. We saw nothing of the other herd during the day, although we looked back constantly. 'They're finished!' Sannat decided complacently. We halted for the night on the gravel-spits near Khileiwa, intending to water the herd there the following morning. It was a silent evening. Far to the east electric lights, yellow and sickly green, marked the Nubian villages along the Nile. We had hobbled the camels and were preparing to eat, when someone said, 'Listen!' We all stopped what we were doing and strained our ears. Out of the darkness came the faint but distinct sound of camel cries and the cracking of whips. Seconds later we heard the ominous shuffle of camels' hooves on the gravel. The sounds grew gradually louder, then suddenly the whole great black apparition of the herd seemed to float out of the night, shrouded in dust, and halted not a dozen yards away.

There were belches and roars from the camels, and the crash of their knees as they were couched in the gravel. A voice called out, 'As salaam 'alaykum!' and my companions answered, 'Welcome! Come and rest!' We heard the sounds of saddles being unloaded, the clink of hobbles and the shouts of herdsmen as we sat and waited. One by one the muffled figures of the Kawahla appeared out of the shadows, each man carrying his camel-whip in his left hand. They greeted us rather stiffly, shaking hands as we stood up to receive them. Then, as they were now formally our guests, we pressed them to eat. After moments they accepted, sitting down gravely by the fire and eating the kisri we offered them.

After everyone had eaten and drunk tea, and the introductions were complete, the Kawahla guide settled down to discuss the situation. He was as big as Bakheit, but much more Arab-looking with bronze-coloured skin. For a moment they sat facing each other across the fire like the captains of rival teams. Then the Kahli said, 'By Almighty God, brothers, there is no profit in racing from here. We shall only kill the camels!' Bakheit agreed, saying, 'We should travel together from here, at least until we get to Isna.' There followed a long discussion, but the good sense of the guides prevailed. It was decided that we should travel together, keeping the herds separate. Each herd would take the lead, day about, until we reached Isna. 'After that it is every man for himself!' said Sannat with a grin.

We watered at Khileiwa the next day. We spent ten days travelling at a leisurely pace along the narrow corridor between the river and the Nubian villages. It was pleasant to move through the drapery of the palm groves and the green gardens after the austerity of the desert. At Dongola we were met by a camel merchant who agreed to buy Wad at Tafashan. He gave me far less than the camel was worth, though I knew that anything was preferable to allowing him to die on the way. As the man led him off, I felt glad that he would not end up on a butcher's block in Cairo.

We left the river again at Lamulay and travelled through a rocky desert broken by tall granite peaks. Here the way was marked by the bones of thousands of dead camels that had expired on the trek to Egypt. Bakheit occasionally pointed to the twisted husks, saying, 'We lost that one three years ago!' and 'That one died suddenly, we had no idea that it was going!' as if these skeletons were old friends.

We crossed featureless ergs of hard-pan sand, climbed over steep walls of gravel and through stony shelves where the rock lay in sharp flakes that stood up at angles from the desert floor. The drivers of previous herds had erected tiny cairns in this stretch of desert; they consisted of a few flat stones over the bones of a dead animal that marked the route as clearly as if it had been a highway.

The Egyptian border was no more than a few days away, and I was apprehensive about border patrols. Bakheit said that the army would change the siting of their posts continually so that no one could tell where they would be.

'Just talk to them as if you are an Arab and say that you know nothing,' Sannat told me. 'Pretend you are Sudanese.'

'I think I am a little too light-skinned for that!'

'Nonsense, some of the Kababish are as fair as you!'

'It is the eyes,' Musa Adam cut in. 'No Kabbashi has green eyes!'

We watered for the last time in Lake Nasser and passed into a massif of broken hills weathered into fantastic shapes by the wind and the blown sand. We travelled through them for two days, and on the morning of the third came over a rise to see, exactly in our path, a military tent with three Egyptian soldiers standing nearby. 'Just keep quiet and let us do the talking,' Sannat said.

We halted the *dabuuka* near the tent and couched our camels. One of the soldiers came directly towards us, carrying an automatic rifle. He was a corporal in untidy khaki with a peaked field-cap and unlaced boots. I pulled my headcloth more tightly over my face, hoping that it would disguise my features. The soldier shuffled around lazily, and for a moment I thought that he would tell us to carry on. Then he looked directly at me and snapped, 'Where is your passport?' I knew then that I should never get away with a deception. I showed him my passport and explained that I was British. Instead of answering me, he shouted, 'Which one is the guide – you.' Old Bakheit admitted with great dignity that the responsibility of the herd was his. 'You should know better than bringing strangers with you!' The soldier went on acidly, 'I am going to arrest you both!'

'The guide is not to blame,' I said. 'He did not know that foreigners are not allowed through the desert.'

'I will take you both to Abu Simbel, by God!' the guard said. Then Sannat stepped forward. 'If you take anyone, you must take us all,' he declared. 'We are companions.'

'If that is what you want,' said the guard, grinning nastily, 'it can be arranged. But Abu Simbel is a long way, and you will not be able to take your camels there.'

'The camels will die,' I said. 'It is my fault and no one else's. Just take me.'

'Very well,' the corporal said. 'You collect your things and come with me. And get those filthy clothes off. You put some European clothes on so we can see who you are.'

It took me only a a few moments to collect my saddle and saddle-bags. I carried them up to the tent, where a Toyota truck was parked. Then I walked back to my companions. The corporal stood looking at me, but did not try to interfere.

'Say the word, and we shall all come with you,' Bakkour said.

'No,' I replied. 'You cannot leave the camels. Anyway I shall be all right. They cannot harm me.'

'Get on with it!' the corporal ordered from the tent. 'You Arabs get moving or I will arrest you all, and damn your camels!' I embraced my companions one by one. Sannat was last. 'God protect you, Omar,' he said.

'God protect us all,' I replied.

I had no heart to watch the *dabuuka* as it moved on into the desert. Instead I went behind the tent and changed into jeans and a shirt, so that the Egyptians should know who I was. A change of clothes meant nothing now; the things I had seen, the things I had learned could not be changed so easily. When I emerged the herd and my companions had gone.

I was taken to Abu Simbel, where I was held for two days. The soldiers who detained me were conscripts who had no desire to be stuck here on Egypt's remotest border. They were friendly, especially when they found out I could speak Arabic. Many times they assured me, guiltily, 'We are only doing our job.' I was then escorted to Aswan and taken before the immigration authorities. I was told that not only had I entered the country illegally, I was also in breach of the currency regulations. I was given five days to go back to Britain.

I emerged from the office a free man, and plunged into the city. Aswan hit me like a wave. There followed a dazed two hours in which I tried to adjust to the new environment. I was confused by the rush of vehicles, the traffic lights and the tourists, my own barbarian race, looking ridiculous and undressed in their shorts and sunhats, with their rucksacks and sleeping-bags. The beautiful Egyptian girls with their black shining hair, the gleaming Nile, the white sails of the feloukas, the smart hotels, the glass-fronted gift shops, American Express, electric lights, ice-cream — I asked myself how all this could exist so near to the world I had left in the desert.

I caught the first train to Cairo, and two days later I had borrowed some money and was flying back to Britain. As the British Airways Trident took off, I had a quick glimpse of the Libyan desert, stretching away west beyond the pyramids. Already my mind was filled with new journeys and new projects.

Part 4
The Search for the Lost Oasis

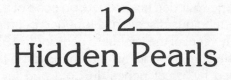

12
Hidden Pearls

The desert is terrible and it is merciless,
but to the desert all those who have
once known it must return.
Ahmad Mohammid Hassanein Bey,
'The Lost Oases'

I spent a restless time in Britain. I was trapped in a flat in London with no money and no chance of returning to the Sudan. I longed to be out of this prison of concrete and glass and back in the desert where the horizons stretched unblemished on all sides and where the works of men left little mark on the landscape.

I filled my empty days scouring the libraries of the Royal Geographical Society and the School of Oriental and African Studies, seeking vicariously what I could not obtain in reality. I pursued the legend of the lost oasis of Zarzura with an avidity born of frustration. Through the plethora of legends and travellers' tales, with their confusing and conflicting reports, I caught a glimpse of the desert as it had appeared to explorers of the past, mysterious, alien and wonderful. There were lost cities and treasure troves, buried rivers and hidden caves. There were stories of lost tribes of black warriors who came out of the sand-mist suddenly, falling like vultures on the people of some sleepy oasis.

The most substantial reference to Zarzura was to be found in an Arabic manuscript of the fifteenth century, *The Book of Hidden Pearls*:

From this last wadi starts a road which will lead you to the city of Zarzura, of which you will find the door closed; the city is white like a pigeon and on the door is carved the effigy of a bird. Take with your hand the key in the beak of the bird, then open the door to the city. Enter and there you will find great riches, also the king and queen asleep in their castle. Do not approach them, but take the treasure.

233

At first the passage sounded far-fetched, an echo of a fairy-tale. Then I thought of the fabulous discoveries that had been made in Upper Egypt in the early years of the twentieth century. In 1926 the Pharaoh Tutankhamun had been found 'asleep' in his tomb behind a sealed door, surrounded by 'great riches' in gold and jewels. It was not unthinkable, certainly to explorers like Hassanein, Kamal ad Din Hussein, Douglas Newbold and William Shaw, that similar legendary sites might be found buried in the desert sands. Newbold and Shaw had led their expedition in search of Zarzura in 1927, only one year after Howard Carter discovered the tomb of Tutankhamun.

Throughout the nineteenth century there were a number of references to Zarzura, and the name cropped up continually in travellers' tales. The general location of the lost oasis was thought to be somewhere in the vast sand-sea to the south of Egypt's Dakhla oasis. These tales were corroborated by reports of medieval Arab geographers such as Al Bakri, who in 1068 wrote of a lost oasis in this region. He told the story of a black giantess from there who was caught stealing dates in the Dakhla oasis. She spoke no known language, and after being released was tracked by her captors, though she outran them in the desert. He tied the story in with a more ancient legend, that of Al Jaza'ir — mystical glades of palm trees concealed in the desert sands, running with water and echoing with the eerie whistling of the jinn.

In the twelfth century another Arab writer, Al Idrisi, told of many deserted oases stretching across the Libyan desert. He quoted reports of a pagan race called the Taguitae, whose capital may have been at El 'Atrun. Vague and insubstantial as these reports seemed, references such as these led to the eventual discovery of oases such as Nukheila and 'Uwaynat in the 1920s.

It was Dr John Bell, the Director of Desert Survey in Cairo, who made the first scientific attempt to solve the riddle of Zarzura. He reckoned that if an oasis existed at all, it must be in a place where the surface was within 100 metres of the sub-surface water-level. From a number of surface-height readings and water-level readings that had been made, he worked out that there were only two areas in the region indicated by the legends where an oasis might possibly be found. One of them lay north of Nukheila oasis, in the region beyond El 'Atrun.

Acting on such information, Douglas Newbold and William Shaw set off in 1927 with a squadron of tribesmen of the Hawawir,

234

not only to discover the lost oasis, but also to make the first detailed exploration of the south Libyan desert. After marching with their camels for thirty-nine days, through El 'Atrun and Nukheila, where they made the first proper survey, they halted in the unknown country to the north. They climbed a steep ridge and gazed over the landscape ahead. If an oasis was likely to be found, then the relief should have fallen sharply. Instead it continued to rise. The two explorers reluctantly gave up their quest for Zarzura at this point. Later Newbold said, 'If it exists it is very probably to be found within a forty-mile radius of this point.'

As I followed the blow by blow accounts of the Zarzura controversy, I became fired with the desire to discover this desert grail. All the accounts indicated that if the oasis existed, it lay behind a barrier of dunes. I had seen the desert as far as El 'Atrun, and I knew that in places it was still as wild and uncharted as it had been in Newbold's day. By the end of summer 1983 I had a new goal. If the oasis of Zarzura was to be found, then I should find it. And I should find it with the help of my Kababish.

Still, I needed money. I was offered a job by ARAMCO, the Arabian-American Oil Company, teaching English to Saudi employees in one of their training centres. I accepted the job and flew to Dhahran.

I was sent to the training centre at Hofuf in the Hasa oasis in the middle of the Ghawar oil field, the largest reservoir of oil on earth. I taught English to students who shared ancestry with the Kababish. They belonged to famous bedouin tribes, the Harb and the 'Ajman, the Murrah, the 'Utayba and perhaps most ancient of all, the Bani Qahtan. Yet these young men were a new generation of bedouin who dressed in spotless white shirts and red-speckled headcloths. They raced away from class revving the engines of their brand-new Chevrolets and Cadillacs. I never found one amongst them who had ridden a camel.

In the evenings I returned to my Portakabin in Udhailiyya. It was a desert camp, surrounded by barbed wire and entered through check-points guarded by armed security men. At weekends I would scale the perimeter fence and walk out in the desert carrying a small rucksack. But the thrill of being outside soon palled. The desert of Arabia was not the wild mysterious place I had known in Africa. Everywhere there were the tracks of bulldozers and excavators, rusty pipelines and derelict gas plants. At night the stars were misted by the blear of oil flares and the sheen of arc lights, and the smell of petrol hung constantly on the breeze. It was more like a gigantic building site than a pristine wilderness.

Once, I drove down with a friend to Jibrin on the edge of the Empty Quarter. I remembered reading Wilfred Thesiger's account of his desperate journey here with the Rashid in 1948. We saw the desert marked with oil drums and littered with the carcasses of burned-out vehicles, abandoned by their owners. Camel herds were being driven by men who did not even bother to get out of their trucks, but just hooted wildly as the beasts ran before them. It seemed ironic that Thesiger should have said: 'Although I had travelled in the deserts of the Sudan and the Sahara, others had been there before me and the mystery was gone . . . The Empty Quarter became for me the promised land.' It was strange that less than a quarter of a century later, I should be standing on the edge of that 'promised land', feeling exactly the opposite emotion. I could hardly bear to look on the desecration that had taken place in this land. I yearned for the unspoiled deserts of the Sudan.

Only ten years before the Murrah, the so-called 'nomads of the nomads', still herded their camels in these sands that were almost untouched by the outside world. Now the old life of Arabia was gone for ever. There were prospecting teams working inside the Empty Quarter, and the Murrah carried their camels to Hofuf market in the back of pick-ups, with cranes to lift and lower them. There were still black tents by the roadside, but they were supplied by mobile generators and furnished with TVs and refrigerators. A few Murrah women in black *tobes* and veils still sat in a corner of Hofuf market selling waterskins and balls of goat's wool that were bought by American and British ARAMCO employees, who carried them back to their homes abroad as mementoes of a forgotten world.

I spent only three and a half months in Arabia, and flew back to the Sudan after a short stay in Kenya. I travelled to El Fasher and in the camel market there bought a superb *ashab* called Wad al Hambati ('Son of the Bandit'). I recrossed Zayadiyya country alone, staying off the track and camping each night in a concealed place. After only seven days I was back in the *dikka* at Umm Sunta.

There was a new order in the camp of the Kababish nazir. Sheikh Hassan had died quietly, and was buried in Omdurman. At Tom was the new nazir, and his relative At Tom Wad al Murr, was deputy. Of the old sheikhs, the sons of Sir Ali Wad at Tom, only Sheikh Ibrahim was a power to be reckoned with. I saw to my dismay that At Tom's first act had been to build a house of mud and thatch in the centre of the camp. He talked avidly of reform and of selling camels to buy motor-vehicles. I thought of the Murrah and of the burned-out cars at Jibrin, and kept quiet.

Many of my old friends were still in the *dikka*. Salim Wad Musa had heard news of me from Sannat on his return from Egypt. Juma' Wad Siniin had just returned from Dongola where he had been arrested for selling camels stolen from the Zayadiyya. He told me that Wad az Ziyadi was dead from an unknown illness. Adam Wad ash Shaham had also been ill and was too weak to ride, and Hamid had committed some peccadillo and was no longer a *ghaffir*. Wad Fadul and Wad Tarabish were still going strong.

I had long ago decided that should I need a companion from these men, I would choose either Wad Siniin or Wad Tarabish. Both were experienced, trustworthy and resilient. Wad Tarabish was occupied with his duties as court baillif and could not travel with me. Wad Siniin's official position was 'forest ranger', which meant that he was not tied down to any specific duties. When I asked him to go with me in search of Zarzura, he agreed at once.

The day after I arrived in the *dikka* there was a wedding. Hassan, the son of Sheikh Musa, and Salim's half-brother, was to be married to his cousin. The periods of mourning for Sheikh Hassan and al Murr were over and there was a great celebration. Amongst the nazir's people weddings were far more lavish than amongst the desert Kababish.

Marriage with first cousins was the rule rather than the exception in Kababish families. A Kababish boy always had first claim on his uncle's daughter, closest to him in age. The girl had no right of refusal. If any other suitor wished to marry her, he first had to secure the permission of her cousin. In general, the arrangement worked well; it prevented the dispersal of the herds and flocks.

I slept in the guest tent near the nazir's new house, and the next morning was woken by the bridegroom himself. There were several other guests, sleeping there, and after we had splashed water over our hands and faces, we walked to Sheikh Musa's tent, where a she-camel was being slaughtered. The slaves and servants began to peel away the skin of the animal, revealing a mass of gelatinous fatty flesh flecked with red, and beneath it the crimson seams of solid muscle.

A little later the meat was taken to the family *tukul*, where the women cooked it in oil over a wood fire. Meanwhile the guests began to arrive, hobbling their camels and donkeys by the tents and saluting the bridegroom and his father. Soon the delicious smell of cooking meat filled the air, and Sheikh Musa invited us into his tent. It had been extended and was decked out with drapes of magenta and white cotton. The ground was spread with hand-stitched carpets. One by one, the sheikhs of the Kababish joined us. Amongst them were many familiar faces.

Soon the platters of raw hump and liver were brought in, with dishes of onion, lemon and red pepper. There were bowls of steaming porridge served with milk, and chunks of cooked meat with delicious gravy. After everyone had eaten, the slaves poured water over our hands and we milled around in the desert outside. A cold wind blew from the north and the tents billowed slightly amongst the sharp claws of the *siyaal* trees.

All day meal followed meal. There was more raw liver, lights and hump; more porridge and roast meat. Sheep and goats were slaughtered to keep up with the scores of guests who came and went. Just before sunset the bridegroom appeared from his father's tent. He was a dark Arab, clad now in a *jibba* of almost luminescent white, with a brilliant white-lace headcloth and cotton *sirwal*. He wore a woollen *tobe* coiled around the pit of his back, with the ends thrown over his shoulders in the Kababish style. In one hand he carried a camel-whip and in the other a silver-hilted sword in a scabbard of leather. On his left wrist he wore a piece of silk and on the other a heavy bracelet of silver. As he emerged, someone brought up a black mare, caparisoned with a high wooden saddle and decorated with a rich saddle-cloth. He mounted the horse, and his sword and whip were passed up to him. Many people called out encouragement, but he maintained a dead-pan expression, laying the sword across his pommel and keeping the whip stiff in his hand as if he were riding out to battle.

As soon as the servants led the mare off, everyone scrambled madly to get on their donkeys and camels, and follow the procession. The men cheered and raised their whips, and the boys wove playful circles around the groom on their small donkeys. The women poured out of the tents dressed in their wedding finery: long swirling dresses of scarlet and blue, *tobes* of purple and lime-green, thick nose-rings of gold, chunks of amber and ivory, and torques of silver, their fine black hair cascading over the neck in plaited *mashat* newly smothered in butter. They chanted and clapped, letting forth shrill ululations as they went, and the serpent of Arabs wound on towards the globe of the dying sun.

Our destination was the *hajil*, the tent specially erected for the newly wedded couple. It was pitched an equal distance between the tents of the groom's family and the bride's.

The bride was still in her father's tent, where she had been confined for the past seven days. During this time her female relations would have prepared her for the marriage. First, they removed all her body hair, using a mixture of sugar, lemon and water as a depilatory. Then they would annoint her with an exotic perfume called *dilka* made of a mixture of spices and sandalwood. The bride would have been made to squat over a hole in which a fire of sweet-smelling herbs and incense had been lit. The woman's hair would be carefully plaited in the *mashat* style and hung with pendants of gold. The Kababish women wore gold in the form of nose-bands and necklaces, but never on their hands. The bride might also be decked in bracelets of twisted silver or ivory and necklaces of amber and cornelian. The nomad women despised the practice of using henna, and never stained their hands and feet as the townswomen did.

When the woman was prepared, she put on her brightest dress and over it her most costly *tobe*, so that she was covered from head to foot. Finally, she donned a small apron of woven leather called a *rahat*, which had a symbolic function in the marriage. Once ready, the bride was carried to the *hajil* by her male relatives.

While we were waiting for the bride to arrive, Hassan took up his position outside the door of the new tent. He was still mounted, though everyone else had dismounted from their animals and stood watching silently. It was just after sunset; there were streaks of gold painted at angles across the sky, in a swelter of lacy grey clouds. The wind had dropped; there was a peaceful silence. Someone brought up the green branch of a tree and planted it in the ground as a symbol of good fortune.

One by one Hassan's closest relations stepped forward, beginning with his father, Sheikh Musa. They touched him ritually on the hand, pledging a number of camels, cattle, goats or sheep as wedding gifts.

After the pledging the bride was carried up like a parcel, completely wrapped in her *tobe*. Her relations carried her around the tent, circling it three times before she was taken inside. Only then did Hassan dismount. As he entered the tent, the crowd surged forward to see what followed. I was just in time to see the bride and groom standing shyly together. Hassan reached out and snatched away the leather *rahat,* which was held in place by a flimsy thread. He cast it out through the door-gap. At once the people around me dodged out of the way and scattered frantically. One young lad of about twelve was not quick enough, and the leather apron struck him. The others began to jeer and point, laughing loudly. Salim Wad Musa told me, 'The Arabs say that anyone hit by the *rahat* will never marry!'

Afterwards we crowded into the tent. It was lit by an oil lamp, but was otherwise stark and bare, devoid of furnishings except for a thick carpet. The bride and groom sat next to each other on the floor near the back of the tent. As the Arabs gathered around them, the women began to sing:

Make your tent-poles steady as iron!
Make your house full of wealth and abundance!

Someone brought in a dish of milk. It was placed between the couple, and at once they dipped their toes into it, then their fingers. The milk was symbolic of the abundance they hoped for. I could hardly make out Hassan's face in the flickering light, but his body was rigid and his attitude formal. The woman remained covered and the pair did not speak.

Then a strange thing happened. An invisible gap in the back of the tent opened suddenly, and three or four men came through it, seizing the bride and making off with her abruptly. I wondered what it meant. The celebrations seemed to have been brought to an unexpected end. Salim Wad Musa said, 'Tonight is only the first part of the wedding. The consummation will be in a week's time.'

For the rest of the week Hassan would sleep in the new tent, which would gradually be decorated by the rich leather work I had seen in other tents. A double bed of palm stalks would be introduced, surrounded by an alcove of woven gazelle hide. By the end of the week the shelter would be transformed from an austere dwelling into a comfortable home for the married couple. The fine leatherwork was made by the women of the bride's family, who were also responsible for making the bridal litter, the *'utfa,* out of light flexible wood.

During the week the groom would feed well on meat, milk and

sorghum beer. On the last day he would lunch with his father, then return to the *hajil* by sunset. On this occasion the bride would arrive on foot, with only a few female relatives. They would enter the tent and sit with the groom. The relatives would flirt, and laugh together. While the bride would maintain a reserved demeanour, making a great show of modesty and reluctance. Eventually the relatives would leave. The bride would rise and try to leave with them, and the man would be obliged to grab her tightly to prevent her. Often there was quite a struggle and the groom might even be pulled across the tent. If he were too slow, she might actually escape and run off into the night. Then he would be forced to chase her, to the great amusement of the onlookers.

Once all the guests had left it was time to consummate the marriage. But even then the couple were not left alone. Friends and relations would remain outside the tent as spectators, shouting bawdy encouragement and beating the tent with their whips. They would even peek under the tent flap to see how things were progressing. The irritation might last for hours, sometimes until dawn. 'The first night is like a battle!' Salim Wad Musa said. 'You have to fight the people outside, chasing them away with your whip, and at the same time stop your bride from escaping. And after all that you have to do your duty!'

Sex was performed without any foreplay or kissing, which the Kababish considered degenerate; there was no touching other than the sexual act itself. The groom was expected to enter the woman in a single act of penetration, and if he failed in this he would be open to ridicule, for the bride would certainly reveal it to her female relatives. It was difficult for both partners because of the custom of female circumcision, which reduced the vagina to a tiny hole.

After the consummation the bride and groom were not supposed to leave the tent for a period that varied from fifteen to forty days, and during that time they were not supposed to wash their clothes. After this they would slaughter an animal and have another celebration. From then on they would live as an ordinary married couple. Generally they would start life with the bride's family, perhaps until the time of the migrations, when they would shift to the groom's people. The man would bring a camel especially to carry his new wife's litter and it would be decked out with ostrich feathers, and leather hangings decorated with cowrie shells. The bride would put on her finest clothes and ride in splendour to the new location.

241

Amongst the Kababish, women had a freedom not found amongst some other Arab tribes. The tent was not divided into male and female parts as those of the Arabian bedouin, and the women were never veiled. It was no disgrace for a woman to be alone in a tent with a male guest except after dark.

I often wondered if circumcision was the price they paid for this freedom. It was practised on girls between the ages of about four and ten. The operation was done by traditional midwives and the men were never present. They used a sharp razor or a knife, and removed the clitoris and the flesh surrounding it. After the operation the sides of the wound were brought together and covered with animal dung. The legs would be tightly bound at the ankle, knees and thigh, and would remain so for up to a month.

The origin of this type of circumcision is unknown. It was practised in ancient Egypt, as certain mummies of the New Kingdom era testify. Though it is still widely practised in the Sudan and Egypt, it is unknown amongst bedouin of Saudi Arabia, Libya and north-west Africa, whose ancestry is cognate with the Kababish.

The day after the wedding I rode to the wells at Umm Sunta with Salim Wad Musa. A large herd belonging to some 'Atawiyya was being watered there, and I wanted to buy from them a good desert camel that Juma' Wad Siniin would ride on our forthcoming journey. It was soon after dawn and the dust was still grey in the air. The iron troughs were already filling up and the 'Atawiyya herdsmen were lining them with salt. These men were from Wadi Howar in the north, and had the chiselled-stone look of desert Arabs, their garments soiled yellow with wear and their headcloths tied flat in the Kababish manner.

One of them showed us a gigantic male camel that was almost red in colour. It was enormously fat and powerful, the best camel in the herd. I agreed to buy it at once, knowing that it was unusual for an Arab to sell his best camel. It was the most expensive camel I had ever bought, and almost the most troublesome.

Later I rode into the market to buy provisions. Umm Sunta had the same bleak look about it, with its verandas and hitching-posts, each the centre point of a circle of camels with saddlery dumped around them. Here the nomads stood shoulder to shoulder in the tiny stores, confronting the merchants and clamouring for attention. The Arabs observed no rules of queuing, nor were they slow to

242

criticize the merchants. The merchants never seemed to mind. The nomads had no choice but to buy from them.

There were some new faces in the market-place, men and women of the Gur'an tribe from the Ennedi hills in Chad. It was the first time I had seen them in the *dar*. The men were tall and black with long narrow faces and fine features. They dressed in shirts slashed at the sides, with their headcloths tightly bound over the lower parts of their faces. The women were small and friendly and brimming with confidence. Two of the men had been employed as herdsmen by the nazir's people. One of them told me that they had migrated from the Ennedi hills as the grazing there had failed.

The Gur'an were the eastern branch of an ancient desert people, known in the north as Teda and in the west as Daza. They were black nomads, and until the 1930s a group of them had been the scourge of the Libyan desert. In small, mobile parties they had sallied forth from their mountain strongholds, using oases and secret wells as stepping-stones and covering vast distances. They had raided oases in the western desert of Egypt and had often attacked the Ga'ab oases near Dongola. I guessed that many of the old legends of giants and mysterious black warriors were connected with the Gur'an.

The Kababish regarded the Gur'an as equals, despite the fact that they were black. This was possibly because they belonged to an aristocratic society consisting of a warrior nobility, with all the chivalry which that implied; the Kababish also saw themselves as natural aristocrats and recognized the same qualities in this other race. Kababish men said that Gur'an women made excellent wives because they were aggressive and self-reliant, capable of herding camels and defending them against attack. Gur'an women carried daggers like men, and were not afraid to use them.

In the *dikka* that afternoon I had a longer talk with Juma' Wad Siniin. He told me frankly that he had never heard of Zarzura, but that he was willing to trust my navigation. I knew that I could ask no more of him. I tried to trace the old man who had first mentioned Zarzura to me, thinking that he must be a survivor of Newbold's expedition. No one seemed to know him, and Salim Wad Musa could not remember who he was. While Juma' and I were talking, Wad Tarabish came up with an Arab of the Awlad Sulayman, called Baaqil. He was from Wadi Howar, and claimed that he knew the desert beyond El 'Atrun better than anyone else. He said that he had once driven some camels to Kufra alone. It soon became clear that he was jealous of Juma' and was trying to persuade me to employ him instead. He had not heard of Zarzura, nor of any of the other remote oases, and he failed to answer several of the questions I asked him. Then he grew angry and said, 'Have you been to Nukheila before? No? Then you will be greeting my mother. And she died ten years ago!' Then he stalked off.

I was up very early the next morning, releasing my camels from their hobbles and letting them browse in the *siyaal* trees. As I watched, the sun came up; framed in the spiked branches, it lingered for a moment, a great orange globe on the edge of the world. Two old women in black cloaks came hobbling out of the nearby *tukul*. One began to beat at a *siyaal* tree with a long pole, knocking down the pods so that the goats could feed; the other began to collect bits of firewood.

It was almost noon when Juma' came out of the thorn groves on his emaciated donkey. Together we assembled our food and equipment. A host of people from the *dikka* gathered around to wish us well. Before we mounted someone said 'Al Fatih', and we presented our hands in supplication. Then we swung into our saddles and rode off at a fast trot towards the wadi.

13
The Last of the Desert Arabs

If a man were to leave the river he might
journey westward and find no human
habitation, except the lonely tent of a
Kababish Arab or the encampment of
a trader's caravan until he reached the
coast of America.
Winston Churchill, The River War, *1899*

The land north of Umm Sunta was deserted except for some scattered families of 'Atawiyya. They had learned to blend in with the arid environment like desert foxes, but many other Arabs had poured out of the steppes and gathered around the wells in the wadi of Abu Bassama. As we rode north, we saw many camel-hair tents pitched in the *siyaal* groves on the wadi-banks. Clouds of dust rose from the animals being watered at the wells.

At noon we halted in the wadi and let the camels browse in the *inderab* leaves that lay like gold flake on the banks. We laid out our equipment and examined it carefully. I was using a riding saddle that I had bought in El Fasher, while Juma' was using a pack saddle. 'You should have changed your saddle,' Juma' said. 'Those riding saddles are no good for the open desert. They put more strain on the camel. We will try to exchange it ahead.' We inspected our water containers. We had four *girbas*, each carrying about five gallons of water. Two of them were full, but the others were new and leaked badly where the stitching was not properly waterproofed. Juma' cut some strips of green *inderab* bark and carefully sealed the leaks one by one. 'The *inderab* is the prince of trees after the date palm,' the Arab declared. 'The wood is hard and flexible, the bark is strong and the leaves are nutritious. Abu Bassama is well known for its *inderab*.' When the waterskins were ready, he took out some old sacks and split them, covering the skins one by one. 'These keep the water cool,' he said. 'And they stop the wind drinking it.'

245

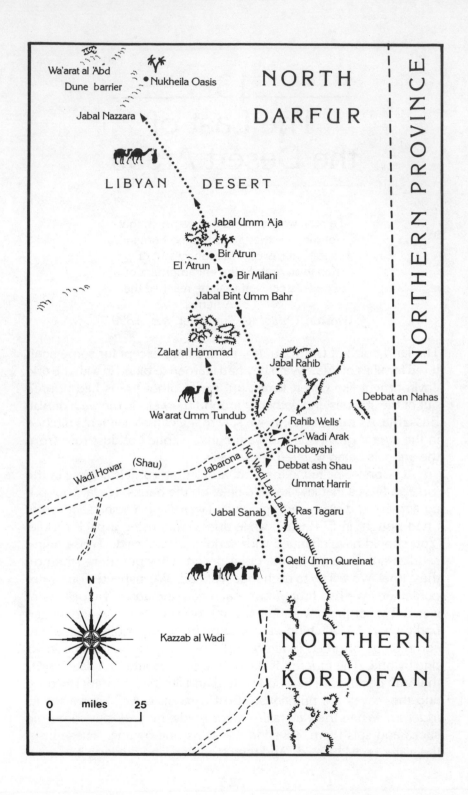

Wa'arat al 'Abd
Dune barrier
• Nukheila Oasis
Jabal Nazzara

NORTH
DARFUR

NORTHERN PROVINCE

LIBYAN DESERT

Jabal Umm 'Aja
• Bir Atrun
El 'Atrun
• Bir Milani
Jabal Bint Umm Bahr

Zalat al Hammad
Jabal Rahib
Debbat an Nahas

Wa'arat Umm Tundub
Rahib Wells'
Wadi Arak
Ghobayshi
Debbat ash Shau
Ummat Harrir

Wadi Howar   (Shau)
Jabarona

Jabal Sanab
Ras Tagaru

Qelti Umm Qureinat

N

Kazzab al Wadi

NORTHERN
KORDOFAN

0   miles   25

It was almost summer. If the temperature remained average, then we should each not need more than six pints of water a day, and our twenty gallons would last us for more than ten days. If summer conditions prevailed, however, our consumption would be double.

Before we set off, Juma' unwrapped his headcloth and put on a khaki army beret. It had a black lining, and he turned it inside out so that this side showed. 'It is to prove that I am a *ghaffir*,' he told me. 'When I have official things to do, I wear it with the other side showing. But until then I shall wear it this way.' I thought of Wad Fadul and his Boy Scout badge, and said nothing.

We rode on into the afternoon, seeing only some 'Atawiyya who were busy watering sheep and goats from a deep-well in the middle of a plain covered in silver *la'ot* trees. They were using two camels to hoist the water, each animal straining alternately in opposite directions. The great cowskin hawsers creaked. The pulleys screamed and spun as the ribbed buckets sailed up to the well-head, to be dragged off by groups of shock-headed Arabs who poured the water into deep stone basins. The flocks crowded around them, pawing at the ground, and the water was finished before the Arabs had even flung the bucket back into the well.

We spent the night near Umm 'Ajayja and the next day pressed on towards the Hattan plateau. At noon we made camp by some *tundub* trees at the foot of the pass, not far from where we had been caught by a freak storm two years before. There were still a few stunted hummocks of grass on the sand-flats that Juma' said were the products of that storm. It had not rained again since that day. We hobbled the camels and turned them into the sparse grazing. Wad al Hambati grazed happily, but the red camel, which we had named Hambarib ('The Little Wind'), fretted continually and turned his head from side to side, looking back forlornly towards Umm Sunta where he had left his herd. He would not eat. 'Hambarib wants camels, not grazing!' Juma' declared. 'His belly is full.'

My companion set to work to mend the pack saddle that had been broken slightly during the morning. I stood and watched Hambarib as he slowly shuffled farther from the camp. He was not interested in the juicy *tundub* shoots and seemed very agitated. I had seen camels behave like this several times before, and it usually preceded something odd. His forefeet, restricted by the *gayd*, were moving very fast. I realized suddenly that he was trying to escape,

247

and ran around a bluff of sand with some ragged vegetation to head him off. It was the worst thing I could have done. Sensing my sudden movement, the camel bounded forward in double-legged strides. A second later the leather hobble snapped and fell uselessly into the sand. Hambarib bellowed a single victory roar, and surged forward, breaking into a gallop. He charged off amongst the hillocks of sand, lifting his legs high and weaving around the scattered trees. Without hesitation I ran back to the camp, shouting, 'The hobble broke! He is running south!' In an instant Juma' had couched the other camel and was saddling him. Moments later he galloped off in pursuit of the monster, leaving me alone with our useless luggage.

I sat down by the trees and waited. Many minutes went past. I reflected that camels always brought me bad luck. Hambarib was the most expensive animal I had ever bought, but still he was unreliable. I was beginning to wonder what I should do if Juma' did not return, when he rode suddenly out of the landscape, dragging the great camel behind his mount on a piece of rope. He slipped down from the saddle grinning happily. 'His heart is sour!' Juma' said. 'That is why they sold him. He is a cunning one, but not as cunning as uncle Juma'!' As I unsaddled Hambati, he led the big camel to a tree and tied him securely. Then he took some strands of plastic rope and made a firm hobble. 'You will not snap this one so easily!' he told the animal. 'We know what you are now. You won't get the chance again, by God!' He hobbled the camel's forelegs with the new rope. 'Plastic rubs the hair off, but it is stronger than leather,' he said.

When we sat down and made tea, Juma' told me how he had captured the beast. 'I picked up his tracks and rode after him at a steady pace,' he said. 'He is a big camel, but he soon got tired. As soon as he slowed down I charged after him at full speed. He thought I should get him, so he galloped off again. Then I slowed down so that he would tire himself out. As soon as he slowed I charged again. I kept it up, charging and slowing, until he was exhausted. Then I just rode up to him in the wadi and lassoed him with the spare rope. He came as quietly as a child! But your *ashab* is fast, by God! I should never have caught him without Hambati!' For the rest of the afternoon the red camel raged to himself, desperately trying to smash the tree and break his headrope. When Juma' saddled him at the end of the break, he dropped a few gobbets of cud to register his disapproval.

We climbed the pass up to Hattan that evening. Gone was the

running water I remembered from my previous expedition. A family of 'Atawiyya were climbing the pass, two men and two boys who wore their hair in masses of curls and carried home-made rifles pitted with rust. They were driving a few goats and sheep and leading two thin camels. A half-grown saluki bitch ran close behind them. We dismounted to lead our camels up the narrow path, watching the goats and sheep scampering away above us.

We camped with the 'Atawiyya in some trees on the plateau summit. They slaughtered a goat for us, and we cooked it in oil and ate together. I asked the 'Atawiyya if they normally grazed in Hattan. 'It is only because of the drought,' answered one of them, a tall man called Salih. 'Or we should still be with our kinsmen north of Khitimai. We move a little further south each year.'

'There is plenty of shooting,' another 'Atawi told us. 'You had better be careful ahead. You know, the grazing in Meidob is finished. The Meidob are in trouble. They have all become bandits and they search the desert for Arab camels. Be on your guard further north!'

These 'Atawiyya lived an incredibly hard life, yet they had none of the suppressed violence I had sensed with the Sarajab. They seemed courageous, confident and dignified. I could not explain why men who lived such similar lives should be so different in character. When I asked Juma' his opinion, he said, 'Of course, it is true. It is like father, like son. It is true of camels. When you breed them you know how they will turn out, or at least you have a good idea. Humans are the same. It is well known that the Sarajab are the rudest Arabs amongst the Kababish, just as it is known that the Barara are honest and the 'Awajda are cowardly. The 'Atawiyya are known as brave fighting men. They are not afraid. They are amongst the best raiders in the Kababish.'

'Who are the others?' I asked him.

'The Nurab, of course,' he answered, grinning.

The following day we travelled with the 'Atawiyya across the face of the mountain. At midday we descended into the pool at Umm Suggura. There was no water in the pool and the trees around it were bare. As we approached we saw that one of the *siyaal* trees was black and smouldering. A group of Arab youths stood around it. At once Juma' took off his beret and replaced it with the official side showing. He pulled it down sharply and with a grim expression rode towards the youths. 'Why have you burned that tree?' he snapped at them.

'No reason,' one of the Arabs answered.

'It is forbidden,' he told them. 'Only last month the nazir gave someone fifty lashes for cutting one branch of a tree, one branch, you understand?' Then he turned to me officiously and said, 'Take their names, Omar! We will report them when we get back.'

'There are plenty of trees!' exclaimed one of the boys.

Juma' bent forwards. 'Remember this my son, and remember it well. Whoever destroys a tree in this land destroys life itself!'

Khitimai valley was now nothing more than light-brown sand edged with the brooding outline of the hills. We rode down from the plateau into the cool of evening, and arrived at the bore-well in darkness. We made camp with some Arabs of the Awlad Sulayman, relations of the guide Baaqil whom we had met in the *dikka*. One of them was an old man who questioned Juma' closely about the route we would take. Then he said to me, with unashamed frankness, 'There is no such place as Zarzura. I was born in the desert and I have never heard of it. You will not even find your way to Nukheila. Juma' does not know the route. He thought Rahib came before Jabarona!' I explained that I should be responsible for navigation and that I had brought Juma' as a companion, not as a guide. Like Baaqil, the Sulaymani claimed he had an excellent knowledge of the desert. He had grazed his camels as far north as Nukheila in the past. 'Some of the Sulayman used to go as far as 'Uwaynat,' he told me. 'But it was much easier in the old days. Then you could find grass scattered through the sands. Now you will never get beyond Nukheila. There is nothing there. The weather is getting hot and your camels will die.'

As we set off the next morning, Juma' said, 'God's curse on all Sulayman. They have plenty of talk, but the truth is they know nothing.'

All day we rode over cherry-pink sand hills scattered with depressions in which sat coarse little clumps of thorn trees, *gafal*, *kitir*, *siyaal* and *sarh*. A string of 'Atawiyya tents stood on the bare side of a hill. Some tiny Arab children played around them in the shrivelling heat. 'See, just like desert foxes!' Juma' said.

As we rose the next morning we saw the cliffs of Tagaru massif in the early light. I had passed east of the inselberg with the Sarajab, but this time we should traverse it from the west and explore it more closely. As we drank tea, Juma' said, 'I have a devil in my head that won't let me sleep. I have had it for years. I am lucky if I snatch a short doze in the night.' He told me that he had awoken in the night and thrown the *khatt*. I had seen him do this many times before. It was a form of divination in which the Arabs made chains of marks in the sand with the thumb and forefinger. 'What did you see?' I asked him.

'I saw a white camel,' he said gravely. 'And a man coming towards me from the back. I did not see him but he saw me. He was a good man!'

We packed up and rode towards the southern toe of Tagaru, known as Qalb al Ba'ir ('The Camel's Heart'). Before us the land dropped into a wide trench of sand filled with trees. It was the Wadi Mafarit that joined the Tagaru plateau with the Meidob hills. It was the richest vein of vegetation in this part of the desert, and the Meidob used it as a highway by which to approach the desert lands.

We had been riding for about two hours when Juma' shouted, 'Look, by God! A white camel!' Far to the east I caught the reflection of a large white body amongst the trees. I remembered Juma's prediction, though it seemed little more than a coincidence. The 'Atawiyya often let their camels graze unattended, and there were probably several white camels browsing in the area. I was not, however, prepared for what happened next. There was a sudden commotion behind us, and turning we saw an angry little Arab carrying a Kalashnikov rifle and wearing a fuzzy mass of hair. He seemed to have materialized out of the desert sands. He ignored our greetings as we couched our camels, and stood there panting. Then he said, 'I have been shouting you for minutes! Why did you not answer? I am dying of thirst! Have you no humanity?'

'We did not hear you!' Juma' answered.

'Give me water!'

We poured out a bowlful of water. The man drank it with slow and appreciative dignity. Then he held up a tiny gazelleskin, and Juma' filled it. 'What is your family?' he asked.

'My family is 'Atawiyya from Wadi Howar,' the man answered. 'But I am taking my camels south in search of pasture. I have not drunk water for five days, by God! I have one she-camel in milk and the milk keeps me going. But you cannot make proper tea out of milk.'

'What about the *geltis* in the mountain?' Juma' asked, referring to the rock pools where water collected. 'Is there no water there?'

'All finished,' the man told us. 'All finished months ago!'

I could not explain how Juma' had been able to predict these events with such accuracy. He told me, 'The *khatt* is unreliable. Sometimes it tells you everything, and sometimes it is completely wrong!'

At mid-morning we stopped in some trees. The heat throbbed over us and Juma' said, 'The summer is coming. There will be the *simoom* soon – the hot winds from the north. If the *simoom* comes we shall never find Zarzura. We shall be lucky to get back to Umm Sunta.' But as we set off later, a beautiful cool wind came down from the desert. We moved towards the great bluffs and spurs of Tagaru, which were now visible before us. As we approached, I saw that the bluffs were higher than they seemed, and after a while I could see the pimples and veins etched in the face of the sandstone. Ridges of sand were piled against the foot of the cliffs, bordered with fields of blue boulders, through which a few straggling *sallam* trees pushed.

Just south of the toe of the mountain we came on a patch of hard ground, which Juma' called a 'city'. There were many ancient grindstones, millions of fragments of shattered bone, arrowheads of flint and stone axes of diorite. There were stones set in the ground that suggested houses, and some that might have been a large enclosure. The large number of milling and grinding stones seemed to indicate that agricultural people had once tilled this hard land.

Little is known of the early history of this part of the Sahara, though rock pictures such as those I had seen at Jabal Musawwira suggested that cattle-rearing pastoralists once roamed the entire area. Despite the great number of milling stones that have been found, scientists believe that these people did not practise agriculture, but made flour from wild grasses such as the *haskanit*, which still grows in abundance on the desert steppes. It is not known for certain which race these men belonged to. The detailed naturalistic rock paintings discovered in places such as Tassili 'n' Ajjer in the north indicate that the pastoralists had some customs still practised by the Fulani peoples of the Sahel.

Whomever they might have been, they were replaced by Semitic-speaking camel nomads who were established in the desert by 1000 BC. The stones at the foot of Tagaru, evidence of the desert's past, were sober reminders of how quickly and completely a culture might disappear.

Tagaru was discovered by Douglas Newbold in 1924. It was an inselberg of sandstone stretching eighty miles through the desert.

The vast area of the interior was crossed by corries and canyons, which still hid addra, gazelle, ostrich and Barbary sheep.

We camped at night near the cliffs, where we found some clumps of *nissa* growing along a shallow wash. We had no firewood, so I took a torch and walked west along the shallow wadi in the darkness. About two kilometres away I found a single *sarh* tree with just enough fragments of wood scattered about to make a fire. I carried it back to Juma' and laid it at his feet triumphantly. He smiled, saying, 'Omar, you are a man!' I knew this was the greatest compliment a Kabbashi could make. A second later, though, he spoiled it by saying, 'The only thing wrong with you is that you have no woman. A man without a woman is like a camel without a nosebag!'

The next day we followed the line of the cliffs, gnarled and weathered, chocolate-brown and rust-red, towering over us like battlements. There were many details to divert us – the fresh track of a hyena, many V-shaped pads of gazelles, the imprint of a riding camel, the old grooves of a salt caravan, and the recent marks of a small grazing herd. 'There are twelve camels in that herd,' Juma' said. 'And they have come from Khitimai in the last few days, because they are well watered. One of them is being ridden. It is a calf, no more than a four-year-old. It might be the Sarajab boy I heard about in Khitimai.'

Later we turned off east into the belly of the massif, so that I might get an impression of its interior. We climbed a steep track up into the plateau. It felt like a fresh new world. There were no tracks or droppings here. From the top of the track we had a magnificent view of the valley beneath. A sheet of bright red sand swept down to the valley floor, where it met a covering of thorn trees. At the very bottom of the gorge stood a perfect circle of stones. It looked like the foundation of an ancient round-house, built long ago, before this land was desert. I tried to imagine what it would be like to live here now. Juma' told me that some of the 'Atawiyya spent weeks amongst the canyons of Tagaru, grazing their camels and drinking camel's milk, drawing water from the hidden *geltis* when they were full, and shooting addra and Barbary sheep on the plateau.

As we descended the side of the valley again, we saw many caves and natural arches cut into the stone along the galleries of red-gold bluffs. Almost at once we picked up the tracks of the small herd once again. 'He is very near,' Juma' said. 'We will catch up with him before dark.' The sun was already sinking over the featureless horizon to the west, when we came upon the herd. There were twelve camels, exactly as my companion had said, and they were being driven by a youth of the Sarajab called Kalklayt. He was about seventeen and rode a trim four-year-old camel, carrying nothing but a goatskin saddle-bag, a set of hobbles and a *kabaros.*

We made camp with Kalklayt that night. I thought his name amusing, but Juma' told me that it was a Kababish word meaning 'kind'. He had seen no one for fifteen days, and had been herding his camels inside Tagaru. 'It is twenty-six days since the camels watered,' he declared. Juma' glanced at the camels and said nothing. 'I know every inch of this desert,' the youth boasted. 'It suits me more than the wadi. But herding your camels alone is difficult. Today I lost my baggage camel in the hills. It had the rest of my hobbles, my cooking pots and my money.' Juma' made porridge, and the boy ate with us, ravenously. Afterwards he drank cup after cup of tea as I poured it out. I admired his toughness, but Juma' shot him questioning glances that I did not understand.

We awoke to the roar of the wind, and arose in a blizzard of dust. It was so powerful we could scarcely stand; it was a struggle to strap on our gear. Kalklayt unhitched his riding beast, saying that he would ride back into the plateau to search for his missing camel. I thought him mad to try in this blizzard, but Juma' made no comment.

It was the most violent sand-storm I had experienced. Visibility was down to a few metres; the great cliffs to the east dissolved into the dust, reappearing occasionally as disjointed humps or tumuli of rock. We plodded on into the wind, winding our headcloths tight around our faces. The camels blinked the sand out of their eyes with their long windscreen-wiper eyelids. There is no animal on earth so well adapted to such storms. Since the heaviest granules of sand moved within six feet of the desert surface, the camel managed to keep its head out of the main blast, and its slit-nostrils could be sealed to prevent the dust entering. We crossed over an elbow of broken detritus and descended into a flat sandy plain bordered by interlocking sayf dunes that were sometimes just visible through the swirling dust. I knew that Juma' could not navigate in this turmoil, and my Silva compass was constantly in my hand. It was as comforting as a brother. It had probably saved my life on at least one occasion.

At noon we found ourselves amongst some stunted *sallam* and tried to rest. The wind lashed us like a cat-o'-nine-tails, ripping down the shelter we tried to erect and baffling all efforts to make a fire. The violence of the wind shocked me. The camels turned their backs to it and waited patiently for the storm to drop. We had no choice but to do the same, lying in the shelter of their great bodies while our clothes filled with sand.

Towards the end of the afternoon the wind dropped mercifully. I was exhausted. Juma' kindled a fire and made tea, hot, thick and tasting of tar. We saddled quickly, and moved over a great sand-sheet of orange, as flat as paper and decorated with nodules of grit, like gazelle droppings. There was the occasional *sarh* tree, leaning over at an acute angle or tilting out of the land like a drunken scarecrow. The sky was white with dust and there was no sound but the rhythmic percussion of the camel's feet, 'ker sho, ker sho, ker sho', on the sand.

For the first time all day we were able to talk again. 'I wonder if Kalklayt found his camel,' was the first thing Juma' said.

'He was crazy to try it in this!'

'There was something odd about that youth,' Juma' declared. 'He said that he had lost his baggage camel, yet did you notice – he was carrying twelve hobbles on his riding beast.'

'He said that he had lost some of his hobbles.'

'Why should he be carrying more than he needed? He had his saddle-bag and his *kabaros* – what more does a herdsman carry? What Arab leaves his money on his baggage camel? I do not believe a word he said. I swear, by God, that those tracks came from Khit-imai, not from inside the mountain. His camels did not look thirsty to me, yet he said they had not drunk for nearly a month. Those Sarajab are bad ones, by Almighty God! There is not an honest man amongst them!'

'Why should he lie?'

'Only God knows! But there is a reason. You can be sure he is hiding something. Perhaps we will find out in Wadi Howar.'

Ras Tagaru was already in sight. Here the cliff wall broke up into a ragged edge and finally degenerated into disconnected lumps of sandstone. We crossed the broken country beyond until the sun sank into the immense sand-sea on our left, and the last thing we saw behind us was the red cliff of Tagaru glowing like molten copper.

It took us five hours next morning to reach Wadi Howar. The wadi was thought to be an ancient drainage system that had carried water from the foot of the Chadian highlands far out into the desert, but no one had ever seen water running in it. It was famous for its game and for its *arak* trees that grew nowhere else in the desert. In good years there was some grass here too, including *'agul*, and *hadd* bushes. The Kababish had sunk many wells along its length. Although the trees were only shadows of their former selves, many families of the Sulayman, the 'Atawiyya and the Awlad Huwal remained here, adamantly refusing to move south. Many of them had spent their entire lives in the desert and knew little of the world outside; to them the nazir was little more than a name and the Sudan was a country that lay somewhere to the south and east.

In Wadi Howar we turned west and picked our way through the bars of sand. I remembered reading of the famous Bedayatt guide, Bidi Awdi, who had led a caravan through this way on his trek to Kufra in 1915. He had been instructed by the Darfur Sultan, Ali Dinar, to take slaves as presents to the Senussi brethren who then occupied the oasis. They had run out of water in Wadi Howar, and the guide had ridden fast to El 'Atrun with two of his men and filled up twelve waterskins. On their return they had found four people dead from thirst, and the rest lying on the sands, jibbering with madness and fear. The camels had scattered into the desert. Such tragedies still happened. Juma' told me of a truck returning from Libya that had run out of petrol south of the wadi only a few years earlier. Some of the passengers had walked off into the sands, while others had remained with the vehicle. One of those who left had eventually been picked up by some nomads who had carried him to the police-post in Wakhaym on their camels. The police had set out in a Land-Rover and found the truck. A few men were still alive, sheltering in the shade of its chassis. All those who had wandered into the desert were found dead.

At Jabarona there were a number of 'Atawiyya families camping around a well. We were welcomed by Ahmad Wad Fadil, an 'Atawi who had been born in the wadi and had lived there all his life. His tent was pitched in a hollow where the sand had been swept off the surface by the wind. It was made of four *shuggas* in the usual way, but was completely open on one side. There was no furniture but a palm-stalk bed that was laid flat in the sand rather than being raised on pegs. One side of the tent was screened by a sheet of gazelleskin, and on the other side was a tiny storehouse that the Arabs called a *khun*. Opposite the tent was a *tukul* of light wood, in which a set of time-blackened cooking pots were hanging.

Ahmad Wad Fadil received us with great dignity, standing out-side his tent as we approached. He was a small, tight-muscled man with a face so fair it was almost red. He had the blue-glazed eyes of the desert Arabs and wore a shirt that looked as if it had been deliber-ately matured for years in the desert sand. He shook hands with us like a lord, saying, 'You grace my house! Welcome in peace!' He called to his herdsman, a tall, slim black youth who belonged to the Gur'an to take our camels and make a small place for us about twenty metres from the tent. Once our gear was unloaded, it was covered with a canvas sheet to protect it from the sun. Then Ahmad invited us to his tent and we made ourselves comfortable. He sum-moned an attractive girl with long plaited hair, telling her to make tea. She busied herself in the *tukul*, lighting a fire and setting a black kettle on it.

'This is how all the Kababish tents used to be,' Juma' com-mented. 'One side for the storehouse and one for the people. The tents in the *dikka* have become too large now, because we hardly ever move.'

I asked Wad Fadil how often his people moved. 'We have no *shogara* like the Arabs in the south,' he explained. 'We are desert Arabs. In the rainy-season we water at Khitimai, but we rarely go further south than that.' He told me that the desert Arabs had more connection with the Nile than with North Kordofan. Their supplies came from the market in Ed Debba, which was twelve days' ride to the east. If they needed to sell camels, they would take them to one of the markets on the river, since there they would fetch a better price than in the south.

Soon the girl brought tea and Wad Fadil served it with ceremony, lacing it with a sprig of cinnamon. As we were drinking, a crowd of Arabs arrived from the other tents. They had seen us arrive and were anxious for news from the outside. News is a luxury that the Arabs crave, and they will travel long distances to hear it. They were as lean and healthy as salukis, sharp little men with eyes keen as knife-blades, little beards and tousled mops of hair. They carried daggers with ornate ivory hilts and their shirts were very short, ending a foot above the knee. All of them carried rifles. The only black face amongst them was that of the Gur'ani herdsman, whose long, drawn features were almost oriental.

Wad Fadil told us that we were not the first and by no means the most impressive visitors they had seen that year. 'The Prince of the

Arabs was here!' he said. 'He had with him nine vehicles as big as mountains. He had an army of slaves, and the biggest tents I have ever seen. There were men of every colour, white, black and brown. Even yellow.' At first I could hardly believe the story, but as he went on I gathered that there had been an expedition here, led by a Saudi prince. 'They came looking for game,' the 'Atawi said. 'They did not want to shoot it, but only to catch it. They wanted to take the animals alive back to their country. They made camp not far from here, and the Prince sent a lorry to fetch me. When I arrived he was sitting in his tent with all his men around him. He said, "Are you the Arab who knows where the game is?" I told him that I could find them addax and addra and gazelle and oryx. I said that the game had gone west because of the dryness, and he would find little in the wadi.'

'Were you afraid of him?' I asked.

'Why should I be afraid? He was just an Arab like me!'

'Did you go with them?'

'Yes, we drove west towards the mountains and we found some addax and some oryx and plenty of gazelle. They caught some of them with ropes, and the others they shot with little arrows. The arrows knocked them out and when they woke they had been tied up. But some of them could not stand it. They died before we got them back here.'

'How was the Prince?'

'He was a very generous man, but you could tell he knew nothing about the desert. He was a city-man.'

The 'Atawiyya were excellent hunters and renowned as the best trackers amongst the Kababish. Almost all the Arabs would recognize the tracks of their own animals, but the 'Atawiyya knew those of every animal they had seen, and could memorize any track after seeing it only once. They knew which tracks belonged to the camels of which tribe, and could tell at a glance the camels of an outsider. No one could pass through their territory without them being aware of it. They did not need to see the travellers: they could form an extremely accurate picture from the tracks alone. Wad Fadil told me how one of his relatives had been travelling in the *jizzu* and had come across the tracks of scores of camels. Amongst them he had recognized the mark of a camel he thought belonged to him. He followed the spoor as far as the Wadi al Milik and caught up with the herd, which was being driven by some Barara. 'Have you a strange camel amongst your herd?' he asked them. 'No, they are all ours,' came the reply. The 'Atawi examined the camels one by one, and singled out the one he thought was his. He brought it to the Barara and said, 'Can you swear by God that this camel is yours?' One of the others answered. 'To say the truth, I found that camel some years ago in the *jizzu*. I came upon a she-camel one day and she had just given birth. She was dying, but the calf was alive so I took it. I reared it with my herd – and here it is.' The two men conferred and the 'Atawi proved that one of his she-camels had been lost in the *jizzu* at the very same time. The camel was returned to him, but he paid a small sum to the Barara in compensation.

Recognizing the track of a camel one had seen many times seemed to be child's play to the 'Atawiyya; the real test was to recognize the track of a camel one had never seen.

The 'Atawiyya could also identify people from their footprints, with or without shoes. The prints revealed a great deal of information. To demonstrate this Wad Fadil later called attention to my own prints in the sand outside. 'These are not the tracks of an Arab,' he told me. 'I should know them anywhere. They are the tracks of a determined man, but not a cautious one. See how straight they are!' Then he pointed to the tracks of Juma' nearby. 'Now those are an Arab's prints. See how the soles are turned outwards as he looks around him while he walks. They belong to a wary man. Everything you do is written in the tracks!' Wad Fadil went on to say that he could easily distinguish a man's tracks from a woman's, and could even tell if the woman was married or pregnant.

Although the conditions in the inner desert were extreme, the 'Atawiyya and the other desert families lived there out of choice. The wadis provided their camels and goats with grazing, and the very remoteness of their pastures meant that little work was involved in herding for most of the year. They would let the camels graze unattended, knowing that they would never leave the wadi, and that they would turn up at the watering-place whenever they were thirsty. During the hot season the only work the Arabs did was watering. I asked Wad Fadil if he was ever afraid of raiders. 'Never!' he replied. 'No bandits would get away with our camels. Someone would pick up their tracks within a very short time. How could they escape? It is a long way to the nearest watering-place, and no one can survive in the desert without visiting the watering-places. Once you see a man's tracks you can tell where he is going. A man driving stolen camels moves slowly. We should catch up with him long before he reached safety.' This reminded me of the Sarajabi, Kalklayt, whom we had met near Tagaru, and I asked Wad Fadil about him.

'Hah!' the 'Atawi said. 'He arrived here yesterday, saying that he lost his baggage camel in Tagaru. That camel happened to be carrying some money that did not belong to him. It was eighty pounds that someone gave him for a Sulayman woman at El 'Atrun.' I learned several lessons from this incident. The Arab grapevine was thorough and perceptive: the area was enormous and the population minute, yet the nomads missed nothing. This great wilderness probed delicately into everyone's weaknesses.

In the late afternoon I walked out into the dunes to bring my camels back. The low sun, reflected in the myriad particles of silicon and quartz, created an unreal aura beside the soft, feminine undulations of the sand and the unadorned bareness of the trees. I watched a woman in a black robe who balanced a can of water on her head while driving a knot of camels back from the well. Six small boys tore about amongst the dunes. There was a large mob of camels at the well, glittering red and white against the amber sand. Wad Fadil's daughter and the Gur'an herdsman were pulling up water in small buckets. I waited there as evening drifted over the desert. One of the 'Atawiyya boys began to play the *zambara*, a pipe of tubular steel, about fourteen inches long, with four holes drilled in it. Its music was reedy and oddly surreal, in perfect harmony with the spirit of the land.

As the darkness came the smell of burning *arak* wood rose from the camps. Each tent was pitched in its own space, some distance from the others, but this night the men gathered around Wad Fadil's tent. He slaughtered a goat for us and brought a dish of flat, unleavened loaves with seasoning. The Arabs called this *gorasa*. It was made of wheat flour that they obtained from the Nubian towns along the river. They supplemented their diet with hunting. There was still plenty of game in the wadi, especially gazelles. The 'Atawiyya would hunt on foot in the early morning, seeking out fresh tracks around the vegetation, stalking the animals and shooting them at close quarters. They had some salukis, trim hunting dogs as fast as greyhounds, quite different from the belligerent guard-dogs the Kababish used to protect their tents. A saluki had wide paws that enabled it to run on sand, and it could outpace a hare or a gazelle. The 'Atawiyya reared their dogs carefully, letting them run everywhere with them, hand-feeding them with lumps of dough and morsels of meat. When hunting with salukis they would ride their camels, casting the dogs after the gazelle. The saluki would chase the quarry for miles. When the gazelle collapsed with exhaustion the dog would seize and hold it until the Arab appeared on his camel to slit its throat. I never saw the 'Atawiyya using gazelle traps as the Sarajab did.

The 'Atawiyya ate gazelle meat both fresh and dried. They staked the carcass out flat, slicing up the flesh and hanging it to dry in the sun from a tent or bush. The meat was much prized by the desert Arabs.

Often I spoke to Wad Fadil's Gur'ani herdsman, whose name I found unpronounceable. He told me that he came from the Ennedi hills, the stronghold of the Gur'an. It was from these hills and those of Mourdi, further north, that the Gur'an had launched their raids on the Nile for centuries. They would appear out of the night and attack a caravan or a quiet village, stealing women and camels. The river dwellers thought of them as evil spirits. They said that their camels made no tracks in the sand, that they lived on snakes and scorpions and the water from their camels' stomachs.

On the morning of the third day Juma' called me over and said, 'Omar, your camel will not eat the *arak* leaves. The big camel was reared in this wadi and is accustomed to them, but Hambati is going hungry. It is better to move on.' He explained that this was the furthest extent of his previous knowledge, and I told him that I should navigate by compass from now on. At night we should travel by the Pole Star, for our way was a few degrees off north. I set a compass-bearing on El 'Atrun and estimated that it would take us twenty hours to get there, which was two days of hard riding.

The 'Atawiyya helped us load and Wad Fadil gave us a hunk of goat. We climbed out of the wadi and into the great sand-sea beyond.

14
Nearing Zarzura

We were now entering a no man's land
where the shadow of governments
hardly falls, and where, when a party of
Arabs espy strange camel-men on the
horizon, they shoot first and inquire
afterwards.
Douglas Newbold and William Shaw,
'An Exploration of the South
Libyan Desert', Sudan Notes and
Records, *1928*

We camped under the sugarloaf of Jabal Toli'a east of the salt-pans
of El 'Atrun. I climbed up once again into the old sangar and scanned
the landscape to the north. I could see little but the weathered sandstone ridges that lay between here and Nukheila. Our destination,
Zarzura, lay far beyond that, in the remotest and most dangerous
part of this desert.

Newbold and Shaw had been the first Europeans to cross this
stretch, in 1928, but Nukheila had been put on the map three years
earlier by Dr John Bell and Prince Kemal ad Din Hussein, who had
reached it from the west in Citroën cars.

Newbold and Shaw had entered the area with nineteen riflemen
of the Hawawir, and had posted scouts to watch for raiders of the
Gur'an. These raiders had terrorized the desert for years and con-
founded all attempts to capture them. It was thought that Nukheila
was used as a base by the Gur'an, especially in summer when the
rest of the desert was hot and lacked grazing for their camels. The
raiders were led by three brothers, the chief of whom was called
Gongoi.

Newbold and Shaw found traces of Gongoi's raiders at Nukheila
but they saw no one. It was winter and the Gur'an had probably
retired into their homelands in the Mourdi depression, sallying forth
only when the explorers had passed. A few months later they
attacked El 'Atrun twice, armed with modern rifles; they killed some

Kababish and stole their camels. So seriously did the British government take this threat that they despatched a motorized machine-gun section to intercept them, but the cars foundered in the desert steppe, and by the time they reached El 'Atrun the raiders had disappeared. They surfaced within a short time, 250 miles away in Chad, where they made three attacks and stirred up the French authorities.

Now, over fifty years later, it could scarcely be said that the shadow of governments fell any darker across this desert than it had in those days. There was no more Gongoi, perhaps, but if anything the condition of the desert was less hospitable than it had been then.

A piece of flying grit touched my face. I heard a deep sigh from far away, as if the earth were sobbing. Over the northern horizon lay an angry red smear of dust. Within an hour the *simoom* hit us.

We lashed our headcloths firmly around us and brought our camels in from the *sallam* groves where they were browsing. We rolled ourselves in shawls and blankets and lay amongst the tamarix bushes as the red sand and dust whipped past.

The storm lasted only till sunset, when we crawled out and lit a fire. 'The summer is with us and no doubt!' Juma' exclaimed. 'It is the wrong season to search for an unknown place. I knew when I saw the Pleiades setting a few nights ago that we were too late.' I knew he was right, yet I was doggedly determined not to give up unless I was forced to. I looked closely at the Arab as he sat amidst the tamarix, wondering if he was going to back out of our agreement. He wore his brown *jibba* and his old army beret with the 'unofficial' black-lining uppermost.

'Many have died in this part of the desert,' he began. 'Often because of the *simoom*. Have you heard the story of Ahmad Wad Mohammid, the brother of Ibrahim who was with us on the Requisition? He was travelling to Kufra with three companions. They had ten camels with them to sell in Libya. They ran into the *simoom* north of Nukheila and lost the way. They soon ran out of water. They killed a camel and drank the water from its guts. When that was gone they slaughtered another, then another. In the end they had killed all the camels in the herd and had to start on the riding animals. Two of them died of thirst and Ahmad and another arrived in 'Uwaynat half crazy. Ahmad told me he would never risk it again. Thirst is a bitch, by God!'

There were many such stories amongst the Kababish. It

263

frequently happened that men rode off in pursuit of raiders or of a lost camel only to get lost in the *simoom* and never return. The mummified corpses would be discovered in the desert, years later perhaps. These stories taught me that the essential factor in surviving the *simoom* was navigation. Without accurate navigation all the waterskins in the world would not save a life. 'We can navigate in the *simoom* with a compass,' I told Juma'. 'Your head may spin in the *simoom*, but the compass-needle doesn't.'

'And will the compass show us how to get to Zarzura?' Juma' asked.

Just then we were interrupted by a woman who approached our camp timidly, carrying a baby that looked sick and malnourished. Hanging on her skirts were two little boys whose ribs pressed through the skin of their chests. The girl was pretty but pitifully thin, her face deeply lined by scarification and her hair in rat's tails. She would not sit down, but told us she belonged to the Awlad Sulayman and that her tent was pitched nearby. 'My husband took our camels to the south four months ago,' she explained. 'And I have heard nothing from him since. My children are hungry. We have only a few goats to live on. You have come from the south. Perhaps you have news of him?' Juma' had no news of him, but he gave her a small amount of money. We watched as she walked sadly back to her tent. I wondered if she would see her husband again.

It was much later, on our return to Wadi Howar, that we learned her full story. The husband was by no means dead. He had sold a camel in Umm Sunta and sent some money to his wife, entrusting it to an Arab who was travelling north and who watered his camels in Wadi Howar. The Arab was none other than the young Sarajabi, Kalklayt. When the husband finally returned to El 'Atrun, his baby had died of starvation.

Next morning we filled our skins at the pits near El 'Atrun and set off north across the rocky plain. It was hard going at first. I felt Hambati wince as his sore feet encountered the rough surface. Eventually Juma' examined the feet of both camels and said, 'Thank God! The soles are not pierced. They are just worn thin. Don't worry, Omar, sore feet never killed a camel yet!' All morning the wind blew on us with its furnace breath. There was little dust, but the heat alone was suffocating, intensified by the rocky ground as if by the refractories in a giant oven.

We crossed a plain towards the weathered sandstone ridges that

I had seen; they formed the ragged edge of an eroded plateau. The plain beneath was covered with metallic debris from extinct volcanoes. We rode over depressions filled with fine blue dust, and places where the rock glittered white as polar ice. To the east the wall of the plateau was bronze and russet-red, cut into fantastic shapes by the forces of the desert. The heat seemed to eat away my skin like acid, even through the folds of my headcloth and the cotton of my shirt. I felt as though a great hand was squeezing my head like a lemon.

At midday we descended into a wadi where there was a single *tundub* growing. We made our camels kneel, hobbling them tightly, and slung our canvas under the branches, anchoring it to our saddles. We laid our sheepskins down and sat on them, trying to summon enough energy to make the meal. We had agreed to take the cooking in turns, and it was my turn. Though the heat had robbed me of my appetite, I knew I must force myself to cook and to eat.

I began to build a fire downwind, collecting a few pieces of wood. I steeled myself against the seductive call of the shade. Taking a strip of sack-cloth from the pack saddle as kindling, I built a shelter against the wind with our saddle-bags and lit the fire with a single match. I noticed with satisfaction that the camels were crunching the shoots of the *tundub*.

We ate the *kisri* an hour later. 'Not bad!' was my companion's verdict. Before we left, he got out the axe and cut three parallel bars and a horizontal one into the trunk of the tree. It was the Nurab camel brand. 'It is the custom,' he told me. 'When you find a good tree for *gayla* – the afternoon rest – you mark it with your brand. There are some famous trees in the *dar* that many people use on their journeys.'

A steep pass led to the plateau. It was walled-in by massive blocks of black stone, and scattered with boulders that looked as if they had been nibbled by giant termites. There were tables of sandstone patterned in purple and white, and on the summit great bars of gravel interspersed with deep sand. The camels floundered and stalled. We were forced to dismount and continue on foot, crossing false valleys and climbing up again into the hills. There were no tracks and not a sign of life. At every step the camels sank in up to their hocks, tottering and almost falling, gasping at the effort. Miraculously they stayed upright as we waded on through the sand.

265

I kept my compass in my hand constantly so that I should not lose the bearing, even though we dropped time and again into deep corries where the walls seemed to have been eroded by time. We clambered out again to cross yet more disjointed groynes of rock. After two exhausting hours we came to a high place from where we glimpsed the horizon. There was a line of hills, no more than dark shadows in the far distance, and between us and them a rubbish dump of stone clusters laid on a bed of sand. It was an enormous, asymmetrical, formless wilderness, as alien in appearance as the moon – the strangest landscape I had ever seen.

At sunset we halted for prayers. The moments of silence were luxury. Neither of us wanted to rise from where we sat on a bed of rippled sand, yet somehow we raised ourselves and rode into the darkness for three more hours.

We made camp on a sheet of flat sand with the silent, unknown wilderness around us. Juma' cooked the dried gazelle meat we had brought with us, and I laid out our canvas sheets before the hobbled camels and fed them sorghum grain, which I poured on to the sheets in handfuls. The animals fought and squabbled over it. Before Hambarib had even finished his own ration, he lurched over to Hambati and tried to drive him away and secure a second meal. I had to separate them with a whip. After we had eaten, we sat in quiet meditation. Juma' thought he heard the hiss of a lorry engine, but it was the sigh of the wind. It was easy to imagine sounds in this eerie silence, but there was nothing here – no insects, no animals, no birds, not a single tree or a single strand of grass. There was no life here, save two human beings – one black, one white – and two camels, one white, one red. We were in an unknown place, marked on no map, on an unknown planet, somewhere spinning silently in space.

Next day the *simoom* started with redoubled force. By the middle of the morning it was so hot that breathing became difficult. The heat seemed to lie on my back like a heavy overcoat. The camels groaned and trembled as their feet touched the sharp, hot rocks. Not even the tracks of small animals showed on the surface of the sand. There were no comforting signs here.

We rode over broken knolls and ridges, where pools of water seemed to lie between the stones, only to evaporate at our approach. Once Juma' spotted a rich clump of *hadd* bushes and made over to them, only to find a field of smooth black boulders. On another occasion I spied a whole forest of trees at the bottom of a valley, but found they were small hummocks of sand that had collected around columns of black rock. The intense heat produced a mood of aggression and cut our patience short. At noon we erected our shelter, digging holes for the wooden uprights we had brought. 'You are digging the holes the wrong shape!' my companion told me. 'They are supposed to be round!'

'What the hell does the shape matter?' I exclaimed angrily. 'It is damned hot! Let's get on with it!' He was right, though, for when we tried to sling our canvas sheets, I discovered that the uprights would not stand firm in my oval holes and tilted over irritatingly. The shelter gave us no protection from the *simoom* that blasted over us as we curled up in our shawls. 'Why do you want to find Zarzura?' Juma' muttered miserably. 'Why enter the desert at this time of year? It is madness!'

'Then you must be mad for agreeing to come!' I answered. I got out the Michelin map I had with me and showed him the entire Sahara. 'Look,' I said. 'If you went westwards from here, you would find the desert like this for thousands of miles as far as the Maghreb. I want to know all that desert. One day I will cross it all!' He shrugged and spat some of his valuable saliva. 'There is nothing in the desert but thirst and heat!'

I already knew that the blinding heat of noon could produce a kind of temporary madness with symptoms of depression, aggression and paranoia. I knew that as soon as the temperature cooled the madness disappeared without trace, and the emotions returned to normal. No one, not even the hardiest of nomads, was immune to the effect. The secret of combating it lay in the knowledge that it would pass.

In the afternoon the going was a little better for the camels. We crossed great sheets of sand with only a smattering of rocks. The wind dropped around sunset and the coolness came over us like a blessing. I looked east as the last rays of the sun burned in the ragged neck of the hills, and thought that if we carried on in the line of my sight for ten or eleven days, we should come to Dongola on the Nile. I thought of how I had arrived there more than five years before and looked across the great desert, wondering what lay within it.

As the darkness came, the stars lit up and we discarded the compass for Polaris, keeping it over our right shoulders. It was very dark. Once Hambarib veered noticeably east and we wondered if he had smelled trees. We both sniffed deeply, hoping to catch the strong scent of *sallam* that would carry far in these wastes, but we found nothing. Disillusioned, we made camp. It was a wretched camp that night. I had hoped that we should be camping in Nukheila. I had worked out that the oasis was only twenty hours' ride from El 'Atrun. We had been riding for nineteen without any sign of the place. I knew that the rocks had slowed us down, and I hoped that our detours had not taken us too far off the bearing. I wondered how accurate our astral navigation was. I had a copy of the 1940 survey map, which showed few features. The *simoom* had sucked away some of our water from the skins despite the covering of sack-cloth and our liquid was dangerously short. To cap it all we had only a limited amount of sorghum for the camels and could not afford to feed them that night. They sniffed hungrily at the saddle-bags and licked their dry lips. Neither of us would have been able to recognize Nukheila from afar and, though I had read the report made by New-bold and Shaw, it was almost impossible to imagine what the place might look like. All I knew was that it lay in a great depression, which might or might not be visible from the south. Both of us knew that if we missed the oasis we should be lost in the most arid stretch of the Sahara. Our chances of survival without Nukheila were precisely nil. It was a bleak prospect.

Then Juma' said suddenly, 'This year will be called by my family, "The Year of Juma''s Trek with the *nasrani* Omar, in Search of Zarzura"!' I could not help laughing. The thought cheered us both up. Afterwards, as I watched Juma' praying, I found a bloated camel tick in my blanket. It made me grin to see the ugly little creature and to think that in all this blighted wilderness the only living thing I could find was this blood-sucker, which I had probably brought with me.

There was no sign of the oasis when we set off at first light. We crossed ridge after ridge of sand and rock and saw nothing. As we climbed each one, I thought, 'Now we shall see it!' but there was only a line of thick crescent dunes stretching like an impenetrable barrier across the way. It took more than two hours to reach them. They jutted out of the plain steeply, tightly fitting together to form a continuous belt. We turned east to skirt around them. After a while Juma' cried, 'Look! *Takhlis!* It only grows where there is moisture!' I looked down to see a single tuft of grass, spiky and quite green; around it were the unmistakable tracks of a jerboa. This one tuft was an oasis in itself, a tiny micro-system. It was life, and life meant water. Somewhere, beyond this barrier of dunes, lay the oasis of Nukheila.

Juma' slipped from the saddle, and I held the camels while he scrambled up the hill of loose sand. In a few moments he slithered back again, saying, 'I can see nothing, but I can find a way through these dunes.'

We led the camels up the slopes. The camels stumbled, but their feet did not sink deeply into the sand. Over the first wall of dunes we came to a flat plain again. We saw more *takhlis* growing amongst the rocks. There was a narrow tunnel leading between another wall of barchans that were moulded into perfect amphi-theatres by the wind. We climbed over the second wall of dunes and descended into a low area where the surface was marred with deep ripples. Here the going became very hard. The camels sank almost to their knees in the sand, floundering about and exhausting them-selves further. Often Juma' thought the way impossible, and we were forced to retrace our steps and work our way around. We ran into more soft sand but had no choice but to struggle through it, leaning heavily on the headropes and hoping dearly that they would not break. It was still early but as excruciatingly hot as the previous day, and the wind blew sand continually into our faces. We climbed a steep slope and fell, panting into the sand. I felt the sun stinging through the back of my shirt. Finally Juma' asked doubtfully, 'Are those trees or rocks?' I looked up. Far to the north were the vague grey shapes of what could have been the heads of palm trees, though they could equally have been columns of rock. We had both made such mistakes on the previous day and had felt foolish: neither of us was willing to commit ourselves again until we were sure.

We mounted our camels and rode down to a lava field. Juma''s gaze read the ground and then spun back to the mysterious grey line ahead. Signs of life grew more numerous. There was the track of a gazelle, and a few old camel droppings, then the carcass of a she-camel, a parcel of untouched bones in a parchment shell of dried skin. A few steps further on we came across a *tundub* tree, then four or five more growing behind a crest of rock. 'This place will be called Omar's *tundub*!' Juma' said. 'This is your route to Nukheila!' We both smiled at each other and our arguments were forgotten. There could be no doubt now: I looked at the grey line ahead. The ghostly shadows had become the heads of huge palm trees. We had arrived.

Half an hour later we were in the great green circle of the southernmost section of the oasis. Newbold and Shaw had named it Wa'arat al 'Abid ('The Oasis of Slaves'), since it was here that they had found traces of occupation. I learned later that the Arabs called it Wa'arat al Ba'ud ('The Oasis of Mosquitoes'). As it turned out, this was a most appropriate name.

There were hundreds of palm trees, some of them huge and ancient, amongst them the smaller frames of *sallam* and *siyaal* and a few tamarix. Underfoot were sharp yellow-green hummocks of *hallif* and *takhlis* – grasses that grow in watery places. There were scores of gazelle tracks, which suggested that no hunters had been here for some time. After the pale, washed-out colours of the desert, this place was a royal feast. We rode gratefully into the umbrella shade of a palm tree and unsaddled. We spread out our canvas sheets and lay still for a moment in the peace of the world.

When we explored the place we found many human and animal tracks, and traces of occupation. A cluster of reed huts, now derelict, had been built outside the palm groves and the ground was covered by the prints and droppings of goats. There were slivers of leather and bark from hobbling-loops, and piles of ash. No doubt these remains were left by the Gur'an who still came here to harvest the date crop in the cool season, bringing with them a large caravan of camels and cutting the dates tree by tree. The harvest must have taken weeks, for there were more than a thousand palms in the oasis, which covered almost fifty square miles. There were no ripe dates in the trees on that day, though many had produced the new crop that was still small and green.

The Gur'an had used this place for generations. More important than the date harvest in the past had been the role the oasis had played as a base for their deep penetration raids across the Libyan desert. These raiders had been the hardiest in the Sahara, sometimes pushing a thousand kilometres through the void to attack the Egyptian oases of Dakhla and Farafra, or riding eleven days east to raid the wells of Al Ga'ab near Dongola. They would attack caravans of traders and salt diggers, coming by night and attacking in a rush with the moon behind them. In 1928 they massacred an Egyptian salt caravan in the Laqiyya Arba'in oasis. The Gur'an had lain in hiding until midnight while the men slept, then crawled forth to slit their throats. Two of the salt diggers escaped off into the desert and walked back to Selima to tell the gory tale.

But discoveries of large caches of water jars in the deserts of Egypt had thrown new light on their achievements. It was possible that the Gur'an had developed a technique of leaving these water dumps buried under the sand in marked places. The dumps were often large, and if replenished often formed an artificial oasis that greatly extended the range of the raiders. Since the Arabic word for water jar, *zir*, was from the same root as the word Zarzura, it is possible that the lost oasis may have been no more than one of these artificial watering-places.

The Gur'an were believed to be the descendants of the ancient Garamantes, who in Roman times were the most powerful nation in the entire Sahara. They drove four-horse chariots and worshipped strange animal-headed gods similar to those of the ancient Egyptians. Their territory once stretched from the hinterlands of the Mediterranean as far east as the Nile. Indeed, the Bayuda desert, just south of the bend in the Nile above Khartoum, had once been known as the 'Desert of the Gur'an'.

When Newbold and Shaw explored Nukheila in 1928, they found the remains of a sacred *siyaal* tree that gave evidence of their pagan practices. The tree was half dead and lying on its side, with two branches sticking up in the air. On one of these they saw a smooth patch, smeared with the fat of a dead camel, and on the other a thong of hide from the same animal. In the crack below they found undigested grasses from the animal's stomach. They surmised that the Gur'an sacrificed a camel to the tree to bring them good fortune in raids. I searched the oasis carefully for the tree, but did not find it.

That night we slept near the palm trees. Juma' threw the *khatt* again; after half an hour of making lines in the sand and rubbing them out, he said with great conviction, 'There are people near. They can see us but we cannot see them. Perhaps they are Gur'an!' In this lonely setting it was difficult to dismiss his words, especially in the light of his former success with the *khatt*. I looked around me uncomfortably. It was an eerie and evil feeling to imagine that we were being watched.

The only raiders we encountered that night were hordes of mosquitoes. They came zooming out of the palm groves and attacked us by the squadron. In the end we were forced to move our bedding on to the higher ground near the abandoned huts; I saw now why the Gur'an had built them outside the trees.

Next morning we moved further north, and within an hour came

271

to the famous water-pool. It was wedge-shaped and the water was bluer than blue, completely encircled by date palms and reeds. The lake was humming with life. The trees harboured swallows and some hawks, and the surface of the water was covered in black-fly larvae. The sand round about was caked with salt and we found that the water was so thick with it that it was nauseous. The black-fly drifted around the surface in living rafts and the air was filled with the sound of their buzzing. To the east of the lake the sand had been piled up into the tallest and most perfect crescent dune I had ever seen. At the base of its slip-face was a field of *hallif* grass. We unloaded by the pool and set the camels to graze by the dune, where we discovered a set of shallow wells that had been scooped out of the sand. The water lay about two feet beneath the surface. Near the pool was an upright stone on which many camel brands had been carved. We found brands of the Zaghawa and Bedayatt as well as the crocodile mark of the Gur'an. Juma' took the axe and added to them the brand of the Nurab.

The heat became unbearable, and the *simoom* came thrashing through the palm trees with a vengeance. We took shelter under some trees, but just as we did so, Juma' exclaimed, 'Oh God! The camels have wandered off! Now we shall have to fetch them!' The animals had forsaken the green grass and shuffled out into the bare sand to the south. They were already two kilometres away and were still going. We had to struggle for more than an hour to bring them back, fighting with the soft sand and the blast of the *simoom*. 'They do not like this place!' my companion said. 'They want to return to Umm Sunta. See how obstinate the camel is!' If we had left them, they would almost certainly have continued shuffling south in their hobbles until they died of thirst or came back to where they had left their herds.

We brought them back to the pool and hobbled them with the knee-hobbles so that they could not shuffle off again. Then we both removed our clothes and bathed in the lake. The water was warm and very soothing after the strains of the journey. As our bodies dried, the salt left a thick white crust on our skin. Juma' said that the water had great medicinal value, and he brought out a plastic container that he filled from the pool. 'I shall drink a little every day!' he declared.

By sundown the camels were flopping over in the grass and snapping madly at the mosquitoes that emerged as the wind dropped. We moved camp into the dunes overlooking the pool, but the mosquitoes followed us. They were huge and voracious and tortured us for hours. Finally we got up and collected armfuls of palm fibre from beneath the trees and lit a huge bonfire up wind. The thick smoke drifted over our camping-place. It made our eyes smart, but it got rid of the mosquitoes.

The *simoom* began at dawn the next day with a whooshing sound that rattled the heads of the palm trees. Within minutes our gear was buried under drifting sand. The sky was obliterated by dust, and the date palms bent over at odd angles in the high wind, which prevented us from making a fire. We decided to move camp again.

We loaded up and headed north away from the pool. Progress was agonizingly slow. The *simoom* clutched at us like a claw and I had difficulty breathing. We sought out the shade of some palms, but visibility was down to a few feet and we could do nothing but wrap ourselves up as always and stay in the lee of the trees, running out now and again to bring back the camels that hopped off into the mist of sand on their three legs. The rustling of the palms, bent over at incredible angles, was deafening. I knew that to continue north in this blizzard would be madness, and reluctantly decided that we should have to abandon the idea of finding the lost oasis. Perhaps it had never existed, or if it had, its water and palm trees had disappeared long ago. When I told Juma' of my decision, he brightened a little and said, 'We will leave tomorrow!'

The next day the *simoom* was fiercer. We moved back to the area of the pool and cut some tamarix trees for firewood. We filled our skins from the sweetest well we could find. I set my compass on a back-bearing, and we moved off south-east across the dunes. The going was easier with the wind behind us, but the dust obscured the face of the barchans and made them very dangerous. Several times we came to a sheer precipice without realizing it until the very last moment. Between the high dunes were more patches of deep sand where the camels trembled and staggered. By noon, though, we were back on the flat hammada, and the camels stepped out, knowing that they were returning. The sky was still dark and visibility limited. Juma' rode slightly ahead while I came behind with my compass, shouting out directions as we rode.

It took two and a half days of hard riding to reach El 'Atrun. We camped in the groves of Bir Milani, near the tent of some 'Atawiyya. As soon as we couched our camels, an old man came out to greet us. A little later he sent out an attractive, buxom daughter with a can of milk for us. She smiled at me, and I asked how she was. When she had gone, Juma' mimicked my voice, saying, 'Why don't you marry her and be done with it!' For a moment or two we grappled together boyishly, but we were too drained for a real wrestling match and lay in the sand, panting. It was almost sunset, and we brought the camels near us. After dark a slave brought us a bowl of porridge drowned in sour milk, and we ate in good spirits.

I was disappointed that I had had to abandon the search for Zarzura, but I knew that the mistake had been to set off at the beginning of the hot season. The weather had defeated us. I knew that, underneath it all, Zarzura had only been a goal I had set myself. The experience of desert life with the desert people was my true interest. If I had really been intent on finding Zarzura I could have hired a Land-Rover or even a plane. I had not found the lost oasis, but I had found many more things of greater value, not the least of which was the company of this Arab, Juma' Wad Siniin, whom I could now call my friend.

After supper that night I felt strangely content. I felt that I belonged here. I remembered the trek with Mohammid Wad Fadlal Mula as no more than a harsh apprenticeship. I had passed that apprenticeship, and tonight I felt that I was reaping my reward. Against all the odds two men from vastly different worlds could be friends and brothers. I had been working towards that end for five long years, and I had never felt closer to it than I did that night.

We stayed with the 'Atawiyya for two days. On the second day we attended a circumcision feast at one of the tents. Soon after sunrise we were escorted across the dunes by a slave. We came to two camel-hair tents, and opposite them a *tukul* of wood. As we approached, the women of the tents greeted us with piercing ululations and ran out with bottles of perfume with which they drenched our moustaches. The boy who was to be circumcised was sitting on a saddle in the shade, looking quite unconcerned. He was about ten, and dressed in clothes of bright new cotton.

At once our host came to greet us. He was called Ali Wad Salih, a slim 'Atawi wearing the usual short tunic with a thick leather belt. He had chosen two goats from his flock for the feast, and he brought them out and slaughtered one immediately. The other wriggled away and dashed off into the dunes, with the boy and another in hot pursuit. They returned in minutes, dragging the animal by the ears.

274

Not long afterwards a host of other guests arrived, bristling with weapons, some of which they fired into the air. We sat down to eat the cooked heart, lungs and ribs of the goat. The tent nearby was very small and tidy. Inside it sat the two girls who had sprayed us with perfume; one was the buxom one who had brought us milk. Both were strikingly beautiful, wearing coloured dresses with garish flower designs and straight underskirts of faded blue cotton. They wore wraps around their breasts, but their copper-bronze shoulders were naked.

In the afternoon more women arrived. All the girls lined up in front of the tent and began to clap their hands, stepping from side to side in a swaying, erotic movement. They began to sing in shrill voices as their bodies swayed. Some of the men jumped up and shouted, waving their rifles and firing them again. Meanwhile Ali lit a roaring fire at the end of the avenue formed by the two tents The old man who was to perform the circumcision arrived. The men formed up in a rough line opposite the women, some of them carrying camel-whips that they brandished above their heads. They began to clap, and to stamp their feet in the sand, singing in deep grating voices as a counterpoint to those of the women. Sometimes they formed a circle, each man stepping forward and backward with a complicated series of movements. They raised their hands to their mouths and made a deep resonating chant in such harmony that the music seemed almost to be coming from outside them; at the same time the women would let rip with their shrill ululation. The boy who was to be circumcised was dragged into the line of men. He held a tiny camel-whip and was told to hold it high and shout with the others. He looked very small and bemused in his spotless new clothes. Soon he was taken inside the tent, for the operation was not performed in public. The singing and dancing reached a new pitch, intended as an encouragement for the painful events taking place inside.

As soon as it was over, he emerged from the tent, still looking bemused. His new clothes were smeared with blood. He was pulled back into the line of dancing men and danced with them till sunset.

The next morning Juma' and I examined our camels to prepare for the rest of the journey south. Both of them had red, sore feet, and Hambati's back was swelling from the riding saddle that I had never managed to exchange. The morning was incredibly hot: I could feel the latent heat lying near the surface even before the sun rose. We set off from Milani at mid-morning, and the *simoom* followed us like an old friend, now in full swing and driving white dust behind us. Its blasts hit us like the flash of a flame-thrower, painful and totally exhausting, crushing the breath out of our bodies. The wind sucked the moisture out of us. I felt my body temperature rising, my brains boiling. I cursed my camel and Juma' silently and without reason, as snatches of personal history, memories and visions of childhood passed through my head.

From far off we saw the shadow of some *sallam* trees, and I prayed that they were real. It seemed hours before we reached them. We couched our camels by the largest tree, working like automatons. We strung up our shelter and hobbled the animals. Juma' then poured out some water; I heard it gurgle into the metal bowl. He handed it to me, and I drank the entire contents without a pause. Then he filled it, and drank himself. Without another word we both collapsed in the shade and lay prone, covered with our shawls from head to foot, trying to trap as much moisture as we could, while the *simoom* played over us like the fingers of the devil.

We did not load again until the afternoon was almost over. We moved off very slowly, walking to preserve the strength of the camels. The cool that came before sunset was unbelievably luscious. I walked barefoot, glad to feel the good crust of the planet under my feet. As I walked, I started to see something new in the surface of this place. I saw the great blue hunks of granite split in half by heat and cold, and the splinters of stone that collected around them. A little further on were the fields of rocks where the splinters had been eroded by the wind and the fluctuations in temperature, broken into yet smaller particles. Further still were even finer gradations of gravel, and then the sand itself, also graded by the size of its granules. This desert seemed a living, changing organism, by no means a dead world.

After two days we reached Rahib. From here we crossed west to the wells at Ghobayshi, where the desert was as smooth as cream, the wind playing over its surface producing a prismatic rainbow effect around the soft edges of the sand-sheet. We moved through another unexpected Stone Age site. There were more grinding mills and arrowheads, flaked bones and flint tools, the last memories of an ancient people who had been born, lived and died with all their joys and agonies on this shelf of land now washed over by these desert sands.

At sunset we came to Ghobayshi, where we found a single tent. We couched our camels nearby and a woman came out and shook hands with us, saying, 'Welcome! Welcome to the guests!' She took the headrope of my camel and led it over to a comfortable, sheltered place. She couched it and began to unload my gear, laying it out neatly. She disappeared for a moment, and came back with some glowing spills of dry wood. She scooped out a hollow in the sand near to where we sat and kindled a fire. She brought out a kettle and a bowl of goat's milk, setting the kettle on the embers of the wood and crouching near the fire as she talked amiably. She told us that her family was Awlad Huwal, and that she was a widow and the daughter of the tribal sheikh. She was a tall, reedy woman, very stately and gracious, with a face seasoned by the elements. She wore a long underskirt from which the colour had faded like old denim, and over it a wrap of rough blue cotton. Her head was covered with a ragged hood of cloth.

When the tea was ready, she asked us to produce our cups. She poured out the hot liquid, adding a few drops of milk to each one. As we sipped she said, 'What is your family?'

'Nurab,' Juma' answered.

'And the *sharif* — is he Nurab too?'

'He has spent a long time with the nazir's people, but he is an Englishman from the English.'

We drank noisily, placing the cups down for refills. When the pot was empty, the woman offered to make more, but we politely declined.

Next morning the Awlad Huwal slaughtered a goat for us, and we were obliged to stay a little longer. During the morning I climbed the slip-face of some great transverse dunes that towered over the camp. From the top Wadi Howar looked endless, and the little tent far below me in its few trees was dwarfed by the vastness of the landscape. To the north, about three kilometres away, was a line of sandy spurs beneath which the Awlad Huwal camels were being watered. They looked as tiny as ants. Beyond them and further west, more than 200 miles away, lay the country of the Gur'an, and the hills of Ennedi and Erdi with the Mourdi depression between them. Beyond those hills were the volcanic pinnacles of Tibesti. All around, the desert lay as boundless as an ocean.

The day was baking hot. I noticed that in the heat the women never ventured from the tents without their headwraps and would not allow the children to run about outside. 'This *simoom* will kill them!' the woman said.

She told me about Wadi Howar as it had been in the past. 'There was no talk of governments then!' she said. 'Sometimes the men would lie in the sand all night waiting for the Gur'an. They would come looking for Kababish camels. But the Arabs were ready for them, by God! They would shoot them down like dogs if they came near our camps!'

We watered our camels in the afternoon and rode south to Tagaru. For four days we followed the shimmering rock wall, and on the fifth we passed Qalb al Ba'ir. Two days later we were camping on the heights above Khitimai with some 'Atawiyya. Their camps were pitched in clusters above the pool where we had once collected camels for the Requisition. There was nothing there now but a disc of dry, red soil circled by a spinney of dead acacias. The 'Atawiyya welcomed us and brought us a bowl of clear water from the bore-well. It tasted sweet and delicious, the first untainted water we had drunk for weeks. It reminded me once again that we were out of the desert and back in the Sudan.

Our host brought us *kisri* and sat with us as we ate. 'The desert is finished,' he told us. 'There is no rain in the south. Now the grazing that came a few years ago has all gone. I am an old man. I have never been south of Hattan. But now we have no choice. There is water in the bore-well, but water in the wells cannot bring grazing.'

Two days later we were crossing Hattan. It was now a dead, dry world. There was no trace of the camps we had seen on the way north. The *siyaal* trees had fallen and turned over, lying on their sides like giant porcupines. There was nothing to see but hardened earth and piles of rocks, rust-red and black, and hidden dry washes where water once ran. At sunset we made camp by a *mukhayyit* bush. We had just brought our camels in and hobbled them, when we heard a scuffling not far away. Juma' picked up his club and went to investigate. A few moments later he was back, whispering, 'It is the Meidob! They are here!'

A minute later eight scrawny camels moved past our camp. Some of them were suffering from mange and all of them looked half starved. With them were two black youths, the oldest about twenty. They were clad in ragged clothes and had no headcloths or camel-whips. As they walked past, they wished us, '*As salaam 'alaykum!*' and they couched the camels about thirty metres away.

278

'Are they bandits?' I asked Juma'.

'They are too poor,' he said. 'Those camels are on their last legs!'

At close quarters the boys seemed even less ferocious, and it was obvious that they were hungry. We made *kisri* and tea and invited them to join us. The youths told us that the grazing in Jabal Meidob had failed almost completely this year and that many head of livestock had died. 'I have just been to Libya,' the older boy said. 'I wanted to get a job to earn some money, but they sent me back. That is a bad road at this time of year. You cannot guess what I found there! The bodies of three men. They were just skeletons with a little dried flesh on, and their clothes in tatters. They were lying in a line, each man on his canvas with his saddle at his head. In front were three camels kneeling just as they had sat down, all stiff and dead. They must have lost their way in the *simoom*, and just gone around in circles until they ran out of water. Then they just lay down and waited to die!'

The vivid picture sent a sudden chill down my spine. I could imagine the scene well. The horror of their lonely death plagued me. I thought of the roasting *simoom* and the boundless eternity of rock and sand we had ridden through for two thousand kilometres, and I thanked God for our safe return.

A week later we were back in Umm Sunta. We came in through the thick *siyaal* trees of the wadi and couched our camels outside Juma''s tent. A plump black woman with a full, rounded face welcomed us and Juma' was pounced upon by four or five tiny children, yet the homecoming seemed without emotion. There was nothing but the stiff unyielding acceptance that the nomads showed to the world.

At once we were made comfortable. A goat was slaughtered, and we ate until we could eat no more. I felt Juma' easing himself back into position as master of the house, as the life of the little camp flowed around him. The story of our journey began to unfold a little at a time.

The news from the south was bad. No rain had fallen and the cattle and sheep had already begun to die. The desert Arabs were moving further south than ever before, and many Kababish had been obliged to sell their stock at the lowest prices they had ever accepted. The bottom had fallen out of the livestock market, and sorghum was up to £S150 a sack. It was that night, perhaps, when the flush of the homecoming had evaporated that I realized the facts.

279

The rains had diminished over the past few years, and this year they had failed completely. The desert and the steppe were no longer inhabitable. The Arabs I had seen out in the desert, the Awlad Huwal, the Sulayman and the 'Atawiyya, were the last survivors of an age that was now ending.

I was filled with sadness. At last, after five years of struggle, I had forged a real link with someone who knew nothing of my people or my environment. Together we had seen the horror and the glory of the lonely sands and skies. Yet in the very moment of my success came the brutal realization that from this land through which I had journeyed by camel for seven thousand miles, life would soon be gone for ever.

Part 5
The Death of Earth

15
The Desert Dies

The Sphinx spoke only once, and the
Sphinx said, 'A grain of sand is a desert
and a desert is a grain of sand. Now let us
be silent again.'
Jibran Khalil Jibran, Sand and Foam,
1926

At the end of May a little rain had fallen in the wadi of Umm Sunta. Within days a carpet of tiny green shoots was hopefully pushing up through the hard-packed dust. Then the sun turned its flame on them, and seared them until they withered and died. That was the last of the rain and the last of the pasture.

The cattle had already begun to die and those that were left were quickly sold at low prices. Then came the turn of the sheep. The cost of sorghum and millet had soared, and the price of livestock fell daily. There had been a poor harvest the previous year, and this year the main grain producing areas along the Blue Nile had not even been planted, because the river was too low. At the *damars* in Kordofan the nomads began selling off their livestock and moving east to the city of Omdurman or to the Gezira. Those in the northern end of the Wadi al Milik moved to the town of Ed Debba on the Nile, and many more settled near El Obeid.

In June the chiefs of the Kababish reported to the regional government that they were facing the worst drought in memory. The regional governor, Al Fatih Mohammid Bishara, continued to advise the central government that all was well. The capital had troubles of its own. President Nimeiri had tried to bolster up his failing regime by declaring martial law. Military courts of 'instantaneous justice' were busy condemning citizens for suspected adultery and holding public mutilations in Omdurman. Occasionally the President himself was to be seen, walking through the market and supervising the wrecking of unlicensed street stalls.

There were clashes on the borders of Darfur and Kordofan. A police patrol confiscated forty-three firearms from the herdsmen of the *nuggara*, and a local police chief stated that he would arrest any Kababish found in his territory. In Darfur itself a third of a million people left their villages and moved south. It was estimated that a further 300,000 would follow them before the year was over. In the east of the Sudan 10,000 nomads of the Beja tribes came down from the Red Sea hills where they had lived for millennia, their livestock dead and their lands devastated.

In Khartoum the government blocked a proposal by the United Nations to make an international call for help. There was, they said, no problem. If there was a food deficit, they claimed, it was due to the thousands of Ethiopians pouring across their borders; everyone knew that the Ethiopians could not manage their country.

In Kordofan the Kababish pressed Al Fatih Mohammid Bishara for help. Bishara, later arrested for involvement in massive corruption, did not make his official report until October, by which time thousands of head of livestock had died or been sold off and thousands more had been eaten. Children and old people perished of starvation, and tens of thousands of nomads were displaced.

The panic selling in the markets went on, and livestock prices plummeted to an all-time low. Those who still had camels packed them and went south. Often there were not enough camels and goats to support the entire family, and the families were forced to split up. Women took the children to the cities while the men took the remainder of the herds into Central Kordofan or South Darfur, where they found the farmers and the cattle-Arabs waiting for them. The farmers guarded wells, and sealed off grazing land. They seized stray animals, and the nomads were obliged to pay ransom for them. Often they refused, and there were ugly clashes. Tempers flared, guns came out. Men and boys died, or never returned from the south. In the Nuba mountains the Arabs encountered new grasses that they did not understand; their animals contracted diseases that they did not recognize. A new and virulent strain of mange appeared, and resisted all methods of treatment.

Back in Kordofan lorry owners were transporting Arab families to the cities. The price of transportation doubled, trebled, and then quadrupled. Eventually nomads were being asked for staggering sums for their tickets. Many despaired of finding transport and began to walk. Some of them, especially children, never made it. Outside

Omdurman, at Abu Zayid and Mwellih, a village of ramshackle tents grew up.

Groups of nomads organized themselves into raiding parties and plundered what was left. They took camels and goats from the fleeing people and slaughtered them there and then. They attacked lorries carrying grain and ruthlessly murdered the drivers. The merchants who had lived under Kababish protection for so long were often forced to move. Raiders from the Sarajab attacked and pillaged the stores at Sawani and at Umm 'Ajayja. Men wandered the ranges hungry and desperate, foraging for their dying children. If caught they had little to lose. The merchants who had built up export *dabuukas* at low prices were continually troubled by attacks on their herds. In the Wadi al Milik the Sarajab lay in wait for them, and in the north they were forced to run the gauntlet of the Umm Mattu. The *dabuukas* ceased racing and began to move in large groups, with many hundreds of camels and scores of men.

By November the Sudan had still not appeared on the UN's list of countries affected by drought.

In September the livestock market collapsed completely. The Kababish were destitute. For the first time in memory they could no longer rely on their innate toughness and their ability to endure. For the first time they were afraid. Animals could not be given away. Sorghum rose to £S200 a sack. The trickle of displaced persons became a flood. Helicopter patrols reported thousands of nomads and villagers moving towards Omdurman. Two major camps were established, at Mwellih and Abu Zayid, holding more than 40,000 people. In other camps there were estimated to be as many as 60,000.

Suddenly the world of the desert and the world of the city were in collision. It had been the policy of the government to pretend that nothing was amiss in the ranges of Kordofan. In the cities life for the affluent had gone on as normal. Now there were fuel shortages and a deficit of bread. There were thousands of displaced people on the city's doorstep. It was a potentially explosive situation. There were protests about food shortages, and in November police used tear-gas to disperse rioting school children in El Obeid. At the beginning of December the President visited Mwellih and Abu Zayid, and was visibly shocked at the extent of the problem.

For the first time the Kababish saw the twentieth century. They saw the cars and the factories, the shops and the cinemas. For the first time the urban population saw proud Arab nomads begging in the streets, and beautiful Kababish girls working as prostitutes. For the first time destitute Arab children foraged in the dustbins of the hotels and hustled along the taxi-ranks, sleeping in the gutters and stealing fruit from the markets.

I spent part of that summer travelling up the Wadi al Milik, as far as Ed Debba. The wadi was silent and grey as a grave. In some places there had been no rain for five years. Everywhere I halted, those Arabs that were left begged me for news of the south. I had no good news to bring them.

I camped for a week at Iided Ahmad with some Sarajab, and spent another week travelling across the desert to Ed Debba. I travelled with a *dabuuka* of a thousand camels and a score of men from the Kawahla and Awlad Rashid. In Ed Debba I found dozens of desert families: from Rahib, El 'Atrun and Wadi Howar. They had pitched their tents along the cliffs overlooking the palm groves. There were many familiar faces.

As I walked in the market someone touched me lightly on the arm. I saw with a shock that it was Mohammid Wad Fadlal Mula. He looked older, and there were lines around his eyes. He seemed out of place in this bustling market-place. We embraced warmly and exchanged a greeting. I asked him what he was doing here.

'Our camels have died,' he told me. 'And our goats and sheep are finished. We lost everything. My sister died. She said she could not go on. Two of her children died with her. My cousin died and his wife too. Our family is finished, by God!'

'What are you doing now?'

'I am working in a palm grove for one of these 'Awwala. My little brother is working in a slave's house, as his servant. They don't give him money, only food! This is no life for us, Omar. We are Arabs of the desert!'

'Then why do you do it?'

'Because the desert is dead. There is nothing else.'

16

Journey
through a Dead Land

The Saraha is getting bigger . . . but not
only is it getting bigger now, it
must have been growing in extent for a very
long time.
Maurice Burton, Deserts, *1974*

I spent a short time in Britain and in December I was back in the
Sudan. The government had still not declared an emergency in
Kordofan. The presence of 100,000 displaced people in Omdurman
was an embarrassment to the government, and at the end of
December they began to ship the nomads back to the ranges in a
fleet of trucks, decorated with banners, proclaiming the 'Glorious
Return!' I happened to be there as the officials began herding the
people towards the trucks. When I tried to photograph the incident,
I was arrested and my film confiscated.

A week later I was back in Ed Debba on the Nile. I had been away
only a few months, but in that time the atmosphere had changed
dramatically. Before there had been a few Arab tents pitched in
clusters on the rocky shoulder that marked the fringes of the desert.
Now the escarpments were packed with shelters, and the Arabs had
moved into the town itself, camping around the market square and
the mud-brick streets. It was the first time in living memory that they
had been forced out of the desert to seek refuge here on the banks
of the Nile.

I arrived in Ed Debba on market day. The place was crowded
with mobs of thin camels and knots of squalling sheep and goats.
A raw wind whipped in from the desert. The Arabs were wrapped up
in *tobes* and threadbare overcoats, their headcloths twisted across
their faces. Horse-drawn carts lumbered across the square, carrying
loads of fresh clover, kicking up a trail of dust that layered the air
like a fog. I watched a caravan of twelve camels stalking through the

287

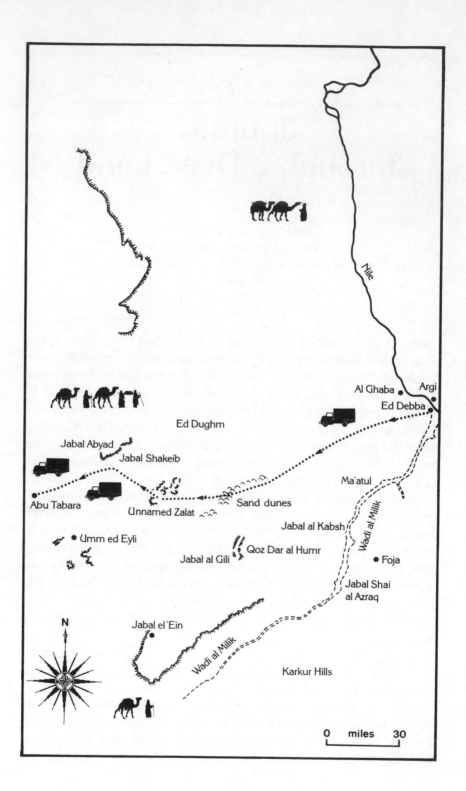

Nile

Al Ghaba   Argi
        Ed Debba

Ed Dughm

Jabal Abyad
        Jabal Shakeib   Ma'atul

Abu Tabara   Wadi al Milik
        Unnamed Zalat   Sand dunes
                                Jabal al Kabsh

• Umm ed Eyli   • Foja

                    Jabal al Gili   Qoz Dar al Humr
                                    Jabal Shai
                                    al Azraq

N

        Jabal el 'Ein

                    Wadi al Milik   Karkur Hills

0   miles   30

sand-mist, led by walking men who were muffled in white hoods. The animals carried loads of firewood.

As I edged my way through the animals and the crowds, an Arab stopped me. His face was shrouded by his headcloth and his body by an army overcoat that was buttoned up to the neck. He loosened the headcloth and I recognized the guide Baaqil, whom I had last seen storming off in a rage one night in the *dikka*. That night was forgotten, and he greeted me with the warmth Arabs always reserved for old acquaintances.

I recalled that Baaqil belonged to the Sulayman and that his tent was pitched in Wadi Howar. When the greetings were finished, I asked him what he was doing in Ed Debba. 'The grazing in Wadi Howar is almost over,' he said. 'Just like everywhere else. There is hardly a *tundub* in leaf between here and Rahib. Even the Arabs of the desert are moving from their homes. Everyone is in Debba.' Then he described how they had waited for news of the rains week after week, but how the rains had not come. He told me how the trees had shrivelled and turned grey, and how the scorched earth had turned to powder. Even the tussock grass had become woody and useless, and the *arak* trees that had grown in the Wadi for years had turned to brittle fibre. The camels and goats had become living skeletons before their eyes and the females had gone dry of milk. Men had come wandering out of the desert like ragged ghosts, thin and sick and grey with hunger. The scouts had ridden south and returned with their bodies racked and trembling with weakness. The rains had still not come. Soon the camels had begun to die, lying down on the bleak sands. The men had started to move either into the semi-desert or east to the Nile with those of their animals that were left. I asked him if there were any families left in the desert west of the Nile. 'Yes, there are a few 'Atawiyya and some Awlad Huwal in Abu Tabara. Apart from that the desert is empty.'

I decided that I must go back to these families, and see how they had managed to survive in this most devastating of droughts. The government had forbidden me to visit Kordofan. I decided that I should travel into the desert, to the wells at Abu Tabara to see how the Kababish who had remained there were faring.

I told Baaqil that I was looking for one of the desert Arabs to travel with me to Abu Tabara to visit the nomads encamped there. 'Hah! You will not find many nomads willing to do that journey now!' he said. 'Most of them are coming from the opposite direction!'

However, he promised to spread the word for me, and a little later I was approached by a man who looked short, lean and incredibly hard. He told me that his name was Jibrin Wad Ali and that he was of the desert Awlad Huwal. His dust-coloured *jibba* was ragged, but he moved with immense grace, almost like a ballet dancer. He wore a tightly bound headcloth, beneath which his face was a perfect oval of copper-bronze, inset with steel-grey eyes and a hooked nose. His expression was solemn and his features were lined with strain, yet there was an unmistakable air of silence about him, the true mark of a man who had spent his life in the desert.

We shook hands and he invited me to his tent. It was pitched very near the market and was spacious inside. On a rope-bed lay a youth covered in sweat and moaning with delirium. 'He has measles,' said Jibrin. 'Upon us be the Prophet! We have been in this city for two weeks, and my cousin is ill and my wife is sick! See how dirty is the town and how clean the desert!' I noticed that he spoke with the slow, measured voice and the clipped accent of the desert Kababish.

We sat down in the shade outside and a woman brought us tea. 'Have you been to Abu Tabara before?' I asked him.

'Yes, my father's tent was pitched there when I was a boy. We used to go there in winter every year.'

'Could you find your way there again?'

'I don't know. It was a long time ago and I only rode from there to Ed Debba once. You see, we had not much need to leave the desert in those days. Mostly we came to Abu Tabara from the south. But I was last there in the "Year of the Great Red Dust" . . . let me see . . . that must be fifteen or sixteen years ago. The desert has changed a lot since then. I cannot promise to find the way.'

I was convinced immediately that Jibrin was a suitable companion. His truthfulness was self-evident. Since navigation was a source of great pride amongst the Kababish, many Arabs would have tried to bluster. I told him that I should use a map and a compass. He looked at me blankly and said, 'You mean that you know the way yourself?' he asked. 'No.' I tried to explain. 'It is a map. Some of my people came this way many years ago. They made a journey to Abu Tabara and they wrote down the directions. It is called a map.'

He looked at me dubiously and said, 'It is better to ask directions from someone who has been there recently. I have some relations who came that way a few days ago. We can ask them. Things have

290

changed since the time of the *Ingleez* and anyway, only the desert Arabs know how to give directions properly.'

I asked Jibrin why he had moved to Ed Debba. 'I come from Ided Ahmad in the Wadi al Milik,' he said. 'There has been no rain in that part of the wadi for five years. This year there was nothing left to feed the animals. There was no growth to replace the old. The camels grew thin – some of them died so we collected together what was left and sent them south. Of course not all of us could travel with the camels. I was left with a few goats and nothing to eat. One day a lorry came along, so I loaded my goats aboard and brought them to market. The price of goats was so low that by the time I had paid the lorry fare there was only enough money to buy one sack of sorghum. I was ashamed. That was all I had to take back to my wife!'

'How long does a sack of grain last you?'

'I have no children. It should last two months or more. But all our neighbours came to ask for some. Why not? They had nothing. They would have shared their food with us. Sharing is the custom of the Arabs. It would have been a disgrace to refuse. But the sorghum was finished in a month, and we had to make our way here. Now I don't even have a camel to ride.'

'Then how will you get to Abu Tabara?'

'My brother-in-law has a camel. It is grazing across the river at Argi. I will ride it, and he and I will share the money.'

'Are you sure this camel will make it to Abu Tabara?'

'If it is well fed it will get there, but we must take grain with us. There is nothing for the camels in the desert now.' I asked Jibrin how he lived, and he told me that he had a job in the palm groves, watering the trees. 'I work for a gypsy,' he said. 'But it pays me little and I hate the work, by God!'

'Why?'

'It is not the work of an Arab! We are camel-men. Our home is the desert. No Arab would do such work out of choice. No Arab would live here in the town except out of necessity. The town is a prison. The desert is hard, but no one who has tasted life there can forget it. In the desert a man is free.' I saw his metallic eyes flash with emotion, and was surprised by the sudden vehemence of his talk.

'How much does your gypsy pay you?' I inquired.

'Fifty pounds a month.'

'I will pay you ten pounds a day and free food.'

'Eleven.'

291

'Agreed.' We shook hands, and Jibrin said he would fetch his camel from Argi the next morning. I told him I would spend the day buying a camel and provisions. As we rose, I thought I saw on his face a momentary look of gratification. Then it was gone, and only the inscrutable desert-rock expression remained.

'What about the gypsy?' I asked.

'Do not worry about the gypsy,' he answered. 'I am already back in the desert!'

The next morning I walked down to the market early and met the Kababish *damin*, Awad Wad Jibrin. He was a bulky, dark-skinned man who belonged to the Awlad 'Ugba. As *damin* he was responsible for all Kababish tribesmen who entered the area. After we had exchanged greetings, I told him that I wanted to buy a good desert camel. 'You will have plenty of choice these days,' he said. 'All the Arabs are selling their animals. They know that they must sell them or let them die. The merchants are out like vultures, and the Arabs are almost giving the stock away. There are herds being sent to Egypt every day almost! Still, I hope the Egyptians will like their meat lean!' I soon saw what he meant. Most of the camels in the market were pitifully thin, the ribs protruding through sagging skin. Others were grey and moulting from the effects of mange. There were several fine riding camels for sale. I knew that this was a sign of the Arabs' desperation: in a good year they would not sell their best camels at any price.

I asked Awad to bid for one of the riding camels. It was a plump *ashab* with the classic light limbs and off-white colour of its race. The owner was a tall, rope-muscled old man with a mahogany face grained with meanness. Awad offered him 300 pounds for the camel. The man shrugged off the price with an expression of scorn. 'May God open!' he said.

'350!' Awad bid. As he did so, a group of Arabs came up to watch the fun. 'May God open!' repeated the seller. The Arabs who had gathered around began to squabble, shouting out and swearing. Several more wandered up to see what the noise was about, and joined in. Awad offered 400 pounds. There were jeers from the spectators and a babble of comment. Two or three more came up. 'By God, it's worth five times that!' someone said.

'Not worth a piastre more than 350!' commented someone else.

'May God open!' said the seller.

Now the transaction was in earnest. There was much pawing

and prodding of the animal. Someone pulled down its lower lip and examined the teeth, describing their characteristics to the world in general. Someone else poked it with a stick. Now the bids went in tens, each one followed by a resolute 'May God open!' from the old man.

Some of the spectators supported the seller and others the buyer. For them it was a fascinating contest. The Arabs loved to watch other people's business, and became as passionately involved as if it were their own. I imagined that many of them came to these markets for just such spectacles and went home, empty-handed but with a satisfied sense of having thoroughly enjoyed themselves. I too enjoyed cattle markets. I had been around them since I could walk with my father, who was a well-known auctioneer and sheep-expert in East Anglia. Like these Arabs though, I enjoyed them a great deal more when it was not my money at stake.

'500!' declared Awad, taking a crisp ten-pound note from his pocket and thrusting it towards the seller. 'Come on! Take it! It is a good price. God knows!'

'Take it! Take it!' repeated some of the audience.

'Don't take it!' admonished others.

With a reluctant smile the old man took the note. We shook hands on the sale. 'It is cheap, by God!' someone cried. I agreed, thinking myself quite lucky to have acquired a thoroughbred at such a low price. It was not until I had actually counted the money into the seller's hand that I discovered my mistake. One of the Arabs watching couched the camel and another ran his hand along its withers. 'It has got a gall!' he shouted. 'Look!' Sure enough, there was a single fleck of pus oozing from an invisible wound on the camel's back. 'He has covered it with flour, the old devil!' the Arab grinned, holding up his hand on which there were traces of yellowish powder. I examined the gall. It was tiny, but I knew that to take a camel like this into absolute desert would be disastrous. After two days of bearing a saddle the animal would be in severe pain and would refuse to go further. In the desert around Ed Debba that would mean death. I told the old man that the camel was no good for me.

'You should have thought about that when you bought it!' was his only comment. There was a surge of exclamation from the crowd. 'Give him his money back you old bandit!' and 'He is a rich *khawaja*, that is his look-out!'

Now the crowd became even bigger as the excitement grew. I

looked at Awad, whose face had remained impassive. 'Of course, he is not obliged to pay you the money back,' he observed. 'But as you are a guest in this country, it is only right.'

He told the old Arab, 'Don't disgrace yourself, Uncle, this man is a guest.'

'Guest or no guest, he does not get a piastre!' said the man, and began to walk away. Two Arabs caught him playfully by the arms, but he pulled away from them, muttering angrily. A few moments later he could be seen glowering on the edge of the square. Awad went off to see him again, and I saw the two men waving their arms about in discussion.

Awad returned and went about some other business. Time passed. Several unofficial delegations went to the old man and returned. Everyone in the market passed an opinion, for or against. At last Awad came back, saying, 'He will return the money, less thirty pounds for his trouble.' I agreed, thinking that if not, I should never get away, but still the matter was not finished. More delegations went to and fro. Another hour passed, then two hours. At last Awad came striding back to where I was, holding the camel. He grabbed the headrope and began to pull the animal angrily out of the market. 'I am taking this camel to the police station!' he shouted, so that everyone could hear. 'By God, it's a disgrace! We have waited hours! Is there an honest man here?' Several Arabs now held him by the arms as they had the old man. 'Let go!' he stormed. 'I am taking it!'

Then someone said, 'He's coming!' Awad continued to march on adamantly. Even when the old Arab appeared out of the crowd and put a restraining hand on the headrope, he refused to stop. For a second there was a struggle. Then, with an air of great reluctance, the *damin* let go. The Arab counted the money back into my hand and walked away with his camel. The crowd of onlookers laughed and cried out. Some patted me on the shoulder and others shook their heads. All in all it seemed that my lost thirty pounds had paid for a good morning's entertainment. Later I bought a superb riding camel named Wad al Bahr. I paid Awad his commission and went off to find Jibrin.

Jibrin's camel was tethered to a post outside his tent, eating millet cane. It looked like a thoroughbred, but it was obviously under-nourished. When I mentioned this to Jibrin, he said, 'He has been too long in the wadi with poor grazing. But he will make it if we feed him grain.' Later we bought provisions in the market and assembled our equipment. We had decided to use pack saddles with crude wooden frames for the journey; I had learned by experience that they were more comfortable than riding saddles over long distances. We filled our saddle-bags with wheat flour, tea, sugar, some onions, seasoning and dried milk. There was a half-sack of sorghum grain for the camels and a bundle of *markh* wood for fuel. Jibrin said that we should find very little in the desert. The most essential items were our waterskins. We had only two, and I worried that they would not be enough. 'If the weather stays cool they will get us there,' Jibrin commented. 'But it would be best to take a little more.'

There were none available for sale in the town, so instead we agreed to use a four-gallon jerrycan of light plastic. We filled all our vessels from a hand-pump and slung them on a tripod outside the tent. Comparing the ancient and modern methods of water-carrying, I realized that both had their advantages. The plastic jerrycan was tough and durable and less inclined to leak, yet the waterskin had stood the test of time. Rock pictures have been found in the Sahara showing cattle-nomads using skins of the same type, some of them dating back to 5000 BC. The skins were comfortable for the camel, and even if they leaked could easily be repaired with a tiny piece of wood, or a fragment of cloth inserted from the inside. They kept the water cool by evaporation, though by the same means a hot wind would deplete them. When I remembered that they were one of the means by which men had survived in arid lands for millennia, I was loath to find fault with them.

Later in the day I changed into Arab clothing. Years ago on my first journeys with the nomads, even throughout my first sojourn with the Kababish, I had felt very self-conscious wearing local dress. I still disliked the long and elegant *jallabiyya* of the townsmen, but I had long ago realized that, like the waterskins, the short Arab shirt and *sirwal* were far better adapted to the desert than anything Europeans had produced. The loose *jibba* and the baggy breeches protected the body from the severe radiation of the desert sun, at the same time allowing the air to circulate beneath so that evaporation of the sweat cooled the skin surface. My main reason for wearing Arab clothes, however, had always been psychological. While I lived with the Kababish I wanted to be accepted as far as possible as one of them. Wearing European dress would have created an unnecessary cultural barrier.

When everything was packed away, we began to load the camels

295

methodically. The loads looked very heavy, but the animals were far from their full capacity. When we were ready the women came out to wish us well. We led the camels out towards the desert.

The town was still and silent at this hour. The market was empty, and the Arabs had returned to their tents amongst the rocks. Girls with shimmering red dresses and long hair were collecting flocks of goats in bubbles of golden dust. We passed through rows of tents and make-shift shelters, some set in the sand beneath the rocky scars, and others pitched on the hard inclines. The first cooking fires twinkled in the mouths of the tents. A slight breeze drew itself across the rocks, carrying with it the scent of burning wood. The sky was grey and full of melting cloudlets.

It was almost dark by the time we had climbed up to the lip of the rock wall, beyond which lay the mighty wasteland of the Libyan desert. It felt as if we were approaching the edge of the world. We mounted our camels and plunged over the ridge. The desert lay in dark relief. A last spill of scarlet flared far away on the western horizon. There was little wind now. The stars came out by the thousand and danced across the dark backcloth of the sky. We did not speak. The camels' feet crunched on the stony ground. We went on for three hours before making camp in a wedge of soft sand between the gravel sheets. We piled up our equipment and hung the skins on the tripod. The animals growled hungrily and I fed them each a few pounds of sorghum while Jibrin lit a fire. Then I sat down to watch my companion go through the 'tea ceremony'.

I looked forward to the ritual now. As I watched, Jibrin let the firewood burn down, then scooped the charcoal embers together in a glowing mass. He filled a white enamel teapot with hot water from a pan, then set it on the embers, adding one mugful of sugar and a little tea. When the mixture was bubbling, he poured a cupful, examined it by the light of the fire, then poured it back in. There was a look of utter concentration on his face. I could see that his mind was focused entirely on the simple task before him. The sequence of the ritual never varied: it had to be carried out in precisely this way. This and the other rituals of desert travel were a powerful means of concentrating the mind into the three or four square metres of space around us. The small tasks that we performed each time we halted prevented our minds from wandering, from dissipating across the awesome emptiness that lay beyond the tiny perimeter of our camp.

When the tea was ready, Jibrin poured us each a cupful and we drank in silence. We drank exactly two and a half cups each. Afterwards he made *kisri* with the same air of absolute concentration. It was a process of the utmost gravity, not to be rushed. When it was ready, we crouched with the steaming pot before us. There was a pause. Everything had its propriety here in the desert. Then we caught each other's eye in a kind of challenge, and Jibrin said, 'Ah — say "In the name of God!" ' It was the usual exhortation to eat, and we plunged our hands into the food simultaneously. It was the first time we had shared food. This ritual somehow sealed the bond of our mutual responsibility. Now we were companions in the Arab sense of the word.

After the meal we sat near the remains of the fire and talked. I noticed that a change had already come over my companion. In the flickering firelight his face looked smooth and relaxed. It was as if being in the familiar surroundings and performing the familiar small rituals had restored his sense of equilibrium.

'You feel better in the desert than the town?' I asked him.

'There is nothing better than the desert,' he answered. 'In a good year it has everything you could ask. There is milk and meat, the animals eat until they are fat. The Arabs are happy.'

I asked him if he thought it a disgrace to settle down.

'It is not a disgrace,' he said. 'But an Arab without animals is nothing. He cannot be a nomad, because without animals he cannot survive in the desert. To lose your animals is not a disgrace, but it is a great misfortune, by God! But — praise be to God — that is life! We cannot make the rain come. As soon as there is grazing in the desert, the Arabs will return.'

'What if all the camels are dead by then?'

'God is generous. God will provide.'

As we lay down to sleep, a sense of peace descended on me. The camels shuffled at their hobbles, wedging themselves closer together in the sand. The last embers of the fire sparkled orange in the hearth. The aurora of Ed Debba cast a coronet of light over the eastern sky, and to the west the star-bejewelled night hid the fathomless expanse of the greatest desert on earth.

The next day we rose before dawn. We saddled and loaded the camels, tying up their headropes and letting them wander before us. The desert was a gently undulating sea of hard-packed pebbles, like cobblestones. Here and there were the stunted remains of *tundub* and *sarh* trees, but there was nothing for the camels to eat. It was cool, and swarms of flies buzzed around their heads, making them sneeze and splutter and rub their muzzles against each other. The flies were parasites that could not live in the desert, but travelled on the backs of men and animals for hundreds of miles. Worst of all were the horseflies that laid their eggs in the camels' nostrils and occasionally plagued them with their powerful sting. Every so often a plump white maggot would drop from the animal's snout and wriggle across the sand. The Arabs believed that these maggots were formed in the camel's brain, and saw no connection between them and the horseflies.

The rocky hammada gradually gave way to a plain of sand. The sun came up casting our shadows before us, gigantic shapes rippling across its surface. The sand looked fresh and pristine as if no other foot had ever trodden there. There were stumps of dead trees and little heaps of deadwood that crumbled to powder at the touch. 'Look at these trees!' Jibrin said. 'This was the famous Sallaym pastures. A few years ago all the Kababish in the north used to collect here. There were *sallam* trees and *tundub* and *siyaal*. The sands were green with grasses. You could not move for camels, and there was as much game as you could hunt. There was gazelle, oryx, even ostrich. I know men that saw herds of them, twenty at a time.'

'What happened?'

'The grazing got less every year, and the rains failed. There was never much rain here, but enough to bring grazing along the wadis. Then the trees died and the Arabs of the Nile came and chopped up the rest for firewood.'

'Will it bloom again?'

'Only God knows, but I don't think it will bloom here. If they had left something, the tops of the trees, and just collected the fallen wood it would have been better. I have seen *sallam* trees go for years without water. You think they are dead, but the spirit is still in them. It just needs a shower of rain and shushsh! They are green again. But this place is a dead place. They have left nothing.'

I tried to imagine how it had been – tall grasses, thick trees, alive with movement. I imagined clusters of tents pitched in the grass, women carrying their infants in decorated litters, the camels bulging with milk and fat with grazing, a galaxy of campfires in the twilight, the herds gliding through the sheen of dusk to be hobbled by the tents. And this had been recently, well within my own lifetime. For hundreds, perhaps thousands of years this plain that seemed so pristine had teemed with life. The traveller Linant de Bellefonds passed through Ed Debba in 1821 and commented in his journal on the wooded nature of the country around. He had heard a lion roaring outside the town. Now the nearest lions were to be found below latitude 10°, over 300 miles south of here.

By mid-morning the heat had become intense, and we mounted our camels. On the horizon I could see a wall of dunes that looked white and insubstantial in the sunlight. By noon we had reached them, and we halted for a drink and a brief rest. During our journey we moved without debate or discussion, stopping as conditions dictated. Each day followed a similar pattern. Our movement was controlled by the natural cycle of the hours, the need of our bodies for food, drink, rest, and the needs of the camels. In the cool of the morning we would drift along behind the animals, our whips across our shoulders, taking in the minutiae of the desert surface – the trail of a lizard or insect, the three stones of an old campfire, the powdered droppings of a camel. Each object had its own story, made more intriguing by the barrenness of the environment. When the sun rose higher, we would mount as the urge took us, riding on for hour after hour in the shimmering haze of the sun and sand. Jibrin was a man of great silences. His eyes were focused far into the distance, sweeping across the horizon. He would suddenly look down, casting his gaze like a fisherman casting a net from side to side around the camels' feet. This was the way of the desert Arabs. They never daydreamed. Their thoughts were always firmly in the present, reading the ground like a code, missing none of the messages that the desert had in store for them. To miss something might spell disaster.

On my first journeys in the desert the vast empty hours had forced me in upon myself. My mind had wandered out of control, drifting from subject to subject, daydream to daydream, along the meaningless void of the day, as the camels rocked gently to and fro. The desert had been an alien and baffling place for me then and I had been like a blind man wandering in its vastness. Experience had trained me to control my thoughts as the Arabs did, to focus them on a single object. That object was survival, and the successful transport of one's body and possessions from water to water. Far from being dull, this concentration kept the mind intensely alive and resilient, and the hours passed with amazing speed. It created a sense of mounting harmony that climaxed in the feeling that everything –

299

men, camels, insects, animals, plants, birds, sand, gravel, dust, even the rocks themselves — had fused into a single harmonious whole. In this state, life and death seemed but two sides of the process of continual and eternal change.

Occasionally we would talk, pointing out to each other objects of interest. Jibrin showed me the tiny corpses of desert larks and sparrows, still feathered and half buried in dust. 'They just drop out of the sky,' he said. 'They used to rest in the trees at Sullaym. Now there is nothing for them to eat or drink, nowhere for them to hide from the afternoon sun. They are dying, like the Arabs.'

On the first afternoon we came across a wide lane of camel tracks, tens of thousands of footprints cut into the firm sand. 'This is the route to Egypt,' my companion told me. 'Some of these camels passed only three days ago.' As I looked at the tracks, I thought of the several occasions on which I had come by this route, and of my very first desert journey here with Abu Sara and his Rizayqat.

We came to a place where the herdsmen had made camp for the night. Each small event of their stay was stamped on the desert surface: the remains of the fire, the places where they had hobbled their riding camels, the depressions where men had slept, the few grains of sorghum where an Arab had hand-fed his mount, the footprints where someone had left the camp at night to relieve himself. The desert sands recorded everything for those who had eyes to see, but the record rarely endured. Soon the wind and drifting sand would wash over the tracks and spoor, creating once again the illusion of a pristine wilderness.

Once, as my eyes swept over the desert floor, I spotted a neolithic hand-axe and stopped to pick it up. It was a smooth boulder of blue basalt, which had been given an edge by some Stone Age craftsman. It was smaller and more finely polished than the diorite axes I had found near Tagaru. It gave me a thrill to imagine that my hand was the first to touch it since it was discarded by its owner millennia before. As I searched around for more objects, I noticed minute fragments of white bone, pieces of pottery with a striated pattern and several large grindstones of the kind still used by the nomads. The axe was of the type belonging to the so-called 'C' group peoples, who had herded cattle in this area thousands of years ago. They were amongst the first nomads to inhabit this desert; they and related races had driven their long-horned cows all over the Sahara. Their way of life had been little different from that of the Kababish who eventually succeeded them. They had lived in temporary shelters that could be easily dismantled for life on the move, carrying all their possessions on the backs of animals, transporting water in sealed skins and spending their lives in search of grazing. Life in the desert had perhaps been a little easier then, the temperature a few degrees lower, the rainfall a few inches higher. But over the millennia the ranges became increasingly arid and the vegetation dwindled, until the nomads were forced to move nearer and nearer to sources of water. Around 2000 BC their way of life ceased. Their cattle could no longer bear the arid conditions, and within a thousand years their culture had been superseded by that of camel-rearing men whose herds were better suited to the new environment.

What fascinated me was the parallel between that time and the present. The cattle-people had been destroyed by desiccation and over-grazing. Now, centuries later, those same processes were destroying the Arab nomads who had inherited the land from that earlier race. Only ten or fifteen years previously the very desert in which we were now travelling had been crowded with nomads and their herds. In colonial times the Kababish had ranged hundreds of miles from where we now were, far north across the plateau of Jabal Abyad. Almost within my own lifetime the vegetation retreated south, taking the herds with it and leaving only a few stragglers like the families we hoped to find in Abu Tabara. The herds moved more and more into the semi-desert, until the failure of the rains came like a *coup de grâce*. Now there were no substantial herds further north than the twelfth parallel, over 400 miles away. Clearly the process of desiccation had not ended with the cattle-people, but had continued almost imperceptibly over the generations, pushing a little further each year.

When I showed the axe to Jibrin, he just said, 'It probably belonged to the Anaj. They were giants in those days. It was long ago before the English came.' He did not mention it again.

In the cool of the first evening we dismounted once again, anxious to spare the camels, and moved on foot for three hours across the erg. The sunset came with dramatic splendour, as if some giant hand had pulled the plug out of the day letting the colours drain away like liquid. The deep blue of the sky poured into the bottle-neck on the horizon, and as the surface shades ran off, the undertones of ultramarine, violet and yellow were exposed. A froth of grey cloud bubbled at its edges and wisps of smoky white drifted across it. Soon

301

there was nothing left but a spark of gold on the edge of the plain, and the black basin of the night across which tumbled the vibrant organisms of the stars.

Not long after sunset we halted. As soon as we unloaded our baggage, the camels flopped down and rolled over in the soft sand, spraying themselves with dust. After we ate, we sat and watched the stars. Jibrin pointed out the planet Venus and told me, 'See, it is the brightest star in the firmament, but it is different from the others. It is the only one that does not cross the sky, apart from the North Star, which stays where it is. They say that it does everything in nines. Once, it did not appear for nine days, but that was long ago.' I thought, as so many times before, how closely these nomads were in tune with nature. I wondered how many people in my own country would even have recognized the planet Venus. The nomads were a practical people. They did not speculate about the meaning of the stars and the planets, but merely accepted that they were part of the beautiful and mysterious workings of the universe. Yet they observed them closely, knowing that their movements imparted knowledge that was useful. Jibrin went on to tell me about the rising and setting of various constellations and their significance in relation to the temperature, the winds and the rainfall. It was complex and I could not follow it all. Yet I was convinced that these desert men had a core of intricate knowledge that more advanced technological societies had lost.

The next morning the sun came up like fire and the desert vibrated with heat. 'We will need shade when we rest today!' Jibrin said. I could see that he was worried; it was the middle of winter, and such a surge in temperature was totally unexpected. We had only one full skin of water, one half full, and the jerrycan. There were still six days of travel ahead. Abu Tabara was the sole source of water in this part of the desert.

By midday we were in rocky country that had become an inferno of heat. At the halt we built a tent, slinging my canvas over the wooden support from which we also slung our waterskins. We threw ourselves down, exhausted, into the shade. 'This is like summer, by God!' Jibrin exclaimed. 'What happened to the winter? If it stays like this, our water will never last us!' I knew that he was right, and I was more troubled than I cared to admit. Water against energy, energy against water – it was the equation with which a desert traveller always had to juggle. In the desert water was life. But to carry too much was as great a mistake as carrying too little, for it exhausted the camels and reduced the distance they could cover.

I unfolded my map. It was a map of the 1940 survey made by Captains Coningham and Whittingham. The map showed a vast flat area, relieved by a sea of sand dunes that was somewhere in front of us, and after that three or four mountain peaks. Because other relief was not shown, the map gave the impression that before us lay a continuous flat plain of sand upon which the few landmarks should have been clearly visible. This was not the case. In front of me I saw very broken country of scattered basalt ridges and shattered rock walls like the backs of half-buried amphibians. None of the landmarks was visible. To cap it all they had improbable names of which Jibrin had never heard; I wondered whether the good Captains' informant, whomever he was, had merely made them up. In Ed Debba I had taken a compass-bearing on the northern edge of the dune-sea, intending to traverse it from that side, but because of the rocky country we had continually turned off-course and there were no features now on which I could reset it.

I asked Jibrin what he remembered of his previous journey, sixteen years previously. 'We came from El 'Atrun with fifteen camels carrying salt,' he said. 'Of course I was only a boy then. I don't remember any of this landscape. I think we came much farther to the south. I remember that the desert was full of Arabs, and almost every night we camped with a different family and drank milk and ate meat. It took us eight days from Abu Tabara to the Nile, but we spent one whole day in a wadi full of *tundub*. It was a forest, by God! There was some grass there too.'

'Did you ask your relations who had come from Rahib?'

'Yes, but you said we should follow that instrument of yours. Now we are too far from the route they described!' I looked at the waterskins. They hung above my head like a pair of black testicles. Neither of them was completely full. I tried to make some mental calculations, but all depended on the temperature. On a cool winter's day we might get away with a quart at the very least, but on a steaming hot day like this one, a gallon would hardly suffice. We also needed water for cooking. I found myself thinking, 'Is this all we have between ourselves and the desert?' I knew that I could have made the decision to turn back at this point, yet I remembered the disappointment I had felt when Juma' and I returned from Nukheila the previous year. We should go on in spite of everything. I said to Jibrin, 'We shall have to ration the water.'

'God is generous!' he said.

Before we set off that afternoon, I scouted around the camp and found the woody stems of some plants, spread out like stars and hugging the surface of the sand. Jibrin told me they were 'umayyi plants. It seemed to me that they were the last souvenirs of a time when this plain had rumbled with the movement of migrating herds, when a traveller could find company every night. I knew how quickly the desert could change, how a single shower could bring to life the ephemeral seeds that had lain dormant for years, painting the matchwood trees with green leaf and nurturing brilliant growths of flowers along the wadi-bottoms. Jibrin snapped off a bit of plant and said, 'The spirit is still in them. You would say they were just wood, but if it rained tomorrow you would see a change.' Both of us stood for a moment in awe at the hardiness of this flora; somewhere, hidden deep within their roots was a tiny reservoir of liquid in which the spirit still pulsed with life. When nature produced such wonders there was always hope.

In the next two days the temperature did not drop, and we moved through a blinding agony of heat. Both of us were perturbed by these freak conditions, and we rationed out the water carefully. Early on the fourth day of the journey we ran into the chain of dunes that stretched north and south across our path. As we approached, I saw that the dunes were crescent-shaped, with steep leeward faces on the south side, so that they presented us with the transverse face. They were linked together and joined by ridges sculpted by the wind into all manner of configurations, seeming to make an impenetrable wall. About their bases I noticed the ripples of loose sand that the Arabs called hayil, in which we might sink up to our calves. I knew that if the dunes extended for any distance, crossing them would be exhausting for ourselves and the camels. We were thirsty, and the day promised no let-up in the powerful radiation of the sun. As we got nearer, we saw a belt of hallif grass. From a distance it looked promising, but when closer we found that the stalks were dry and useless. A little further on, though, we discovered two hadd bushes like prickly toadstools. While the camels fed, Jibrin walked forward to inspect the dunes. I watched him struggling through the deep sand. Once he was forced to steady himself from falling. I wondered how we should get the camels through it. Jibrin climbed the side of

304

the dune and disappeared over its lip. He reappeared, and I watched him racing down towards me, kicking up spurts of amber sand. As he came up, he said, 'We have come right into the middle of it. If we try to go round we might lose a day. Our water cannot stand that. We have to go over.' I asked him how far it extended. 'As far as I can see,' he answered. 'But there are flat spaces between.' Then he grabbed his camel's headrope. 'Come on!' he said.

We hauled the camels forwards, but as we reached the *hayil* they began to flounder, jerking back on the ropes. Jibrin's camel was a few feet in front of me, and I saw its legs trembling as it hesitated. It let out a wail of displeasure. 'Come on, you son of the forbidden!' Jibrin yelled. I gave the animal a sharp whack across the rear-quarters, which sent it lurching forwards. Its legs sank deeper into the sand, and before I could do anything it stumbled and toppled over on to its side. There was a slight crack, and I thought, 'God! The jerrycan!' I kicked the camel frantically and as it dragged its body up I saw a runnel of precious water darkening the sand.

The vessel was still intact, but its screw top had flown off and about a quarter of the liquid had splashed out. It was tragic to see it dripping away down the side of the can. Jibrin cursed and couched the camel in the deep sand. He took the screw top and examined the neck of the jerrycan. It was made of cheap commercial plastic and had previously been used for peanut oil. When we tried the cap, we saw it was loose. Jibrin cut a piece of sacking from one of the saddle-pads and screwed the cap over it. 'It will drip,' he said. 'But it is the best we can do now.'

The sun was already high as we dragged the camels up the slope. We panted, catching our breath in the heat. After a few minutes we reached the crest of the dune, and I saw an ocean of sand stretching out west as far as the skyline. The surface glistened with a soft glow of quartz pink. We manhandled the animals down the other side and crossed a flat of firm ground littered with nuggets of basalt and quartz.

All day we fought a desperate battle with the awful physics of the blown sand, striding on until the going became agonizing and our throats too dry for anything except growling at the camels. As we climbed the crest of each dune, it seemed that there was always another one waiting mercilessly beyond it. My arms ached from grasping the headrope and my calves from the constant struggle with the loose sand. Finally, as the sun began to sink and its heat to die, the dunes became gentler, until they were no more than ripples in the sand a foot high. We couched our camels and threw ourselves between them, our bodies craving rest and water. Jibrin drew a little water from one of the skins and we drank a mugful each. Then we made a sobering discovery. Searching the bag that had held our firewood, we found that there was none left. 'We cannot eat!' Jibrin said. I was too tired to do anything but grimace. I doubted if I should have been able to stomach *kisri* now anyway.

In the morning we descended into a horseshoe-shaped amphi-theatre of rock, perhaps five miles wide. Its floor was covered in cream-coloured sand, and its walls were a melted crust of blue rock with terraces of scattered boulders along its sides. Across the sand were strange groups of oval stones and other boulders perched on slender platforms like exotic sculpture. To the north Jibrin pointed out a flash of green, and insisted on investigating it. As we came near, we saw that it was an *arak* tree, a tall, stout specimen in imperial green with a perfectly rounded canopy of leaves. Its presence was like an illusion in this desolation of rock and sand.

We brought the camels up and let them browse. At the base of the tree were the spiral tracks of many snakes that probably lived among its roots. The sand was scarred by the stitchlike patterns of lizards, and several darkling beetles scuttered away at our approach. A single black and white bird flitted off in alarm and perched on a rock nearby. I picked up one of the beetles and examined it. Its legs kicked the air violently as I turned it over. Of all desert creatures these were the hardiest. Their thick cuticle prevented water loss and their modified wing-covers, no longer adapted for flying, trapped a layer of air that insulated them from the heat. They could survive almost anywhere, and unlike most desert fauna emerged during the day as well as at night.

We were content to let our camels feed, though we were still plagued by thirst. 'I say we could find water here if we dug a hole,' I said to Jibrin.

The Arab laughed condescendingly. 'I hope you are prepared to dig for a week. The roots of trees like this go on for ever. You will die of exhaustion before you even get near it!'

For the rest of the day we moved through a maze of rock that closed in on us from all sides. Enormous ridges towered above us, their surface weathered into all manner of surreal shapes: pillars, balls, ovals and wedges. There were scars of granite that had been cracked by the fluctuations of heat and cold, shattering into a billion glittering fragments of geological refuse. In the crevices were the grey bones of *sallam* and *siyaal*, but they bore no leaves and were useless even for firewood.

At noon we stopped as usual and lay down in the shade of our tiny shelter. The camels rested their heavy skulls on the sand in exhaustion, their eyes blinking in the heat. The sun streamed down from an unblemished sky, and the heat seemed to rise from the ground in a visible cloud of vapour. For a moment I dozed and dreamt of an Arctic river flowing with ice-cold melt-water. I opened my eyes and felt the thirst gouging my stomach like nausea. I would have given much for a mug of water from the Nile. I knew that I could not drink until evening, and I was worried about our navigation. The rocky terrain had now taken us way off course, and neither Jibrin nor I knew where we were. At Abu Tabara there was only one well and probably no more than two or three tents. If we missed it, we should have to make for Rahib or Umm Grayn. Both were four or five days' journey from Abu Tabara and we should have to cover the distance with thirsty, exhausted camels without any drinking water for ourselves. I asked Jibrin how long he thought we could last without water in this heat. 'I once went three days without drinking,' he told me. 'It was in the *jizzu* – some raiders took three of our camels and I rode off so quickly that I had no time to take any water. Once I was after them, I did not want to leave the trail. But they outrode me. I was just about to give up when I came to an 'Atawiyya camp. They gave me milk and water. But it was a bitter time, by God! There is nothing so bad as thirst.'

'Could we make it to Umm Grayn if we miss Abu Tabara?'

'The question is the camels. As long as the spirit is in your body and you can hang on to your camel, then it is possible. Many an Arab has been saved by his camel. But if your camel goes down, you are finished. Ours are thirsty already.'

'Is Abu Tabara easy to see from a distance?'

'No, by God! It is the most difficult of places. It is hidden in a belly of great stones which goes on for a long distance. There are no palm trees, and nothing can be seen from a long way off.'

'God willing, we well find some people there.'

'Amen!'

I had another look at the map. It told me almost nothing, and I cursed Captains Coningham and Whittingham and wondered where the hell they had learned to survey. Jibrin noticed my expression and commented, 'Those maps are rubbish! How could those *Ingleez* know the desert when they came here only once?'

'You are right, brother,' I agreed.

In the late afternoon we broke out through the wall of rock and came upon a vast plain if ice-cream pink, broken by seams of black stone. Below us was a wadi with a few dry *sarh* trees. We halted the camels and cut off some of their lower branches with an axe. I knew this was desecration, and that such practices as these had helped to destroy the desert. But it was one thing to pronounce on the evils of deforestation when one was sitting at home with a full stomach, and quite another here in this dangerous void when one was fighting for survival – and possibly losing.

The land rose slightly to the horizon, where I could see a pyramid-shaped hill and a ridge with a flat top. Time passed and the camels paced on. There was silence between us. There was nothing but the slap of the camels' feet and the washing ebb-tide of the wind, like the sea on the shore. There was no life in this land but us. There was no sign of any creature: no foxes, no hares, not even a jerboa. As night came and the embers of the sun flared across the ridge, Venus appeared. It was a pulsing beacon of hypnotic light. Suddenly, as if some hypnotist had snapped his fingers, I had a strange out-of-body-experience. It was as if I were looking down on myself and my companion from somewhere up near Venus. For a moment I watched two full-grown men riding two grotesque animals across a wasteland, for no good reason. I found myself saying, from way up there, 'They do it. And it even seems important!'

That evening we camped on a rock shelf beyond the ridge. We cooked porridge, but our mouths were too dry to enjoy it. As the next day dawned I saw to the north a long wall of black rock. It looked no more than ten kilometres away, and had two rock chimneys rising above it. I guessed that it was the southern edge of the legendary Jabal Abyad 'The White Mountain', where Kababish herds had grazed in past times. There was a high peak marked on the map as Burj al Hatab, but this was nowhere to be seen. The country to the west was hammada with patches of sand rising to naked peaks of basalt here and there. The day was another hot one, without the solace of a cloud to veil the full power of the sun. We had been riding for six days, most of them under summer conditions, and the camels were tired and thirsty. Working in these temperatures they needed to drink every three or four days, and the grain we fed them increased their thirst. As the day grew hotter, I felt my spirits sink. The lining of my stomach felt tight with a sick, acid sensation. I could think of nothing but water. The thirst was an acute pain, like a nagging tooth-ache that all my powers of concentration could not dismiss. We rode through a region where the rocks were weathered into the shapes of nightmare creatures and strange deformed reptiles. It was a dead, dry, moonscape world where men did not belong. By the middle of the morning, on that sixth day, I was almost dropping from my camel with thirst, my body bent and hunched up over the saddle-horns. I guessed Jibrin felt the same, for he had assumed the same hunched position. I knew now that the ability to resist thirst was psychological, not physiological. Experiments had proved that an acclimatized European has exactly the same water requirements in the desert as a nomad. One had to have the will to endure it.

Jibrin exclaimed, 'By God, it is hot!'

'Let's drink,' I said. We couched our camels and drew a single mug of water, half each. At once I felt the moisture seeping into my blood and reactivating my cells and muscles, uncloying and lubricating the tight walls of my stomach that had seized up and fused together.

'Let's go,' Jibrin said, and on we went, crossing the huge boulder-strewn plain, two tiny black specks in its midst.

Once we came across the tracks of two men and eight camels. Jibrin grew excited. 'These are the tracks of my relations!' he said. We followed them a short way, but they veered drunkenly from side to side in great sweeps and soon petered out amongst the rocks. Still, it was cheering to know that we were on the right trajectory, and our spirits rose a little. But by the time the darkness came our optimism had faded.

The night closed in around us. We ate porridge, chewing it mechanically and retching from its dryness. We drank a little water afterwards, but not enough to quench our thirst. I looked at our remaining supply. Both waterskins were empty and there remained about a gallon in the jerrycan. I could hardly believe that we had used so much. That gallon would last us for the next morning; it might last us all day if we did not eat. That meant that it was essential to find Abu Tabara sometime during the next day. We had no leeway. The chances would be firmly against us, even if the weather changed.

In all my travels in the desert by camel, I had never been in a position as serious as this. I had been thirsty before; I had gone for days without drinking, but then the temperature had been relatively low and our navigation assured. I thought longingly of the bulging skins I had seen in Ed Debba. Why had I not persuaded someone to sell me one? I remembered bathing in the shallow inlets on the waterfront at Debba, and thought of the water pots the river people left outside their houses. I could think of nothing else. I said to Jibrin, 'If we do not find Abu Tabara tomorrow we are in big trouble!'

'We shall all die when it is time for us to die,' the Arab said. 'God is generous.'

I rolled over on to my stomach and switched on my torch. The way ahead looked grim, and I felt angry with myself. My navigation had failed. My map had failed. Even Jibrin's knowledge had failed. How on earth could we find Abu Tabara? Now all we could do was to resign ourselves to what came, or fight back. Jibrin, true to his culture, had chosen resignation. I, true to mine, wrote in my journal: 'As long as there is the will in me, I shall struggle to survive.'

Later we curled up in our blankets. After about half an hour I was still awake when I heard the distant growl of a motor-vehicle. The sound swelled and died, then swelled again. It sounded like a truck that had got bogged down in the sand. I jumped up and woke Jibrin. He sat up reluctantly. The sound came again, unmistakably. 'Don't you hear it?' I asked him. 'No,' he replied dully. The sound suddenly ceased, and the desert was quiet again. 'There is nothing,' my companion said. 'You imagined it. It is strange what thirst will do. Go back to sleep. You will need your sleep if we are to find Abu Tabara tomorrow.' I lay down straining my ears. There was no sound but the humming breath of the camels. Perhaps I had imagined it after all. I reasoned that Jibrin's senses must be more acute than mine. I did not know that he had suffered mumps as a boy, and was deaf in one ear.

Our departure next morning was grim and silent. We moved off, walking as usual through the mystical landscape of moulded rock and drifting sand. My eyes had become accustomed to the washed-out, pastel hues of the desert scenery, so when my gaze swept over the landscape ahead, I picked out a brilliant yellow and silver shape amongst the rocks. I was drawn to it like a magnet. A few paces further on I realized that it was certainly something man-made. Then Jibrin said, 'It *is* a truck, by Almighty God! There are two of them!'

310

As we approached, we saw that there were two silver-grey Fiats parked amongst the boulders. They were loaded with sacks and carried yellow covers. There were six men with the vehicles, who gathered together to stare at us when we approached. We left our camels hobbled at some distance and went to greet them.

The two drivers were fat townsmen with black faces and fuzzy hair. Their faces dropped in amazement when they realized I was a European. I greeted them formally in the manner of the nomads and ignored their expressions. This was enough to prevent too many tedious questions. They were friendly and called for tea. They told us that they had come from El 'Atrun and were taking rock salt for sale in Dongola. They had not been to Abu Tabara, but they thought it was ahead.

'What grazing have you seen on the way?' Jibrin asked. I was dying to ask for water and could hardly stand the tension, but I thought it better to let my companion talk.

'Well, there was some grass and trees about half an hour from here,' said one of the drivers.

'What kind of trees?' Jibrin asked.

'Thorny ones,' answered the other.

I saw Jibrin smile almost pityingly. We drank the tea that the lorry-boys brought us and squatted down in the hearth with them. Jibrin behaved formally and with great dignity. He sipped his tea as if it were his fifth cup. I took my cue from him, even though I was desperate. I realized that it would be a disgrace to display thirst before these townsmen. After we had drunk, Jibrin casually mentioned that we needed some water. The driver told one of the boys to half fill one of our skins. The squelching vessel was laid in front of us. I tried to avoid looking at it. Instead I thanked the men and told them our names.

'Why don't you travel by lorry? It's much easier!' said one of the drivers.

'You can't learn anything in a lorry,' I told him. 'If you are in a lorry you are not in the desert.' He looked at me in bewilderment, but Jibrin's eyes glowed in understanding.

The men climbed aboard the great machines and started the engines. The desert was filled with the sound of their buzzing, and with fumes of oil. The drivers waved and wished us good luck, and we thanked them again. We grabbed the headropes of our camels to

311

prevent them bolting as the vehicles lumbered off, billowing smoke, slowly gathering speed until they disappeared into the landscape.

Then Jibrin poured out a mugful of water and held it out to me. I was too thirsty to worry about protocol. I drank it down greedily in steady gulps. It tasted like cream. When it was finished, I exclaimed, 'Praise be to God!' and meant it. Then Jibrin drank. As we reloaded the camels, he muttered, 'Those people don't even know they are travelling. There are some trees here . . . some grass there . . . "thorny ones" indeed! They know nothing of the desert!'

'You cannot know the desert if you travel by motor-vehicle,' I said.

'Yes,' he agreed. 'There is nothing better than a camel in the desert. The lorry is fast but you cannot enjoy it.' I had always hated motor-vehicles, yet I knew that this time they had saved my life.

We walked for almost four hours over the carcass of the desert. Soon the rocks gave way to a basin of brown dust with a great edifice of jagged black rock on the horizon. We mounted up as the time passed, not daring to halt, for the half-skin of water would soon be used up and we could waste no time. In the middle of the plain was a withered *tundub* and at its base lay the tangled skeleton of a camel, the dry hide twisted around the bones. There were a few leaves on the tree and we let our camels browse. Jibrin joked, 'Was this camel a male or a female? It doesn't matter much now does it! Was it brown or red? Who cares anyway!'

We pressed on, but now the camels were faltering. 'This one will be dead soon if we do not find water!' Jibrin declared. At midday we crossed a dune and saw from the top a depression filled with massive slabs of rock, black and silver, weathered and carved into weird figures and half-buried by furrows of sand. The sun was so hot it took our breath away. As we descended the dune-slope, Jibrin said, 'It must be here.'

I knew he was right. This was the lowest land as far as I could see, and the water course must be in a depression. Then we saw a trail of droppings scattered in the sand. They looked very old. We moved on, weaving in and out of the boulders. There were no other signs of humans or herds, and I was beginning to wonder if this was really the place when Jibrin cried, 'See the last of the tents! This is it!' Looking down, I saw many pieces of torn *shuggas*, half covered in sand, with broken pots, useless leather buckets, split saddle-bags. 'This is Abu Tabara,' Jibrin said, smiling. We climbed a hump of sand, and he showed me the single well, covered in flat stones. 'They have all gone,' he said. 'They must have left only days ago.' It was disappointing to find the place uninhabited, but the survival instinct was stronger: I was overjoyed to find water.

Near the well we spied an immense block of granite that had split in half. The fissure was easily large enough to take us and all our luggage. As we sat down in the shade both of us said, 'Praise be to God!' and were silent for a moment. Jibrin exclaimed 'By Almighty God! This is where we were, all that time ago! There were Awlad Huwal and Hamdab here then. I wonder what happened to them all!'

I walked down to the well head. There was a basin of dried clay, and the well was covered with five flat stones. I crouched down and removed them carefully. Then I dropped a pebble into the gaping hole. The 'plunk!' and the rippling of water was a holy sound in this appalling dryness. Abu Tabara was a holy shrine devoted to this end. Jibrin brought the well-bucket and hoisted up some of the liquid. It was clean and clear and its taste as untainted as the desert wind. It seemed like a miracle. Here, in the middle of the most dangerous desert on earth, there was water. Here there was life.

Epilogue

In summer 1985 I made a brief visit to Hamrat ash Sheikh.

The first person I saw in the market-place was Juma' Wad Siniin. It was almost as if he had been waiting for me. We embraced warmly, but the pleasure of seeing him again was marred by the shock of his appearance. When we had ridden to Nukheila only a year before, he had been a nomad in his prime, tough, proud and aggressive. Now he looked like an old beggar. His flesh was drawn and bloodless, his hair bleached white, his body frail, his clothes dirty and ragged. He leaned heavily on a stick as we talked. 'I knew you would come, Omar,' he said. 'I saw it in the *khatt!*'

We went up to the lonely court-house on the hill, where the deputy nazir, At Tom Wad al Murr, greeted me. With him were his half-brother Ali Sheikh and about fifteen other Kababish. Amongst them I was amazed to see the sheikhs of the Haworab and the 'Atawiyya. They looked half starved, their eyes sunken with malnutrition, their teeth rotten and their gums pink with anaemia. At Tom told me that three-quarters of the Kababish livestock had been lost in the drought. The Arabs had nothing but the American grain that was being shipped from Omdurman. Little of it got through to the *dar*; the lorry drivers who brought it refused to cross the Wadi al Milik without extra cash from the people.

'You remember those few sheep I had?' Juma' asked me. 'Those went months ago. I caught an old man slaughtering one of them in the wadi, by Almighty God! He almost cried when I caught him. "I must have it!" he told me. "My children are dying!" What could I do? The beast was dead. If I had taken him before the nazir, he would have had no money to pay me! I just left him to it.'

314

News of old friends was equally dismal. At Tom Wad Hassan
was in El Fasher seeking blood money on behalf of two 'Atawiyya
who had been shot dead by police. Salim Wad Hassan was in Darfur
with what was left of the sheep. Salim Wad Musa had lost two of his
wives in the famine, and a third had recently given birth to a still-
born child. Mohammid Wad Ali had died of a mysterious illness, and
Adam Wad ash Shaham was at death's door. The *nuggara* herds
had been attacked badly by the new strain of mange.

'You have not heard about Mohammid Wad Fadlal Mula?' Juma'
asked me. 'He is in prison. He attacked a store in Umm 'Ajayja with
his cousin. They cleaned it out. But they were stupid enough to
return for more, and the police got them. What a fight Mohammid
put up, by God! It took three men to take his shotgun off him. When
I saw the gun I could hardly believe it. I said, "That is Omar's shotgun
and no doubt. The one he bought from Dagalol!" '

Later I walked up to where a mud-walled dome covered the
grave of Sir Ali Wad at Tom. Below me, to the north, a group of Arab
boys were driving a single she-camel towards the thorn groves; even
from where I stood the black patches of mange were clearly visible
on the camel's skin.

I remembered how, three years before, I had come trudging out
of those thorn groves on my way back from El 'Atrun, weak with
exhaustion, Wad at Tafashan galled and limping. I remembered how
I had despaired of ever being accepted by the Kababish. I had
learned the lessons of this harsh land and learned them well, but I
had only half succeeded. I had become a man of two cultures and
an outcast of both.

My eyes followed the boys until they were black commas on the
landscape. A gust of wind rattled the branches in a nearby *sarh* tree.
A grey falcon swooped down and took shelter amongst them. On
the distant horizon, far beyond the dwarf-dots of the nomads, some
daubs of mist fused and formed into steel-blue clouds of rain.

List of Tribes Composing the Kababish

Tribal names have collective and singular forms. All collective forms are given, with those singular forms used in the text.

NURAB	Nurabi	Nas ash Sheikh (nazir's people)
		Awlad Awad Sid
		Awlad al Kir
		Awlad Fahal
		Nas Graysh
		Dar Umm Bakheit
		Dar Kibir
		Dar Sa'id
AWLAD HUWAL		
AWLAD TARAYF		
AWLAD SULAYMAN	Sulaymani	
AWLAD 'UGBA		
BARARA	Bari	
HAMDAB		
HAMMADAB		
HAWORAB		
GHILAYAN		
RUWAHLA	Rahli	
RIBAYGAT	Ribaygi	
SARAJAB	Sarajabi	
SHILAYWAB		

ZANARKHA
'ATAWIYYA   'Atawi
'AWAJDA   'Aidi
'UDUSA
UMM MATTU

Sections of:

KAWAHLA   Kahli   ZAGHAWA OF KAJMAR
HASSANIYYA   (Nas Wad Haydar)
DUWAYIH
BANI JARRAR

317

Glossary

'anafi	hybrid Kababish camel
'angareb	rope-bed
'arabi	heavy breed of camel
'aragi	a spirit found all over the East from Morocco to Tibet, usually 'arak' in English
ashab	thoroughbred camel
'Atrana	salt diggers
'Awwala	'slaves'
dabuuka	export camel herd
damar	nomads' semi-permanent camp
damin	tribal guarantor
dar	territory or house
darat	short season between rains and winter
dia	blood money
dikka	camp, especially the nazir's camp
dilka	perfume made of sandalwood and spices
dobbayt	four-line rhyming verse that is sung
fahal	dominant bull-camel
fula	seasonal water-pool
gaaris	sour camel's milk
gayd	front-leg hobble for camel
gayla	afternoon rest
gelti	rock cistern where water collects
ghaffir	guard, watchman or court baillif
girbas	waterskin
gom	raiding party
gontar	unit of weight equalling 100 pounds
gorasa	flat bread made of wheat flour
goz	undulating sand hills

hajil	bridal tent
halib	fresh camels' milk
hawayya	pack saddle
hawd	mud drinking-basin
hayil	ripples of loose sand
hurr	literally 'free'; also anything of good quality
ilbil	collective name for camels
'imma	headcloth
Ingleez	British
jabal	a mountain or a hill
jadi	young gazelle
jallabiyya	long shirt worn by townsmen
jibba	short shirt worn by nomads
jizzu	ephemeral pastures on edges of the desert
jumaal	riding and baggage camels
kabaros	carved wooden milking-vessel
karama	the act of hospitality
kibjan	monitor lizard
kisri	polenta of millet or sorghum
khatt (al ramil)	divination by making depressions in sand
khesh	matting of black goat-hair
khun	storage tent
mashat	braided hair-style
muhawwadin	literally 'those who race to the water basins'
nahas	tribal kettle drums
nasrani	Christian
nuggara	wooden drum
'Ol	household slaves
rahat	leather bridal apron
sawani	deep-wells
shakima	straw mask worn by camel
sharif	'noble' man
shogara	migration to the Sahel
shugga	length of woven wool used for tents
simoom	hot wind of summer
sirwal	cloth breeches
taya	camp of herdsmen or travellers
tobe	(1) woollen garment worn by men, (2) colourful robe worn by women
tukul	cabin of brushwood used as kitchen
tulba	annual herd tax
umbasha	corporal
umm	literally 'the mother of'

Umm Duffan	bread made by being buried under hot ashes
'uqal	knee-hobble
'urf	Arab law
'utfa	Kababish litter for women
zabata	weakness of camels' shoulder
zalat	an area of rocky cliffs and gorges in the desert, or just a stony area
zambara	herdsman's pipe
zariba	enclosure
zikra	repetition of a sound

List of
Botanical Species

'agul	*Fagonia cretica*
arak	*Salvadora persica*
baghayl	*Blepharis linariaefolia*
diffir	*Brachiaria sp.*
gafal	*Commiphora africana*
gau	*Aristida adscensionis*
gutub	*Cien fuegosia digitata*
hadd	*Cornulaca monocantha*
hallif	*Desmo-stachya cynosuroides*
handal	*Colocynthis vulgaris*
harjal	*Solenostemma argel*
haskanit	*Cenchrus biflorus*
hejlij	*Balanites aegyptiaca*
inderab	*Cordia rothii*
jibayn	*Solanum dubium*
kitir	*Acacia mellifera*
la'ot	*Acacia nubica*
markh	*Leptadenia spartium*
mukhayyit	*Boscia senegalensis*
nabak	*Zizyphus abyssinica*
nissa	*Aristida ciliata*
sa'adan	*Neurada procumbens*
sallam	*Acacia ehren-bergiana*
sarh	*Maerua rigida*
siyaal	*Acacia spirocarpa*
tomam	*Panicum turgidum*
tundub	*Capparis aphylla*
'ushur	*Calotropis procera*

Index

323